W9-BFO-205

QUANTITATIVE MODELS FOR PERFORMANCE EVALUATION AND BENCHMARKING

Data Envelopment Analysis with Spreadsheets and DEA Excel Solver

INTERNATIONAL SERIES IN
OPERATIONS RESEARCH & MANAGEMENT SCIENCE
Frederick S. Hillier, Series Editor   Stanford University

QUANTITATIVE MODELS FOR PERFORMANCE EVALUATION AND BENCHMARKING
Data Envelopment Analysis with Spreadsheets and DEA Excel Solver

by

Joe Zhu
Worcester Polytechnic Institute, U.S.A.

 Springer

Joe Zhu
Worcester Polytechnic Institute
Massachusetts, USA

Library of Congress Control Number: 2003268638

ISBN-10: 1-4020-7082-9 (HB)
ISBN-13: 978-1-4020-7082-2 (HB)

Printed on acid-free paper.

Printed in the United States of America.

9 8 7 6 5 4

springer.com

To my wife

Contents

List of Tables

Chapter 5

Chapter 6

Chapter 7

Chapter 8

Chapter 9

Chapter 10

Chapter 11

Chapter 12

List of Figures

Chapter 1

Chapter 2

Chapter 3

Chapter 4

Chapter 5

Chapter 6

Chapter 9

Chapter 10

Chapter 11

Chapter 12

Preface

Managers are often under great pressure to improve the performance of their organizations. To improve performance, one needs to constantly evaluate operations or processes related to producing products, providing services, and marketing and selling products. Performance evaluation and benchmarking are a widely used method to identify and adopt best practices as a means to improve performance and increase productivity, and are particularly valuable when no objective or engineered standard is available to define efficient and effective performance. For this reason, benchmarking is often used in managing service operations, because service standards (benchmarks) are more difficult to define than manufacturing standards.

Benchmarks can be established but they are somewhat limited as they work with single measurements one at a time. It is difficult to evaluate an organization's performance when there are multiple inputs and outputs to the system. The difficulties are further enhanced when the relationships between the inputs and the outputs are complex and involve unknown tradeoffs. It is critical to show benchmarks where multiple measurements exist. The current book introduces the methodology of data envelopment analysis (DEA) and its uses in performance evaluation and benchmarking under the context of multiple performance measures.

DEA uses mathematical programming techniques and models to evaluate the performance of peer units (e.g., bank branches, hospitals and schools) in terms of multiple inputs used and multiple outputs produced. DEA examines the resources available to each unit and monitors the "conversion" of these resources (inputs) into the desired outputs. Since DEA was first introduced in 1978, over 2000 DEA-related articles have been published. Researchers in a number of fields have quickly recognized that DEA is an excellent methodology for modeling operational processes. DEA's empirical orientation and absence of *a priori* assumptions have resulted in its use in a number of studies involving efficient frontier estimation in the nonprofit sector, in the regulated sector, and in the private sector. DEA applications involve a wide range of contexts, such as education, health care, banking, armed forces, auditing, market research, retail outlets, organization effectiveness, transportation, public housing, and manufacturing.

The motivation for this book is three-fold. First, as DEA is being applied to a variety of efficiency evaluation problems, managers may want to conduct performance evaluation and analyze decision alternatives without the help of sophisticated modeling programs. For this purpose, spreadsheet modeling is a suitable vehicle. In fact, spreadsheet modeling has been recognized as one of the most effective ways to evaluate decision alternatives. It is easy for the managers to apply various DEA models in spreadsheets. The book introduces spreadsheet modeling into DEA, and shows how various conventional and new DEA approaches can be implemented using Microsoft® Excel and Solver. With the assistant of the developed DEA spreadsheets, the user can easily develop new DEA models to deal with specific evaluation scenarios.

Second, new models for performance evaluation and benchmarking are needed to evaluate business operations and processes in a variety of contexts. After briefly presenting the basic DEA techniques, the current book introduces new DEA models and approaches. For example, a context-dependent DEA measures the relative attractiveness of competitive alternatives. Sensitivity analysis techniques can be easily applied, and used to identify critical performance measures. Value chain efficiency models deal with multi-stage efficiency evaluation problems. DEA benchmarking models incorporate benchmarks and standards into DEA evaluation.

All these new models can be useful in benchmarking and analyzing complex operational efficiency in manufacturing organizations as well as evaluating processes in banking, retail, franchising, health care, e-business, public services and many other industries. For example, information technology (IT) has been used extensively in every single industry in the world to improve performance and productivity. Yet there are still relatively few means of measuring the exact impact of IT investments on productivity. The value chain efficiency and DEA benchmarking models can be utilized to examine how efficiently organizations are using their IT investments, and how these investments affect the productivity and profitability of their everyday operations.

Third, although the spreadsheet modeling approach is an excellent way to build new DEA models, an integrated easy-to-use DEA software can be helpful to managers, researchers, and practitioners. I therefore develop a DEA Excel Solver which is a DEA Add-In for Microsoft® Excel. DEA Excel Solver offers the user the ability to perform a variety of DEA models and approaches – it provides a custom Excel menu which calculates more than 150 different DEA models. The DEA Excel Solver requires Excel 97 or later versions, and does not set limit on the number of units, inputs or outputs. With the capacity of Excel Solver engines, this allows the user to deal with large sized performance evaluation problems.

I would like to offer my sincere thanks to my mentor, friend and collaborator, Dr. Lawrence M. Seiford who helped and enabled me to contribute to dual areas of DEA methodology and applications, and to Dr. William W. Cooper who constantly supports my DEA research. I also want to thank Dr. Frederick S. Hiller – the series Editor, and Roberts Apse and Gary Folven of Kluwer Publishers for their support in publishing the book. However, any errors in the book are entirely my responsibility, and I would be grateful if anyone would bring any such errors to my attention.

Joe Zhu, April 2002.

Chapter 1

Basic DEA Models

1.1 Performance Evaluation, Tradeoffs, and DEA

All business operations/processes involve transformation – adding values and changes to materials and turning them into goods and services that customers want. The transformation involves the use of inputs made up of labor, materials, energy, machines, and other resources, and the generation of outputs of finished products, services, customer satisfaction, and other outcomes. Consider hospital operations, for example. The inputs include doctors, nurses, medical supplies, equipment, laboratories, beds and others, and outputs include number of patients treated, number of interns and residents trained, and others. Managers are often interested in evaluating how efficiently various processes operate with respect to multiple inputs and outputs. For example, in a buyer-seller supply chain, the buyer may be interested in comparing the performance of several sellers with respect to response time, costs, flexibility, customer service, quality, and customization. Eliminating or improving inefficient operations decreases the cost of inputs and increases productivity. Performance evaluation and benchmarking help business operations/processes to become more productive.

Performance evaluation is an important continuous improvement tool for staying competitive and plays an important role in the high-technology world of computers and telecommunications where competition is intense and grows more so each day. Performance evaluation and benchmarking positively force any business unit to constantly evolve and improve in order to survive and prosper in a business environment facing global competition. Through performance evaluation, one can (i) reveal the strengths and weaknesses of business operations, activities, and processes; (ii) better prepare the business to meet its customers' needs and requirements; and (iii) identify opportunities to improve current operations and processes, and create new products, services and processes.

Single-measure based gap analysis is often used as a fundamental method in performance evaluation and benchmarking. However, as pointed out by Camp (1995), one of the dilemmas that we face is how to show benchmarks where multiple measurements exist. It is rare that one single measure can suffice for the purpose of performance evaluation. The single output to input financial ratios, such as, return on investment (ROI) and return on sales (ROS), may be used as indices to characterize the financial performance. However, they are unsatisfactory discriminants of "best-practice", and are not sufficient to evaluate operating efficiency. Since a business unit's performance is a complex phenomenon requiring more than a single criterion to characterize it. For example, as pointed out by Sherman (1984), a bank branch may be profitable when profit reflects the interest and the revenues earned on funds generated by the branch less the cost of these funds and less the costs of operating the branch. However, this profit measure does not indicate whether the resources used to provide customer services are being managed efficiently.

Further, the use of single measures ignores any interactions, substitutions or tradeoffs among various performance measures. Each business operation has specific performance measures with tradeoffs. For example, consider the tradeoff between total supply chain cost and supply chain response time, measured by the amount of time between an order and its corresponding delivery. Figure 1.1 illustrates alternate supply chain operations S1, S2, S3, and S, and the efficient frontier or tradeoff curve determined by them. A supply chain whose performance (or strategy) is on the efficient frontier is non-dominated (efficient) in the sense that no alternate supply chain's performance is strictly better in both cost and response time. Through performance evaluation, the efficient frontier that represents the best practice is identified, and an inefficient strategy (e.g., point S) can be improved (moved to the efficient frontier) with suggested directions for improvement (to S1, S2, S3 or other points along the frontier).

Optimization techniques can be used to estimate the efficient frontier if we know the functional forms for the relationships among various performance measures. For example, stockout levels and inventory turns are two mutually dependent variables with performance tradeoffs. Technological and process innovations can shift the cost tradeoff curves by reducing the cost of achieving lower inventories at a particular stockout level or the cost of achieving lower stockouts at a particular inventory level. Unfortunately, such information is usually not completely available.

Without *a priori* information on the tradeoffs, the functional forms cannot be specified. Consequently, we cannot fully characterize the business operations and processes. Note that the objective of performance evaluation is to evaluate the current business operation internally and to benchmark against similar business operations externally to identify the best practice. Thus, such best-practices can be empirically identified. We can empirically estimate the efficient frontier based upon observations on one business operation/process over time or similar business operations at a specific time period.

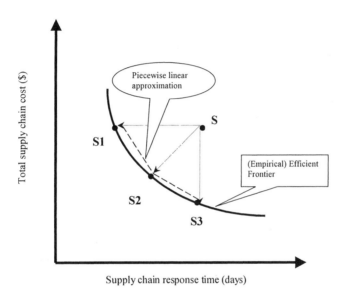

Figure 1.1. Efficient Frontier of Supply Chain Operations

Throughout the book, we use decision making units (DMUs) to represent business operations or processes . Each DMU has a set of inputs and outputs, representing multiple performance measures. Consider a set of n observations on the DMUs. Each observation, DMU_j $(j = 1, ..., n)$, uses m inputs x_{ij} $(i = 1, 2, ..., m)$ to produce s outputs y_{rj} $(r = 1, 2, ..., s)$.

The (empirical) efficient frontier or best-practice frontier is determined by these n observations. The following two properties ensure that we can develop a piecewise linear approximation to the efficient frontier and the area dominated by the frontier.

Property 1.1 *Convexity.* $\sum_{j=1}^{n} \lambda_j \, x_{ij}$ $(i = 1, 2, ..., m)$ and $\sum_{j=1}^{n} \lambda_j \, y_{rj}$ $(r = 1, 2, ..., s)$ are possible inputs and outputs achievable by the DMU$_j$, where λ_j $(j = 1, ..., n)$ are nonnegative scalars such that $\sum_{j=1}^{n} \lambda_j = 1$.

Property 1.2 *Inefficiency.* The same y_{rj} can be obtained by using $\hat{x}_{ij}$, where $\hat{x}_{ij} \geq x_{ij}$ (i.e., the same outputs can be produced by using more inputs); The same x_{ij} can be used to obtain $\hat{y}_{rj}$, where $\hat{y}_{rj} \leq y_{rj}$ (i.e., the same inputs can be used to produce less outputs).

Consider Figure 1.1 where total supply chain cost and supply chain response time represent two inputs. Applying Property 1.1 to S1, S2, and S3 yields the piecewise linear approximation to the curve shown in Figure 1.1. Applying both properties expands the line segments S1S2 and S2S3 into the area dominated by the curve.

For specific x_i $(i = 1, 2, ..., m)$ and y_i $(r = 1, 2, ..., s)$, we have

$$\begin{cases} \sum_{j=1}^{n} \lambda_j x_{ij} \leq x_i & i = 1, 2, ..., m \\ \sum_{j=1}^{n} \lambda_j y_{rj} \geq y_i & r = 1, 2, ..., s \\ \sum_{j=1}^{n} \lambda_j = 1 \end{cases} \tag{1.1}$$

The next step is to estimate the empirical (piecewise linear) efficient frontier characterized by (1.1). Data Envelopment Analysis (DEA) has been proven an effective tool in identifying such empirical frontiers and in evaluating relative efficiency. DEA uses mathematical programming to implicitly estimate the tradeoffs inherent in the empirical efficient frontier.

DEA was designed to measure the relative efficiency where market prices are not available (see, e.g., Charnes, Cooper and Rhodes, 1981; Johnson and Zhu, 2002). However, by its ability to model multiple-input and multiple-output relationships without *a priori* underlying functional form assumption, DEA has also been widely applied to other areas. For example, Bank failure prediction (Barr and Siems, 1997), electric utilities evaluation (Färe, Grosskopf, Logan and Lovell, 1985), textile industry performance (Zhu, 1996c), steel industry productivity (Ray, Seiford and Zhu, 1998), highway maintenance efficiency (Cook, Roll and Kazakov, 1990), individual physician practice (Chilingerian, 1995), software development (Banker and Kemerer, 1989), spatial efficiency (Desai and Storbeck, 1990), sports (Anderson and Sharp, 1997), logistics systems (Kleinsorge, Schary and Tanner, 1989) among others. See Charnes, Cooper, Lewin and Seiford (1994) for a collection of DEA applications. Such previous DEA studies provide useful managerial information on improving the performance. In particular, DEA is an excellent tool for improving the productivity of service businesses (Sherman, 1984).

In the current book, we present various DEA approaches that can be used in empirical efficient frontier estimation and further in performance evaluation and benchmarking. For readers who are interested in detailed discussion on fundamental DEA, please refer to Cooper, Seiford and Tone (2000) and Thanassoulis (2001).

1.2 Envelopment Model

1.2.1 Envelopment Models with Variable Returns to Scale

Two alternative approaches are available in DEA to estimate the efficient frontier characterized by (1.1). One is input-oriented, and the other output-oriented.

The following DEA model is an input-oriented model where the inputs are minimized and the outputs are kept at their current levels.

$$
\begin{aligned}
&\theta^* = \min \theta \\
&\text{subject to} \\
&\sum_{j=1}^{n} \lambda_j x_{ij} \le \theta x_{io} \qquad i = 1,2,\dots,m; \\
&\sum_{j=1}^{n} \lambda_j y_{rj} \ge y_{ro} \qquad r = 1,2,\dots,s; \\
&\sum_{j=1}^{n} \lambda_j = 1 \\
&\lambda_j \ge 0 \qquad\qquad j = 1,2,\dots,n.
\end{aligned}
\qquad (1.2)
$$

where DMU_o represents one of the n DMUs under evaluation, and x_{io} and y_{ro} are the ith input and rth output for DMU_o, respectively.

Since $\theta = 1$ is a feasible solution to (1.2), the optimal value to (1.2), $\theta^* \le 1$. If $\theta^* = 1$, then the current input levels cannot be reduced (proportionally), indicating that DMU_o is on the frontier. Otherwise, if $\theta^* < 1$, then DMU_o is dominated by the frontier. θ^* represents the (input-oriented) efficiency score of DMU_o.

Consider a simple numerical example shown in Table 1.1 where we have five DMUs (supply chain operations). Within a week, each DMU generates the same profit of $2,000 with a different combination of supply chain cost and response time.

Table 1.1. Supply Chain Operations Within a Week

DMU	Cost ($100)	Response time (days)	Profit ($1,000)
1	1	5	2
2	2	2	2
3	4	1	2
4	6	1	2
5	4	4	2

Figure 1.2 presents the five DMUs and the piecewise linear frontier. DMUs 1, 2, 3, and 4 are on the frontier. If we calculate model (1.2) for DMU5,

$$\text{Min } \theta$$

Subject to
$$1\,\lambda_1 + 2\lambda_2 + 4\lambda_3 + 6\lambda_4 + 4\lambda_5 \leq 4\theta$$
$$5\,\lambda_1 + 2\lambda_2 + 1\lambda_3 + 1\lambda_4 + 4\lambda_5 \leq 4\theta$$
$$2\,\lambda_1 + 2\lambda_2 + 2\lambda_3 + 2\lambda_4 + 2\lambda_5 \geq 2$$
$$\lambda_1 + \lambda_2 + \lambda_3 + \lambda_4 + \lambda_5 = 1$$
$$\lambda_1,\, \lambda_2,\, \lambda_3, \lambda_4,\, \lambda_5 \geq 0$$

we obtain a set of unique optimal solutions of $\theta^* = 0.5$, $\lambda_2^* = 1$, and $\lambda_j^* = 0$ ($j \neq 2$), indicating that DMU2 is the benchmark for DMU5, and DMU5 should reduce its cost and response time to the amounts used by DMU2.

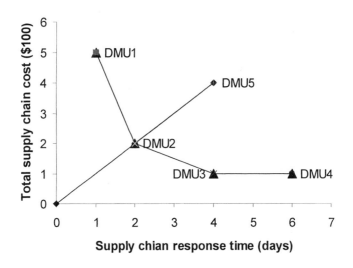

Figure 1.2. Five Supply Chain Operations

Now, if we calculate model (1.2) for DMU4, we obtain $\theta^* = 1$, $\lambda_4^* = 1$, and $\lambda_j^* = 0$ ($j \neq 4$), indicating that DMU4 is on the frontier. However, Figure 1.2 indicates that DMU4 can still reduce its response time by 2 days to reach DMU3. This individual input reduction is called input slack.

In fact, both input and output slack values may exist in model (1.2). Usually, after calculating (1.2), we have

$$\begin{cases} s_i^- = \theta^* x_{io} - \sum_{j=1}^{n} \lambda_j x_{ij} & i = 1,2,...,m \\ s_r^+ = \sum_{j=1}^{n} \lambda_j y_{rj} - y_{ro} & r = 1,2,...,s \end{cases} \qquad (1.3)$$

where s_i^- and s_r^+ represent input and output slacks, respectively. An alternate optimal solution of $\theta^* = 1$ and $\lambda_3^* = 1$ exists when we calculate model (1.2) for DMU4. This leads to $s_1^- = 2$ for DMU4. However, if we obtain $\theta^* = 1$ and $\lambda_4^* = 1$ from model (1.2), we have all zero slack values. i.e., because of possible multiple optimal solutions, (1.3) may not yield all the non-zero slacks.

Therefore, we use the following linear programming model to determine the possible non-zero slacks after (1.2) is solved.

$$\max \sum_{i=1}^{m} s_i^- + \sum_{r=1}^{s} s_r^+$$
subject to
$$\sum_{j=1}^{n} \lambda_j x_{ij} + s_i^- = \theta^* x_{io} \qquad i = 1,2,...,m;$$
$$\sum_{j=1}^{n} \lambda_j y_{rj} - s_r^+ = y_{ro} \qquad r = 1,2,...,s; \qquad (1.4)$$
$$\sum_{j=1}^{n} \lambda_j = 1$$
$$\lambda_j \geq 0 \qquad j = 1,2,...,n.$$

For example, applying (1.4) to DMU4 yields

$$\text{Max } s_1^- + s_2^- + s_1^+$$
$$\text{Subject to}$$
$$1\lambda_1 + 2\lambda_2 + 4\lambda_3 + 6\lambda_4 + 4\lambda_5 + s_1^- = 4\theta^* = 4$$
$$5\lambda_1 + 2\lambda_2 + 1\lambda_3 + 1\lambda_4 + 4\lambda_5 + s_2^- = 4\theta^* = 4$$
$$2\lambda_1 + 2\lambda_2 + 2\lambda_3 + 2\lambda_4 + 2\lambda_5 - s_1^+ = 2$$
$$\lambda_1 + \lambda_2 + \lambda_3 + \lambda_4 + \lambda_5 = 1$$
$$\lambda_1, \lambda_2, \lambda_3, \lambda_4, \lambda_5, s_1^-, s_2^-, s_1^+ \geq 0$$

with optimal slacks of $s_1^{-*} = 2$, $s_2^{-*} = s_1^{+*} = 0$.

DMU_o is efficient if and only if $\theta^* = 1$ and $s_i^{-*} = s_r^{+*} = 0$ for all i and r. DMU_o is weakly efficient if $\theta^* = 1$ and $s_i^{-*} \neq 0$ and (or) $s_r^{+*} \neq 0$ for some i and r. In Figure 1.2, DMUs 1, 2, and 3 are efficient, and DMU 4 is weakly efficient. (The slacks obtained by (1.4) are called DEA slacks, see Definition 9.2 in Chapter 9.)

In fact, models (1.2) and (1.4) represent a two-stage DEA process involved in the following DEA model.

$$\min \theta - \varepsilon \left(\sum_{i=1}^{m} s_i^- + \sum_{r=1}^{s} s_r^+ \right)$$

subject to

$$\sum_{j=1}^{n} \lambda_j x_{ij} + s_i^- = \theta x_{io} \qquad i = 1,2,...,m;$$

$$\sum_{j=1}^{n} \lambda_j y_{rj} - s_r^+ = y_{ro} \qquad r = 1,2,...,s; \qquad (1.5)$$

$$\sum_{j=1}^{n} \lambda_j = 1$$

$$\lambda_j \geq 0 \qquad j = 1,2,...,n.$$

The presence of the non-Archimedean ε in the objective function of (1.5) effectively allows the minimization over θ to preempt the optimization involving the slacks, s_i^- and s_r^+. Thus, (1.5) is calculated in a two-stage process with maximal reduction of inputs being achieved first, via the optimal θ^* in (1.2); then, in the second stage, movement onto the efficient frontier is achieved via optimizing the slack variables in (1.4).

In fact, the presence of weakly efficient DMUs is the cause of multiple optimal solutions. Thus, if weakly efficient DMUs are not present, the second stage calculation (1.4) is not necessary, and we can obtain the slacks using (1.3). However, priori to calculation, we usually do not know whether weakly efficient DMUs are present.

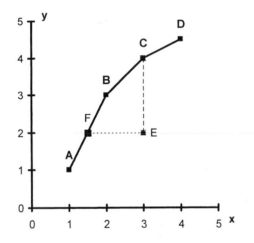

Figure 1.3. VRS Frontier

Note that the frontier determined by model (1.5) exhibits variable returns to scale (VRS). Model (1.5) is called input-oriented VRS envelopment model. (see Chapter 3 for a detailed discussion on DEA and Returns-to-Scale (RTS).)

Consider Figure 1.3 where we have 5 DMUs (A, B, C, D, and E) with one input and one output. The VRS frontier consists of DMUs A, B, C, and D. AB exhibits increasing RTS (IRS), B exhibits constant RTS (CRS), and BC and CD exhibit decreasing RTS (DRS).

Based upon (1.5), DMU E is inefficient and is compared to F (a convex combination of A and B) on the VRS frontier, i.e., E should reduce its input to F, or F is the efficient target for E. If we use an output-oriented model, E is compared to C by increasing output.

The output-oriented VRS envelopment model can be expressed as

$$\max \phi - \varepsilon \left(\sum_{i=1}^{m} s_i^- + \sum_{r=1}^{s} s_r^+ \right)$$

subject to

$$\sum_{j=1}^{n} \lambda_j x_{ij} + s_i^- = x_{io} \qquad i = 1, 2, \ldots, m;$$

$$\sum_{j=1}^{n} \lambda_j y_{rj} - s_r^+ = \phi y_{ro} \qquad r = 1, 2, \ldots, s; \qquad (1.6)$$

$$\sum_{j=1}^{n} \lambda_j = 1$$

$$\lambda_j \geq 0 \qquad\qquad j = 1, 2, \ldots, n.$$

Model (1.6) is also calculated in a two-stage process. First, we calculate ϕ^* by ignoring the slacks, and then we optimize the slacks by fixing the ϕ^* in the following linear programming problem.

$$\max \sum_{i=1}^{m} s_i^- + \sum_{r=1}^{s} s_r^+$$

subject to

$$\sum_{j=1}^{n} \lambda_j x_{ij} + s_i^- = x_{io} \qquad i = 1, 2, \ldots, m;$$

$$\sum_{j=1}^{n} \lambda_j y_{rj} - s_r^+ = \phi^* y_{ro} \qquad r = 1, 2, \ldots, s; \qquad (1.7)$$

$$\sum_{j=1}^{n} \lambda_j = 1$$

$$\lambda_j \geq 0 \qquad\qquad j = 1, 2, \ldots, n.$$

DMU_o is efficient if and only if $\phi^* = 1$ and $s_i^{-*} = s_r^{+*} = 0$ for all i and r. DMU_o is weakly efficient if $\phi^* = 1$ and $s_i^{-*} \neq 0$ and (or) $s_r^{+*} \neq 0$ for some i and r. If weakly efficient DMUs are not present, then we need not to calculate (1.7), and we can obtain the slacks via

$$\begin{cases} s_i^- = x_{io} - \sum_{j=1}^{n} \lambda_j x_{ij} & i = 1,2,...,m \\ s_r^+ = \sum_{j=1}^{n} \lambda_j y_{rj} - \phi^* y_{ro} & r = 1,2,...,s \end{cases}$$

Note that $\phi^* \geq 1$, and $\phi^* = 1$ if and only if $\theta^* = 1$. This indicates that models (1.5) and (1.6) identify the same frontier. Also, $\theta^* = 1/\phi^*$ (see Lemma 3.2 in Chapter 3).

Figure 1.2 shows an input efficient frontier when outputs are fixed at their current levels. Similarly, we can obtain an output efficient frontier when inputs are fixed at their current levels. Consider the four DMUs shown in Figure 1.4 where we have two outputs.

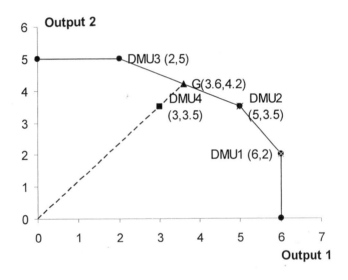

Figure 1.4. Output Efficient Frontier

In Figure 1.4, DMUs 1, 2 and 3 are efficient. If we calculate model (1.6) for DMU4, we have

$$\begin{aligned} &\text{Max } \phi \\ &\text{Subject to} \\ &\lambda_1 + \lambda_2 + \lambda_3 + \lambda_4 \leq 1 \\ &6\lambda_1 + 5\lambda_2 + 2\lambda_3 + 3\lambda_4 \geq 3\phi \\ &2\lambda_1 + 3.5\lambda_2 + 5\lambda_3 + 3.5\lambda_4 \geq 3.5\phi \\ &\lambda_1 + \lambda_2 + \lambda_3 + \lambda_4 = 1 \\ &\lambda_1, \lambda_2, \lambda_3, \lambda_4 \geq 0 \end{aligned}$$

The optimal solution is $\phi^* = 1.2$, $\lambda_2^* = 8/15$, and $\lambda_3^* = 7/15$. i.e., DMU4 is inefficient and is compared to G in Figure 1.4, or DMU4 should increase its two output levels to G.

1.2.2   Other Envelopment Models

The constraint on $\sum_{j=1}^{n} \lambda_j$ actually determines the RTS type of an efficient frontier. If we remove $\sum_{j=1}^{n} \lambda_j = 1$ from models (1.5) and (1.6), we obtain CRS envelopment models where the frontier exhibits CRS. Figure 1.5 shows an CRS frontier – ray OB. Based upon this CRS frontier, only B is efficient.

If we replace $\sum_{j=1}^{n} \lambda_j = 1$ with $\sum_{j=1}^{n} \lambda_j \leq 1$, then we obtain non-increasing RTS (NIRS) envelopment models. In Figure 1.6, the NIRS frontier consists of DMUs B, C, D and the origin.

If we replace $\sum_{j=1}^{n} \lambda_j = 1$ with $\sum_{j=1}^{n} \lambda_j \geq 1$, then we obtain non-decreasing RTS (NDRS) envelopment models. In Figure 1.7, the NDRS frontier consists of DMUs, A, B, and the section starting with B on ray OB.

Table 1.2 summarizes the envelopment models with respect to the orientations and frontier types. The last row presents the efficient target (DEA projection) of a specific DMU under evaluation.

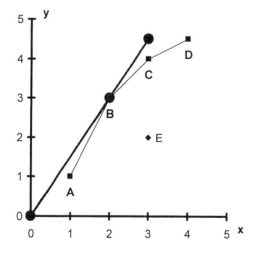

Figure 1.5. CRS Frontier

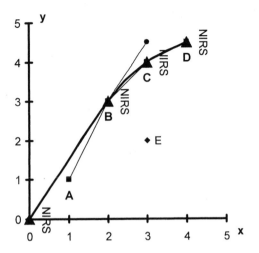

Figure 1.6. NIRS Frontier

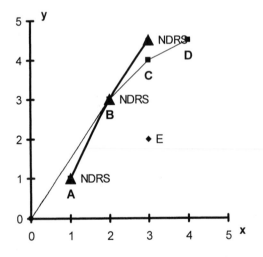

Figure 1.7. NDRS Frontier

Table 1.2. Envelopment Models

Frontier Type	Input-Oriented		Output-Oriented	
	$\min \theta - \varepsilon(\sum\limits_{i=1}^{m} s_i^- + \sum\limits_{r=1}^{s} s_r^+)$ subject to		$\max \phi - \varepsilon(\sum\limits_{i=1}^{m} s_i^- + \sum\limits_{r=1}^{s} s_r^+)$ subject to	
CRS	$\sum\limits_{j=1}^{n} \lambda_j x_{ij} + s_i^- = \theta x_{io}$ $i=1,2,...,m;$ $\sum\limits_{j=1}^{n} \lambda_j y_{rj} - s_r^+ = y_{ro}$ $r=1,2,...,s;$ $\lambda_j \geq 0$ $j=1,2,...,n.$		$\sum\limits_{j=1}^{n} \lambda_j x_{ij} + s_i^- = x_{io}$ $i=1,2,...,m;$ $\sum\limits_{j=1}^{n} \lambda_j y_{rj} - s_r^+ = \phi y_{ro}$ $r=1,2,...,s;$ $\lambda_j \geq 0$ $j=1,2,...,n.$	
VRS	Add $\sum_{j=1}^{n} \lambda_j = 1$			
NIRS	Add $\sum_{j=1}^{n} \lambda_j \leq 1$			
NDRS	Add $\sum_{j=1}^{n} \lambda_j \geq 1$			
Efficient Target	$\begin{cases} \hat{x}_{io} = \theta^* x_{io} - s_i^{-*} & i=1,2,...,m \\ \hat{y}_{ro} = y_{ro} + s_r^{+*} & r=1,2,...,s \end{cases}$		$\begin{cases} \hat{x}_{io} = x_{io} - s_i^{-*} & i=1,2,...,m \\ \hat{y}_{ro} = \phi^* y_{ro} + s_r^{+*} & r=1,2,...,s \end{cases}$	

The interpretation of the envelopment model results can be summarized as

i) If $\theta^* = 1$ or $\phi^* = 1$, then the DMU under evaluation is a frontier point. i.e., there is no other DMUs that are operating more efficiently than this DMU. Otherwise, if $\theta^* < 1$ or $\phi^* > 1$, then the DMU under evaluation is inefficient. i.e., this DMU can either increase its output levels or decrease its input levels.

ii) The left-hand-side of the envelopment models is usually called the "Reference Set", and the right-hand-side represents a specific DMU under evaluation. The non-zero optimal λ_j^* represent the benchmarks for a specific DMU under evaluation. The Reference Set provides coefficients (λ_j^*) to define the hypothetical efficient DMU. The Reference Set or the efficient target shows how inputs can be decreased and outputs increased to make the DMU under evaluation efficient.

1.3 Envelopment Models in Spreadsheets

Table 1.3 presents 15 companies from the top Fortune Global 500 list in 1995. We have three inputs: (1) number of employees, (2) assets ($ millions), and (3) equity ($ millions), and two outputs: (1) profit ($ millions), and (2) revenue ($ millions).

1.3.1   Input-oriented VRS Envelopment Spreadsheet Model

The input-oriented VRS envelopment model (model (1.5)) requires 15 calculations – one for each company. We illustrate how to formulate this efficiency evaluation problem in a spreadsheet, and then illustrate how Excel Solver can be used to calculate the efficiency scores for the 15 companies.

We begin by organizing the data in Table 1.3 in a spreadsheet (see Figure 1.8). A spreadsheet model of an envelopment model contains the following four major components: (1) cells for the decision variables (e.g., λ_j and θ); (2) cell for the objective function (efficiency) (e.g., θ); (3) cells containing formulas for computing the DEA reference set (the right-hand-side of the constraints) ($\sum_{j=1}^{n} \lambda_j x_{ij}, \sum_{j=1}^{n} \lambda_j y_{rj}$, and $\sum_{j=1}^{n} \lambda_j$); and (4) cells containing formulas for computing the DMU under evaluation (left-hand-side of the constraints) (e.g., θx_{io} and y_{ro}).

Table 1.3. Fortune Global 500 Companies

Company	Assets	Equity	Employees	Revenue	Profit
Mitsubishi	91920.6	10950	36000	184365.2	346.2
Mitsui	68770.9	5553.9	80000	181518.7	314.8
Itochu	65708.9	4271.1	7182	169164.6	121.2
General Motors	217123.4	23345.5	709000	168828.6	6880.7
Sumitomo	50268.9	6681	6193	167530.7	210.5
Marubeni	71439.3	5239.1	6702	161057.4	156.6
Ford Motor	243283	24547	346990	137137	4139
Toyota Motor	106004.2	49691.6	146855	111052	2662.4
Exxon	91296	40436	82000	110009	6470
Royal Dutch/Shell Group	118011.6	58986.4	104000	109833.7	6904.6
Wal-Mart	37871	14762	675000	93627	2740
Hitachi	91620.9	29907.2	331852	84167.1	1468.8
Nippon Life Insurance	364762.5	2241.9	89690	83206.7	2426.6
Nippon Telegraph & Telephone	127077.3	42240.1	231400	81937.2	2209.1
AT&T	88884	17274	299300	79609	139

In Figure 1.8, cells I2 through I16 represent λ_j (j = 1, 2, ..., 15). Cell F19 represents the efficiency score θ which is the objective function.

For the DEA reference set (left-hand-side of the envelopment model), we enter the following formulas that calculate the weighted sums of inputs and outputs across all DMUs, respectively.

Cell B20 =SUMPRODUCT(B2:B16,$I$2:$I$16)
Cell B21 =SUMPRODUCT(C2:C16,$I$2:$I$16)
Cell B22 =SUMPRODUCT(D2:D16,$I$2:$I$16)
Cell B23 =SUMPRODUCT(F2:F16,$I$2:$I$16)
Cell B24 =SUMPRODUCT(G2:G16,$I$2:$I$16)

For the DMU under evaluation (DMU1: Mitsubishi), we enter the following formulas into cells D20:D24.

Cell D20 =$F$19*INDEX(B2:B16,E18,1)
Cell D21 =$F$19*INDEX(C2:C16,E18,1)
Cell D22 =$F$19*INDEX(C2:C16,E18,1)
Cell D23 =INDEX(F2:F16,E18,1)
Cell D24 =INDEX(G2:G16,E18,1)

	A	B	C	D	E	F	G	H	I	J	K
1	Company	Assets	Equity	Employees		Revenue	Profit		λ	changing cell	
2	Mitsubishi	91920.6	10950	36000		184365.2	346.2		1	changing cell	
3	Mitsui	68770.9	5553.9	80000		181518.7	314.8		0	changing cell	
4	Itochu	65708.9	4271.1	7182		169164.6	121.2		0	changing cell	
5	General Motors	217123.4	23345.5	709000		168828.6	6880.7		0	changing cell	
6	Sumitomo	50268.9	6681	6193		167530.7	210.5		0	changing cell	
7	Marubeni	71439.3	5239.1	6702		161057.4	156.6		0	changing cell	
8	Ford Motor	243283	24547	346990		137137	4139		0	changing cell	
9	Toyota Motor	106004.2	49691.6	146855		111052	2662.4		0	changing cell	
10	Exxon	91296	40436	82000		110009	6470		0	changing cell	
11	Royal Dutch/Shell Group	118011.6	58986.4	104000		109833.7	6904.6		0	changing cell	
12	Wal-Mart	37871	14762	675000		93627	2740		0	changing cell	
13	Hitachi	91620.9	29907.2	331852		84167.1	1468.8		0	changing cell	
14	Nippon Life Insurance	364762.5	2241.9	89690		83206.7	2426.6		0	changing cell	
15	Nippon Telegraph & Telephone	127077.3	42240.1	231400		81937.2	2209.1		0	changing cell	
16	AT&T	88884	17274	299300		79609	139		0	changing cell	
17								Reserved to indicate			
18		Reference		DMU under	1	Efficiency		the DMU under			
19	Constraints	set		Evaluation		1		evaluation.			
20	Assets	91920.6	≤	91920.6							
21	Equity	10950	≤	10950		Efficiency; θ;					
22	Employees	36000	≤	36000		A changing cell;					
23	Revenue	Constraint on Σλ		184365.2		Target cell in Solver					
24	Profit	346.2	≥	346.2							
25	Σλ	1	=	1							

Figure 1.8. Input-oriented VRS Envelopment Spreadsheet Model

Finally, we enter the formula for $\sum_{j=1}^{n} \lambda_j = 1$ into cells B25 (=SUM(I2:I16)) and D25 (=1), respectively.

Cell E18 is reserved to indicate the DMU under evaluation. The function INDEX(array,row number,column number) returns the value in the specified row and column of the given array. Because cell E18 contains the current value of 1, the INDEX function in cell D23 returns the value in first row and first column of the Revenue array F2:F16 (or the value in cell F2, the Revenue output for DMU1). When the value in cell E18 changes from 1 to 15, the INDEX functions in cells D20:D24 return the input and output values for a specific DMU under evaluation. This feature becomes obvious and useful when we provide the Visual Basic for Applications (VBA) code to automate the DEA computation.

1.3.2   Using Solver

After the DEA model is set up in the spreadsheet, we can use Solver to find the optimal solutions. First, we need to invoke Solver in Excel by using the Tools/Solver menu item, as shown in Figure 1.9.

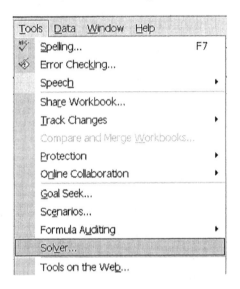

Figure 1.9. Display Solver Parameters Dialog Box

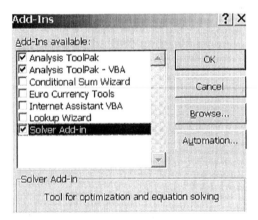

Figure 1.10. Solver Add-In

If Solver does not exist in the Tools menu, you need to select Tools/Add-Ins, and check the Solver box, as shown in Figure 1.10.

(If Solver does not show in the Add-Ins, you need to install the Solver first.)

Now, you should see the Solver Parameters dialog box shown in Figure 1.11.

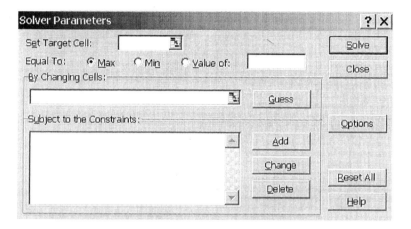

Figure 1.11. Solver Parameters Dialog Box

1.3.3 Specifying the Target Cell

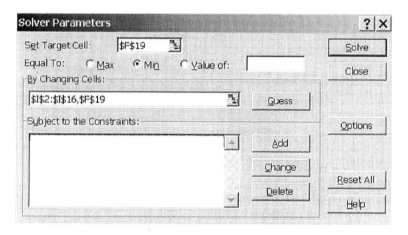

Figure 1.12. Specifying Target Cell and Changing Cells

Set Target Cell indicates the objective function cell in the spreadsheet, and whether its value should be maximized or minimized. In our case, the target cell is the DEA efficiency represented by cell F19, and its value should be minimized, because we use the input-oriented VRS envelopment model (1.5) (see Figure 1.12).

1.3.4   Specifying Changing Cells

Changing Cells represent the decision variables in the spreadsheet. In our case, they represent the λ_j (j = 1,2, ..., 15) and θ, and should be cells I2:I16 and F19, respectively (see Figure 1.12).

1.3.5   Adding Constraints

Constraints represent the constraints in the spreadsheet. In our case, they are determined by cells B20:B25 and D20:D25. For example, click the Add button shown in Figure 1.12, you will see the Add Constraint dialog box shown in Figure 1.13.

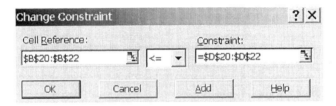

Figure 1.13. Adding Constraints

In the spreadsheet model shown in Figure 1.8, we have six constraints. The "Cell Reference" corresponds to the DEA Reference Set, and "Constraint" corresponds to the DMU under evaluation. The first three constraints are related to the three inputs (see Figure 1.13). Click the Add button to add additional constraints (output constraints and $\sum_{j=1}^{n} \lambda_j = 1$), and click the OK button when you have finished adding the constraints. The set of the constraints are shown in Figure 1.15.

1.3.6   Non-Negativity and Linear Model

Note that λ_j and θ are all non-negative, and the envelopment model is a linear programming problem. This can be achieved by clicking the Option button in Figure 1.12, and then checking the Assume Non-Negative and Assume Linear Model boxes, as shown in Figure 1.14. This action should be performed for each DEA model. In the rest of the book, we will not show the Solver Options dialog box.

When the Assuming Linear Model option is checked, Solver conducts a number of internal tests to see if the model is truly linear. When the data are poorly scaled, Solver may show that the conditions for linearity are not satisfied. To circumvent this, we may check the box of "Use Automatic Scaling" in the Solver Options dialog box.

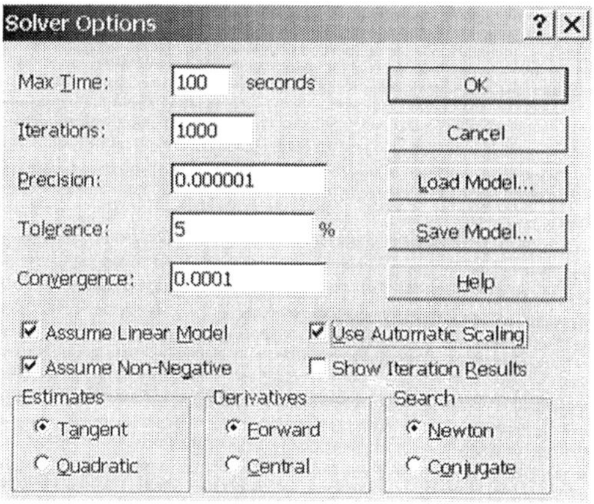

Figure 1.14. Non-Negative and Linear Model

1.3.7   Solving the Model

Now, we have successfully set up the Solver Parameters dialog box, as shown in Figure 1.15. Click the Solve button to solve the model. When Solver finds an optimal solution, it displays the Solver Results dialog box, as shown in Figure 1.16.

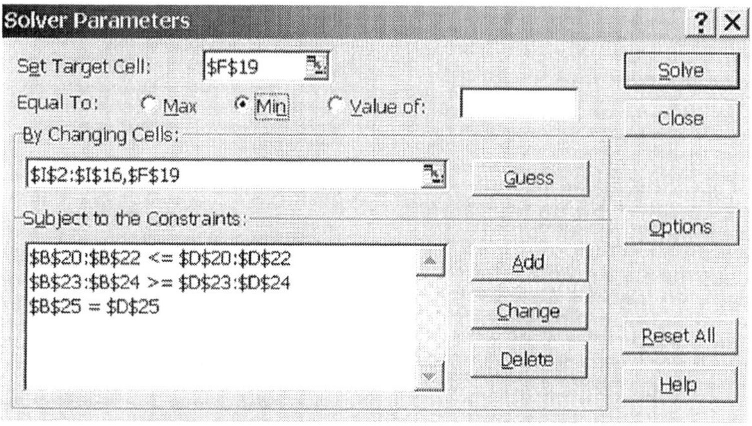

Figure 1.15. Solver Parameters for Input-oriented VRS Envelopment Model

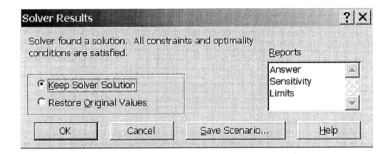

Figure 1.16. Solver Results Dialog Box

1.3.8   Automating the DEA Calculation

To complete the analysis for the remaining 14 companies, one needs to manually change the value in cell E18 to 2, 3, …, 15 and use Solver to re-optimize the spreadsheet model for each company and record the efficiency scores (in column J, for instance). When the number of DMUs becomes large, the manual process is apparently cumbersome.

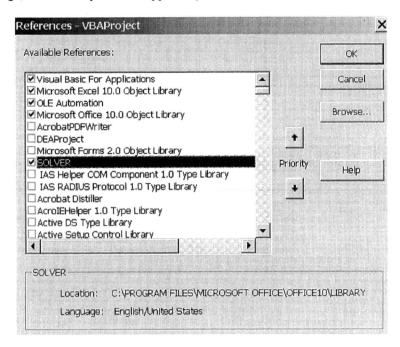

Figure 1.17. Adding Reference to Solver Add-In

Note that exactly the same Solver settings will be used to find the optimal solutions for the remaining DMUs. This allows us to write a simple VBA code to carry out the process automatically.

Before we write the VBA code, we need to set a reference to Solver Add-In in Visual Basic (VB) Editor. Otherwise, VBA will not recognize the Solver functions and you will get a "Sub or function not defined" error message.

We may follow the following procedure to set the reference. Enter the VB Editor by pressing *Alt-F11* key combination (or using the Tools/Macro/Visual Basic Editor menu item). Open the Tools/References menu in the VB Editor. This brings up a list of references. One of these should be **Solver.xla** (see Figure 1.17).

To add the reference, simply check its box. If it says "Missing: Solver.xla", then click the Browse button and search for **Solver.xla**. If you are using Excel XP, the **Solver.xla** is usually located at C:\Program Files\Microsoft Office\Office10\Library\ Solver. Otherwise, the **Solver.xla** is usually located at C:\Program Files\Microsoft Office\Office\Library\ Solver. However, this depends on where the Microsoft® Office is installed.

After the Solver reference is added, we should see "Reference to Solver.xla" under the "References" in the VBA Project Explorer window shown in Figure 1.18. (The file "envelopment spreadsheet.xls" in the CD contains the spreadsheet model.)

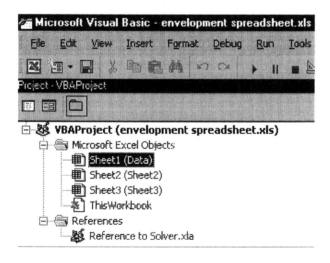

Figure 1.18. Reference to Solver Add-In in VBA Project

Next, select the Insert/Module menu item in the VB Editor (Figure 1.19). This action will add a Module (e.g., Module1) into the Excel file. (You can change the name of the inserted module in the Name property of the module.)

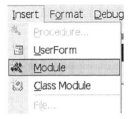

Figure 1.19. Insert a Module

Now, we can insert the VBA code into the Module1. Type "Sub DEA()" in the code window. This generates a VBA procedure called DEA which is also the Macro name (see Figure 1.21). Figure 1.20 shows the VBA code for automating the DEA calculation.

The Macro statement "SolverSolve UserFinish:=True" tells the Solver to solve the DEA problem without displaying the Solver Results dialog box. The "Offset(*rowOffset, columnOffset*)" property takes two arguments that correspond to the relative position from the upper-left cell of the specified Range. When we evaluate the first DMU, i.e., DMUNo = 1, Range("J1").Offset(1,0) refers to cell J2. The statements "With Range("J1")" and ".Offset(DMUNo, 0)=Range("F19")" take the optimal objective function value (efficiency score) in cell F19 and place it in cell J "DMUNo" (that is, cell J2, J3, …, J16).

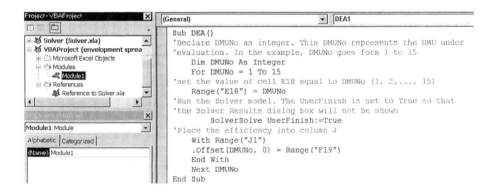

Figure 1.20. VBA Code for Input-oriented VRS Envelopment Model

Enter the Run Macro dialog box by pressing *Alt-F8* key combination (or using the Tools/Macro/Macros menu item). You should see "DEA", as shown in Figure 1.21. Select "DEA" and then click the Run button. This action will generate the efficiency scores (cells J2:J16) for the 15 companies, as shown in Figure 1.22.

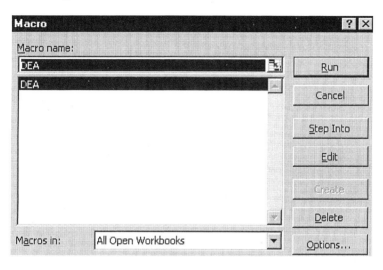

Figure 1.21. Run "DEA" Macro

	A	B	C	D	E	F	G	H	I	J
1	Company	Assets	Equity	Employees		Revenue	Profit		λ	Efficiency
2	Mitsubishi	91920.6	10950	36000		184365.2	346.2		0	1
3	Mitsui	68770.9	5553.9	80000		181518.7	314.8		0	1
4	Itochu	65708.9	4271.1	7182		169164.6	121.2		0	1
5	General Motors	217123.4	23345.5	709000		168828.6	6880.7		0	1
6	Sumitomo	50268.9	6681	6193		167530.7	210.5		0.77	1
7	Marubeni	71439.3	5239.1	6702		161057.4	156.6		0	1
8	Ford Motor	243283	24547	346990		137137	4139		0	0.737556
9	Toyota Motor	106004.2	49691.6	146855		111052	2662.4		0	0.603245
10	Exxon	91296	40436	82000		110009	6470		0	1
11	Royal Dutch/Shell Group	118011.6	58986.4	104000		109833.7	6904.6		0	1
12	Wal-Mart	37871	14762	675000		93627	2740		0.23	1
13	Hitachi	91620.9	29907.2	331852		84167.1	1468.8		0	0.557596
14	Nippon Life Insurance	364762.5	2241.9	89690		83206.7	2426.6		0	1
15	Nippon Telegraph & Telephone	127077.3	42240.1	231400		81937.2	2209.1		0	0.470611
16	AT&T	88884	17274	299300		79609	139		0	0.533544
17										
18		Reference		DMU under	15	Efficiency				
19	**Constraints**	set		Evaluation		0.533544				
20	Assets	47423.482	≤	47423.482						
21	Equity	8535.6544	≤	9216.4308						
22	Employees	159689.58	≤	159689.58						
23	Revenue	150569.21	≥	79609						
24	Profit	791.04056	≥	139						
25	Σλ	1	=	1						

Figure 1.22. Input-oriented VRS Envelopment Efficiency

Ten companies are efficient (on the VRS frontier). For the inefficient companies, the non-zero optimal λ_j indicate the benchmarks. For example, the efficiency score for AT&T is 0.53354 and the benchmarks for AT&T are Sumitoma ($\lambda_5 = 0.77$ in cell I6) and Wal-Mart ($\lambda_{11} = 0.23$ in cell I12).

The previous macro "DEA" does not record the optimal λ_j in the worksheet. This can be done by the adding a VBA procedure named "DEA1" into the existing module.

```
Sub DEA1()
'Declare DMUNo as integer. This DMUNo represents the DMU under
'evaluation. In the example, DMUNo goes form 1 to 15
    Dim DMUNo As Integer
    For DMUNo = 1 To 15
'set the value of cell E18 equal to DMUNo (1, 2,..., 15)
    Range("E18") = DMUNo
'Run the Solver model. The UserFinish is set to True so that
'the Solver Results dialog box will not be shown
    SolverSolve UserFinish:=True
'Place the efficiency into column J
    Range("J" & DMUNo + 1) = Range("F19")
'Select the cells containing the optimal lambdas
    Range("I2:I16").Select
'copy the selected lambdas and paste them to row "DMUNo+1"
'(that is row 2, 3, ..., 16) starting with column K
Selection.Copy
Range("K" & DMUNo + 1).Select
Selection.PasteSpecial Paste:=xlPasteValues, Transpose:=True
Next DMUNo
End Sub
```

In the Run Macro dialog box, select "DEA1" and then click the Run button. The procedure "DEA1" will record both the efficiency scores and the related optimal values on λ_j ($j = 1, 2, \ldots, 15$) (see file "envelopment spreadsheet.xls" in the CD).

1.3.9   Calculating Slacks

Based upon the efficiency scores and the optimal values on λ_j ($j = 1, 2, \ldots, 15$), we can calculate the slack values using (1.3). However, because of possible multiple optimal solutions, we need to use model (1.4) to optimize the input and output slacks.

Figure 1.23 shows the spreadsheet model for calculating the slacks after the efficiency scores are obtained. This spreadsheet model is built upon the spreadsheet model shown in Figure 1.18 with efficiency scores reported in column J.

	A	B	C	D	E	F	G	H	I	J
1	Company	Assets	Equity	Employees		Revenue	Profit		λ	Efficiency
2	Mitsubishi	91920.6	10950	36000		184365.2	346.2		1	1
3	Mitsui	68770.9	5553.9	80000		181518.7	314.8		0	1
4	Itochu	65708.9	4271.1	7182		169164.6	121.2		0	1
5	General Motors	217123.4	23345.5	709000		168828.6	6880.7		0	1
6	Sumitomo	50268.9	6681	6193		167530.7	210.5		0	1
7	Marubeni	71439.3	5239.1	6702		161057.4	156.6		0	1
8	Ford Motor	243283	24547	346990		137137	4139		0	0.737556
9	Toyota Motor	106004.2	49691.6	146855		111052	2662.4		0	0.603245
10	Exxon	91296	40436	82000		110009	6470		0	1
11	Royal Dutch/Shell Group	118011.6	58986.4	104000		109833.7	6904.6		0	1
12	Wal-Mart	37871	14762	675000		93627	2740		0	1
13	Hitachi	91620.9	29907.2	331852		84167.1	1468.8		0	0.557596
14	Nippon Life Insurance	364762.5	2241.9	89690		83206.7	2426.6		0	1
15	Nippon Telegraph & Telephone	127077.3	42240.1	231400		81937.2	2209.1		0	0.470611
16	AT&T	88884	17274	299300		79609	139		0	0.533544
17						Reserved to indicate the DMU under evaluation.				
18		Reference		DMU under	1					
19	Constraints	set		Evaluation						
20	Assets	91920.6	≤	91920.6		0	slack; changing cell			
21	Equity	10950	≤	10950		0	slack; changing cell			
22	Employees	36000	≤	36000		0	slack; changing cell			
23	Revenue	184365.2	≥	184365.2		0	slack; changing cell			
24	Profit	346.2	≥	346.2		0	slack; changing cell			
25	Σλ	1	=	1		0	Objective function Sum of slacks			

Figure 1.23. Second-stage Slack Spreadsheet Model

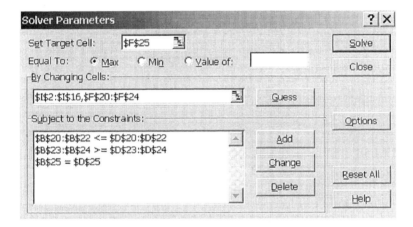

Figure 1.24. Solver Parameters for Calculating Slacks

Cells F20:F24 are reserved for input and output slacks (changing cells). The formulas for cells B25 and D25 remain unchanged. The formulas for Cells B20:B24 are changed to

Cell B20 =SUMPRODUCT(B2:B16,$I$2:$I$16)+F20
Cell B21 =SUMPRODUCT(C2:C16,$I$2:$I$16)+F21
Cell B22 =SUMPRODUCT(D2:D16,$I$2:$I$16)+F22
Cell B23 =SUMPRODUCT(F2:F16,$I$2:$I$16)-F23
Cell B24 =SUMPRODUCT(G2:G16,$I$2:$I$16)-F24

The formulas for cells D21:D24 are

Cell D20 =INDEX(J2:J16,E18,1)*INDEX(B2:B16,E18,1)
Cell D21 =INDEX(J2:J16,E18,1)*INDEX(C2:C16,E18,1)
Cell D22 =INDEX(J2:J16,E18,1)*INDEX(C2:C16,E18,1)
Cell D23 =INDEX(F2:F16,E18,1)
Cell D24 =INDEX(G2:G16,E18,1)

After the Solver parameters are set up, as shown in Figure 1.24, the VBA procedure "DEASlack" is inserted into the existing module to automate the slack calculations for the 15 companies (see file "envelopment spreadsheet.xls" in the CD for the results).

```
Sub DEASlack()
'Declare DMUNo as integer. This DMUNo represents the DMU under
'evaluation. In the example, DMUNo goes form 1 to 15
    Dim DMUNo As Integer
    For DMUNo = 1 To 15
'set the value of cell E18 equal to DMUNo (1, 2,..., 15)
    Range("E18") = DMUNo
'Run the Slack Solver model
    SolverSolve UserFinish:=True
'Select the cells containing the slacks
    Range("F20:F24").Select
'copy the selection (slacks) and paste it to row "DMUNo+1"
'(that is, row 2,3, ...,16) starting column L
Selection.Copy
Range("L" & DMUNo + 1).Select
Selection.PasteSpecial Paste:=xlPasteValues, Transpose:=True
Next DMUNo
End Sub
```

1.3.10   Other Input-oriented Envelopment Spreadsheet Models

Figures 1.8 and 1.15 represent the input-oriented VRS envelopment model. By changing the constraint on $\sum_{j=1}^{n} \lambda_j$, we immediately obtain other input-oriented envelopment models.

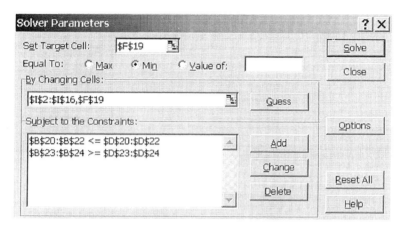

Figure 1.25. Solver Parameters for Input-oriented CRS Envelopment Model

	A	B	C	D	E	F	G	H	I	J
1	Company	Assets	Equity	Employees		Revenue	Profit		λ	Efficiency
2	Mitsubishi	91920.6	10950	36000		184365.2	346.2		0	0.662832
3	Mitsui	68770.9	5553.9	80000		181518.7	314.8		0	1
4	Itochu	65708.9	4271.1	7182		169164.6	121.2		0	1
5	General Motors	217123.4	23345.5	709000		168828.6	6880.7		0	1
6	Sumitomo	50268.9	6681	6193		167530.7	210.5		0.47	1
7	Marubeni	71439.3	5239.1	6702		161057.4	156.6		0	0.971967
8	Ford Motor	243283	24547	346990		137137	4139		0	0.737166
9	Toyota Motor	106004.2	49691.6	146855		111052	2662.4		0	0.524558
10	Exxon	91296	40436	82000		110009	6470		0	1
11	Royal Dutch/Shell Group	118011.6	58986.4	104000		109833.7	6904.6		0	0.841424
12	Wal-Mart	37871	14762	675000		93627	2740		0.01	1
13	Hitachi	91620.9	29907.2	331852		84167.1	1468.8		0	0.386057
14	Nippon Life Insurance	364762.5	2241.9	89690		83206.7	2426.6		0	1
15	Nippon Telegraph & Telephone	127077.3	42240.1	231400		81937.2	2209.1		0	0.348578
16	AT&T	88884	17274	299300		79609	139		0	0.270382
17										
18		Reference		DMU under	15	Efficiency				
19	**Constraints**	set		Evaluation		0.270382				
20	Assets	24032.613	≤	24032.613						
21	Equity	3338.6447	≤	4670.5747						
22	Employees	12922.984	≤	80925.264						
23	Revenue	79609	≥	79609						
24	Profit	139	≥	139						
25	Σλ	0.4817465								

Figure 1.26. Input-oriented CRS Envelopment Efficiency

For example, if we select $B$25 = $D$25 and click the Delete button in Figure 1.15 (i.e., we remove $\sum_{j=1}^{n} \lambda_j = 1$), we obtain the Solver parameters for the input-oriented CRS envelopment model, as shown in Figure 1.25.

If we click the Change button, and replace $B$25 = $D$25 with $B$25 <= $D$25 (or $B$25 >= $D$25), we obtain the input-oriented NIRS (or NDRS) envelopment model.

During this process, the spreadsheet shown in Figure 1.15 and the VBA procedures remain unchanged. For example, if we run the Macro "DEA" for the input-oriented CRS envelopment model, we have the CRS efficiency scores shown in Figure 1.26. Seven DMUs are on the CRS efficient frontier.

1.3.11   Output-oriented Envelopment Spreadsheet Models

We next consider the output-oriented envelopment models. The spreadsheet model should be similar to the one in Figure 1.15, but with a different set of formulas for the DMU under evaluation. Figure 1.27 shows a spreadsheet for the output-oriented VRS envelopment model.

To make the spreadsheet more understandable, we use "range names" in the formulas. Select a range that needs to be named, and then type the desirable range name in the upper left "name box" in the Excel. This "name box" is just above the column A heading (see Figure 1.27). For example, we select cells B2:D16 containing the inputs, and then type "InputUsed" in the "name box" (see Figure 1.27). An alternative way is to use the Insert/Name/Define menu item. We can then refer to the inputs by using "InputUsed" in stead of cells B2:D16.

InputUsed	f_x	91920.6								
	A	B	C	D	E	F	G	H	I	J	K
1	Company	Assets	Equity	Employees		Revenue	Profit		λ	Name cells I2:I16
2	Mitsubishi	91920.6	10950	36000		184365.2	346.2		1	"Lambdas"
3	Mitsui	68770.9	5553.9	80000		181518.7	314.8		0	
4	Itochu	65708.9	4271.1	7182		169164.6	121.2		0	
5	General Motors	217123.4	23345.5	709000		168828.6	6880.7		0	
6	Sumitomo	50268.9	6681	6193		167530.7	210.5		0	
7	Marubeni	71439.3	5239.1	6702		161057.4	156.6		0	
8	Ford Motor	243283	24547	346990		137137	4139		0	
9	Toyota Motor	106004.2	49691.6	146855		111052	2662.4		0	
10	Exxon	91296	40436	82000		110009	6470		0	
11	Royal Dutch/Shell Group	118011.6	58986.4	104000		109833.7	6904.6		0	
12	Wal-Mart	37871	14762	675000		93627	2740		0	
13	Hitachi	91620.9	29907.2	331852		84167.1	1468.8		0	
14	Nippon Life Insurance	364762.5	2241.9	89690		83206.7	2426.6		0	
15	Nippon Telegraph & Telephone	127077.3	42240.1	231400		81937.2	2209.1		0	
16	AT&T	88884	17274	299300		79609	139		0	
17										
18		Reference		DMU under	1	Efficiency		Reserved to indicate the DMU under evaluation.		
19	Constraints	set		Evaluation		1				
20	Assets	91920.6	<	91920.6						
21	Equity	Constraint on Σλ	10950	<	10950		Efficiency; ↑;			
22	Employees	The cell is named	36000	<	36000		A changing cell;			
23	Revenue	"SumLambda"	184365.2	>	184365.2		Target cell in Solver			
24	Profit		346.2	>	346.2					
25	Σλ		1	=	1					

Figure 1.27. Output-oriented VRS Envelopment Spreadsheet Model

We name the cells F2:G16 containing the outputs as "OutputProduced". We also name the changing cells I2:I16 and F19 "Lambdas" and "Efficiency", respectively. As a result, the formulas on $\sum_{j=1}^{n} \lambda_j$ can be expressed as Cell B25 =SUM(Lambdas), and the formulas for the DEA reference set can be expressed as

Cell B20 = SUMPRODUCT(INDEX(InputUsed,0,1),Lambdas)
Cell B21 = SUMPRODUCT(INDEX(InputUsed,0,2),Lambdas)
Cell B22 = SUMPRODUCT(INDEX(InputUsed,0,3),Lambdas)
Cell B23 = SUMPRODUCT(INDEX(OutputProduced,0,1),Lambdas)
Cell B24 = SUMPRODUCT(INDEX(OutputProduced,0,2),Lambdas)

Note that we use "0" for the "row number" in the INDEX function. This returns the whole column in the specified array in the INDEX function. For example, INDEX(InputUsed,0,1) returns the first input across all DMUs in cells B2:B16.

We assign a range name of "DMU" to cell E18, the cell representing the DMU under evaluation. The formulas for the DMU under evaluation then can be expressed as

Cell D20 =INDEX(InputUsed,DMU,1)
Cell D21 =INDEX(InputUsed,DMU,2)
Cell D22 =INDEX(InputUsed,DMU,3)
Cell D23 = Efficiency*INDEX(OutputProduced,DMU,1)
Cell D24 = Efficiency*INDEX(OutputProduced,DMU,2)

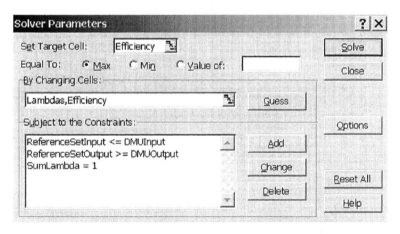

Figure 1.28. Solver Parameters for Output-oriented VRS Envelopment Model

The cells "B20:B22", "B23:B24", "B25", "D20:D22", "D23:D24" are named as "ReferenceSetInput", "ReferenceSetOutput", "SumLambda", "DMUInput", and "DMUOutput", respectively. Based upon these range names, we obtain the Solver parameters shown in Figure 1.28. Since it is an output-oriented envelopment model, "Max" is selected to maximize the efficiency (ϕ).

We can still apply the previous Excel macros ("DEA" or "DEA1") to this spreadsheet model shown in Figure 1.27 with the Solver parameters shown in Figure 1.28. We next present an alternative approach to automate the DEA calculation.

First, turn on the Control Toolbox command bar by selecting the View/Toolbars/Control Toolbox menu item. Then click the Command Button icon on the Control Toolbox, and drag it on to your worksheet (see Figure 1.29).

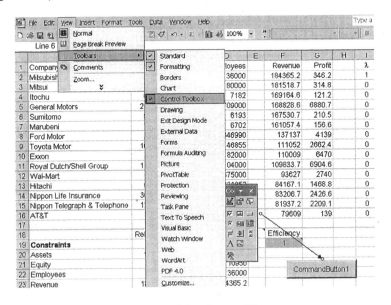

Figure 1.29. Adding Command Button

While the command button is selected, you can change its properties by clicking the Properties button on the Control Toolbox toolbar. For example, setting the TakeFocusOnClick to False leaves the worksheet selection unchanged when the button is clicked. You can change the name of this Command Button by changing the Caption property with "Output-oriented VRS" (see Figure 1.30).

Double click the command button. This should launch the VB Editor and bring up the code window for the command button's click event. Insert the statements shown in Figure 1.31.

The word Private before the macro name "CommandButton1_Click" means that this macro will not appear in the Run Macro dialog box. The macro is only available to the worksheet "output VRS" containing the model (see Figure 1.31).

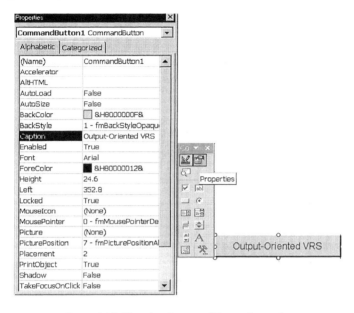

Figure 1.30. Changing Command Button Properties

Figure 1.31. VBA Code for Output-oriented VRS Envelopment Model

In the macro, we introduce three variables, NDMUs, NInputs, and NOutputs, representing the number of DMUs, inputs and outputs, respectively. In the current example, NDMUs = 15, NInputs = 3, and NOutputs = 2. For a different set of DMUs, set these variables to different values, and the macro should still work.

	A	B	C	D	E	F	G	H	I	J
1	Company	Assets	Equity	Employees		Revenue	Profit		λ	Efficiency
2	Mitsubishi	91920.6	10950	36000		184365.2	346.2		0.87	1
3	Mitsui	68770.9	5553.9	80000		181518.7	314.8		0.13	1
4	Itochu	65708.9	4271.1	7182		169164.6	121.2		0	1
5	General Motors	217123.4	23345.5	709000		168828.6	6880.7		0	1
6	Sumitomo	50268.9	6681	6193		167530.7	210.5		0	1
7	Marubeni	71439.3	5239.1	6702		161057.4	156.6		0	1
8	Ford Motor	243283	24547	346990		137137	4139		0	1.158415
9	Toyota Motor	106004.2	49691.6	146855		111052	2662.4		0	1.371588
10	Exxon	91296	40436	82000		110009	6470		0	1
11	Royal Dutch/Shell Group	118011.6	58986.4	104000		109833.7	6904.6		0	1
12	Wal-Mart	37871	14762	675000		93627	2740		0	1
13	Hitachi	91620.9	29907.2	331852		84167.1	1468.8		0	1.898939
14	Nippon Life Insurance	364762.5	2241.9	89690		83206.7	2426.6		0	1
15	Nippon Telegraph & Telephone	127077.3	42240.1	231400		81937.2	2209.1		0	1.892917
16	AT&T	88884	17274	299300		79609	139		0	2.311194
17										
18		Reference		DMU under	16	Efficiency				
19	**Constraints**	set		Evaluation		2.311194				
20	Assets	88884	≤	88884						
21	Equity	10242.181	≤	17274		Output-Oriented VRS				
22	Employees	41771.582	≤	299300						
23	Revenue	183991.82	≥	183991.82						
24	Profit	342.08119	≥	321.25592						
25	Σλ		1							

Figure 1.32. Output-oriented VRS Envelopment Efficiency

Close the VB Editor and click the Exit Design Mode icon on the Control Toolbox. The selection handles disappear from the command button. The macro runs when you click the command button. Note that if the Control Toolbox toolbar is closed before clicking the Exit Design Mode icon, the Excel is still in design mode and the macro will not run. Figure 1.32 shows the results (see file "envelopment spreadsheet.xls" in the CD).

In a similar manner, we can set up other output-oriented envelopment spreadsheet models. For example, if we remove "SumLambda=1" from Figure 1.28, we obtain the Solver parameters for output-oriented CRS envelopment model.

If one wants to use the macros established for the input-oriented envelopment spreadsheet models, one can proceed as follows.

First, we select the View/Toolbars/Forms menu item (or right-click on any toolbar in Excel) (see Figure 1.29). The fourth item on the Forms toolbar is for creating buttons to run macros (VBA procedures). Click and drag the button onto your worksheet containing the output-oriented CRS envelopment spreadsheet and the Solver parameters. You will immediately be asked to assign a macro to this button. Select "DEA1". At this point, the button is selected. You may also want to change the caption on the button to "Output-oriented CRS', for example (see Figure 1.33). To run the selected macro, you have to deselect the button by clicking anywhere else on the worksheet. You can always assign a different macro to the button by right-clicking on the button and selecting "Assign Macro". Figure 1.34 shows the output-oriented CRS efficiency scores.

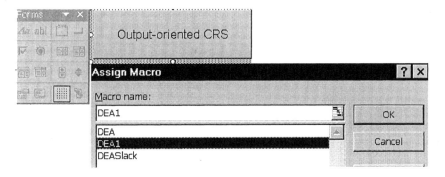

Figure 1.33. Adding a Button with Macro

	A	B	C	D	E	F	G	H	I	J
1	Company	Assets	Equity	Employees		Revenue	Profit		λ	Efficiency
2	Mitsubishi	91920.6	10950	36000		184365.2	346.2		0	1.508679
3	Mitsui	68770.9	5553.9	80000		181518.7	314.8		0	1
4	Itochu	65708.9	4271.1	7182		169164.6	121.2		0	1
5	General Motors	217123.4	23345.5	709000		168828.6	6880.7		0	1
6	Sumitomo	50268.9	6681	6193		167530.7	210.5		1.73	1
7	Marubeni	71439.3	5239.1	6702		161057.4	156.6		0	1.028842
8	Ford Motor	243283	24547	346990		137137	4139		0	1.356546
9	Toyota Motor	106004.2	49691.6	146855		111052	2662.4		0	1.906368
10	Exxon	91296	40436	82000		110009	6470		0	1
11	Royal Dutch/Shell Group	118011.6	58986.4	104000		109833.7	6904.6		0	1.188462
12	Wal-Mart	37871	14762	675000		93627	2740		0.05	1
13	Hitachi	91620.9	29907.2	331852		84167.1	1468.8		0	2.590289
14	Nippon Life Insurance	364762.5	2241.9	89690		83206.7	2426.6		0	1
15	Nippon Telegraph & Telephone	127077.3	42240.1	231400		81937.2	2209.1		0	2.8688
16	AT&T	88884	17274	299300		79609	139		0	3.698474
17										
18		Reference		DMU under	15	Efficiency				
19	Constraints	set		Evaluation		3.698474				
20	Assets	88884	≤	88884						
21	Equity	12347.891	≤	17274		Output-oriented CRS				
22	Employees	47795.324	≤	299300						
23	Revenue	294431.83	≥	294431.83						
24	Profit	514.08791	≥	514.08791						
25	Σλ	1.7817269								

Figure 1.34. Output-oriented CRS Envelopment Efficiency

1.4   Multiplier Model

The dual linear programming problems to the envelopment models are called multiplier models as shown in Table 1.4.

The dual variables v_i and μ_r are called multipliers. A DMU is on the frontier if and only if $\sum_{r=1}^{s} \mu_r y_{ro} + \mu = 1$ (or $\sum_{i=1}^{m} v_i x_{io} + v = 1$) in optimality. The ε in the envelopment model essentially requires that v_i and μ_r are positive in the multiplier models. The constraint $\sum_{i=1}^{m} v_i x_{io} = 1$ (or $\sum_{r=1}^{s} \mu_r y_{ro} = 1$) is known as a normalization constraint. In DEA, the weighted input and output of $\sum_{i=1}^{m} v_i x_{ij}$ and $\sum_{r=1}^{s} \mu_r y_{rj}$ are called virtual input and virtual output, respectively. See Seiford and Thrall (1990) for a detailed discussion on these models.

Table 1.4. Multiplier Models

Frontier Type	Input-Oriented	Output-Oriented
	$\max \sum_{r=1}^{s} \mu_r y_{ro} + \mu$ subject to $\sum_{r=1}^{s} \mu_r y_{rj} - \sum_{i=1}^{m} v_i x_{ij} + \mu \le 0$ $\sum_{i=1}^{m} v_i x_{io} = 1$ $\mu_r, v_i \ge 0(\varepsilon)$	$\min \sum_{i=1}^{m} v_i x_{io} + v$ subject to $\sum_{i=1}^{m} v_i x_{ij} - \sum_{r=1}^{s} \mu_r y_{rj} + v \ge 0$ $\sum_{r=1}^{s} \mu_r y_{ro} = 1$ $\mu_r, v_i \ge 0(\varepsilon)$
CRS	where $\mu = 0$	where $v = 0$
VRS	where μ free	where v free
NIRS	where $\mu \le 0$	where $v \ge 0$
NDRS	where $\mu \ge 0$	where $v \le 0$

1.5   Multiplier Models in Spreadsheets

Figure 1.35 presents the input-oriented CRS multiplier spreadsheet model. We name the cells C2:E16 containing the inputs as "InputUsed" and the cells G2:H16 containing the outputs as "OutputProduced". Cells C19:E19 and G19:H19 are reserved for the decision variables – input and output multipliers, and are named "InputMultiplier" and "OutputMultiplier", respectively. Cells A2:A16 are reserved for DMU numbers which are used in the formulas in cells I2:I16.

Cell I2 contains the formula "= SUMPRODUCT(OutputMultiplier, INDEX (OutputProduced,A2,0))-SUMPRODUCT(InputMultiplier,INDEX (InputUsed,A2,0))" which represents the difference between weighted output and weighted input for DMU1. This value will be set as non-negative in the Solver parameters.

The function INDEX(array,row number,0) returns the entire row in the array. For example, the value for cell A2 is one, therefore INDEX(OutputProduced,A2,0) returns the first outputs across all DMUs, i.e., cells G2:H2.

	A	B	C	D	E	F	G	H	I	J
1	DMU	Company	Assets	Equity	Employees		Revenue	Profit	**Constraints**	Efficiency
2	1	Mitsubishi	91920.6	10950	36000		184365.2	346.2	45840.8	
3	2	Mitsui	68770.9	5553.9	80000		181518.7	314.8	27508.7	
4	3	Itochu	65708.9	4271.1	7182		169164.6	121.2	92123.8	
5	4	General Motors	217123.4	23345.5	709000		168828.6	6880.7	-773759.6	
6	5	Sumitomo	50268.9	6681	6193		167530.7	210.5	104598.3	
7	6	Marubeni	71439.3	5239.1	6702		161057.4	156.6	77833.6	
8	7	Ford Motor	243283	24547	346990		137137	4139	-473544	
9	8	Toyota Motor	106004.2	49691.6	146855		111052	2662.4	-188836.4	
10	9	Exxon	91296	40436	82000		110009	6470	-97253	
11	10	Royal Dutch/Shell Group	118011.6	58986.4	104000		109833.7	6904.6	-164259.7	
12	11	Wal-Mart	37871	14762	675000		93627	2740	-631266	
13	12	Hitachi	91620.9	29907.2	331852		84167.1	1468.8	-367744.2	
14	13	Nippon Life Insurance	364762.5	2241.9	89690		83206.7	2426.6	-371061.1	
15	14	Nippon Telegraph & Telephone	127077.3	42240.1	231400		81937.2	2209.1	-316571.1	
16	15	AT&T	88884	17274	299300		79609	139	-325710	
17									138870.6	
18										
19		**Multipliers**	1	1	1		1	1	Weighted inputs for	
20		DMU under evaluation	1						DMU under	
21		Efficiency	184711.1		Input multipliers		Output multipliers		evaluation	
22		efficiency			changing cells		changing cells			
23		weighted output			reserved to indicate					
24		Target cell			the DMU under evaluation					

Figure 1.35. Input-oriented CRS Multiplier Spreadsheet Model

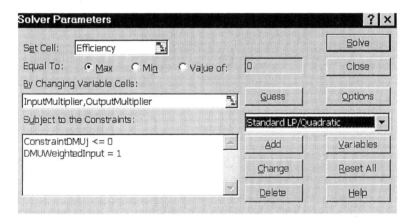

Figure 1.36. Premium Solver Parameters for Input-oriented CRS Multiplier Model

The formula in cell I2 is then copied into cells I3:I16. Cells I2:I16 are named "ConstraintDMUj".

The formula for cell I17 is "= SUMPRODUCT (InputMultiplier, INDEX (InputUsed,DMU,0))", where DMU is a range name for cell C20, indicating the DMU under evaluation. The value of cell I17 will be set equal to one in the Solver parameters. Cell I17 is named "DMUWeightedInput".

The target cell is C21 which represents the efficiency – weighted output for the DMU under evaluation. The cell C21 is named "Efficiency". Its formula is "= SUMPRODUCT(OutputMultiplier,INDEX(OutputProduced, DMU,0))".

Note that initial values of one are entered into the cells for the multipliers. As a result, some of the constraints are violated, and the value in cell C20 (efficiency) is greater than one. However, once the Solver solves, these values will be replaced by optimal solutions.

Figure 1.36 shows the Premium Solver parameters for the spreadsheet model in Figure 1.35. If one uses the Premium Solver, one should select "Standard LP/Quadratic" solver engine. In the Options, check the "Assume Non-Negative" box.

	Efficiency		f_x =SUMPRODUCT(OutputMultiplier, INDEX(OutputProduced,DMU,0))							
	A	B	C	D	E	F	G	H	I	J
1	DMU	Company	Assets	Equity	Employees		Revenue	Profit	Constraints	Efficiency
2	1	Mitsubishi	91920.6	10950	36000		184365.2	346.2	-0.33716826	0.662832
3	2	Mitsui	68770.9	5553.9	80000		181518.7	314.8	-0.00211303	1
4	3	Itochu	65708.9	4271.1	7182		169164.6	121.2	-3.2196E-15	1
5	4	General Motors	217123.4	23345.5	709000		168828.6	6880.7	-1.9984E-14	1
6	5	Sumitomo	50268.9	6681	6193		167530.7	210.5	0	1
7	6	Marubeni	71439.3	5239.1	6702		161057.4	156.6	-0.08918393	0.971967
8	7	Ford Motor	243283	24547	346990		137137	4139	-0.95350243	0.737166
9	8	Toyota Motor	106004.2	49691.6	146855		111052	2662.4	-1.7278984	0.524558
10	9	Exxon	91296	40436	82000		110009	6470	-0.16903775	1
11	10	Royal Dutch/Shell Group	118011.6	58986.4	104000		109833.7	6904.6	-1.01666407	0.841424
12	11	Wal-Mart	37871	14762	675000		93627	2740	0	1
13	12	Hitachi	91620.9	29907.2	331852		84167.1	1468.8	-1.24683922	0.386057
14	13	Nippon Life Insurance	364762.5	2241.9	89690		83206.7	2426.6	-1.21742056	1
15	14	Nippon Telegraph & Telephone	127077.3	42240.1	231400		81937.2	2209.1	-1.75723797	0.348578
16	15	AT&T	88884	17274	299300		79609	139	-1.05154525	0.270382
17									1	
18										
19		Multipliers	5.546E-06	4.38E-05	2.827E-07		3.07E-06	0.00028		
20		DMU under evaluation	1							
21		Efficiency	0.6628317							
22										
23										
24		CRS Multiplier								

Figure 1.37. Input-oriented CRS Multiplier Efficiency

Figure 1.37 shows the optimal solutions for DMU1 with an efficiency of 0.66283. To calculate the CRS efficiencies for the remaining DMUs, we insert a VBA procedure "MultiplierCRS" to automate the computation, as shown in Figure 1.38. Note that the name of the module is changed to "MultiplierDEA". This VBA procedure works for other sets of DMUs when setting the "NDMUs", "NInputs", and "NOutputs" equal to proper values. In the current example, this VBA procedure takes the efficiency in cell C21 and places it into cells J2:J16, and also takes the optimal multipliers and places them into cells K2:M16 and O2:P16 for 15 DMUs. Select and run the macro

"MultiplierCRS" in the Run Macro dialog box will generate the efficiency results. You may also create a button in Forms toolbar and assign macro "MultiplierCRS" to the button (see file "multiplier spreadsheet.xls" in the CD).

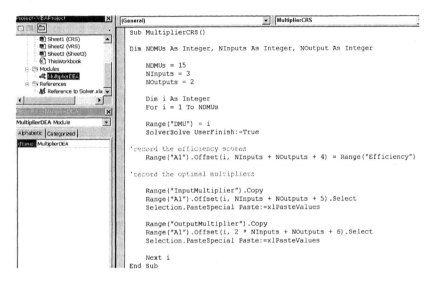

Figure 1.38. VBA Code for Input-oriented CRS Multiplier Model

Spreadsheets for other multiplier models can be set up in a similar manner. For example, Figure 1.39 shows a spreadsheet model for the input-oriented VRS multiplier model.

Because we have a decision variable that is free in sign, we need to introduce two variables in cells I19 and J19. The free variable in the VRS multiplier model is represented by cell J18 with a formula of "=I19-J19". In the Solver parameters, cells I19 and J19 (not cell J18) along with cells C19:E19 and G19:H19 are changing cells.

The formula for cell I2 is

Cell I2 =SUMPRODUCT(G2:H2,$G$19:$H$19)-
SUMPRODUCT(C2:E2,$C$19:$E$19)+$I$19-$J$19

Cells for the multipliers and free variables are used as absolute references indicated by the dollar sign. This allows us to copy the formula in cell I2 to cells I3:I16. Figure 1.40 shows the Solver parameters for the input-oriented VRS multiplier spreadsheet model.

	A	B	C	D	E	F	G	H	I	J
1	DMU	Company	Assets	Equity	Employees		Revenue	Profit	**Constraints**	Efficiency
2	1	Mitsubishi	91920.6	10950	36000		184365.2	346.2	-7.9936E-15	
3	2	Mitsui	68770.9	5553.9	80000		181518.7	314.8	0	
4	3	Itochu	65708.9	4271.1	7182		169164.6	121.2	-0.42009487	
5	4	General Motors	217123.4	23345.5	709000		168828.6	6880.7	-4.3521E-14	
6	5	Sumitomo	50268.9	6681	6193		167530.7	210.5	-0.2847084	
7	6	Marubeni	71439.3	5239.1	6702		161057.4	156.6	-0.7938799	
8	7	Ford Motor	243283	24547	346990		137137	4139	-2.19408313	
9	8	Toyota Motor	106004.2	49691.6	146855		111052	2662.4	-2.22252322	
10	9	Exxon	91296	40436	82000		110009	6470	0	
11	10	Royal Dutch/Shell Group	118011.6	58986.4	104000		109833.7	6904.6	-0.098082	
12	11	Wal-Mart	37871	14762	675000		93627	2740	-3.39289316	
13	12	Hitachi	91620.9	29907.2	331852		84167.1	1468.8	-4.22139918	
14	13	Nippon Life Insurance	364762.5	2241.9	89690		83206.7	2426.6	-5.96194306	
15	14	Nippon Telegraph & Telephone	127077.3	42240.1	231400		81937.2	2209.1	-4.06208857	
16	15	AT&T	88884	17274	299300		79609	139	-5.00032337	
17									1	
18									free variable	-6.81693
19		**Multipliers**	1.001E-05	0	2.217E-06		4.14E-05	0.00052	0	5.816927
20		DMU under evaluation	1							
21		Efficiency	1							

Figure 1.39. Input-oriented VRS Multiplier Spreadsheet Model

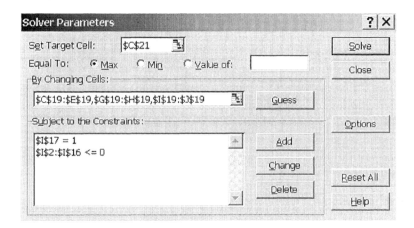

Figure 1.40. Solver Parameters for Input-oriented CRS Multiplier Model

Insert the VBA procedure "MultiplierVRS" shown in Figure 1.41 into the existing module "MultiplierDEA". The macro records the efficiency score in cells J2:J16, optimal free variable in cells K2:K16, and optimal multipliers in cells L2:N16 and P2:Q16 for 15 DMUs (see file "multiplier spreadsheet.xls" in the CD).

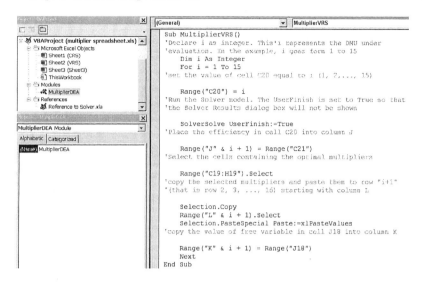

Figure 1.41. VBA Code for the Input-oriented VRS Multiplier Model

1.6 Slack-based Model

The input-oriented DEA models consider the possible (proportional) input reductions while maintaining the current levels of outputs. The output-oriented DEA models consider the possible (proportional) output augmentations while keeping the current levels of inputs. Charnes, Cooper, Golany, Seiford and Stutz (1985) develop an additive DEA model which considers possible input decreases as well as output increases simultaneously. The additive model is based upon input and output slacks. For example,

$$\max \sum_{i=1}^{m} s_i^- + \sum_{r=1}^{s} s_r^+$$
$$\text{subject to}$$
$$\sum_{j=1}^{n} \lambda_j x_{ij} + s_i^- = x_{io} \qquad i = 1,2,...,m; \tag{1.8}$$
$$\sum_{j=1}^{n} \lambda_j y_{rj} - s_r^+ = y_{ro} \qquad r = 1,2,...,s;$$
$$\lambda_j, s_i^-, s_r^+ \geq 0$$

Note that model (1.8) assumes equal marginal worth for the nonzero input and output slacks. Therefore, caution should be excised in selecting the units for different input and output measures. Some *a priori* information may be required to prevent an inappropriate summation of non-commensurable measures. Previous management experience and expert opinion, which prove important in productivity analysis, may be used (see Seiford and Zhu (1998c)).

Model (1.8) therefore is modified to a weighted CRS slack-based model as follows (Ali, Lerme and Seiford, 1995; Thrall, 1996).

$$\max \sum_{i=1}^{m} w_i^- s_i^- + \sum_{r=1}^{s} w_r^+ s_r^+$$

subject to   (1.9)

$$\sum_{j=1}^{n} \lambda_j x_{ij} + s_i^- = x_{io} \qquad i = 1,2,...,m;$$

$$\sum_{j=1}^{n} \lambda_j y_{rj} - s_r^+ = y_{ro} \qquad r = 1,2,...,s;$$

$$\lambda_j, s_i^-, s_r^+ \geq 0$$

where w_i^- and w_r^+ are user-specified weights obtained through value judgment. The DMU_o under evaluation will be termed efficient *if and only if* the optimal value to (1.9) is equal to zero. Otherwise, the nonzero optimal s_i^{-*} identifies an excess utilization of the ith input, and the non-zero optimal s_r^{+*} identifies a deficit in the rth output. Thus, the solution of (1.9) yields the information on possible adjustments to individual outputs and inputs of each DMU. Obviously, model (1.9) is useful for setting targets for inefficient DMUs with *a priori* information on the adjustments of outputs and inputs.

Table 1.5. Slack-based Models

Frontier type	Slack-based DEA Model
CRS	$\max \sum_{i=1}^{m} w_i^- s_i^- + \sum_{r=1}^{s} w_r^+ s_r^+$ subject to $\sum_{j=1}^{n} \lambda_j x_{ij} + s_i^- = x_{io} \qquad i = 1,2,...,m;$ $\sum_{j=1}^{n} \lambda_j y_{rj} - s_r^+ = y_{ro} \qquad r = 1,2,...,s;$ $\lambda_j, s_i^-, s_r^+ \geq 0$
VRS	Add $\sum_{j=1}^{n} \lambda_j = 1$
NIRS	Add $\sum_{j=1}^{n} \lambda_j \leq 1$
NDRS	Add $\sum_{j=1}^{n} \lambda_j \geq 1$

One should note that model (1.9) does not necessarily yield results that are different from those obtained from the model (1.8). In particular, it will not change the classification from efficient to inefficient (or vice versa) for any DMU.

Model (1.9) identifies a CRS frontier, and therefore is called CRS slack-based model. Table 1.5 summarizes the slack-based models in terms of the frontier types.

1.7   Slack-based Models in Spreadsheets

Figure 1.42 shows a spreadsheet model for the CRS slack-based model when DMU1 is under evaluation. Cells I2:I16 are reserved for λ_j. Cells F20:F24 are reserved for input and output slacks. The weights on slacks are entered into Cells G20:G24. Currently, the weights are all equal to one.

	A	B	C	D	E	F	G	H	I
1	Company	Assets	Equity	Employees		Revenue	Profit		λ
2	Mitsubishi	91920.6	10950	36000		184365.2	346.2		0
3	Mitsui	68770.9	5553.9	80000		181518.7	314.8		0
4	Itochu	65708.9	4271.1	7182		169164.6	121.2		0.2901
5	General Motors	217123.4	23345.5	709000		168828.6	6880.7		0
6	Sumitomo	50268.9	6681	6193		167530.7	210.5		1.4476
7	Marubeni	71439.3	5239.1	6702		161057.4	156.6		0
8	Ford Motor	243283	24547	346990		137137	4139		0
9	Toyota Motor	106004.2	49691.6	146855		111052	2662.4		0
10	Exxon	91296	40436	82000		110009	6470		0.001
11	Royal Dutch/Shell Group	118011.6	58986.4	104000		109833.7	6904.6		0
12	Wal-Mart	37871	14762	675000		93627	2740		0
13	Hitachi	91620.9	29907.2	331852		84167.1	1468.8		0
14	Nippon Life Insurance	364762.5	2241.9	89690		83206.7	2426.6		0
15	Nippon Telegraph & Telephone	127077.3	42240.1	231400		81937.2	2209.1		0
16	AT&T	88884	17274	299300		79609	139		0
17									
18		Reference		DMU under	1				
19	**Constraints**	set		Evaluation		**Slack**	**Weights**		
20	Assets	91920.6	=	91920.6		0	1		
21	Equity	10950	=	10950		0	1		
22	Employees	36000	=	36000		24871.42	1		
23	Revenue	184365.2	=	184365.2		107334.9	1		
24	Profit	346.2	=	346.2		0	1		
25						132206.4			

Figure 1.42. CRS Slack-based DEA Spreadsheet Model

Cells B20:B24 contain the following formulas

Cell B20 =SUMPRODUCT(B2:B16,$I$2:$I$16)+F20
Cell B21 =SUMPRODUCT(C2:C16,$I$2:$I$16)+F21
Cell B22 =SUMPRODUCT(D2:D16,$I$2:$I$16)+F22
Cell B23 =SUMPRODUCT(F2:F16,$I$2:$I$16)-F23
Cell B24 =SUMPRODUCT(G2:G16,$I$2:$I$16)-F24

The input and output values of the DMU under evaluation are placed into cells D20:D24 via the following formulas

Cell D20 =INDEX(B2:B16,E18,1)
Cell D21 =INDEX(C2:C16,E18,1)
Cell D22 =INDEX(C2:C16,E18,1)
Cell D23 =INDEX(F2:F16,E18,1)
Cell D24 =INDEX(G2:G16,E18,1)

Cell F25 is the target cell which represents the weighted slack. The formula for cell F25 is

Cell F25 =SUMPRODUCT(F20:F24,G20:G24)

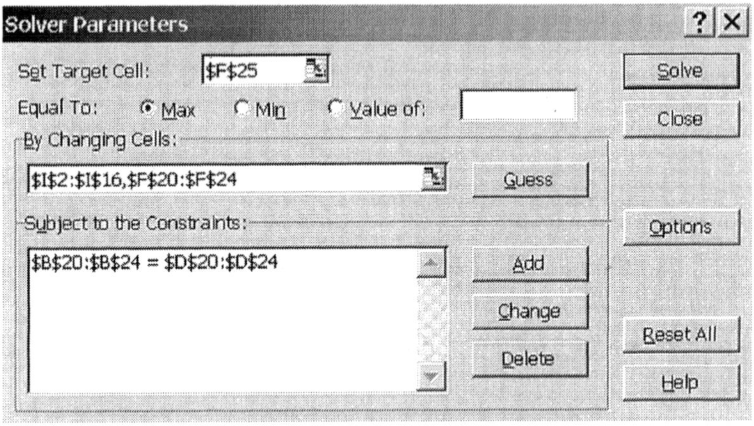

Figure 1.43. Solver Parameters for CRS Slack-based Model

Figure 1.43 shows the Solver parameters. Figure 1.42 shows the optimal slack values when DMU1 is under evaluation. Next, we insert a VBA procedure "CRSSlack" to calculate the optimal slacks for the remaining DMUs. Figure 1.44 shows the results.

```
Sub CRSSlack()
Dim NDMUs As Integer, NInputs As Integer, NOutputs As Integer
Dim i As Integer
    For i = 1 To 15
'set the value of cell E18 equal to i (=1, 2,..., 15)
    Range("E18") = i
'Run the Slack Solver model
    SolverSolve UserFinish:=True
'Select the cells containing the slacks
    Range("F20:F24").Select
'record optimal slacks in cells K2:O16
Selection.Copy
Range("K" & i + 1).Select
Selection.PasteSpecial Paste:=xlPasteValues, Transpose:=True
```

```
Next
End Sub
```

	J	K	L	M	N	O
1	Company	Assets	Equity	Employees	Revenue	Profit
2	Mitsubishi	0	0	24871.423	107334.9	0
3	Mitsui	0	0	-3.988E-10	0	0
4	Itochu	3.69E-11	0	0	-8.6E-14	1.75E-13
5	General Motors	0	0	-1.649E-10	0	0
6	Sumitomo	0	2.27E-12	1.99E-13	-2.1E-13	-7.1E-14
7	Marubeni	12794.2	0	0	5857.514	0.812974
8	Ford Motor	0	0	267229.26	112833	0
9	Toyota Motor	0	25289.03	108011.55	171436.8	0
10	Exxon	0	8.49E-12	2.118E-11	5.85E-11	0
11	Royal Dutch/Shell Group	0	13499.36	14957.88	78912.18	0
12	Wal-Mart	0	0	0	0	0
13	Hitachi	0	12685.39	307952.81	186551.3	0
14	Nippon Life Insurance	-1E-10	0	0	-1.9E-10	0
15	Nippon Telegraph & Telephone	0	17554.49	196254.33	288061.8	0
16	AT&T	0	5460.851	288349.72	216613.9	233.1999
17						
18						
19						
20						
21	CRS Slack					

Figure 1.44. CRS Slacks

	A	B	C	D	E	F	G	H	I
1	Company	Assets	Equity	Employees		Revenue	Profit		λ
2	Mitsubishi	91920.6	10950	36000		184365.2	346.2		1
3	Mitsui	68770.9	5553.9	80000		181518.7	314.8		0
4	Itochu	65708.9	4271.1	7182		169164.6	121.2		0
5	General Motors	217123.4	23345.5	709000		168828.6	6880.7		0
6	Sumitomo	50268.9	6681	6193		167530.7	210.5		0
7	Marubeni	71439.3	5239.1	6702		161057.4	156.6		0
8	Ford Motor	243283	24547	346990		137137	4139		0
9	Toyota Motor	106004.2	49691.6	146855		111052	2662.4		0
10	Exxon	91296	40436	82000		110009	6470		0
11	Royal Dutch/Shell Group	118011.6	58986.4	104000		109833.7	6904.6		0
12	Wal-Mart	37871	14762	675000		93627	2740		0
13	Hitachi	91620.9	29907.2	331852		84167.1	1468.8		0
14	Nippon Life Insurance	364762.5	2241.9	89690		83206.7	2426.6		0
15	Nippon Telegraph & Telephone	127077.3	42240.1	231400		81937.2	2209.1		0
16	AT&T	88884	17274	299300		79609	139		0
17									
18		Reference		DMU under	1				
19	**Constraints**	set		Evaluation		**Slack**	**Weights**		
20	Assets	91920.6	=	91920.6		0	1		
21	Equity	10950	=	10950		0	1		
22	Employees	36000	=	36000		0	1		
23	Revenue	184365.2	=	184365.2		0	1		
24	Profit	346.2	=	346.2		0	1		
25	Σλ	1	=	1		0			

Figure 1.45. VRS Slack-based Spreadsheet Model

By adding an additional constraint on $\sum_{j=1}^{n} \lambda_j$, we can obtain spreadsheet models for other slack-based models (see Excel file slack-based spreadsheet.xls in the CD). For example, Figure 1.45 shows a spreadsheet model for the VRS slack-based DEA model.

Range names are used in Figure 1.45. Cells B2:D16 are named "InputUsed" and cells F2:G16 are named "OutputProduced". We also name cells I2:I16 "Lambdas", cells F20:F24 "Slacks", G20:G24 "Weights", and cell E18 "DMU". Accordingly, we have formulas

Cell B20 = SUMPRODUCT(INDEX(InputUsed,0,1),Lambdas)+Slacks
Cell B21 = SUMPRODUCT(INDEX(InputUsed,0,2),Lambdas)+Slacks
Cell B22 = SUMPRODUCT(INDEX(InputUsed,0,3),Lambdas)+Slacks
Cell B23 = SUMPRODUCT(INDEX(OutputProduced,0,1),Lambdas)-Slacks
Cell B24 = SUMPRODUCT(INDEX(OutputProduced,0,2),Lambdas)-Slacks
Cell B25 = SUM(Lambdas)
Cell F25 = SUMPRODUCT(Slacks,Weights)

We then name cells B20:B24 "ReferenceSet", cells D20:D24 "DMUEvaluation", B25 "SumLambda", and cell F25 "SumSlack". Figure 1.46 shows the Solver parameters for the VRS slack-based model.

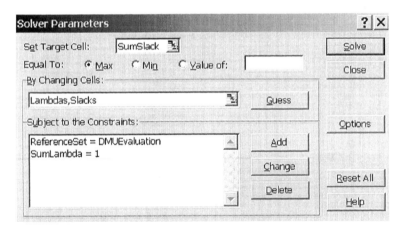

Figure 1.46. Solver Parameters for VRS Slack-based Model

Since range names are used in the Solver model, we can modify "CRSSlack" into a VBA procedure that can be applied to other data sets. The modified VBA procedure is called "Slack".

```
Sub Slack()
Dim NDMUs As Integer, NInputs As Integer, NOutputs As Integer
```

```
      NDMUs = 15
      NInputs = 3
      NOutputs = 2
Dim i As Integer
For i = 1 To NDMUs
Range("DMU") = i
SolverSolve UserFinish:=True
Range("Slacks").Copy
Range("A1").Offset(i, NInputs + NOutputs + 5).Select
Selection.PasteSpecial Paste:=xlPasteValues, Transpose:=True
Next
End Sub
```

Chapter 2

Measure-specific DEA Models

2.1 Measure-specific Models

Although DEA does not need *a priori* information on the underlying functional forms and weights among various input and output measures, it assumes proportional improvements of inputs or outputs. This assumption becomes invalid when a preference structure over the improvement of different inputs (outputs) is present in evaluating (inefficient) DMUs (see Chapter 4). We need models where a particular set of performance measures is given pre-emptive priority to improve.

Let $I \subseteq \{1,2, \ldots, m\}$ and $O \subseteq \{1,2, \ldots, s\}$ represent the sets of specific inputs and outputs of interest, respectively. Based upon the envelopment models, we can obtain a set of measure-specific models where only the inputs associated with I or the outputs associated with O are optimized (see Table 2.1).

The measure-specific models can be used to model uncontrollable inputs and outputs (see Banker and Morey (1986)). The controllable measures are related to set I or set O.

A DMU is efficient under envelopment models if and only if it is efficient under measure-specific models. i.e., both the measure-specific models and the envelopment models yield the same frontier. However, for inefficient DMUs, envelopment and measure-specific models yield different efficient targets.

Consider Figure 1.1. If the response time input is of interest, then the measure-specific model will yield the efficient target of S1 for inefficient S. If the cost input is of interest, S3 will be the target for S. The envelopment model projects S to S2 by reducing the two inputs proportionally.

Table 2.1. Measure-specific Models

Frontier Type	Input-Oriented	Output-Oriented
	$\min \theta - \varepsilon(\sum_{i=1}^{m} s_i^- + \sum_{r=1}^{s} s_r^+)$	$\max \phi - \varepsilon(\sum_{i=1}^{m} s_i^- + \sum_{r=1}^{s} s_r^+)$
	subject to	subject to
CRS	$\sum_{j=1}^{n} \lambda_j x_{ij} + s_i^- = \theta x_{io} \quad i \in I;$ $\sum_{j=1}^{n} \lambda_j x_{ij} + s_i^- = x_{io} \quad i \notin I;$ $\sum_{j=1}^{n} \lambda_j y_{rj} - s_r^+ = y_{ro} \quad r = 1,2,...,s;$ $\lambda_j \geq 0 \qquad\qquad j = 1,2,...,n.$	$\sum_{j=1}^{n} \lambda_j x_{ij} + s_i^- = x_{io} \quad i = 1,2,...,m;$ $\sum_{j=1}^{n} \lambda_j y_{rj} - s_r^+ = \phi y_{ro} \quad r \in O;$ $\sum_{j=1}^{n} \lambda_j y_{rj} - s_r^+ = y_{ro} \quad r \notin O;$ $\lambda_j \geq 0 \qquad\qquad j = 1,2,...,n.$
VRS	Add $\sum_{j=1}^{n} \lambda_j = 1$	
NIRS	Add $\sum_{j=1}^{n} \lambda_j \leq 1$	
NDRS	Add $\sum_{j=1}^{n} \lambda_j \geq 1$	
Efficient Target	$\begin{cases} \hat{x}_{io} = \theta^* x_{io} - s_i^{-*} & i \in I \\ \hat{x}_{io} = x_{io} - s_i^{-*} & i \notin I \\ \hat{y}_{ro} = y_{ro} + s_r^{+*} & r = 1,2,...,s \end{cases}$	$\begin{cases} \hat{x}_{io} = x_{io} - s_i^{-*} & i = 1,2,...,m \\ \hat{y}_{ro} = \phi^* y_{ro} + s_r^{+*} & r \in O \\ \hat{y}_{ro} = y_{ro} + s_r^{+*} & r \notin O \end{cases}$

2.2   Measure-specific Models in Spreadsheets

Since the measure-specific models are closely related to the envelopment models, the spreadsheet models can be modified from the envelopment spreadsheet models.

Figure 2.1 shows an input-oriented VRS measure-specific spreadsheet model where the Assets input is of interest. We only need to change the formulas in cells D21:D22 (representing Equity and Employee for the DMU under evaluation) in the input-oriented VRS envelopment spreadsheet model shown in Figure 1.8 to

Cell D21 =INDEX(C2:C16,E18,1)
Cell D22 =INDEX(C2:C16,E18,1)

The Solver parameters remain the same, as shown in Figure 1.15. All the VBA procedures developed for the envelopment models can be used. In Figure 2.1, the VBA procedure "DEA1" is assigned to the button "Measure-Specific".

If we apply the same formula changes in the Second-stage Slack Spreadsheet Model shown in Figure 1.23, with the same Solver parameters shown in Figure 1.24 and with the macro "DEASlack", we can optimize the slacks for the spreadsheet model shown in Figure 2.1 after we obtain the efficiency scores. Figure 2.2 shows the results (see Excel file measure-specific spreadsheet.xls in the CD).

	A	B	C	D	E	F	G	H	I	J
1	Company	Assets	Equity	Employees		Revenue	Profit		λ	Efficiency
2	Mitsubishi	91920.6	10950	36000		184365.2	346.2		0	1
3	Mitsui	68770.9	5553.9	80000		181518.7	314.8		0	1
4	Itochu	65708.9	4271.1	7182		169164.6	121.2		0	1
5	General Motors	217123.4	23345.5	709000		168828.6	6880.7		0	1
6	Sumitomo	50268.9	6681	6193		167530.7	210.5		0.56	1
7	Marubeni	71439.3	5239.1	6702		161057.4	156.6		0	1
8	Ford Motor	243283	24547	346990		137137	4139		0	0.377606
9	Toyota Motor	106004.2	49691.6	146855		111052	2662.4		0	0.578288
10	Exxon	91296	40436	82000		110009	6470		0	1
11	Royal Dutch/Shell Group	118011.6	58986.4	104000		109833.7	6904.6		0	1
12	Wal-Mart	37871	14762	675000		93627	2740		0.44	1
13	Hitachi	91620.9	29907.2	331852		84167.1	1468.8		0	0.484837
14	Nippon Life Insurance	364762.5	2241.9	89690		83206.7	2426.6		0	1
15	Nippon Telegraph & Telephone	127077.3	42240.1	231400		81937.2	2209.1		0	0.42684
16	AT&T	88884	17274	299300		79609	139		0	0.504427
17										
18		Reference		DMU under	15	Efficiency				
19	Constraints	set		Evaluation		0.504427				
20	Assets	44835.477	<	44835.477						
21	Equity	10222.526	<	17274						
22	Employees	299300	<	299300			Measure-Specific			
23	Revenue	135142.15	>	79609						
24	Profit	1319.0622	>	139						
25	Σλ	1	=	1						

Figure 2.1. Input-oriented VRS Measure-specific Spreadsheet Model

	E	F	G	H	I	J	K	L	M	N	O	P
1		Revenue	Profit		λ	Efficiency		Assets	Equity	Employees	Revenue	Profit
2		184365.2	346.2		0	1		0	0	0	0	0
3		181518.7	314.8		0	1		0	0	0	0	0
4		169164.6	121.2		0	1		0	0	0	0	0
5		168828.6	6880.7		0	1		0	0	0	0	0
6		167530.7	210.5		0.7705	1		0	0	0	0	0
7		161057.4	156.6		0	1		0	0	0	0	0
8		137137	4139		0	0.737556		75728.26	0	220277.5	0	0
9		111052	2662.4		0	0.603245		0	30247.6	58265.4	29763.39	0
10		110009	6470		0	1		0	0	0	0	0
11		109833.7	6904.6		0	1		0	0	0	0	0
12		93627	2740		0.2295	1		0	0	0	0	0
13		84167.1	1468.8		0	0.557596		0	17865.99	146812.7	58813.12	0
14		83206.7	2426.6		0	1		0	0	0	0	0
15		81937.2	2209.1		0	0.470611		0	25465.33	122500.6	60995.79	0
16		79609	139		0	0.533544		0	8738.346	139610.4	70960.21	652.0406
17												
18	16											
19		Slack										
20		0										
21		8738.346										
22		139610.4		Slack								
23		70960.21										
24		652.0406										
25		219961										

Figure 2.2. Second-stage Slacks for Input-oriented VRS Measure-specific Model

2.3   Performance Evaluation of Fortune 500 Companies

Fortune magazine analyzes the financial performance of companies by eight measures: revenue, profit, assets, number of employees (employees), stockholders' equity (equity), market value (MV), earnings per share (EPS) and total return to investors (TRI).

In order to obtain an overall performance index, we employ DEA to reconcile these eight measures via a two-stage transformation process described in Figure 2.3. Each stage is defined by a group of "inputs (x)" and "outputs (y)".

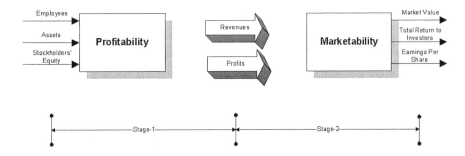

Figure 2.3. Input-output System for Fortune 500 Companies

The performance in the first stage (stage-1) may be viewed as profitability, i.e., a company's ability to generate the revenue and profit in terms of its current labor, assets and capital stock. The performance in the second stage (stage-2) may be viewed as (stock) marketability, i.e., a company's performance in stock market by its revenue and profit generated.

The data of 1995 is used. The DMU numbers correspond to the ranks by the magnitude of revenues. Because some data on MV, profit and equity are not available for some companies, we exclude these companies, and analyze the performance of the 364 companies.

2.3.1   Identification of Best Practice Frontier

Because the Fortune 500 list consists of a variety of companies representing different industries, we assume that the best-practice frontier exhibits VRS. We use the input-oriented VRS envelopment model to identify the best-practice.

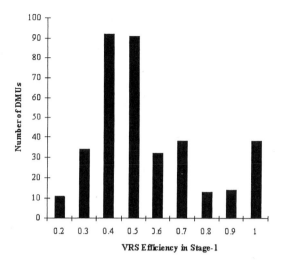

Figure 2.4. Profitability VRS Efficiency Distribution

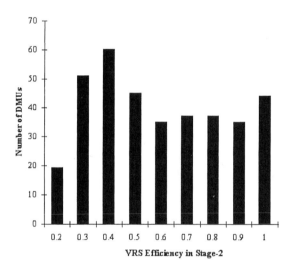

Figure 2.5. Marketability VRS Efficiency Distribution

Figures 2.4 and 2.5 report the distributions of VRS efficiency scores. 30 and 16 DMUs are VRS-efficient in profitability (stage-1) and marketability (stage-2), respectively. In stage-1, most VRS scores are distributed over [0.27, 0.51]. In stage-2, the VRS scores are almost evenly distributed over [0.16, 1]. Only four companies, namely, General Electric (DMU7), Coca-

Cola (DMU48), Nash Finch (DMU437), and CompUSA (DMU451) are on the best-practice frontiers of stage-1 and stage-2.

2.3.2   Measure-specific Performance[1]

Proportional reductions of all inputs are used to determine the best practice frontier for the Fortune 500 companies. However, in an evaluation of inefficient DMUs, non-proportional input (output) improvement may be more appropriate. Therefore, we seek an alternative way to further characterize the performance of inefficient companies by measure-specific models.

Because we have already obtained the VRS best-practice frontier and the measure-specific models yield the same frontier, we modify the VRS measure-specific models for a particular inefficient DMU_d,

$$\theta_d^{k*} = \min \theta_d^k \quad d \in \mathbf{N}$$
subject to
$$\sum_{j \in \mathbf{E}} \lambda_j^d x_{kj} = \theta_d^k x_{kd} \qquad k \in \{1,...,m\}$$
$$\sum_{j \in \mathbf{E}} \lambda_j^d x_{ij} \le x_{id} \qquad i \ne k \qquad\qquad (2.1)$$
$$\sum_{j \in \mathbf{E}} \lambda_j^d y_{rj} \ge y_{rd} \qquad r = 1,...,s$$
$$\sum_{j \in \mathbf{E}} \lambda_j^d = 1$$
$$\lambda_j^d \ge 0, \ j \in \mathbf{E}.$$

$$\phi_d^{q*} = \max \phi_d^q \quad d \in \mathbf{N}$$
subject to
$$\sum_{j \in \mathbf{E}} \lambda_j^d y_{qj} = \phi_d^q y_{qd} \qquad q \in \{1,...,s\}$$
$$\sum_{j \in \mathbf{E}} \lambda_j^d y_{rj} \ge y_{rd} \qquad r \ne q \qquad\qquad (2.2)$$
$$\sum_{j \in \mathbf{E}} \lambda_j^d x_{ij} \le x_{id} \qquad i = 1,...,m$$
$$\sum_{j \in \mathbf{E}} \lambda_j^d = 1$$
$$\lambda_j^d \ge 0, \ j \in \mathbf{E}.$$

where $\mathbf{E}$ and $\mathbf{N}$ represent the index sets for the efficient and inefficient companies, respectively, identified by the VRS envelopment DEA model.

Models (2.1) and (2.2) determine the maximum potential decrease of an input and increase of an output while keeping other inputs and outputs at current levels.

Tables 2.2 and 2.3 report the results for the top-20 companies. Recall that revenue and profit are two factors served as the two outputs in stage-1 and the two inputs in stage-2. Therefore, we have two measure-specific efficiency scores for each revenue and each profit.

Table 2.2. Profitability Measure-specific Efficiency

DMU No.	Company Name	Profitability				
		employees	assets	equity	revenue	profit
1	General Motors	1.000	1.000	1.000	1.000	1.000
2	Ford Motors	1.000	1.000	1.000	1.000	1.000
3	Exxon	1.000	1.000	1.000	1.000	1.000
4	Wal-Mart Stores	1.000	1.000	1.000	1.000	1.000
5	AT&T	0.479	0.503	0.653	1.172	41.670
6	IBM	0.304	0.598	0.573	1.307	1.397
7	General Electric	1.000	1.000	1.000	1.000	1.000
8	Mobil	1.000	1.000	1.000	1.000	1.000
9	Chrysler	0.805	0.735	0.906	1.060	1.381
10	Philip Morris	1.000	1.000	1.000	1.000	1.000
13	Du Pont De Nemours	0.933	0.950	0.976	1.015	1.039
14	Texaco	0.933	0.862	0.936	1.046	2.475
15	Sears Roebuck	1.000	1.000	1.000	1.000	1.000
17	Procter & Gamble	0.325	0.743	0.654	1.291	1.413
18	Chevron	0.493	0.469	0.444	1.716	4.100
19	Citicorp	0.285	0.096	0.385	2.237	1.415
20	Hewlett-Packard	0.286	0.772	0.535	1.287	1.443
Average		0.755	0.808	0.827	1.184	3.784

Table 2.3. Marketability Measure-specific Efficiency

DMU No.	Company Name	Marketability				
		Revenue	Profit	MV	TRI	EPS
1	General Motors	0.025	0.010	3.207	9.258	84.743
2	Ford Motors	0.028	0.013	3.314	33.754	170.670
3	Exxon	0.155	0.088	1.284	3.022	41.071
4	Wal-Mart Stores	0.058	0.029	2.011	43.768	447.912
5	AT&T	1.000	1.000	1.000	1.000	1.000
6	IBM	0.114	0.032	1.690	7.235	59.740
7	General Electric	1.000	1.000	1.000	1.000	1.000
8	Mobil	0.068	0.052	2.401	6.494	103.697
9	Chrysler	0.057	0.020	4.388	17.559	115.283
10	Philip Morris	0.239	0.095	1.408	2.465	47.335
13	Du Pont De Nemours	0.122	0.023	2.342	8.748	107.288
14	Texaco	0.080	0.059	3.202	7.863	243.004
15	Sears Roebuck	0.079	0.020	4.737	9.926	135.778
17	Procter & Gamble	0.168	0.127	1.789	5.644	138.595
18	Chevron	0.122	0.059	2.035	11.386	427.273
19	Citicorp	0.118	0.017	3.000	4.154	82.197
20	Hewlett-Packard	0.172	0.111	1.839	3.268	111.866
Average		0.212	0.162	2.391	10.385	136.379

Table 2.4. Profitability Measure-specific Industry Efficiency

Industries	Employees	Assets	Equity	Revenue	Profit
Aerospace	0.12 (0.11)	0.30 (0.35)	0.24 (0.23)	1.98 (2.26)	3.85 (4.16)
Airlines	0.12 (0.12)	0.24 (0.29)	0.24 (0.27)	1.95 (2.37)	4.54 (5.36)
Beverages	0.34 (0.33)	0.56 (0.46)	0.56 (0.39)	1.71 (2.17)	1.72 (4.96)
Chemicals	0.46 (0.32)	0.56 (0.46)	0.46 (0.31)	1.91 (2.54)	1.83 (2.46)
Commercial Banks	0.13 (0.13)	0.06 (0.05)	0.31 (0.24)	3.66 (4.26)	2.62 (3.24)
Computer and Data Services	0.20 (0.30)	0.57 (0.54)	0.36 (0.31)	2.93 (3.12)	1.69 (2.39)
Computers, Office Equipment	0.25 (0.26)	0.60 (0.59)	0.48 (0.38)	1.51 (2.00)	1.77 (3.33)
Diversified Financials	0.15 (0.38)	0.62 (0.39)	0.39 (0.43)	2.46 (3.09)	2.08 (2.40)
Electric & Gas Utilities	0.30 (0.32)	0.18 (0.18)	0.16 (0.15)	3.73 (3.85)	2.69 (4.03)
Electronics, Electrical Equipment	0.41 (0.30)	0.86 (0.53)	0.69 (0.38)	1.68 (2.35)	1.57 (3.12)
Entertainment	0.12 (0.16)	0.20 (0.24)	0.15 (0.25)	3.24 (3.06)	4.33 (7.86)
Food	0.29 (0.35)	0.45 (0.55)	0.32 (0.43)	1.84 (2.01)	2.49 (6.26)
Food & Drug Stores	0.35 (0.23)	0.70 (0.64)	0.44 (0.41)	1.49 (1.83)	2.39 (3.34)
Forest & Paper Products	0.16 (0.17)	0.30 (0.36)	0.21 (0.18)	2.47 (2.83)	3.44 (7.88)
General Merchandisers	0.65 (0.32)	0.85 (0.65)	0.65 (0.43)	1.35 (2.16)	1.95 (3.52)
Health Care	0.07 (0.30)	0.34 (0.47)	0.23 (0.32)	2.69 (2.75)	3.61 (4.94)
Industrial & Farm Equipment	0.14 (0.13)	0.33 (0.36)	0.24 (0.18)	2.43 (2.89)	2.78 (3.59)
Insurance: Life & Health (stock)	0.15 (0.25)	0.06 (0.07)	0.19 (0.22)	2.57 (2.97)	4.72 (5.23)
Insurance: Property & Causality (stock)	0.29 (0.37)	0.29 (0.27)	0.47 (0.35)	2.26 (2.76)	1.84 (2.64)
Metal Products	0.12 (0.11)	0.43 (0.42)	0.19 (0.17)	3.04 (3.28)	2.82 (4.83)
Motor Vehicles & Parts	0.77 (0.32)	0.92 (0.51)	0.84 (0.39)	1.19 (2.11)	1.36 (2.67)
Petroleum Refining	0.64 (0.51)	0.71 (0.50)	0.73 (0.44)	1.29 (1.72)	1.85 (6.28)
Pharmaceuticals	0.38 (0.41)	0.63 (0.64)	0.52 (0.54)	2.02 (2.14)	1.44 (1.59)
Pipelines	0.63 (0.57)	0.51 (0.44)	0.59 (0.50)	1.76 (1.91)	1.40 (2.64)
Publishing, Printing	0.13 (0.20)	0.39 (0.43)	0.16 (0.21)	3.35 (3.44)	2.77 (2.84)
Soaps, Cosmetics	0.40 (0.47)	0.64 (0.64)	0.58 (0.58)	1.40 (1.45)	1.67 (3.00)
Special Retailers	0.24 (0.27)	0.69 (0.66)	0.35 (0.40)	1.72 (2.11)	2.39 (4.28)
Telecommunications	0.36 (0.25)	0.41 (0.34)	0.42 (0.33)	1.70 (2.45)	3.72 (10.19)
Temporary Help	0.50 (0.56)	0.84 (0.87)	0.68 (0.68)	1.30 (1.31)	1.39 (1.31)
Wholesalers	0.54 (0.58)	0.69 (0.74)	0.38 (0.55)	1.34 (1.46)	2.37 (2.08)

* The number in parenthesis represents the arithmetic average.

We may use the average measure-specific efficiency scores (optimal values to (2.1) or (2.2)) within each industry to characterize the measure-specific industry efficiency. However, different companies with different sizes may exist in each industry. Therefore arithmetic averages may not be a good way to characterize the industry efficiency. Usually, one expects large input and output levels, e.g., assets and revenue, form relatively big companies.

Table 2.5. Marketability Measure-specific Industry Efficiency

Industries	Revenue	Profit	MV	TRI	EPS
Aerospace	0.21 (0.29)	0.06 (0.06)	3.44 (4.51)	5.88 (6.39)	102.60 (131.24)
Airlines	0.35 (0.55)	0.34 (0.38)	4.73 (4.10)	2.66 (5.80)	35.65 (54.23)
Beverages	0.64 (0.61)	0.80 (0.37)	1.37 (2.67)	4.57 (4.94)	102.55 (95.84)
Chemicals	0.32 (0.52)	0.06 (0.11)	3.55 (4.16)	9.63 (13.37)	84.31 (100.13)
Commercial Banks	0.34 (0.51)	0.07 (0.13)	3.94 (4.05)	6.40 (5.98)	85.39 (104.16)
Computer and Data Services	0.82 (0.85)	0.83 (0.66)	1.20 (1.52)	4.01 (5.68)	38.83 (38.77)
Computers, Office Equipment	0.24 (0.50)	0.09 (0.02)	2.37 (3.90)	4.28 (8.59)	84.83 (86.03)
Diversified Financials	0.33 (0.47)	0.13 (0.17)	2.82 (3.79)	5.24 (7.31)	6.88 (117.12)
Electric & Gas Utilities	0.56 (0.65)	0.08 (0.14)	4.99 (5.00)	10.34 (11.68)	128.75 (126.03)
Electronics, Electrical Equipment	0.63 (0.54)	0.47 (0.19)	2.14 (3.54)	6.34 (14.22)	86.56 (87.05)
Entertainment	0.40 (0.50)	0.41 (0.39)	1.49 (1.56)	6.96 (10.07)	248.91 (285.42)
Food	0.30 (0.42)	0.09 (0.20)	3.42 (3.28)	8.83 (16.35)	145.47 (143.31)
Food & Drug Stores	0.28 (0.44)	0.10 (0.21)	5.52 (5.31)	6.24 (25.35)	83.66 (86.30)
Forest & Paper Products	0.49 (0.59)	0.06 (0.16)	4.24 (5.14)	11.63 (26.57)	67.17 (66.03)
General Merchandisers	0.12 (0.32)	0.04 (0.08)	3.48 (4.33)	17.41 (24.60)	129.62 (152.9)
Health Care	0.50 (0.66)	0.16 (0.28)	2.68 (2.91)	8.95 (13.56)	98.43 (95.67)
Industrial & Farm Equipment	0.39 (0.52)	0.08 (0.15)	4.19 (4.20)	7.56 (13.39)	98.35 (103.26)
Insurance: Life & Health (stock)	0.37 (0.53)	0.10 (0.14)	4.86 (5.16)	6.25 (6.58)	57.71 (65.72)
Insurance: Property & Causality (stock)	0.28 (0.47)	0.05 (0.08)	4.09 (5.55)	6.42 (8.49)	71.85 (80.33)
Metal Products	0.63 (0.70)	0.30 (0.36)	2.22 (2.12)	7.47 (8.89)	103.54 (96.76)
Motor Vehicles & Parts	0.07 (0.32)	0.02 (0.08)	41.19 (5.72)	13.26 (30.38)	77.53 (77.95)
Petroleum Refining	0.17 (0.36)	0.07 (0.16)	2.41 (4.21)	9.94 (18.53)	102.81 (122.06)
Pharmaceuticals	0.44 (0.44)	0.33 (0.29)	1.75 (2.00)	4.77 (5.65)	163.58 (193.30)
Pipelines	0.51 (0.65)	0.07 (0.13)	4.38 (4.22)	5.22 (6.47)	46.10 (103.94)
Publishing, Printing	0.67 (0.73)	0.21 (0.22)	3.23 (3.19)	14.35 (19.16)	69.09 (73.99)
Soaps, Cosmetics	0.25 (0.37)	0.13 (0.12)	1.89 (2.23)	10.04 (11.98)	101.42 (109.16)
Special Retailers	0.40 (0.60)	0.15 (0.30)	3.19 (3.90)	6.79 (20.26)	103.34 (98.36)
Telecommunications	0.68 (0.44)	0.12 (0.25)	1.85 (2.53)	7.19 (61.16)	188.16 (214.68)
Temporary Help	0.69 (0.78)	0.32 (0.36)	3.68 (3.52)	18.87 (93.62)	30.83 (30.48)
Wholesalers	0.37 (0.47)	0.18 (0.30)	3.95 (4.61)	6.64 (8.83)	49.55 (49.33)

* The number in parenthesis represents the arithmetic average.

Thus, we define weighted measure-specific scores within each industry by considering the sizes of the companies.

(size-adjusted) kth input-specific industry efficiency measure for industry **F**

$$I_k^{\mathbf{F}} = \sum_{d \in \mathbf{F}} \theta_d^{k*} \cdot \frac{x_{kd}}{\sum_{d \in \mathbf{F}} x_{kd}} = \frac{\sum_{d \in \mathbf{F}} \hat{x}_{kd}}{\sum_{d \in \mathbf{F}} x_{kd}} \qquad (2.3)$$

(size-adjusted) qth output-specific industry efficiency measure for industry **F**

$$O_q^F = \sum_{d\in F} \phi_d^{q^*} \cdot \frac{y_{qd}}{\sum_{d\in F} y_{qd}} = \frac{\sum_{d\in F} \hat{y}_{qd}}{\sum_{d\in F} y_{qd}}$$

(2.4)

where $\hat{x}_{kd}$ ($= \theta_d^{k^*} x_{kd}$) and $\hat{y}_{qd}$ ($= \phi_d^{q^*} y_{qd}$) are, respectively, the projected (potentially efficient) levels for kth input and qth output of DMU_d, $d\in$ **F**.

The weights in (2.3) ($\frac{x_{kd}}{\sum_{d\in F} x_{kd}}$, $d\in$ **F**) and (2.4) ($\frac{y_{qd}}{\sum_{d\in F} y_{qd}}$, $d\in$ **F**) are normalized, therefore a specific industry F achieves 100% efficiency, i.e., $I_k^F = 1$ and $O_q^F = 1$, if and only if, all of its companies are located on the best-practice frontier.

Tables 2.4 and 2.5 report the industry efficiency scores for the 30 selected industries where the number in parenthesis represents the corresponding arithmetic mean of measure-specific efficiency scores.

A relatively large discrepancy between weighted and arithmetic average scores is detected for six industries – General Merchandiser, Health Care, Motor Vehicles & Parts, Petroleum Refining, Pipelines, and Telecommunications. Since (2.3) and (2.4) determine the industry efficiency by considering the size of each company, this may imply that efficiency may highly correlate with size in these industries.

2.3.3 Benchmark Share

Non-zero λ_j^* indicates that DMU_j is used as a benchmark. As an efficient company, the role it plays in evaluating inefficiency companies is to be of interest. One wants to know the importance of each efficient DMU in measuring the inefficiencies of inefficient DMUs. Based upon the non-zero λ_j^*, we develop benchmark-share measures for each efficient company via (2.1) and (2.2).

We define the kth input-specific benchmark-share for each efficient DMU_j, $j \in$ **E**,

$$\Delta_j^k = \frac{\sum_{d\in N} \lambda_j^{d^*} (1-\theta_d^{k^*}) x_{kd}}{\sum_{d\in N} (1-\theta_d^{k^*}) x_{kd}}$$

(2.5)

where $\lambda_j^{d^*}$ and $\theta_d^{k^*}$ are optimal values in (2.1).

We define the qth output-specific benchmark-share for each efficient $DMU_j, j \in \mathbf{E}$,

$$\Pi_j^q = \frac{\sum\limits_{d \in N} \lambda_j^{d*}(\phi_d^{q*} - 1)y_{qd}}{\sum\limits_{d \in N}(\phi_d^{q*} - 1)y_{qd}} \tag{2.6}$$

where λ_j^{d*} and ϕ_d^{q*} are optimal values in (2.2).

The benchmark-share Δ_j^k (or Π_j^q) depends on the values of λ_j^{d*} and θ_d^{k*} (or λ_j^{d*} and ϕ_d^{q*}). Note that $(1 - \theta_d^{k*})x_{kd}$ and $(\phi_d^{q*} - 1)y_{qd}$ characterize the potential decrease on kth input and increase on qth output, respectively.

Δ_j^k and Π_j^q are weighted λ_j^* across all inefficient DMUs. The weights,

$\dfrac{(1 - \theta_d^{k*})x_{kd}}{\sum\limits_{d \in N}(1 - \theta_d^{k*})x_{kd}}$ in (2.5) and $\dfrac{(\phi_d^{q*} - 1)y_{qd}}{\sum\limits_{d \in N}(\phi_d^{q*} - 1)y_{qd}}$ in (2.7) are normalized.

Therefore, we have $\sum\limits_{j \in \mathbf{E}} \Delta_j^k = 1$ and $\sum\limits_{j \in \mathbf{E}} \Pi_j^q = 1$. (Note that $\sum\limits_{j \in \mathbf{E}} \lambda_j^{d*} = 1$ in (2.1) and (2.2).)

It is very clear form (2.5) and (2.6) that an efficient company which does not act as a referent DMU for any inefficient DMU will have zero benchmark-share. The bigger the benchmark-share, the more important an efficient company is in benchmarking.

Table 2.6 reports the benchmark-shares for 12 selected VRS-efficient companies. The benchmark-shares for the remaining VRS-efficient companies are less than 0.01%. Of the total 60 benchmark-shares, 12 are greater than 10%. Particularly, DMU48 (Coca-Cola), DMU156 (General Mills) and DMU281 (Bindley Western) have the biggest benchmark-share with respect to employees, equity and profit, respectively. This means that, e.g., General Mills plays a leading role in setting a benchmark with respect to equity input given the current levels of employees and assets. Note that General Mills had the highest returns on equity in 1995.

In Table 2.7, DMU226 (Continental Airlines) and DMU292 (Berkshire Hathaway) are two important companies in TRI and EPS benchmarking, respectively. (Note that Continental Airlines and Berkshire Hathaway had the highest TRI and EPS in 1995.) Although Berkshire Hathaway was ranked 18 in terms of MV levels by the Fortune magazine, the benchmark-share of 39.99% indicates that it had an outstanding performance in terms of MV given other measures at their current levels. This indicates that single financial performance alone is not sufficient to characterize a company's performance.

Finally, note that, e.g., DMU292 and DMU474 both acted as a referent DMU in 63% of the inefficient DMUs when measuring the revenue-specific efficiency. However, the benchmark-share indicates that DMU474 is more important.

Table 2.6. Benchmark-share for Profitability

DMU No.	Company Name	Employees	Assets	Equity	Revenue	Profit
8	Mobil	3.07%	1.51%	0.76%	**16.00%**	0.15%
32	Fed. Natl. Mortgage	2.78%	0	2.76%	0.89%	0.10%
44	Loews	7.17%	0.14%	0	0.95%	1.41%
48	Coca-Cola	2.58%	**12.54%**	10.65%	2.88%	**40.65%**
94	IBP	0	**22.51%**	0.07%	13.16%	0.80%
153	Bergen Brunswig	0.60%	0	0.16%	5.91%	0.17%
156	General Mills	1.86%	0.01%	**60.91%**	17.19%	7.85%
168	Cardinal Health	3.12%	2.82%	0.01%	10.89%	0
281	Bindley Western	**52.91%**	4.79%	2.93%	5.97%	2.86%
419	Micron Technology	0.17%	**28.37%**	0.24%	0.29%	**11.04%**
437	Nash Finch	0	**10.16%**	0.02%	0.24%	0.27%
447	Williams	8.68%	0	0	0.02%	8.62%
Total		82.94%	82.85%	78.51%	74.39%	73.92%

Table 2.7. Benchmark-share for Marketability

DMU No.	Company Name	Revenue	Profit	MV	TRI	EPS
5	AT&T	0	**12.33%**	6.95%	2.22%	0
7	IBM	0	0.20%	3.83%	6.39%	0.79%
48	Coca-Cola	5.44%	0.80%	**11.37%**	0.13%	0.11%
78	Kimberly-Clark	0.04%	**36.66%**	6.96%	0	0.10%
210	Burlington Northern Santa FE	0.05%	4.29%	6.39%	0	0
219	Microsoft	8.46%	0	9.97%	0	0
226	Continental Airlines	0.44%	0.69%	1.30%	**81.91%**	0.87%
292	Berkshire Hathaway	**23.56%**	8.37%	**39.99%**	0.18%	**73.96%**
312	Chiquita Brands International	0.00%	**15.49%**	0.07%	0.17%	**11.41%**
376	Consolidated Natural Gas	0.99%	**11.29%**	4.89%	0.05%	0.00%
417	Oracle	0.00%	0.00%	1.37%	0	0
437	Nash Finch	0.09%	0.51%	0	0	3.56%
451	CompUSA	1.43%	7.22%	0.88%	8.85%	4.11%
474	Computer Associates	**29.90%**	0.04%	1.69%	0.00%	0.00%
494	Foundation Health	5.21%	2.07%	4.25%	0.07%	2.58%
495	State Street Boston Corp.	**24.39%**	0.04%	0.09%	0.03%	2.51%
Total		100%	100%	100%	100%	100%

We here explore the multidimensional financial performance of the Fortune 500 companies. Revenue-top-ranked companies do not necessarily have top-ranked performance in terms of profitability and (stock) marketability. Most companies exhibited serious inefficiencies. The measure-specific models enable us to study the performance based upon a specific measure while keeping the current levels of other measures. See Zhu (2000a) for more discussion on measuring the performance of Fortune 500 companies.

[1] The material in this section is adapted from European Journal of Operational Research, Vol 123, Zhu, J., Multi-factor Performance Measure Model with An Application to Fortune 500 Companies, 105-124, 2000, with permission from Elsevier Science.

Chapter 3

Returns-to-Scale

3.1 Introduction

As demonstrated in Figure 1.3, the VRS envelopment model identifies the VRS frontier with DMUs exhibiting IRS, CRS, and DRS. In fact, the economic concept of RTS has been widely studied within the framework of DEA. RTS have typically been defined only for single output situations. DEA generalizes the notion of RTS to the multiple-output case. This, in turn, further extended the applicability of DEA.

Seiford and Zhu (1999a) demonstrate that there are at least three equivalent *basic* methods of testing a DMU's RTS nature which have appeared in the DEA literature. Based upon the VRS multiplier models, the sign of the optimal free variable (μ^* or v^*) indicates the RTS (Banker, Charnes and Cooper, 1984). Based upon the CRS envelopment models, the magnitude of optimal $\sum_j^n \lambda_j$ indicates the RTS (Banker, 1984). These two methods may fail when DEA models have alternate optimal solutions. The third method is based upon the scale efficiency index (Färe, Grosskopf and Lovell, 1994). The scale efficiency index method does not require information on μ^* or v^* or $\sum_j^n \lambda_j^*$, and is robust even when there exist multiple optima. However, the scale efficiency index method requires the calculation of three DEA models.

3.2 RTS Regions

It is meaningful to discuss RTS for DMUs located on the VRS frontier. We discuss the RTS for non-frontier DMUs by their VRS efficient targets as indicated in Table 1.1. Because a VRS envelopment model can be either input-oriented or output-oriented, we may obtain different efficient targets and RTS classifications for a specific non-frontier DMU.

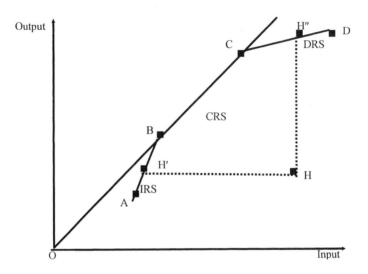

Figure 3.1. RTS and VRS Efficient Target

Suppose we have five DMUs, A, B, C, D, and H as shown in Figure 3.1. Ray OBC is the CRS frontier. AB, BC and CD constitute the VRS frontier, and exhibit IRS, CRS and DRS, respectively. B and C exhibit CRS. On the line segment AB, IRS prevail to the left of B. On the line segment CD, DRS prevail to the right of C.

Consider non-frontier DMU H. If the input-oriented VRS envelopment model is used, then H′ is the efficient target, and the RTS classification for H is IRS. If the output-oriented VRS envelopment model is used, then H″is the efficient target, and the RTS classification for H is DRS.

However some IRS, CRS and DRS regions are uniquely determined no matter which VRS model is employed. They are region 'I' – IRS, region 'II' – CRS, and region 'III' – DRS. In fact, we have six RTS regions as shown in Figure 3.2. Two RTS classifications will be assigned into the remaining regions IV, V and VI. Region 'IV' is of IRS (input-oriented) and of CRS (output-oriented). Region 'V' is of CRS (input-oriented) and of DRS (output-oriented). Region 'VI' is of IRS (input-oriented) and of DRS (output-oriented).

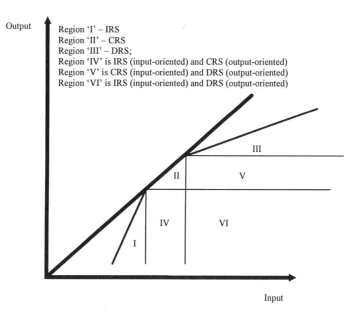

Output

Region 'I' – IRS
Region 'II' – CRS
Region 'III' – DRS;
Region 'IV' is IRS (input-oriented) and CRS (output-oriented)
Region 'V' is CRS (input-oriented) and DRS (output-oriented)
Region 'VI' is IRS (input-oriented) and DRS (output-oriented)

Input

Figure 3.2. RTS Region

3.3   RTS Estimation

3.3.1   VRS and CRS RTS Methods

Let μ^* represent the optimal value of μ in the input-oriented VRS multiplier model, and v^* the optimal value of v in the output-oriented VRS multiplier model, then we have the VRS RTS method.

Theorem 3.1
(i) If $\mu^* = 0$ (or $v^* = 0$) in *any* alternate optima, then CRS prevail on DMU_o.
(ii) If $\mu^* > 0$ (or $v^* < 0$) in *all* alternate optima, then IRS prevail on DMU_o.
(iii) If $\mu^* < 0$ (or $v^* > 0$) in *all* alternate optima, then DRS prevail on DMU_o.

Note that the VRS frontier can be expressed as $\sum_{r=1}^{s} \mu_r y_{rj} = \sum_{i=1}^{m} v_i x_{ij} - \mu$ (or $\sum_{r=1}^{s} \mu_r y_{rj} = \sum_{i=1}^{m} v_i x_{ij} + v$). Thus, geometrically, in the case of single output, $-\mu^*$ (or v^*) represents the y-intercept on the output axis. Consider Figure 3.1. The intercept is positive for line segment CD so $\mu^* < 0$ (or $v^* >$

0) and RTS is decreasing for any DMU on CD (excluding C), whereas the intercept is negative for line segment AB so $\mu^* > 0$ (or $v^* < 0$) and RTS is increasing for any DMU on AB (excluding B). The intercept for line OBC is zero so $\mu^* = 0$ (or $v^* = 0$) and RTS is constant. However, in computation, we may not obtain the unique optimal solution (the frontier), and we may obtain supporting hyperplanes at VRS frontier DMUs. Consequently, we have to check all optimal solutions as indicated in Theorem 3.1.

Table 3.1 presents five VRS frontier DMUs with two inputs and one output. The last column indicates the RTS classification.

Table 3.1. DMUs for RTS Estimation

DMU	input 1 (x1)	input 2 (x2)	output (y)	RTS
1	2	5	2	CRS
2	2	2	1	CRS
3	4	1	1	CRS
4	2	1	1/2	IRS
5	6	5	5/2	DRS

The second column of Table 3.2 reports the optimal μ^*. μ^* can take all the optimal values in the interval $[\mu^-, \mu^+]$. $\mu^* = 0$ is found in DMUs 1, 2, and 3, therefore the three DMUs exhibit CRS. All μ^* are positive and negative in DMU5 and DMU6, respectively, therefore IRS and DRS prevail on DMU5 and DMU6, respectively.

Table 3.2. Optimal Values for RTS Estimation

DMU	$\mu^* \in [\mu^-, \mu^+]$	λ_j^*
1	[-7, 1]	$\lambda_1^* = 1$; $\sum_{j=1}^6 \lambda_j^* = 1$
2	[0, 1]	solution 1: $\lambda_2^* = 1$; $\sum_{j=1}^6 \lambda_j^* = 1$
		solution 2: $\lambda_1^* = 1/3$, $\lambda_3^* = 1/3$; $\sum_{j=1}^6 \lambda_j^* = 2/3$
3	[-5/3, 1]	$\lambda_3^* = 1$; $\sum_{j=1}^6 \lambda_j^* = 1$
4	[1/2, 1]	$0 \le \lambda_1^* \le 1/12$, $\lambda_2^* = 1/4 - 3\lambda_1^*$, $\lambda_3^* = 1/4 + \lambda_1^*$
		$5/12 \le \sum_{j=1}^6 \lambda_j^* \le 1/2$
5	(-∞, -3/37]	$\lambda_1^* = 35/48 - \lambda_2^*/3$, $0 \le \lambda_2^* \le 35/16$, $\lambda_3^* = 25/24 - \lambda_2^*/3$
		$85/48 \le \sum_{j=1}^6 \lambda_j^* \le 15/6$

The above RTS method uses the VRS multiplier models. In fact, we can use CRS envelopment models to estimate the RTS classification (Zhu, 2000c). Let λ_j^* be the optimal values in CRS envelopment models. We have

Theorem 3.2
(i) If $\sum_j^n \lambda_j^* = 1$ in *any* alternate optima, then CRS prevail on DMU_o.
(ii) If $\sum_j^n \lambda_j^* < 1$ for *all* alternate optima, then IRS prevail on DMU_o.
(iii) If $\sum_j^n \lambda_j^* > 1$ for *all* alternate optima, then DRS prevail on DMU_o.

From Table 3.2, we see that DMU2 has alternate optimal λ_j^*. Nevertheless, there exists an optimal solution such that $\sum_j^n \lambda_j^* = 1$ indicating CRS. DMU4 exhibits IRS because $\sum_j^n \lambda_j^* < 1$ in all optima, and DMU5 exhibits DRS because $\sum_j^n \lambda_j^* > 1$ in all optima.

3.3.2 Improved RTS Method

In real world applications, the examination of alternative optima is a laborious task, and one may attempt to use a single set of resulting optimal solutions in the application of the RTS methods. However, this may yield erroneous results. For instance, if we obtain $\lambda_1^* = \lambda_3^* = 1/3$, or $\mu^* = 1$ for DMU2, then DMU2 may erroneously be classified as having IRS because $\sum \lambda_j^* < 1$ or $\mu^* > 0$ in one particular alternate solution.

A number of methods have been developed to deal with multiple optimal solutions in the VRS multiplier models and the CRS envelopment models. Seiford and Zhu (1999a) show the following results with respect to the relationship amongst envelopment and multiplier models, respectively.

Theorem 3.3
(i) The CRS efficiency score is equal to the VRS efficiency score *if and only if* there exists an optimal solution such that $\sum_j^n \lambda_j^* = 1$. If The CRS efficiency score is not equal to the VRS efficiency score, then
(ii) The VRS efficiency score is greater than the NIRS efficiency score *if and only if* $\sum_j^n \lambda_j^* < 1$ in all optimal solutions of the CRS envelopment model.
(iii) The VRS efficiency score is equal to the NIRS efficiency score *if and only if* $\sum_j^n \lambda_j^* > 1$ in all optimal solutions of the CRS envelopment model.

Theorem 3.4
(i) The CRS efficiency score is equal to the VRS efficiency score *if and only if* there exists an optimal solution $\mu^* = 0$ (or $v^* = 0$). If The CRS efficiency score is not equal to the VRS efficiency score, then
(ii) The VRS efficiency score is greater than the NIRS efficiency score *if and only if* $\mu^* > 0$ (or $v^* < 0$) in all optimal solutions.
(iii) The VRS efficiency score is equal to the NIRS efficiency score *if and only if* $\mu^* < 0$ (or $v^* > 0$) in all optimal solutions.

Based upon Theorems 3.3 and 3.4, we have

Theorem 3.5
(i) If DMU_o exhibits IRS, then $\sum_j^n \lambda_j^* < 1$ for *all* alternate optima.
(ii) If DMU_o exhibits DRS, then $\sum_j^n \lambda_j^* > 1$ for *all* alternate optima.

The significance of Theorem 3.5 lies in the fact that the possible alternate optimal λ_j^* obtained from the CRS envelopment models only affect the estimation of RTS for those DMUs that truly exhibit CRS, and have nothing to do with the RTS estimation on those DMUs that truly exhibit IRS or DRS. That is, if a DMU exhibits IRS (or DRS), then $\sum_j^n \lambda_j^*$ must be less (or greater) than one, no matter whether there exist alternate optima of λ_j.

Further, we can have a very simple approach to eliminate the need for examining all alternate optima.

Theorem 3.6
(i) The CRS efficiency score is equal to the VRS efficiency score *if and only if* CRS prevail on DMU_o. Otherwise,
(ii) $\sum_j^n \lambda_j^* < 1$ *if and only if* IRS prevail on DMU_o.
(iii) $\sum_j^n \lambda_j^* > 1$ *if and only if* DRS prevail on DMU_o.

Thus, in empirical applications, we can explore RTS in two steps. First, select all the DMUs that have the same CRS and VRS efficiency scores regardless of the value of $\sum_j^n \lambda_j^*$. These DMUs are in the CRS region. Next, use the value of $\sum_j^n \lambda_j^*$ (in any CRS envelopment model outcome) to determine the RTS for the remaining DMUs. We observe that in this process we can safely ignore possible multiple optimal solutions of λ_j.

Similarly, based upon VRS multiplier models, we have

Theorem 3.7
(i) The CRS efficiency score is equal to the VRS efficiency score *if and only if* CRS prevail on DMU_o. Otherwise,
(ii) $\mu^* > 0$ (or $v^* < 0$) if and only if IRS prevail on DMU_o.
(iii) $\mu^* < 0$ (or $v^* > 0$) if and only if DRS prevail on DMU_o.

3.3.3   Spreadsheets for RTS Estimation

We here develop spreadsheet models for RTS estimation based upon Theorem 3.6. The RTS spreadsheet model uses VRS and CRS envelopment spreadsheets. Figure 3.3 shows a spreadsheet for the input-oriented CRS envelopment model where CRS efficiency scores and the optimal $\sum_j^n \lambda_j^*$ are recorded in columns J and K, respectively. The button "Input-oriented CRS (RTS)" is linked to a VBA procedure "RTS".

```
Sub RTS()
    Dim i As Integer
    For i = 1 To 15
'set the value of cell E18 equal to i (1, 2,..., 15)
```

```
    Range("E18") = i
'Run the Solver model. The UserFinish is set to True so that
'the Solver Results dialog box will not be shown
    SolverSolve UserFinish:=True
'Place the efficiency into column J
    Range("J" & i + 1) = Range("F19")
'Place the sum of lambdas into column K
    Range("K" & i + 1) = Range("B25")
    Next i
End Sub
```

	A	B	C	D	E	F	G	H	I	J	K
1	Company	Assets	Equity	Employees		Revenue	Profit		λ	CRS Efficiency	Σλ
2	Mitsubishi	91920.6	10950	36000		184365.2	346.2		0	0.662831738	1.101942
3	Mitsui	68770.9	5553.9	80000		181518.7	314.8		0	1	1
4	Itochu	65708.9	4271.1	7182		169164.6	121.2		0	1	1
5	General Motors	217123.4	23345.5	709000		168828.6	6880.7		0	1	1
6	Sumitomo	50268.9	6681	6193		167530.7	210.5		0.47	1	1
7	Marubeni	71439.3	5239.1	6702		161057.4	156.6		0	0.971966637	0.956252
8	Ford Motor	243283	24547	346990		137137	4139		0	0.737166307	0.99751
9	Toyota Motor	106004.2	49691.6	146855		111052	2662.4		0	0.524557613	0.819264
10	Exxon	91296	40436	82000		110009	6470		0	1	1
11	Royal Dutch/Shell Group	118011.6	58986.4	104000		109833.7	6904.6		0	0.841423731	1.067172
12	Wal-Mart	37871	14762	675000		93627	2740		0.01	1	1
13	Hitachi	91620.9	29907.2	331852		84167.1	1468.8		0	0.386057261	0.62692
14	Nippon Life Insurance	364762.5	2241.9	89690		83206.7	2426.6		0	1	1
15	Nippon Telegraph & Telephone	127077.3	42240.1	231400		81937.2	2209.1		0	0.348577853	0.619252
16	AT&T	88884	17274	299300		79609	139		0	0.270381772	0.481746
17											
18		Reference		DMU under	16	Efficiency					
19	**Constraints**	set		Evaluation		0.270382					
20	Assets	24032.61	≤	24032.613							
21	Equity	3338.645	≤	4670.5747		Input-oriented					
22	Employees	12922.98	≤	80925.264		CRS (RTS)					
23	Revenue	79609	≥	79609							
24	Profit	139	≥	139							
25	Σλ	0.481746									

Figure 3.3. Input-oriented RTS Classification Spreadsheet Model

In order to obtain the RTS classification, we need also to calculate the input-oriented VRS envelopment model. This can be achieved by using the spreadsheet model shown in Figure 1.8 (Chapter 1). We then copy the VRS efficiency scores into column L, as shown in Figure 3.4. Cells M2:M16 contain formulas based upon Theorem 3.6. The formula for cell M2 which is copied into cells M3:M16 is

=IF(J2=L2,"CRS",IF(AND(J2<>L2,K2<1),"IRS",IF(AND(J2<>L2,K2>1),"DRS")))

To obtain the output-oriented RTS classification, we use the spreadsheet for output-oriented CRS envelopment model. Figure 3.5 shows the spreadsheet, and Figure 3.6 shows the Solver parameters. Note that range names are used in the spreadsheet shown in Figure 3.5 as in the spreadsheet for output-oriented VRS envelopment model shown in Figure 1.27. For example, cell E18 is named as "DMU", cell F19 is named as "Efficiency", and cell B25 is named as "SumLambda". The button "Output-oriented CRS" is linked to a VBA procedure "GeneralRTS" which automates the calculation, and records the efficiency score and $\sum_j^n \lambda_j^*$ into columns K and L, respectively.

```
Sub GeneralRTS()
Dim NDMUs As Integer, NInputs As Integer, NOutputs As Integer
    NDMUs = 15
    NInputs = 3
    NOutputs = 2
    Dim i As Integer
    For i = 1 To NDMUs
    Range("DMU") = i
    SolverSolve UserFinish:=True
Range("A1").Offset(i,NInputs+NOutputs+4) = Range("Efficiency")
Range("A1").Offset(i, NInputs+NOutputs+5) = Range("SumLambda")
    Next
End Sub
```

M2			f_x	=IF(J2=L2,"CRS",IF(AND(J2<>L2,K2<1),"IRS",IF(AND(J2<>L2,K2>1),"DRS")))			
	J	K	L	M	N	O	P
1	CRS Efficiency Σλ		VRS Efficiency	RTS	Company		
2	0.662831738	1.101942	1	DRS	Mitsubishi		
3	1	1	1	CRS	Mitsui		
4	1	1	1	CRS	Itochu		
5	1	1	1	CRS	General Motors		
6	1	1	1	CRS	Sumitomo		
7	0.971966637	0.956252	1	IRS	Marubeni		
8	0.737166307	0.99751	0.737555958	IRS	Ford Motor		
9	0.524557613	0.819264	0.603245345	IRS	Toyota Motor		
10	1	1	1	CRS	Exxon		
11	0.841423731	1.067172	1	DRS	Royal Dutch/Shell Group		
12	1	1	1	CRS	Wal-Mart		
13	0.386057261	0.62692	0.557595838	IRS	Hitachi		
14	1	1	1	CRS	Nippon Life Insurance		
15	0.348577853	0.619252	0.470610997	IRS	Nippon Telegraph & Telephone		
16	0.270381772	0.481746	0.533543522	IRS	AT&T		

Figure 3.4. Input-oriented RTS Classification

Note that we can assign "RTS" to the button "Output-oriented CRS (RTS)". In fact, when the range names are used, Range("DMU"), Range("Efficiency"), and Range("SumLambda") are equivalent to Range("E18"), Range("F19"), and Range("B25"), respectively. The procedure "GeneralRTS" can be applied to other data sets with the range names.

With the output-oriented VRS efficiency scores and Theorem 3.7, we can obtain the output-oriented RTS classification shown in Figure 3.7.

Based upon Figures 3.4 and 3.7, we obtain the RTS regions (see column O in Figure 3.7).

	A	B	C	D	E	F	G	H	I	J	K
1	Company	Assets	Equity	Employees		Revenue	Profit		λ	CRS Efficiency	Σλ
2	Mitsubishi	91920.6	10950	36000		184365.2	1		0	1.58488945	1.74138
3	Mitsui	68770.9	5553.9	80000		181518.7	314.8		0	1	1
4	Itochu	65708.9	4271.1	7182		169164.6	121.2		0	1	1
5	General Motors	217123.4	23345.5	709000		168828.6	6880.7		0	1	1
6	Sumitomo	50268.9	6681	6193		167530.7	210.5		1.73	1	1
7	Marubeni	71439.3	5239.1	6702		161057.4	156.6		0	1.028841898	0.983832
8	Ford Motor	243283	24547	346990		137137	4139		0	1.356545993	1.353168
9	Toyota Motor	106004.2	49691.6	146855		111052	2662.4		0	1.906368292	1.561819
10	Exxon	91296	40436	82000		110009	6470		0	1	1
11	Royal Dutch/Shell Group	118011.6	58986.4	104000		109833.7	6904.6		0	1.188461846	1.268293
12	Wal-Mart	37871	14762	675000		93627	2740		0.05	1	1
13	Hitachi	91620.9	29907.2	331852		84167.1	1468.8		0	2.590289318	1.623905
14	Nippon Life Insurance	364762.5	224	*Reserved to indicate the DMU under evaluation.*		83206.7	2426.6		0	1	1
15	Nippon Telegraph & Telephone	127077.3	4224			81937.2	2209.1		0	2.868799584	1.77651
16	AT&T	88884	172			79609	139		0	3.698474165	1.781727
17											
18		Reference		DMU under	15	Efficiency					
19	**Constraints**	set		Evaluation		3.698474					
20	Assets	88884	≤	88884							
21	Equity	12347.89	≤	17274		Output-oriented CRS					
22	Employees	47795.32	≤	299300		(RTS)					
23	Revenue	294431.8	≥	294431.83							
24	Profit	514.0879	≥	514.08791							
25	Σλ	1.781727									

Name cells I2:I16 "Lambdas"

Efficiency; φ; A changing cell; Target cell in Solver

Σλ The cell is named "SumLambda"

Figure 3.5. Output-oriented RTS Classification Spreadsheet Model

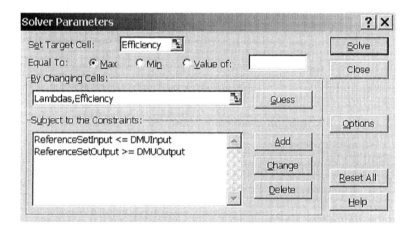

Figure 3.6. Solver Parameters for Output-oriented CRS Envelopment Model

M2			f_x	=IF(J2=L2,"CRS",IF(AND(J2<>L2,K2<1),"IRS",IF(AND(J2<>L2,K2>1),"DRS")))		
	J	K	L	M	N	O	P
1	CRS Efficiency	Σλ	VRS Efficiency	RTS	Company	RTS Region	
2	1.58488945	1.74138	1	DRS	Mitsubishi	Region III	
3	1	1	1	CRS	Mitsui	Region II	
4	1	1	1	CRS	Itochu	Region II	
5	1	1	1	CRS	General Motors	Region II	
6	1	1	1	CRS	Sumitomo	Region II	
7	1.028841898	0.983832	1	IRS	Marubeni	Region I	
8	1.356545993	1.353168	1.158414974	DRS	Ford Motor	Region VI	
9	1.906368292	1.561819	1.371588284	DRS	Toyota Motor	Region VI	
10	1	1	1	CRS	Exxon	Region II	
11	1.188461846	1.268293	1	DRS	Royal Dutch/Shell Group	Region III	
12	1	1	1	CRS	Wal-Mart	Region II	
13	2.590289318	1.623905	1.898938938	DRS	Hitachi	Region VI	
14	1	1	1	CRS	Nippon Life Insurance	Region II	
15	2.868799584	1.77651	1.892916538	DRS	Nippon Telegraph & Telephone	Region VI	
16	3.698474165	1.781727	2.311193684	DRS	AT&T	Region VI	

Figure 3.7. Output-oriented RTS Classification

3.4   Scale Efficient Targets

By using the most productive scale size (MPSS) concept (Banker, 1984), we can develop linear programming problems to set unique scale efficient target. Consider the following linear program when the input-oriented CRS envelopment model is solved (Zhu, 2000b).

$$\min \sum_{j=1}^{n} \lambda_j$$
subject to
$$\sum_{j=1}^{n} \lambda_j x_{ij} \le \theta^* x_{io} \quad i = 1,2,...,m; \tag{3.1}$$
$$\sum_{j=1}^{n} \lambda_j y_{rj} \ge y_{ro} \quad r = 1,2,...,s;$$
$$\lambda_j \ge 0. \quad j = 1,2,...,n.$$

where θ^* is the input-oriented CRS efficiency score.

Based upon the optimal values from (3.1) (i.e., $\sum \lambda_j^*$), the MPSS concept yields the following scale-efficient target for DMU_o corresponding to the largest MPSS

$$\text{MPSS}_{\max} : \begin{cases} \tilde{x}_{io} = \theta^* x_{io} / \sum \lambda_j^* \\ \tilde{y}_{ro} = y_{ro} / \sum \lambda_j^* \end{cases} \tag{3.2}$$

where (~) represents the target value.

If we change the objective of (3.1) to maximization,

$$\max \sum_{j=1}^{n} \hat{\lambda}_j$$

subject to

$$\sum_{j=1}^{n} \hat{\lambda}_j x_{ij} \leq \theta^* x_{io} \quad i = 1,2,...,m; \tag{3.3}$$

$$\sum_{j=1}^{n} \hat{\lambda}_j y_{rj} \geq y_{ro} \quad r = 1,2,...,s;$$

$$\hat{\lambda}_j \geq 0. \quad j = 1,2,...,n.$$

then we have the scale efficient target corresponding to the smallest MPSS.

$$\text{MPSS}_{\min} : \begin{cases} \widetilde{x}_{io} = \theta^* x_{io} / \sum \hat{\lambda}_j^* \\ \widetilde{y}_{ro} = y_{ro} / \sum \hat{\lambda}_j^* \end{cases} \tag{3.4}$$

Note that models (3.1) and (3.3) are based upon the input-oriented CRS envelopment model. However, by using the relationship between the input-oriented and output-oriented CRS envelopment models (see Lemma 3.2), it is trivial to show that $\text{MPSS}_{\max}$ ($\text{MPSS}_{\min}$) remains the same under both orientations. Consequently, $\text{MPSS}_{\max}$ and $\text{MPSS}_{\min}$ are uniquely determined by θ^* and $\sum \lambda_j^*$ ($\sum \hat{\lambda}_j^*$).

We can select the largest or the smallest MPSS target for a particular DMU under consideration based upon the RTS preference over performance improvement. For example, one may select the smallest MPSS for an IRS DMU and the largest MPSS for a DRS DMU. Further, if the CRS envelopment models yield the unique optimal solutions, then the $\text{MPSS}_{\max}$ and $\text{MPSS}_{\min}$ are the same.

The spreadsheet model for calculating the scale efficient target involves (i) calculating CRS envelopment model, and (ii) calculating model (3.1). We demonstrate (ii) using the input-oriented CRS envelopment model shown in Figure 3.3.

In Figure 3.8, the target cell is B25, and contains the formula "=SUM(I2:I16)", representing the $\sum \lambda_j^*$. Cell F19 is no longer a changing cell, and contains the formula "=INDEX(J2:J16,E18,1)". This formula returns the CRS efficiency score of a DMU under evaluation from column J.

The changing cells are I2:I16. The constraints in the Solver parameters for the input-oriented CRS envelopment model shown in Figure 1.24 remain the same. Figure 3.8 also shows the Solver parameters for calculating the model (3.1). Select "Max" if model (3.3) is used.

To automate the computation, we remove the statement Range("J"& i+1)=Range("F19") from the procedure "RTS", and name the new procedure "MPSS".

```
Sub MPSS()
  Dim i As Integer
    For i = 1 To 15
'set the value of cell E18 equal to i (1, 2,..., 15)
    Range("E18") = i
'Run the Solver model. The UserFinish is set to True so that
'the Solver Results dialog box will not be shown
    SolverSolve UserFinish:=True
'Place the sum of lambdas into column K
    Range("K" & i + 1) = Range("B25")
    Next i
End Sub
```

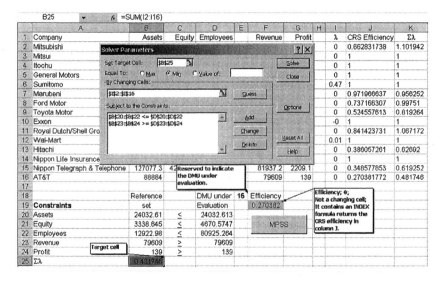

Figure 3.8. Largest MPSS Spreadsheet Model

It can be seen that the maximum $\sum \lambda_j^*$ is the same as that obtained from the input-oriented CRS envelopment model shown in Figure 3.3. This is due to the fact that we have unique optimal solutions on λ_j^*. As a result, minimum $\sum \hat{\lambda}_j$ = maximum $\sum \lambda_j^*$. We can apply (3.2) or (3.4) to obtain the scale efficient targets for the 15 DMUs.

3.5   RTS Classification Stability

Seiford and Zhu (1999b) develop several linear programming formulations for investigating the stability of RTS classifications. A by-product of their RTS sensitivity analysis measure is an alternative method for characterizing RTS.

Let J denote the set of n DMUs and E_o the set of CRS frontier DMUs, i.e., $E_o = \{j \,|\, \lambda_j > 0$ for some optimal solutions for $DMU_o\}$. The set of DMU_j $(j \in E_o)$ may be different for each different DMU_o under evaluation. As a result, the input-oriented CRS envelopment model can be expressed as

$$\min \theta$$
subject to
$$\sum_{j \in E_o} \lambda_j x_{ij} \leq \theta x_{io} \quad i = 1,2,...,m; \tag{3.5}$$
$$\sum_{j \in E_o} \lambda_j y_{rj} \geq y_{ro} \quad r = 1,2,...,s;$$
$$\lambda_j \geq 0 \quad j \in E_o$$

The output-oriented CRS envelopment model can be expressed as

$$\max \phi$$
subject to
$$\sum_{j \in E_o} \lambda_j x_{ij} \leq x_{io} \quad i = 1,2,...,m; \tag{3.6}$$
$$\sum_{j \in E_o} \lambda_j y_{rj} \geq \phi y_{ro} \quad r = 1,2,...,s;$$
$$\lambda_j \geq 0 \quad j \in E_o$$

Based upon (3.5) and (3.6), we have

Lemma 3.1 For a DMU_o, if we have $\lambda_j^{*(1)}$ $(j \in E_o)$ with $\sum \lambda_j^{*(1)} < 1$ and $\lambda_j^{*(2)}$ $(j \in E_o)$ with $\sum \lambda_j^{*(2)} > 1$ in (3.5) (or (3.6)), then we must have λ_j^* $(j \in E_o)$ with $\sum \lambda_j^* = 1$, where (*) represents optimal value.

[Proof]: Let $\sum \lambda_j^{*(1)} = d_1$ and $\sum \lambda_j^{*(2)} = d_2$. Define $d = (1-d_1)/(d_2-d_1)$. Obviously $0 < d < 1$ and $(1-d)d_1 + dd_2 = 1$.

Let $\lambda_j^* = (1-d)\lambda_j^{*(1)} + d\lambda_j^{*(2)} (j \in E_o)$. Then $\sum \lambda_j^* = 1$ and
$$\sum \lambda_j^* x_{ij} \leq \sum [(1-d)\lambda_j^{*(1)} + d\lambda_j^{*(2)}]x_{ij} \leq \theta^* x_{io}$$
$$\sum \lambda_j^* y_{rj} = \sum [(1-d)\lambda_j^{*(1)} + d\lambda_j^{*(2)}]y_{rj} \geq (1-d)y_{ro} + dy_{ro} = y_{ro}$$
Thus, λ_j^* $(j \in E_o)$ with $\sum \lambda_j^* = 1$ is an optimal solution. ∎

Lemma 3.2 Suppose λ_j^* $(j \in E_o)$ and θ^* is an optimal solution to (3.5). There exists a corresponding optimal solution $\tilde{\lambda}_j^*$ $(j \in E_o)$ and ϕ^* to (3.6) such that $\tilde{\lambda}_j^* = \lambda_j^*/\theta^*$ and $\theta^* = 1/\phi^*$, or equivalently, $\lambda_j^* = \tilde{\lambda}_j^*/\phi^*$ and $\phi^* = 1/\theta^*$.

Note that a change in input levels for DMU_o in (3.5) or a change of output levels in (3.6) does not alter the RTS nature of DMU_o unless it is moved onto the CRS frontier. Therefore we limit our investigation to the effect of output changes under (3.5) and the effect of input changes under (3.6) on the RTS classification for DMU_o.

Note also that CRS efficient DMUs continue to exhibit CRS if they are still efficient after data variations. Therefore we may use the sensitivity analysis procedure for the robustness of efficient DMUs in Zhu (1996b) and Seiford and Zhu (1998d) to investigate the stability of RTS estimation on CRS frontier DMUs. Hence, we only address the sensitivity of RTS classifications for CRS inefficient DMUs.

3.5.1   Input-oriented RTS Classification Stability

Note that under (3.5), if DMU_o exhibits IRS, then decreases in outputs cannot change its IRS nature. Likewise, if DMU_o exhibits DRS, increases in outputs cannot change its DRS nature unless DMU_o reaches the CRS frontier. Therefore, we only consider output increases and decreases for IRS and DRS DMUs, respectively.

Because the estimation of RTS in DEA usually considers the proportional change (increase or decrease) in all the outputs of DMU_o achieved by a proportional change in all its inputs, we consider proportional perturbations for all the outputs of DMU_o. Denote the proportional increase by $\alpha \geq 1$ and the proportional decrease by $\beta \leq 1$, i.e., DMU_o may increase or decrease its outputs by α and β up to αy_{ro} and βy_{ro} ($r = 1, 2,..., s$), respectively, and the RTS classification remains the same.

In order to calculate the values of α and β, we first define the set T_o for DMU_j ($j \in E_o$)

$$T_o = \{(x, y): \sum_{j \in E_o} \lambda_j x_{ij} \leq x_i, i = 1,2,..., m;$$
$$\sum_{j \in E_o} \lambda_j y_{rj} \geq y_r, \ r = 1,2,..., s;$$
$$\sum_{j \in E_o} \lambda_j = 1; \lambda_j \geq 0, \ \ j \in E_o\}$$

Based upon T_o, we define the following measure

$$\varphi_o^* = \max\{\varphi_o : (x_o, \varphi_o y_o) \in T_o\} \tag{3.7}$$

where (x_o, y_o) represents the input and output vector of DMU_o and φ_o^* can be calculated as the solution to the linear programming problem

$$\varphi_o^* = \max \varphi_o$$

subject to

$$\sum_{j \in E_o} \lambda_j x_{ij} \le x_{io} \qquad i = 1, 2, ..., m;$$

$$\sum_{j \in E_o} \lambda_j y_{rj} \ge \varphi_o y_{ro} \qquad r = 1, 2, ..., s;$$

$$\sum_{j \in E_o} \lambda_j = 1$$

$$\lambda_j \ge 0 \qquad j \in E_o$$

The above formulation is similar to the output-oriented VRS envelopment model but the reference set is restricted to the CRS frontier DMUs. Four possible cases are associated with (3.7), that is, $\varphi_o^* = 1$, $\varphi_o^* < 1$, $\varphi_o^* > 1$ or (3.7) is infeasible.

Lemma 3.3 If DMU_o exhibits DRS, then (3.7) is feasible.

[Proof]: We introduce a set of new variables:
Let $\hat{\varphi}_o = \hat{\theta}\varphi_o = 1$ so $\hat{\theta} = \varphi_o^{-1} > 0$, $\hat{\lambda}_j = \hat{\theta}\lambda_j = \varphi_o^{-1}\lambda_j$ $(j \in E_o)$
Multiplying all constraints by $\hat{\theta}$ in (3.7) gives

$$\min \hat{\theta}$$

subject to

$$\sum_{j \in E_o} \hat{\lambda}_j x_{ij} \le \hat{\theta} x_{io} \qquad i = 1, 2, ..., m;$$

$$\sum_{j \in E_o} \hat{\lambda}_j y_{rj} \ge y_{ro} \qquad r = 1, 2, ..., s; \qquad (3.8)$$

$$\sum_{j \in E_o} \hat{\lambda}_j = \sum_{j \in E_o} \lambda_j \varphi_o^{-1} = \varphi_o^{-1} = \hat{\theta}$$

$$\hat{\lambda}_j, \lambda_j \ge 0 \qquad j \in E_o$$

Because DMU_o exhibits DRS, $\sum \lambda_j^* > 1$ in (3.5). Let $\sum \lambda_j^* = \tilde{\theta}$. Obviously, $\tilde{\theta} > \theta$ is a feasible solution to (3.5). Therefore $\lambda_j^*(j \in E_o)$ and $\tilde{\theta}$ are also a feasible solution to (3.8). Thus, (3.7) is feasible. ∎

From Lemma 3.1 we know that if the following regularity condition is true, then RTS classifications can be uniquely determined by $\sum \lambda_j^*$ in any optimal solution to (3.5) (or (3.6)).

Regularity Condition (RC1)
$\sum \lambda_j^* = 1$ in all possible optimal solutions for the CRS DMUs.

Note that multiple optimal solutions of λ_j may occur even under RC1. We also require the following regularity condition (RC2) on the convexity of the CRS efficient facet. RC2 is closely related to the concept of "face regularity" of Thrall (1996).

Regularity Condition (RC2)
Suppose E_o forms an efficient facet. Then, any convex combination of CRS frontier DMUs in E_o is still on the same facet.

Theorem 3.8 Suppose regularity conditions RC1 and RC2 hold. Then
(i) CRS prevail for DMU_o if and only if $\varphi_o^* = 1$.
(ii) DRS prevail for DMU_o if and only if $\varphi_o^* < 1$.
(iii) IRS prevail for DMU_o if and only if $\varphi_o^* > 1$ or (3.7) is infeasible.

[Proof]: Suppose $\varphi_o^* = 1$. Because $DMU_j (j \in E_o)$ exhibits CRS, by RC2, DMU_o has an optimal solution to (3.5) with $\Sigma \lambda_j^* = 1$ and $\theta^* = 1$. Therefore, DMU_o exhibits CRS.

Next, if $DMU_o = (x_o, y_o)$ exhibits CRS, then $DMU_o(\delta) = (\delta x_o, y_o)$ also exhibits CRS under (3.5), where $\theta^* \le \delta < +\infty$, and θ^* is the optimal value to (3.5). Suppose $\varphi_o^* \ne 1$. Let $\lambda_j^* = \varphi_o^* \lambda_j$, where λ_j ($j \in E_o$) is an optimal solution to (3.7) associated with φ_o^*. We have

$$\sum_{j \in E_o} \lambda_j x_{ij} \le \frac{1}{\varphi_o^*} x_{io} \qquad i = 1,2,...,m;$$

$$\sum_{j \in E_o} \lambda_j y_{rj} \ge y_{ro} \qquad r = 1,2,...,s;$$

$$\sum_{j \in E_o} \lambda_j = \frac{1}{\varphi_o^*} < 1 \qquad j \in E_o.$$

If $1/\varphi_o^* \le \theta^*$, then the optimality of θ^* is violated. If $1/\varphi_o^* > \theta^*$, then let $1/\varphi_o^* = \delta \theta^*$. Obviously, $1/\varphi_o^*$ is the optimal value to (3.5) when evaluating $(\delta x_o, y_o)$, where $\theta^* \le \delta < +\infty$. However, $\Sigma \lambda_j^* < 1$ violating RC1. Therefore $\varphi_o^* = 1$ must hold. This completes the proof of (i).

If $\varphi_o^* < 1$, then the optimal value to (3.7) is equal to one for $DMU_o' = (x_o, \varphi_o^* y_o)$. From (i), we know that CRS prevail for DMU_o'. Thus, DMU_o cannot exhibit IRS. (We cannot decrease the outputs and cause a IRS DMU to exhibit CRS). Therefore, DRS prevail for DMU_o. This completes the *if* part of (ii).

From Lemma 3.3 and (i), we know that if (3.7) is infeasible, then IRS must prevail for DMU_o. If $\varphi_o^* > 1$, then similar to the proof of the *if* part of (ii), DMU_o cannot exhibit DRS. Therefore, IRS prevail for DMU_o. This completes the proof of the *if* part of (iii).

The *only if* part of (ii) and (iii) follows directly from the mutually exclusive and exhaustive conditions specified in the theorem. ■

Under RC1, any proportional output change in a CRS-inefficient DMU exhibiting CRS will alter its RTS nature. The *only if* parts of (ii) and (iii) are true without RC1. We see that if $\varphi_o^* < 1$, then DMU_o will also be termed as having DRS by (3.6). Thus, (3.7) is an indicator of the identical DRS regions under (3.5) and (3.6). Theorem 3.8 gives an alternative approach for estimating the RTS.

Theorem 3.9 Suppose DMU_o exhibits DRS. If $\varphi_o^* < \beta \leq 1$ then the DRS classification still holds for a proportional decrease of amount β.

[Proof]: Suppose the outputs of DMU_o decrease to $\hat{\beta} y_{ro}$ $(r = 1, 2, ..., s)$ where $\varphi_o^* < \hat{\beta} \leq 1$, and the RTS on DMU_o becomes CRS or IRS.
  Consider the following linear programming problem

$$\hat{\varphi}_o^* = \max \hat{\varphi}_o$$
$$\text{subject to}$$
$$\sum_{j \in E_o} \lambda_j x_{ij} \leq x_{io} \qquad i = 1,2,...,m;$$
$$\sum_{j \in E_o} \lambda_j y_{rj} \geq \hat{\varphi}_o \hat{\beta} y_{ro} \qquad r = 1,2,...,s; \qquad (3.9)$$
$$\sum_{j \in E_o} \lambda_j = 1$$
$$\lambda_j \geq 0 \qquad j \in E_o$$

Obviously, (3.9) has a feasible solution of λ_j ($j \in E_o$) and $\hat{\varphi}_o = \varphi_o^*/\hat{\beta}$. Thus, either $\hat{\varphi}_o^* = 1$ or $\hat{\varphi}_o^* > 1$ will violate the optimality of φ_o^*. Therefore, DRS still prevail on DMU_o. ∎

Theorem 3.10 Suppose DMU_o exhibits IRS and (3.7) is feasible. If $1 \leq \alpha < \varphi_o^*$ then the IRS classification continues to hold for an increase of amount α.

[Proof]: The proof is analogous with that of Theorem 3.9 and is omitted. ∎

Thus, when (3.7) is feasible, the optimal value to (3.7) determines the maximum possible output proportional changes for IRS and DRS DMUs which preserve their RTS classifications.
  If (3.7) is infeasible, then these IRS DMUs do not belong to T_o. In this situation, we consider the output-oriented CRS envelopment model (3.6) to determine the maximum allowable perturbation.

Theorem 3.11 Suppose (3.7) is infeasible. Let α satisfy $1 \leq \alpha < \phi^*$, where ϕ^* is the optimal value to (3.6) when evaluating DMU_o. Then IRS continue to hold for DMU_o for an increase of amount α.

[Proof]: Suppose the output of DMU_o is increased to $\hat{\alpha}$, where $1 \le \alpha < \phi^*$, and the resulting DMU exhibits CRS or DRS. Then we have an optimal solution, λ_j^* ($j \in E_o$) and θ^* to (3.5) such that

$$\sum_{j \in E_o} \lambda_j^* x_{ij} \le \theta^* x_{io} \qquad i = 1, 2, ..., m;$$

$$\sum_{j \in E_o} \lambda_j^* y_{rj} \le \hat{\alpha} y_{ro} \qquad r = 1, 2, ..., s;$$

$$\sum_{j \in E_o} \lambda_j^* \ge 1 \qquad j \in E_o.$$

Obviously, $\lambda_j = \lambda_j / \sum \lambda_j^*$ and $\varphi_o = \hat{\alpha} / \sum \lambda_j^*$ is a feasible solution to (3.7) violating the infeasibility of (3.7). ∎

In this situation, DMU_o is moved toward the CRS frontier. Theorem 3.11 indicates that if (3.7) is infeasible then the input-oriented and output-oriented DEA models both classify DMU_o as IRS. Thus, (3.7) is also an indicator of the identical IRS regions yielded by (3.5) and (3.6).

It can be seen that (3.7) not only analyzes the stability of the RTS classifications but also gives the RTS classifications. i.e., both the RTS classification of a specific DMU and its stability can be obtained from one model.

The previous developments assume that (3.5) has $\sum \lambda_j^* = 1$ in all possible optimal solutions for CRS DMUs. If this does not hold, then $\sum \lambda_j^*$ may also be either greater or less than one for the CRS DMUs. Consequently, φ_o^* in (3.7) may also be larger or smaller than one. Therefore, some data perturbations in the CRS DMUs can be allowed. We next further discuss the RTS sensitivity analysis without requiring RC1 and RC2. Note that if $\varphi_o^* > 1$ for DRS DMUs, then RC2 is violated.

Suppose DMU_o exhibits CRS. Let $(\tau_o^*)^{-1}$ and $(\sigma_o^*)^{-1}$ be the optimal values to (3.1) and (3.3), respectively. Since DMU_o exhibits CRS, therefore $\tau_o^* = (\sum \hat{\lambda}_j^*)^{-1} \ge 1$ ($\sigma_o^* = (\sum \hat{\lambda}_j^*)^{-1} \le 1$) where $\hat{\lambda}_j^*$ ($j \in E_o$) represent optimal solutions to (3.1) ((3.3)). Obviously $\hat{\lambda}_j^*$ ($j \in E_o$) with $\sum \hat{\lambda}_j^* \le 1$ ($\sum \hat{\lambda}_j^* \ge 1$) is also an optimal solution to (3.5) ((3.6)).

Theorem 3.12 Suppose DMU_o exhibits CRS. If $\chi \in \mathbf{R}^{\text{CRS}} = \{ \chi : \min\{1, \sigma_o^*\} \le \chi \le \max\{1, \tau_o^*\} \}$. The CRS classification continues to hold, where χ represents a proportional change of all outputs, $\hat{y}_{ro} = \chi y_{ro}$ ($r = 1, 2, ..., s$).

[Proof]: We know that ($\theta^* \tau_o^* x_o$, $\tau_o^* y_o$) and ($\theta^* \sigma_o^* x_o, \sigma_o^* y_o$) both exhibit CRS. Consequently, (x_o, $\tau_o^* y_o$) and ($x_o, \sigma_o^* y_o$) exhibit CRS. Therefore, if $\min\{1, \sigma_o^*\} \le \chi \le \max\{1, \tau_o^*\}$, then DMU_o ($= x_o, \chi y_o$) exhibits CRS. ∎

If $\sum \lambda_j \ge 1$ for all alternate optima to (3.5), then $\sigma_o^* = \varphi^* = 1$ and no proportional output increase is allowed. If $\sum \lambda_j \le 1$ for all alternate optima to (3.5), then $\tau_o^* = 1$ and no proportional output decrease is allowed. If $\sum \lambda_j$ can be equal to, larger than, or less than one, then both proportional increases and decreases of output are possible. If RC2 holds, then $\mathbf{R}^{CRS} = \{\chi: \min\{1,\sigma_o^*\} \leq \chi \leq \max\{1,\tau_o^*,\varphi_o^*\}\}$. Furthermore, if only RC1 is violated, Theorem 3.8 (i) should be modified to read: CRS prevail for *DMU$_o$* *if and only if* there exist some E_o such that $\varphi^* = 1$ in (3.7).

Next we discuss the RTS sensitivity analysis for IRS DMUs. If *DMU$_o$* exhibits IRS, then $\sum \lambda_j < 1$ in all optimal solutions to (1). Thus $\sigma_o^* > 1$.

Theorem 3.13 Suppose *DMU$_o$* exhibits IRS. The IRS classification continues to hold for $\alpha \in \mathbf{R}^{IRS} = \{\alpha: 1 \leq \alpha < \sigma_o^*\}$, where α represents the proportional increase of all outputs, $\hat{y}_{ro} = \alpha y_{ro}$ ($r = 1, 2, ..., s$).

[Proof]: Suppose $DMU_o' = (x_o, \alpha y_o)$ and DMU_o' exhibits CRS or DRS. Then $DMU_o'' = (\alpha \theta^* x_o, \alpha y_o)$ must also exhibit CRS or DRS. Furthermore, we have

$$\sum_{j \in E_o} \lambda_j^* x_{ij} \leq \gamma^* \alpha \theta^* x_{io} \leq \alpha \theta^* x_{io} \qquad i = 1,2,...,m;$$
$$\sum_{j \in E_o} \lambda_j^* y_{rj} \leq \alpha y_{ro} \qquad\qquad r = 1,2,...,s;$$
$$\sum_{j \in E_o} \lambda_j^* \geq 1 \qquad\qquad\qquad j \in E_o.$$

where γ^* is the optimal value to (3.5) when evaluating DMU_o''. Obviously, λ_j^*/α ($j \in E_o$) is a feasible solution to (3.3). Thus $(\sum \lambda_j^*/\alpha) \geq (1/\alpha) > (1/\sigma_o^*)$ violating the optimality of (3.3). ∎

From the proof of Theorem 3.11, we know that Theorem 3.11 holds in the absence of RC1 and RC2. Therefore, if (3.7) is infeasible for *DMU$_o$*, then the RTS stability region is $\mathbf{R}^{IRS} = \{\alpha : 1 \leq \alpha < \max\{\phi^*, \sigma_o^*\}\}$, where ϕ^* is the optimal value to (3.6).

Next, we consider the DRS DMUs.

Lemma 3.4 If *DMU$_o$* exhibits DRS in (3.5), then *DMU$_o$* must exhibit DRS in (3.6).

[Proof]: Suppose *DMU$_o$* exhibits CRS or IRS in (3.6). Then by Lemma 3.2, we have $\sum \lambda_j^* < \theta^* \leq 1$, where λ_j^* ($j \in E_o$) and θ^* is an optimal solution to (3.5). Because *DMU$_o$* exhibits DRS in (3.5), $\sum \lambda_j^* > 1$ in all alternative optimal solutions to (3.5). Thus, $\theta^* > 1$, a contradiction. ∎

The following Lemma is obvious. Note that φ_o does not necessarily represent the optimal value to (3.7).

Lemma 3.5 If CRS prevail for DMU_o, then there exists some E_o such that $\varphi_o = 1$ in (3.7).

Theorem 3.14 Suppose DMU_o exhibits DRS and $\varphi_o^* < 1$. The DRS classification continues to hold for $\varphi_o^* < \beta \leq 1$, where β represents the proportional change of all outputs, $\hat{y}_{ro} = \beta y_{ro}$ $(r =1, 2, ..., s)$ and φ_o^* is the optimal value to (3.7).

[Proof]: By Lemma 3.4, DMU_o exhibits DRS under (3.6). Next, let $DMU_o' = (x_o, \beta y_o)$. Then DMU_o' still exhibits DRS under (3.6). Thus

$$\begin{aligned} \sum_{j \in E_o} \lambda_j^* x_{ij} &\leq x_{io} & i &= 1,2,...,m; \\ \sum_{j \in E_o} \lambda_j^* y_{rj} &\leq \vartheta^* \beta y_{ro} & r &= 1,2,...,s; \\ \sum_{j \in E_o} \lambda_j^* &> 1 & j &\in E_o. \end{aligned}$$

where ϕ^* is the optimal value to (3.6) when evaluating DMU_o'.

If DMU_o' exhibits IRS in (3.5), then, by Lemma 3.2, $(\sum \lambda_j^* / \phi^*)< 1$. Thus $\varphi_o = (\phi^* \beta / \sum \lambda_j^*) > \varphi_o^*$ is a feasible solution to (3.7), violating the optimality of φ_o^*.

If DMU_o' exhibits CRS, then, by Lemma 3.5, we have $\varphi_o = 1$ when calculating (3.7) for DMU_o'. Thus $\beta > \varphi_o^*$, violating the optimality of φ_o^*. ∎

However, one may also use the optimal value to (3.1), $\tau_o^* < 1$, to determine the stability region, particularly in the case of $\varphi_o^* > 1$ for a DRS DMU_o. This is characterized by the following theorem.

Theorem 3.15 Suppose DMU_o exhibits DRS. Then the DRS classification continues to hold for $\beta \in \mathbf{R}^{DRS} = \{ \beta : \tau_o^* < \beta \leq 1 \}$, where β represents the proportional change of all outputs, $\hat{y}_{ro} = \beta y_{ro}$ $(r =1, 2, ..., m)$.

[Proof]: The proof is analogous with that of Theorem 3.13 and is omitted. ∎

Now, we can use τ_o^* and σ_o^* to estimate the RTS classifications.

Theorem 3.16
(i) CRS prevail for DMU_o if and only if $\sigma_o^* \leq 1 \leq \tau_o^*$.
(ii) DRS prevail for DMU_o if and only if $\tau_o^* < 1$.
(iii) IRS prevail for DMU_o if and only if $\sigma_o^* > 1$.

[Proof]: The *only if* parts of (ii) and (iii) are obvious. Next, if $\tau_o^* < 1$, then $\sum \hat{\lambda}_j^* > 1$, where $\sum \hat{\lambda}_j^*$ is the optimal value to (3.1). This indicates that $\sum \lambda_j^*$

> 1 in all alternative optimal solutions to (3.5). Thus DRS prevail for DMU_o. This completes the proof of the *if* part of (ii). The proof of the *if* part of (iii) is similar. The *if* and the *only if* parts of (i) follow directly. ∎

Next, we consider an example taken from Zhu and Shen (1995) with $m = 2$, $s = 1$, $n = 4$ (See Table 3.3).

Table 3.3. RTS Sensitivity Numerical Example

DMU	x1	x2	y
1	0.1	0.25	0.1
2	2	2	1
3	40	10	10
4	3	2	1

DMUs 1, 2 and 3 are CRS-efficient and are on the same efficient facet given by $x_1 + 2x_2 = 6y$. Obviously, RC2 is satisfied. DMU4 is inefficient with $\theta^* = 6/7$. We obtain $E_o = \{DMU1, DMU2, DMU3\}$ where $DMU2 = \frac{2}{3} DMU1 + \frac{1}{30} DMU3$. Multiple optimal lambda solutions are detected in evaluating DMU4 using (3.5) (see Zhu and Shen (1995)).

For DMU4, we first calculate (3.7), that is

$$\varphi_o^* = \max \varphi_o$$
subject to
$$0.1\ \lambda_1 + 2\lambda_2 + 40\lambda_3 \le 3$$
$$0.25\lambda_1 + 2\lambda_2 + 10\lambda_3 \le 2$$
$$0.1\ \lambda_1 + \ \lambda_2 + 10\lambda_3 \ge \varphi_o$$
$$\lambda_1 + \lambda_2 + \lambda_3 = 1$$
$$\lambda_1, \lambda_2, \lambda_3 \ge 0$$

The optimal value is $\varphi_o^* = 7/6$. Next, we calculate (3.1)

$$(\tau_o^*)^{-1} = \min \lambda_1 + \lambda_2 + \lambda_3$$
subject to
$$0.1\ \lambda_1 + 2\lambda_2 + 40\lambda_3 \le 3 \times \frac{6}{7} = \frac{18}{7}$$
$$0.25\lambda_1 + 2\lambda_2 + 10\lambda_3 \le 2 \times \frac{6}{7} = \frac{12}{7}$$
$$0.1\ \lambda_1 + \ \lambda_2 + 10\lambda_3 \ge 1$$
$$\lambda_1, \lambda_2, \lambda_3 \ge 0$$

We have $\tau_o^* = 70/52$ with $\lambda_1^* = 0$, $\lambda_2^* = 5/7$, and $\lambda_3^* = 2/70$.

If we calculate (3.3), we have $\sigma_o^* = 210/1011$ with $\lambda_1^* = 100/21$, $\lambda_2^* = 0$ and $\lambda_3^* = 11/210$. Therefore the stability region for the CRS classification is $\{\chi: 210/1011 \le \chi \le 70/52\}$.

3.5.2   Output-oriented RTS Classification Stability

We now consider input perturbations in DMU_o. Note that under (3.6), if DMU_o exhibits DRS, then increases in inputs cannot change its DRS nature. Likewise, if DMU_o exhibits IRS, decreases in inputs cannot change its IRS nature unless DMU_o reaches the CRS frontier. Therefore, we only consider input increases and decreases for IRS and DRS DMUs, respectively.

Suppose that DMU_o may proportionally increase and decrease its inputs, respectively, by $\eta \geq 1$ and $\xi \leq 1$, up to ηx_{io} and ξx_{io} ($i = 1, 2, ..., m$) while its RTS classification still holds. Suppose also that the RC1 and RC2 are true.

In order to calculate η and ξ, we define the following measure

$$\omega_o^* = \min\{\omega_o : (\omega_o x_o, y_o) \in T_o\} \tag{3.10}$$

where (x_o, y_o) represents the input and output vector for DMU_o, and ω_o^* can be calculated as the optimal value to the linear programming problem

$$
\begin{aligned}
&\omega_o^* = \min \omega_o \\
&\text{subject to} \\
&\sum_{j \in E_o} \lambda_j x_{ij} \leq \omega_o x_{io} \quad i = 1,2,...,m; \\
&\sum_{j \in E_o} \lambda_j y_{rj} \geq y_{ro} \quad r = 1,2,...,s; \\
&\sum_{j \in E_o} \lambda_j = 1 \\
&\lambda_j \geq 0 \quad\quad\quad j \in E_o
\end{aligned}
$$

Note that the above model is the input-oriented VRS envelopment model if $E_o = J$. Four possible cases are associated with (3.10), that is, $\omega_o^* = 1$, $\omega_o^* > 1$, $\omega_o^* < 1$ or (3.10) is infeasible. Similar to Theorem 3.8, we have

Theorem 3.17 Suppose regularity conditions RC1 and RC2 hold. Then
(i) CRS prevail for DMU_o *if and only if* $\omega_o^* = 1$.
(ii) IRS prevail for DMU_o *if and only if* $\omega_o^* > 1$.
(iii) DRS prevail for DMU_o *if and only if* $\omega_o^* < 1$ or (3.10) is infeasible.

Obviously, no input changes are allowed in DMU_o if CRS prevail when RC1 holds. The *only if* parts of (ii) and (iii) are true without RC1. If (3.10) is infeasible, then DRS must prevail on DMU_o. If $\omega_o^* > 1$, then DMU_o will also be termed as having IRS by (3.5). i.e., (3.10) finds out the identical IRS regions generated by (3.5) and (3.6). Theorem 3.17 gives an alternative RTS method under the output-oriented DEA technique.

Furthermore, we have

Theorem 3.18 Suppose DMU_o exhibits IRS. For an input increase of amount η, if $1 \le \eta < \omega_o^*$, then the IRS classification continues to hold.

Theorem 3.19 Suppose DMU_o exhibits DRS and (3.10) is feasible. For an input decrease amount of ξ, if $\omega_o^* < \xi \le 1$, then the DRS classification continues to hold.

Thus, when (3.10) is feasible, the optimal value to (3.10) determines the maximum possible input proportional changes for IRS and DRS DMUs which preserve their RTS classifications.

If (3.10) is infeasible, then these DRS DMUs do not belong to T_o. In this situation, we consider the input-oriented VRS envelopment model (3.5).

Theorem 3.20 Suppose (3.10) is infeasible. For an input decrease amount of ξ, where $\theta^* < \xi \le 1$ then DRS still prevail for DMU_o, where θ^* is the optimal value to (3.5) when evaluating DMU_o.

Theorem 3.20 indicates that if (3.10) is infeasible then the input-oriented and output-oriented DEA models both declare DMU_o as DRS. Thus, (3.10) indicates the identical DRS regions yielded by (3.5) and (3.6).

From the above discussion, we see that model (3.10) can also be used to estimate the RTS classification for DMU_o in addition to its role in sensitivity analysis.

We next discuss the sensitivity of output-oriented RTS classification without the requirement of RC1 and RC2. Note that if $\omega_o^* < 1$ for IRS DMUs, then RC2 is violated.

Consider the following two linear programming models

$$(\tilde{\tau}_o^*)^{-1} = \min \sum_{j \in E_o} \tilde{\lambda}_j$$

subject to

$$
\begin{array}{ll}
\sum_{j \in E_o} \tilde{\lambda}_j x_{ij} \le x_{io} & i = 1,2,...,m; \\
\sum_{j \in E_o} \tilde{\lambda}_j y_{rj} \ge \phi^* y_{ro} & r = 1,2,...,s; \\
\tilde{\lambda}_j \ge 0 & j \in E_o.
\end{array}
\tag{3.11}
$$

$$(\tilde{\sigma}_o^*)^{-1} = \max \sum_{j \in E_o} \tilde{\lambda}_j$$

subject to

$$
\begin{array}{ll}
\sum_{j \in E_o} \tilde{\lambda}_j x_{ij} \le x_{io} & i = 1,2,...,m; \\
\sum_{j \in E_o} \tilde{\lambda}_j y_{rj} \ge \phi^* y_{ro} & r = 1,2,...,s; \\
\tilde{\lambda}_j \ge 0 & j \in E_o.
\end{array}
\tag{3.12}
$$

where ϕ^* is the optimal value to (3.6) when evaluating DMU_o.

Suppose DMU_o exhibits CRS. Then $\sum \tilde{\lambda}_j^* \leq 1$ in (3.11) and $\sum \tilde{\tilde{\lambda}}_j^* \geq 1$ in (3.12), i.e., $\tilde{\tau}_o^* \geq 1$ and $\tilde{\sigma}_o^* \leq 1$, respectively. Similar to Theorem 3.12, we have

Theorem 3.21 Suppose DMU_o exhibits CRS. If $\gamma \in \mathbf{R}^{\mathbf{CRS}} = \{\gamma : \min\{1, \sigma_o^*\} \leq \chi \leq \max\{1, \tau_o^*\}\}$. The CRS classification continues to hold, where γ represents the proportional change of all inputs, $\hat{x}_{io} = \gamma x_{io}$ ($i = 1, 2, ..., m$), and $\tilde{\tau}_o^*$ and $\tilde{\sigma}_o^*$ are defined in (3.11) and (3.12), respectively.

If $\sum \lambda_j \geq 1$ in all alternate optima to (3.6), then $\tilde{\sigma}^* = 1$ and no proportional input increase is allowed. If $\sum \lambda_j \leq 1$ in all alternate optima to (3.6), then $\tilde{\tau}_o^* = 1$ and $\omega_o^* = 1$ and no proportional input decrease is allowed. If $\sum \lambda_j$ can be equal to, larger than, or less than one, then both proportional input increase and decrease are possible. In this situation, E_o in (3.10) is identified by the different optimal basis sets associated with non-zero λ_j in (3.6). If RC2 holds, then $\mathbf{R}^{\mathbf{CRS}} = \{\gamma : \min\{1, \sigma_o^*, \phi_o^*\} \leq \chi \leq \max\{1, \tau_o^*\}\}$. Furthermore, if only RC1 is violated, Theorem 3.17 (i) should be modified to read: CRS prevail for DMU_o *if and only if* there exists a E_o such that $\omega^* = 1$ in (3.10).

If DMU_o exhibits DRS, then $\sum \tilde{\lambda}_j^* > 1$, i.e., $\tilde{\tau}^* < 1$ in (3.11) and similar to Theorem 3.13, we have

Theorem 3.22 Suppose DMU_o exhibits DRS. The DRS classification continues to hold for $\xi \in \mathbf{R}^{\mathbf{DRS}} = \{\xi : \tilde{\tau}_o^* < \xi \leq 1\}$, where ξ represents the proportional decrease of all inputs, $\hat{x}_{io} = \xi x_{io}$ ($i = 1, 2, ..., m$), and $\tilde{\tau}_o^*$ is defined in (3.11).

Theorem 3.20 holds for the situation without RC1 and RC2. Therefore if (3.10) is infeasible, then the RTS stability region is $\mathbf{R}^{\mathbf{DRS}} = \{\xi : \min\{\theta^*, \tilde{\tau}_o^*\} < \xi \leq 1\}$, where θ^* is the optimal value to (3.5) when evaluating DMU_o.

For IRS DMUs, we have

Theorem 3.23 Suppose DMU_o exhibits IRS and $\omega_o^* > 1$. Then the IRS classification continues to hold for $1 \leq \eta < \omega_o^*$, where η represents the proportional change of all inputs, $\hat{x}_{io} = \eta x_{io}$ ($i = 1, 2, ..., m$) and ω_o^* is the optimal value to (3.10).

However, one may also use the optimal value to (3.12) to determine the IRS stability region, particularly in the case of $\omega_o^* > 1$ for DMU_o. This is characterized by the following theorem.

Theorem 3.24 Suppose DMU_o exhibits IRS. Then the IRS classification continues to hold for $\eta \in \mathbf{R}^{\mathrm{IRS}} = \{\eta : 1 \le \eta < \tilde{\sigma}_o^* \}$, where η represents the proportional change of all inputs, $\hat{x}_{io} = \eta x_{io}$ ($i = 1, 2, ..., m$), and $\tilde{\sigma}_o^*$ is defined in (3.12).

Finally, based upon Lemma 3.2, we have

Theorem 3.25 $(\tau_o^*)^{-1} = \theta^* (\tilde{\tau}^*)^{-1}$ and $(\sigma_o^*)^{-1} = \theta^* (\tilde{\sigma}_o^*)^{-1}$, where $\theta^* = (\phi^*)^{-1}$.

3.5.3   Spreadsheets for RTS Sensitivity Analysis

Since Theorems 3.12, 3.13, 3.15, 3.21, 3.22, and 3.24 present the RTS sensitivity analysis without the RC1 and RC2, we develop the RTS sensitivity spreadsheet models for models (3.1), (3.3), (3.11) and (3.12).

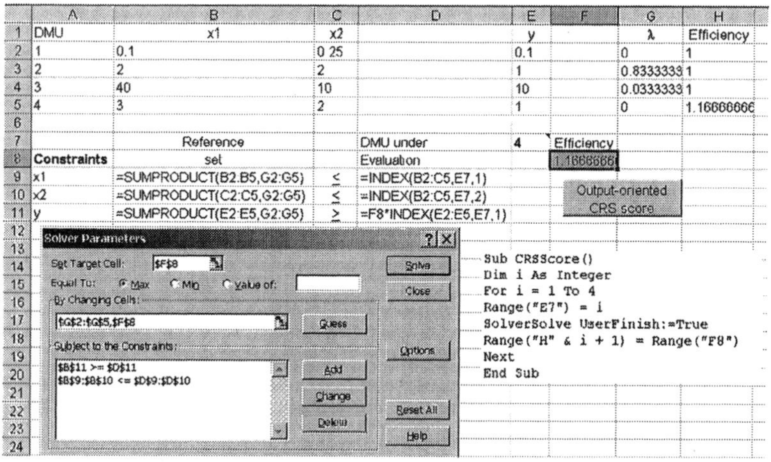

Figure 3.9. Spreadsheet for RTS Sensitivity Numerical Example

The spreadsheet models for (3.1) and (3.3) are discussed in setting the MPSS targets, therefore, we here discuss the RTS sensitivity spreadsheets based upon (3.11) and (3.12) which use the output-oriented CRS efficiency score. Figure 3.9 presents the spreadsheet model for calculating the output-oriented CRS scores for the numerical example presented in Table 3.3. Figure 3.9 also shows the formulas, the Solver parameters, and the VBA procedure "CRSScore".

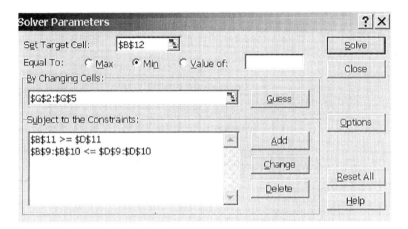

Figure 3.10. Solver Parameters for RTS Stability Region Bounds

A	B	C	D	E	F	G	H	I	J	K
DMU	x1	x2		y		λ	Efficiency	minΣλ	τ	
1	0.1	0.25		0.1		0	1.00	1	1	
2	2	2		1		0.833333	1.00	1	1	
3	40	10		10		0.033333	1.00	1	1	
4	3	2		1		0	1.17	0.866667	1.153846	
	Reference		DMU unde	4			Sub RTSBound()			
Constrain	set		Evaluation				Dim i As Integer			
x1	3	≤	3			RTS Upper	For i = 1 To 4			
x2	2	≤	2			Bound	Range("E7") = i			
y	1.166667	≥	1.166667				SolverSolve UserFinish:=True			
Σλ	0.866667						Range("I" & i + 1) = Range("B12")			
							Next			

A	B	C	D	E	F	G	H	I	J
DMU	x1	x2		y		λ	Efficiency	maxΣλ	δ
1	0.1	0.25		0.1		5.555556	1.00	1	1
2	2	2		1		0	1.00	6.7	0.149254
3	40	10		10		0.061111	1.00	1	1
4	3	2		1		0	1.17	5.616667	0.178042
	Reference		DMU under	4					
Constrain	set		Evaluation						
x1	3	≤	3			RTS Lower			
x2	2	≤	2			Bound			
y	1.166667	≥	1.1666667						
Σλ	5.616667								

Figure 3.11. Spreadsheet Model for RTS Stability Region Bounds

Note that (3.11) and (3.12) determine the upper and lower bounds for RTS stability region, respectively. Figure 3.10 shows the Solver parameters for the two spreadsheets for models (3.11) and (3.12) shown in Figure 3.11. Cells B9:B12, C9:C11 contain the following formulas.

Cell B9 =SUMPRODUCT(B2:B5,G2:G5)
Cell B10 = SUMPRODUCT(C2:C5,G2:G5)

Cell B11 =SUMPRODUCT(E2:E5,G2:G5)
Cell B12 = SUM(G2:G5)
Cell C9 =INDEX(B2:C5,E7,1)
Cell C10 =INDEX(B2:C5,E7,2)
Cell C11 =INDEX(H2:H5,E7,1)*INDEX(E2:E5,E7,1)

The VBA procedure "RTSBound" records the optimal $\sum \lambda_j^*$ in cells I2:I5. Cells J2:J5 are reciprocals of the values in cells I2:I5, representing the lower and upper bounds for the RTS stability region. For example, the RTS classification of DMU4 continues to hold if the input change lies in [0.178, 1.154]. Note that the current result is based upon the output-oriented RTS classification. Thus, the stability region for DMU4 is different from that obtained in section 3.5.1. However, based on Theorem 3.25, we can obtain the RTS stability region for DMU4 when input-oriented RTS classification is used.

3.6   Use of RTS Sensitivity Analysis

Seiford and Zhu (1999d) describe a use of RTS sensitivity analysis in process improvement where a two-stage efficiency improvement is involved as shown in Figure 2.3. In a study of top US commercial banks, Seiford and Zhu (1999d) find that a bank can improve its performance in the second stage via (i) increasing its MV, TRI, and EPS (proportionally), or (ii) decreasing its revenue and profit (proportionally). If the bank chooses to improve its performance with plan (ii), then it may no longer be efficient in stage 1 profitability. In addition, a bank may not have direct control over all stage 2 outputs, i.e., its performance in the stock market. Thus, to improve performance over stage 1 and stage 2, Seiford and Zhu (1999d) focus on maximizing revenue and profit.

However, increases in revenue and profit may affect the scale efficiency in stage 2. Figures 3.12 and 3.13 illustrate this with employees (input) and profit (output) in stage 1, and profit (input) and market value (output) in stage 2. If maximizing profit is a major goal, then a bank will increase its current profit level to point S (Figure 3.12). Note that being positioned in an IRS region is ideal for economic viability. Therefore, one should avoid the situation that a profit increase (AS) in stage-1 would move the bank into a DRS region in stage-2, i.e., AS should not be greater than UV. If AS > UV, then one may wish to investigate alternative approaches to performance improvement in stage-1. For example, one may move the bank onto best practice point G by increasing the profit to P and then by reducing the number of employees to G.

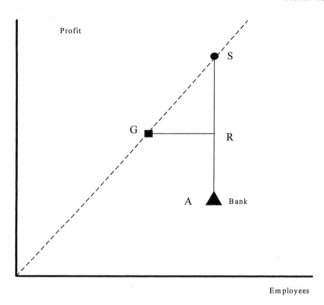

Figure 3.12. Process Improvement Stage-1

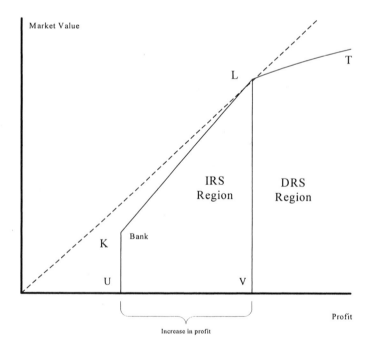

Figure 3.13. Process Improvement Stage-2

The preference for maintaining viability while improving a bank's profitability is formalized as (Seiford and Zhu, 1999d)

Process Improvement Rule The increase in revenue and profit for stage-1 improvement should not move an IRS bank in stage-2 into a DRS region.

It can be seen that in order to implement the process improvement rule, we must determine an IRS stability region which preserves the IRS nature of a bank. We apply (3.3) to an IRS bank DMU_o, in stage-2,

$$(\sigma_o^*)^{-1} = \max \sum_{j=1}^{n} \tilde{\lambda}_j$$

subject to

$$\sum_{j=1}^{n} \tilde{\lambda}_j x_{ij} \leq x_{io} \qquad i = 1,2,...,m; \tag{3.13}$$

$$\sum_{j=1}^{n} \tilde{\lambda}_j y_{rj} \geq \phi_o^{2*} y_{ro} \qquad r = 1,2,...,s;$$

$$\tilde{\lambda}_j \geq 0.$$

where ϕ_o^{2*} is the optimal value to the output-oriented CRS envelopment model for DMU_o in stage-2.

We now can implement the process improvement rule as follows.

<u>Step 1</u>: For an IRS bank, DMU_o, in stage-2 which is CRS-inefficient in stage-1, calculate (3.13).
(i) If $\phi_o^{1*} \leq \sigma_o^*$, improve profitability performance by setting

$$\text{stage-1} \begin{cases} Employees^{stage-1} = employees - s_{employees}^{-*} \\ Assets^{stage-1} = assets - s_{assets}^{-*} \\ Equity^{stage-1} = equity - s_{equity}^{-*} \\ Revenue^{stage-1} = \phi_o^{1*} revenue + s_{revenue}^{+*} \\ Profit^{stage-1} = \phi_o^{1*} profit + s_{profit}^{+*} \end{cases}$$

where (*) represents the optimal value in the output-oriented CRS envelopment model;
(ii) If $\phi_o^{1*} > \sigma_o^*$, then improve the profitability performance by computing the following input-oriented CRS envelopment model

$$\theta_o^* = \min \theta_o$$

subject to

$$\sum_{j=1}^{n} \lambda_j Employees_j + s_{employees}^{-} = \theta_o Employees_o$$

$$\sum_{j=1}^{n} \lambda_j Assets_j + s_{assets}^{-} = \theta_o Assets_o$$

$$\sum_{j=1}^{n} \lambda_j Equity_j + s_{equity}^- = \theta_o Equity_o$$

$$\sum_{j=1}^{n} \lambda_j Revenue_j - s_{revenue}^+ = \tau_o^* Revenue_o$$

$$\sum_{j=1}^{n} \lambda_j Profit_j - s_{profit}^+ = \tau_o^* Profit_o$$
$$\lambda_j \geq 0$$

We first increase DMU_o's current output levels by σ_o^* (moving the bank onto point P as in Figure 3.12), then decrease the three input levels by an input-oriented CRS envelopment model (moving the bank onto point G in Figure 3.12).

Finally, we obtain an efficient input-output level in stage-1 by setting

$$\text{stage-1} \begin{cases} Employees^{stage-1} = \theta_o^* employees - s_{employees}^{-*} \\ Assets^{stage-1} = \theta_o^* assets - s_{assets}^{-*} \\ Equity^{stage-1} = \theta_o^* equity - s_{equity}^{-*} \\ Revenue^{stage-1} = \sigma_o^* revenue + s_{revenue}^{+*} \\ Profit^{stage-1} = \sigma_o^* profit + s_{profit}^{+*} \end{cases}$$

<u>Step 2</u>: Apply case (i) to other banks and obtain the corresponding efficient input-output levels.

<u>Step 3</u>: Calculate the output-oriented CRS envelopment model again with the new $Revenue^{stage-1}$ and $Profit^{stage-1}$ levels obtained from steps 1 and 2 as new input levels in stage-2. We then obtain the following efficient input-output levels for DMU_o in stage-2:

$$\text{stage-2} \begin{cases} MV^{stage-2} = \phi_o^{2*} MV + s_{MV}^{+*} \\ TRI^{stage-2} = \phi_o^{2*} TRI + s_{TRI}^{+*} \\ EPS^{stage-2} = \phi_o^{2*} EPS + s_{EPS}^{+*} \\ Revenue^{stage-2} = Revenue^{stage-1} - s_{revenue}^{-*} \\ Profit^{stage-2} = Profit^{stage-1} - s_{profit}^{-*} \end{cases}$$

The above steps improve the profitability and marketability and satisfy the process improvement rule. Note that the only difference between the $Revenue^{stage-1}$ ($Profit^{stage-1}$) and $Revenue^{stage-2}$ ($Profit^{stage-2}$) is possible nonzero input slacks in stage-2.

Chapter 4

DEA with Preference

4.1 Non-radial DEA Models

We can call the envelopment DEA models as radial efficiency measures, because these models optimize all inputs or outputs of a DMU at a certain proportion. Färe and Lovell (1978) introduce a non-radial measure which allows nonproportional reductions in positive inputs or augmentations in positive outputs. Table 4.1 summarizes the non-radial DEA models with respect to the model orientation and frontier type.

Table 4.1. Non-radial DEA Models

Frontier Type	Input-Oriented		Output-Oriented	
	$\min(\dfrac{1}{m}\sum\limits_{i=1}^{m}\theta_i - \varepsilon\sum\limits_{r=1}^{s}s_r^+)$ subject to		$\max(\dfrac{1}{s}\sum\limits_{r=1}^{s}\phi_r - \varepsilon\sum\limits_{r=1}^{s}s_r^+)$ subject to	
	$\sum\limits_{j=1}^{n}\lambda_j x_{ij} = \theta_i x_{io}$	$i=1,2,...,m;$	$\sum\limits_{j=1}^{n}\lambda_j x_{ij} + s_i^- = x_{io}$	$i=1,2,...,m;$
CRS	$\sum\limits_{j=1}^{n}\lambda_j y_{rj} - s_r^+ = y_{ro}$	$r=1,2,...,s;$	$\sum\limits_{j=1}^{n}\lambda_j y_{rj} = \phi_r y_{ro}$	$r=1,2,...,s;$
	$\theta_i \le 1$	$i=1,2,...,m;$	$\phi_i \ge 1$	$r=1,2,...,s;$
	$\lambda_j \ge 0$	$j=1,2,...,n.$	$\lambda_j \ge 0$	$j=1,2,...,n.$
VRS	Add $\sum_{j=1}^{n}\lambda_j = 1$			
NIRS	Add $\sum_{j=1}^{n}\lambda_j \le 1$			
NDRS	Add $\sum_{j=1}^{n}\lambda_j \ge 1$			
Efficient Target	$\begin{cases}\hat{x}_{io} = \theta_i^* x_{io} \\ \hat{y}_{ro} = y_{ro} + s_r^{+*}\end{cases}$	$\begin{aligned}i&=1,2,...,m \\ r&=1,2,...,s\end{aligned}$	$\begin{cases}\hat{x}_{io} = x_{io} - s_i^{-*} \\ \hat{y}_{ro} = \phi_r^* y_{ro}\end{cases}$	$\begin{aligned}i&=1,2,...,m \\ r&=1,2,...,s\end{aligned}$

The slacks in the non-radial DEA models are optimized in a second-stage model where θ_i^* or ϕ_r^* are fixed. For example, under CRS we have

Input Slacks for Output-oriented Non-radial DEA Model

$$\max \sum_{r=1}^{s} s_r^+$$
subject to
$$\sum_{j=1}^{n} \lambda_j x_{ij} = \theta_i^* x_{io} \qquad i = 1,2,\dots,m;$$
$$\sum_{j=1}^{n} \lambda_j y_{rj} - s_r^+ = y_{ro} \qquad r = 1,2,\dots,s;$$
$$\lambda_j \geq 0 \qquad\qquad j = 1,2,\dots,n.$$

Output Slacks for Input-oriented Non-radial DEA Model

$$\max \sum_{i=1}^{m} s_i^-$$
subject to
$$\sum_{j=1}^{n} \lambda_j x_{ij} + s_i^- = x_{io} \qquad i = 1,2,\dots,m;$$
$$\sum_{j=1}^{n} \lambda_j y_{rj} = \phi_r^* y_{ro} \qquad r = 1,2,\dots,s;$$
$$\lambda_j \geq 0 \qquad\qquad j = 1,2,\dots,n.$$

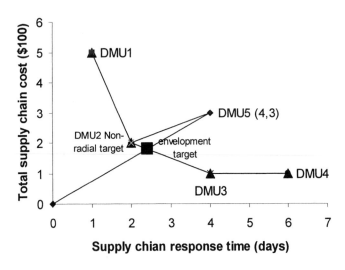

Figure 4.1. Efficient Targets

Note that input slacks do not exist in the input-oriented non-radial DEA models, and output slacks do not exist in the output-oriented non-radial DEA models.

Because $\theta_i^* \leq 1$ ($\phi_r^* \geq 1$), $\frac{1}{m}\sum_{i=1}^{m}\theta_i^* \leq 1$ and $\frac{1}{m}\sum_{i=1}^{m}\theta_i^* = 1$ if and only if $\theta_i^* = 1$ for all i ($\frac{1}{s}\sum_{r=1}^{s}\phi_r^* \geq 1$ and $\frac{1}{s}\sum_{r=1}^{s}\phi_r^* = 1$ if and only if $\phi_r^* = 1$ for all r). Thus, $\frac{1}{m}\sum_{i=1}^{m}\theta_i^*$ ($\frac{1}{s}\sum_{r=1}^{s}\phi_r^*$) can be used as an efficiency index.

Both the envelopment models and the non-radial DEA models yield the same frontier, but may yield different efficient targets (even when the envelopment models do not have non-zero slacks). For example, if we change the second input from 4 to 3 for DMU5 in Table 1.1 (Chapter 1), the input-oriented CRS envelopment model yields the efficient target of $x1 = 2.4$ and $x2 = 1.8$ (with $\lambda_2^* = 0.8$, $\lambda_3^* = 0.2$, and all zero slacks). Whereas the input-oriented CRS non-radial DEA model yields DMU2 as the efficient target for DMU5 (see Figure 4.1). Note that both models yield the same target of DMU3 for DMU4.

4.2   DEA with Preference Structure

Both the envelopment models and the non-radial DEA models yield efficient targets for inefficient DMUs. However, these targets may not be preferred by the management or achievable under the current management and other external conditions. Therefore, some other targets along the efficient frontier should be considered as preferred ones. This can be done by constructing preference structures over the proportions by which the corresponding current input levels (output levels) can be changed. Zhu (1996a) develops a set of weighted non-radial DEA models where various efficient targets along with the frontier can be obtained.

Let A_i ($i = 1, 2, \ldots, m$) and B_r ($r = 1, 2,\ldots, s$) be user-specified preference weights which reflect the relative degree of desirability of the adjustments of the current input and output levels, respectively. Then we can have a set of weighted non-radial DEA models based upon Table 4.1 by changing the objective functions $\frac{1}{m}\sum_{i=1}^{m}\theta_i$ and $\frac{1}{s}\sum_{r=1}^{s}\phi_r$ to $\sum_{i=1}^{m}A_i\theta_i / \sum_{i=1}^{m}A_i$ and $\sum_{r=1}^{s}B_r\phi_r / \sum_{r=1}^{s}B_r$, respectively.

Further, if we remove the constraint $\theta_i \leq 1$ ($\phi_r \geq 1$), we obtain the DEA/preference structure (DEA/PS) models shown in Table 4.2 (Zhu, 1996a).

If some $A_i = 0$ ($B_r = 0$), then set the corresponding $\theta_i = 1$ ($\phi_r = 1$). But at least one of such weights should be positive. Note that for example, the bigger the weight A_i, the higher the priority DMU_o is allowed to adjust its ith input amount to a lower level. i.e., when inefficiency occurs, the more one wants to adjust an input or an output, the bigger the weight should be attached to θ_i or ϕ_r. If we can rank the inputs or outputs according to their relative importance, then we can obtain a set of ordinal weights. One may use Delphi-like techniques, or Analytic Hierarchy Process (AHP) to obtain the weights. However, caution should be paid when we convert the ordinal weights into preference weights. For example, if an input (output) is relatively more important and the DMU does not wish to adjust it with a higher rate, we should take the reciprocal of the corresponding ordinal weight as the preference weight. Otherwise, if the DMU does want to adjust the input (output) with a higher rate, we can take the ordinal weight as the preference weight. Also, one may use the principal component analysis to derive the information on weights (Zhu, 1998).

Note that in the DEA/PS models, some θ_i^* (ϕ_r^*) may be greater (less) than one under certain weight combinations. i.e., the DEA/PS models are *not* restricted to the case where 100% efficiency is maintained through the input decreases or output increases.

Table 4.2. DEA/Preference Structure Models

Frontier Type	Input-Oriented	Output-Oriented
CRS	$\min(\dfrac{\sum\limits_{i=1}^{m} A_i \theta_i}{\sum\limits_{i=1}^{m} A_i} - \varepsilon \sum\limits_{r=1}^{s} s_r^+)$ subject to $\sum\limits_{j=1}^{n} \lambda_j x_{ij} = \theta_i x_{io} \quad i=1,2,...,m;$ $\sum\limits_{j=1}^{n} \lambda_j y_{rj} - s_r^+ = y_{ro} \quad r=1,2,...,s;$ $\lambda_j \geq 0 \qquad j=1,2,...,n.$	$\max(\dfrac{\sum\limits_{r=1}^{s} \phi_r}{\sum\limits_{r=1}^{s} B_r} - \varepsilon \sum\limits_{r=1}^{s} s_r^+)$ subject to $\sum\limits_{j=1}^{n} \lambda_j x_{ij} + s_i^- = x_{io} \quad i=1,2,...,m;$ $\sum\limits_{j=1}^{n} \lambda_j y_{rj} = \phi_r y_{ro} \quad r=1,2,...,s;$ $\lambda_j \geq 0 \qquad j=1,2,...,n.$
VRS	Add $\sum_{j=1}^{n} \lambda_j = 1$	
NIRS	Add $\sum_{j=1}^{n} \lambda_j \leq 1$	
NDRS	Add $\sum_{j=1}^{n} \lambda_j \geq 1$	
Efficient Target	$\begin{cases} \hat{x}_{io} = \theta_i^* x_{io} & i=1,2,...,m \\ \hat{y}_{ro} = y_{ro} + s_r^{+*} & r=1,2,...,s \end{cases}$	$\begin{cases} \hat{x}_{io} = x_{io} - s_i^{-*} & i=1,2,...,m \\ \hat{y}_{ro} = \phi_r^* y_{ro} & r=1,2,...,s \end{cases}$

Now, in order to further investigate the property of DEA/PS models, we consider the dual program to the input-oriented CRS DEA/PS model.

$$\max \sum_{r=1}^{s} u_r y_{ro}$$
subject to
$$\sum_{r=1}^{s} \mu_r y_{rj} - \sum_{i=1}^{m} v_i x_{ij} \leq 0 \quad j=1,...,n; \tag{4.1}$$
$$v_i x_{io} = A_i / \sum_{i=1}^{m} A_i \quad i=1,...,m;$$
$$\mu_r, v_i \geq 0$$

We see that the normalization condition $\sum_{i=1}^{m} v_i x_{io} = 1$ is also satisfied in (4.1). The DEA/PS model is actually a DEA model with fixed input multipliers.

Let p_i^o denote the *i*th input price for DMU_o and $\tilde{x}_{io}$ represents the *i*th input that minimizes the cost. Consider the following DEA model for calculating the "minimum cost".

$$\min \sum_{i=1}^{m} p_i^o \tilde{x}_{io}$$

subject to

$$\sum_{j=1}^{n} \lambda_j x_{ij} \leq \tilde{x}_{io} \qquad i = 1,...,m \tag{4.2}$$

$$\sum_{j=1}^{n} \lambda_j y_{rj} \geq y_{ro} \qquad r = 1,...,s$$

$$\lambda_j, \tilde{x}_{io} \geq 0$$

The dual program to (4.2) is

$$\max \sum_{r=1}^{s} u_r y_{ro}$$

subject to

$$\sum_{r=1}^{s} \mu_r y_{rj} - \sum_{i=1}^{m} v_i x_{ij} \leq 0 \qquad j = 1,...,n; \tag{4.3}$$

$$0 \leq v_i \leq p_i^o \qquad i = 1,...,m;$$

$$\mu_r, v_i \geq 0$$

By the complementary slackness condition of linear programming, we have that if $\tilde{x}_{io}^* > 0$ then $p_i^o = v_i^*$. Thus, v_i^* can be interpreted as p_i^o. Consequently, the input prices can be used to develop the preference weights.

In the DEA literature, we have a concept called "cost efficiency" which is defined as (see also Chapter 12)

$$\frac{\sum_{i=1}^{m} p_i^o \tilde{x}_{io}^*}{\sum_{i=1}^{m} p_i^o x_{io}}$$

The following development shows that the related DEA/PS model can be used to obtain exact the cost efficiency scores. Because the actual cost – $\sum_{i=1}^{m} p_i^o x_{io}$ is a constant for a specific DMU_o, cost efficiency can be directly calculated by the following modified (4.2).

$$\min \frac{\sum\limits_{i=1}^{m} p_i^o \tilde{x}_{io}}{\sum\limits_{i=1}^{m} p_i^o x_{io}}$$

subject to

$$\sum_{j=1}^{n} \lambda_j x_{ij} \leq \tilde{x}_{io} \quad i = 1,2,...,m; \tag{4.4}$$

$$\sum_{j=1}^{n} \lambda_j y_{rj} \geq y_{ro} \quad r = 1,2,...,s;$$

$$\lambda_j \geq 0 \qquad\quad j = 1,2,...,n.$$

Let $\tilde{x}_{io} = \theta_i x_{io}$. Then (4.4) is equivalent to the input-oriented CRS DEA/PS model with $A_i = p_i^o x_{io}$. This indicates that if one imposes a proper set of preference weights for each DMU under consideration, then the DEA/PS model yields cost efficiency measure. (see Seiford and Zhu (2002a) for an empirical investigation of DEA efficiency and cost efficiency.)

Similarly, the output-oriented DEA/PS model can be used to obtain the "revenue efficiency" which is defined as (see also Chapter 12)

$$\frac{\sum\limits_{r=1}^{s} q_r^o \tilde{y}_{ro}^*}{\sum\limits_{r=1}^{s} q_r^o y_{ro}}$$

where q_r^o indicates output price for DMU_o and $\tilde{y}_{ro}$ represents the rth output that maximizes the revenue in the following linear programming problem.

$$\max \sum_{r=1}^{s} q_r^o \tilde{y}_{ro}$$

subject to

$$\sum_{j=1}^{n} \lambda_j x_{ij} \leq x_{io} \quad i = 1,2,...,m \tag{4.5}$$

$$\sum_{j=1}^{n} \lambda_j y_{rj} \geq \tilde{y}_{ro} \quad r = 1,2,...,s$$

$$\lambda_j, \tilde{y}_{ro} \geq 0$$

Let $\tilde{y}_{ro} = \phi_r y_{ro}$ and $B_r = q_r^o y_{ro}$ in the output-oriented DEA/PS model. We have

$$\max \frac{\sum_{r=1}^{s} q_r^o \tilde{y}_{ro}}{\sum_{r=1}^{s} q_r^o y_{ro}}$$

subject to

$$\sum_{j=1}^{n} \lambda_j x_{ij} \le x_{io} \qquad i = 1,2,...,m;$$

$$\sum_{j=1}^{n} \lambda_j y_{rj} \ge \tilde{y}_{ro} \qquad r = 1,2,...,s;$$

$$\lambda_j \ge 0 \qquad\qquad j = 1,2,...,n.$$

which calculates the revenue efficiency.

4.3   DEA/Preference Structure Models in Spreadsheets

Figure 4.2 shows an input-oriented VRS DEA/PS spreadsheet model. Cells I2:I16 are reserved for λ_j. Cells F20:F22 are reserved for θ_i. These are the changing cells in the Solver parameters shown in Figure 4.3.

	A	B	C	D	E	F	G	H	I
1	Company	Assets	Equity	Employees		Revenue	Profit		λ
2	Mitsubishi	91920.6	10950	36000		184365.2	346.2		1
3	Mitsui	68770.9	5553.9	80000		181518.7	314.8		0
4	Itochu	65708.9	4271.1	7182		169164.6	121.2		0
5	General Motors	217123.4	23345.5	709000		168828.6	6880.7		0
6	Sumitomo	50268.9	6681	6193		167530.7	210.5		0
7	Marubeni	71439.3	5239.1	6702		161057.4	156.6		0
8	Ford Motor	243283	24547	346990		137137	4139		0
9	Toyota Motor	106004.2	49691.6	146855		111052	2662.4		0
10	Exxon	91296	40436	82000		110009	6470		0
11	Royal Dutch/Shell Group	118011.6	58986.4	104000		109833.7	6904.6		0
12	Wal-Mart	37871	14762	675000		93627	2740		0
13	Hitachi	91620.9	29007.2	331852		84107.4	1168.9		0
14	Nippon Life Insurance	364762.5	Reserved to indicate the DMU under evaluation.			83	Efficiency; Weighted sum of individual θi		0
15	Nippon Telegraph & Telephone	127077.3	4			81			0
16	AT&T	88884	17274	299300		79609	139		0
17									
18		Reference		DMU under	1	Efficiency			
19	**Constraints**	set		Evaluation		3	Weights		
20	Assets	91920.6	=	91920.6		1	1		
21	Equity	10950	=	10950		1	1		
22	Employees	36000	=	36000		1	1		
23	Revenue	184365.2	≥	184365.2			Changing cells; Individual θi		
24	Profit	346.2	≥	346.2					
25	Σλ	1							

Figure 4.2. Input-oriented VRS DEA/PS Spreadsheet Model

The target cell is cell F19 which contains the following formula

Cell F19 =SUMPRODUCT(F20:F22,G20:G22)/SUM(G20:G22)

where cells G20:G22 are reserved for the input weights.

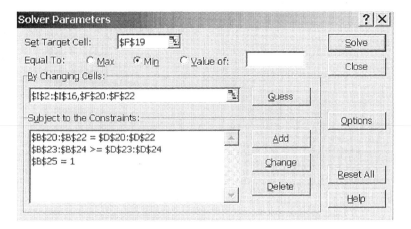

Figure 4.3. Solver Parameters for Input-oriented VRS DEA/PS Model

	B	C	D	E	F	G	H	I	J	K	L	M
1	Assets	Equity	Employees		Revenue	Profit		λ	Efficiency	Assets	Equity	Employees
2	91	Sub DEAPS()							1	1	1	1
3	68								1	1	1	1
4	65	Dim i As Integer							1	1	1	1
5	217	For i = 1 To 15							1	1	1	1
6	50	Range("E18") = i							1	1	1	1
7	71	SolverSolve UserFinish:=True							0.948271	0.83411	0.9975806	1.013122
8	2	Range("J" & i + 1) = Range("F19")							0.561535	0.340581	1.1085533	0.23547
9	106	'place the individual thetas into columns K,L,M							0.423575	0.62582	0.400533	0.244372
10		Range("K" & i + 1) = Range("F20")							1	1	1	1
11	118	Range("L" & i + 1) = Range("F21")							1	1	1	1
12		Range("M" & i + 1) = Range("F22")							1	1	1	1
12		Next										
13	91	End Sub							0.384513	0.638678	0.4502766	0.064583
14	364762.5	2241.9	89690		83206.7	2426.6	0		1	1	1	1
15	127077.3	42240.1	231400		81937.2	2209.1	0		0.347781	0.498661	0.4133195	0.131363
16	88884	17274	299300		79609	139	0		0.324338	0.565556	0.3867662	0.020692
17												
18	Reference		DMU under	16	Efficiency							
19	set		Evaluation		0.324338	Weights						
20	50268.9	=	50268.9		0.565556	1						
21	6681	=	6681		0.386766	1						
22	6193	=	6193		0.020692	1		DEA/PS				
23	167530.7	≥	79609									
24	210.5	≥	139									

Figure 4.4. Efficiency Result for Input-oriented VRS DEA/PS Model

The formulas for cells B20:B25 are

Cell B20 =SUMPRODUCT(B2:B16,$I$2:$I$16)
Cell B21 =SUMPRODUCT(C2:C16,$I$2:$I$16)
Cell B22 =SUMPRODUCT(D2:D16,$I$2:$I$16)

Cell B23 =SUMPRODUCT(F2:F16,$I$2:$I$16)
Cell B24 =SUMPRODUCT(G2:G16,$I$2:$I$16)
Cell B25 =SUM(I2:I16)

The formulas for cells D20:D24 are

Cell D20 =F20*INDEX(B2:B16,E18,1)
Cell D21 =F21*INDEX(C2:C16,E18,1)
Cell D22 =F22*INDEX(D2:D16,E18,1)
Cell D23 =INDEX(F2:F16,E18,1)
Cell D24 =INDEX(G2:G16,E18,1)

	B	C	D	E	F	G	H	I	J	K	L	M
1	Assets	Equity	Employees		Revenue	Profit		λ	Efficiency	Assets	Equity	Employees
2	91920.6	10950	36000		184365.2	346.2		0	1	1	1	1
3	Solver Parameters							?|X| 1	1	1	1
4	Set Target Cell: $F$19						Solve		1	1	1	1
5	Equal To: Max Min Value of:								1	1	1	1
6	By Changing Cells:						Close		1	1	1	1
7	$I$2:$I$16,$F$20:$F$22						Guess		1	1	1	1
8	Subject to the Constraints:								0.597152	0.42628	1	0.365176
9								Options	0.423575	0.62582	0.400533	0.244372
10	$B$20:$B$22 = $D$20:$D$22						Add		1	1	1	1
11	$B$23:$B$24 >= $D$23:$D$24								1	1	1	1
12	$B$25 = 1						Change		1	1	1	1
13	$F$20:$F$22 <= 1						Reset All		0.384513	0.638678	0.4502766	0.064583
14							Delete	Help	1	1	1	1
15									0.347781	0.498661	0.4133195	0.131363
16	88884	17274	299300		79609	139		0	0.324338	0.565556	0.3867662	0.020692
17												
18	Reference		DMU under	16	Efficiency							
19	set		Evaluation		0.324338	Weights						
20	50268.9	=	50268.9		0.565556	1						
21	6681	=	6681		0.386766	1			DEAPS			
22	6193	=	6193		0.020692	1						
23	167530.7	≥	79609									
24	210.5	≥	139									

Figure 4.5. Efficiency Result for Input-oriented VRS Non-radial DEA Model

Figure 4.4 shows the results and the VBA procedure "DEAPS" which automates the calculation.

Note that the θ_i ($i = 1,2,3$) are not restricted in Figure 4.3. If we add $\theta_i \leq$ 1 ($F$20:FF22 <=1), then we obtain the results shown in Figure 4.5.

4.4 DEA and Multiple Objective Linear Programming

Charnes, Cooper, Golany, Seiford and Stutz (1985) describe the relationship between DEA frontier and Pareto-Koopmans efficient empirical production frontier. This work points out the relation of efficiency in DEA and pareto optimality in multiple criteria decision making (MCDM) or Multiple Objective Linear Programming (MOLP). The relationship between

DEA and MOLP is again raised by Belton and Vickers (1993), Doyle and Green (1993) and Stewart (1994) in their discussion of DEA and MCDM. Joro, Korhonen and Wallenius (1998) provide a structure comparison of DEA and MOLP.

In fact, as shown in Chen and Zhu (2002), the DEA/PS models have a strong relationship with MOLP. To demonstrate this, we use vector presentation of $\mathbf{x}_j = (x_{1j},...,x_{mj})$ and $\mathbf{y}_j = (y_{1j},...,y_{sj})$.

4.4.1   Output-oriented DEA

Consider the following MOLP model

$$\max_{\lambda_j}(\sum_{j=1}^{n}\lambda_j\mathbf{y}_j) = (\sum_{j=1}^{n}\lambda_j y_{1j},...,\sum_{j=1}^{n}\lambda_j y_{sj})$$

subject to

$$\sum_{j=1}^{n}\lambda_j x_{ij} \le x_{io} \quad i = 1,...,m;$$
$$\lambda_j \ge 0, \qquad j = 1,...,n.$$

(4.6)

where $\mathbf{x}_o = (x_{1o},...,x_{mo})$ represents the input vector of DMU_o among others.

If all DMUs produce only one output, i.e., $\mathbf{y}_j$ is a scalar rather than a vector, then (4.6) is a single objective linear programming problem

$$\max_{\lambda_j}(\sum_{j=1}^{n}\lambda_j y_j)$$

subject to

$$\sum_{j=1}^{n}\lambda_j x_{ij} \le x_{io} \quad i = 1,...,m;$$
$$\lambda_j \ge 0, \qquad j = 1,...,n.$$

(4.7)

Let $\lambda_j y_j = \lambda_j'$, then (4.7) turns into

$$\max_{\lambda_j'} \sum_{j=1}^{n}\lambda_j'$$

subject to

$$\sum_{j=1}^{n}\lambda_j' x_{ij}' \le x_{io}' \quad i = 1,...,m;$$
$$\lambda_j' \ge 0, \qquad j = 1,...,n.$$

(4.8)

where $x_{ij}' = x_{ij}/y_j$ and $x_{io}' = x_{io}/y_o$.

As shown in Charnes, Cooper and Rhodes (1978), model (4.8) is equivalent to the output-oriented CRS envelopment model

$$\max_{\lambda_j, z_o} z_o$$

subject to

$$\sum_{j=1}^{n} \lambda_j y_j \geq z_o y_o$$

$$\sum_{j=1}^{n} \lambda_j x_{ij} \leq x_{io} \quad i = 1,...,m;$$

$$\lambda_j \geq 0, \quad j = 1,...,n.$$

Next, if $\mathbf{y}_j$ is a vector with s components, then we define

$$\sum_{j=1}^{n} \lambda_j y_{rj} = \sigma_r y_{ro} \tag{4.9}$$

As a result, (4.6) becomes

$$\max_{\lambda_j \sigma_r} (\sigma_1 y_{1o},...,\sigma_s y_{so})$$

subject to

$$\sum_{j=1}^{n} \lambda_j y_{rj} = \sigma_r y_{ro} \quad r = 1,...,s; \tag{4.10}$$

$$\sum_{j=1}^{n} \lambda_j x_{ij} \leq x_{io}, \quad i = 1,...,m;$$

$$\lambda_j \geq 0, \quad j = 1,...,n.$$

Let $\mathbf{W} = \{w \mid w \in \mathbf{R}^s, w_r \geq 0 \text{ and } \sum_{r=1}^{s} w_r\}$ be the set of nonnegative weights. The weighting problem associated with (4.10) is defined for some $w \in \mathbf{W}$ as

$$\max_{\lambda_j \sigma_r} \sum_{r=1}^{s} w_r \sigma_r y_{ro}$$

subject to

$$\sum_{j=1}^{n} \lambda_j y_{rj} = \sigma_r y_{ro} \quad r = 1,...,s; \tag{4.11}$$

$$\sum_{j=1}^{n} \lambda_j x_{ij} \leq x_{io} \quad i = 1,...,m;$$

$$\lambda_j \geq 0 \quad j = 1,...,n.$$

Furthermore, let $\overline{w}_r = w_r y_{ro}$ for all $r = 1, ..., s$, then (4.11) is equivalent to the following linear programming problem

$$\max_{\lambda_j \sigma_r} \sum_{r=1}^{s} \overline{w}_r \sigma_r$$

subject to

$$\sum_{j=1}^{n} \lambda_j y_{rj} = \sigma_r y_{ro} \quad r = 1,...,s; \tag{4.12}$$

$$\sum_{j=1}^{n} \lambda_j x_{ij} \leq x_{io} \quad i = 1,...,m;$$

$$\lambda_j \geq 0 \quad j = 1,...,n.$$

Model (4.12) is exactly the output-oriented CRS DEA/preference model. However, if we wish output level cannot be decreased to reach the efficient frontier, we specify (4.13) instead of (4.9).

$$\sum_{j=1}^{n} \lambda_j y_{rj} = \sigma_r y_{ro} \text{ such that } \sigma_r \geq 1 \text{ for all } r = 1, ..., s. \quad (4.13)$$

We see that for a specific DMU_o, $\lambda_o^* = 1$ and $\lambda_j^* = 0 \ (j \neq o)$ is an optimal solution to (4.12), when $\sigma_r^* = 1$ for all $r = 1, ..., s$. Note that if some $\sigma_r^* \neq 1$, then $\lambda_o^* = 0$ is an optimal solution to (4.12). Therefore, (4.6) can be interpreted as follows: when $\mathbf{x}_o = (x_{1o}, ..., x_{mo})$ is regarded as resource, if the resource $\mathbf{x}_o$ can be used among other DMUs (associated with $\lambda_j^* \neq 0$), then more desirable or preferred output level $\mathbf{y}^*$ is produced and $\mathbf{y}_o$ is not a pareto solution to (4.6).

It can be seen that weighted non-radial DEA model (4.12) is equivalent to an MOLP problem. If we impose an additional on $\sum_{j=1}^{n} \lambda_j$ in (4.6), then we obtain other output-oriented DEA models.

4.4.2   Input-oriented DEA

Similar to (4.6), we write the following MOLP model.

$$\min_{\lambda_j}(\sum_{j=1}^{n} \lambda_j \mathbf{x}_j) = (\sum_{j=1}^{n} \lambda_j x_{1j}, ..., \sum_{j=1}^{n} \lambda_j x_{mj})$$
$$\text{subject to} \quad\quad\quad\quad\quad\quad\quad\quad\quad\quad\quad\quad\quad (4.14)$$
$$\sum_{j=1}^{n} \lambda_j y_{rj} \leq y_{ro} \quad\quad r = 1, ..., s;$$
$$\lambda_j \geq 0, \quad\quad\quad\quad j = 1, ..., n.$$

where $\mathbf{y}_o = (y_{1o}, ..., y_{so})$ represents the output vector of DMU_o. If all DMUs use only one input, i.e., $\mathbf{x}_j$ is a scalar, then (4.14) is a single objective linear programming problem and is equivalent to the input-oriented CRS envelopment model with single input.

Let $\mathbf{G} = \{g \mid g \in \mathbf{R}^m, g_i \geq 0 \text{ and } \sum_{i=1}^{m} g_i = 1\}$ be the set of nonnegative weights. Then model (4.14) can be transformed into the following linear programming problem.

$$\min_{\lambda_j \tau_i} \sum_{i=1}^{m} \overline{g}_i \tau_i$$
$$\text{subject to}$$
$$\sum_{j=1}^{n} \lambda_j x_{ij} = \tau_i x_{io} \quad\quad i = 1, ..., m; \quad\quad\quad (4.15)$$
$$\sum_{j=1}^{n} \lambda_j y_{rj} \geq y_{ro} \quad\quad r = 1, ..., s;$$
$$\lambda_j \geq 0 \quad\quad\quad\quad j = 1, ..., n.$$

where $\bar{g}_i = g_i x_{io}$ for all $i = 1, \ldots, m$, and τ_i is defined in (4.16) or (4.17).

$$\sum_{j=1}^{n} \lambda_j x_{ij} = \tau_i x_{io} \qquad (4.16)$$

$$\sum_{j=1}^{n} \lambda_j x_{ij} = \tau_i x_{io} \text{ such that } \tau_i \leq 1 \text{ for all } i = 1, \ldots, m. \qquad (4.17)$$

Model (4.15) is a weighted non-radial DEA model incorporated with preference over the adjustment of input levels. If we use (4.16), then there is no restrictions on τ_i and model (4.15) is the input-oriented CRS DEA/PS model.

Note that for a specific DMU_o, $\lambda_o^* = 1$ and $\lambda_j^* = 0 \,(j \neq o)$ is an optimal solution to (4.15), when $\tau_i^* = 1$ for all $i = 1, \ldots, m$. Note also that if some $\tau_i^* \neq 1$, then $\lambda_o^* = 0$ is an optimal solution to (4.15). If we impose an additional on $\sum_{j=1}^{n} \lambda_j$ in (4.15), then we obtain other input-oriented DEA models.

4.4.3 Non-Orientation DEA

Consider the following MOLP model.

$$\max_{\lambda_j}(\sum_{j=1}^{n} \lambda_j \mathbf{y}_j) = (\sum_{j=1}^{n} \lambda_j y_{1j}, \ldots, \sum_{j=1}^{n} \lambda_j y_{sj})$$

$$\min_{\lambda_j}(\sum_{j=1}^{n} \lambda_j \mathbf{x}_j) = (\sum_{j=1}^{n} \lambda_j x_{1j}, \ldots, \sum_{j=1}^{n} \lambda_j x_{mj}) \qquad (4.18)$$

subject to
$$\lambda_j \geq 0 \qquad j = 1, \ldots, n.$$

We have the following equivalent linear programming model

$$\max_{\lambda_j, \sigma_r, \tau_i} \sum_{r=1}^{s} \overline{w}_r \sigma_r - \sum_{i=1}^{m} \overline{g}_i \tau_i$$

subject to
$$\sum_{j=1}^{n} \lambda_j x_{ij} = \tau_i x_{io} \qquad i = 1, \ldots, m;$$
$$\sum_{j=1}^{n} \lambda_j y_{rj} = \sigma_r y_{ro}, \qquad r = 1, \ldots, s; \qquad (4.19)$$
$$\tau_i \leq 1, \qquad i = 1, \ldots, m;$$
$$\sigma_r \geq 1, \qquad r = 1, \ldots, s;$$
$$\lambda_j \geq 0, \qquad j = 1, \ldots, n.$$

Note that $\sigma_r \geq 1$ and $\tau_i \leq 1$ in (4.19). Therefore, we have $\tau_i x_{io} = x_{io} - s_i^-$ and $\sigma_r y_{ro} = y_{ro} + s_r^+$, where s_i^-, $s_r^+ \geq 0$. Then, (4.19) becomes

$$\max_{\lambda_j, s_i^-, s_r^+} \sum_{r=1}^{s} w_r s_r^+ + \sum_{i=1}^{m} g_i s_i^- - \sum_{i=1}^{m} \overline{g}_i + \sum_{r=1}^{s} \overline{w}_r$$

subject to

$$\sum_{j=1}^{n} \lambda_j x_{ij} + s_i^- = x_{io} \qquad i = 1,...,m;$$

$$\sum_{j=1}^{n} \lambda_j y_{rj} - s_r^+ = y_{ro} \qquad r = 1,...,s;$$

$$s_i^-, s_r^+, \lambda_j \geq 0.$$

which is a weighted slack-based DEA model (see also Seiford and Zhu (1998c)).

Chapter 5

Modeling Undesirable Measures

5.1   Introduction

Both desirable (good) and undesirable (bad) outputs and inputs may be present. For example, the number of defective products is an undesirable output. One wants to reduce the number of defects to improve the performance. If inefficiency exists in production processes where final products are manufactured with a production of wastes and pollutants, the outputs of wastes and pollutants are undesirable and should be reduced to improve the performance.

Note that in the conventional DEA models, e.g., the VRS envelopment models, it is assumed that outputs should be increased and the inputs should be decreased to improve the performance or to reach the best-practice frontier. If one treats the undesirable outputs as inputs so that the bad outputs can be reduced, the resulting DEA model does not reflect the true production process.

Situations when some inputs need to be increased to improve the performance are also likely to occur. For example, in order to improve the performance of a waste treatment process, the amount of waste (undesirable input) to be treated should be increased rather than decreased as assumed in the conventional DEA models.

Seiford and Zhu (2002b) develop an approach to treat undesirable input/outputs in the VRS envelopment models. The key to their approach is the use of DEA classification invariance under which classifications of efficiencies and inefficiencies are invariant to the data transformation.

Suppose that the inputs and outputs are transformed to $\bar{x}_{ij} = x_{ij} + u_i$ and $\bar{y}_{rj} = y_{rj} + v_r$, where u_i and v_r are nonnegative. Then the input-oriented and the output-oriented VRS envelopment models become

$$\min \theta - \varepsilon (\sum_{i=1}^{m} s_i^- + \sum_{r=1}^{s} s_r^+)$$
subject to
$$\sum_{j=1}^{n} \lambda_j \bar{x}_{ij} + s_i^- = \theta \bar{x}_{io} \qquad i = 1,2,...,m;$$
$$\sum_{j=1}^{n} \lambda_j \bar{y}_{rj} - s_r^+ = \bar{y}_{ro} \qquad r = 1,2,...,s; \qquad\qquad (5.1)$$
$$\sum_{j=1}^{n} \lambda_j = 1$$
$$\lambda_j \geq 0 \qquad\qquad j = 1,2,...,n.$$

$$\max \phi - \varepsilon (\sum_{i=1}^{m} s_i^- + \sum_{r=1}^{s} s_r^+)$$
subject to
$$\sum_{j=1}^{n} \lambda_j \bar{x}_{ij} + s_i^- = \bar{x}_{io} \qquad i = 1,2,...,m;$$
$$\sum_{j=1}^{n} \lambda_j \bar{y}_{rj} - s_r^+ = \phi \bar{y}_{ro} \qquad r = 1,2,...,s; \qquad\qquad (5.2)$$
$$\sum_{j=1}^{n} \lambda_j = 1$$
$$\lambda_j \geq 0 \qquad\qquad j = 1,2,...,n.$$

Ali and Seiford (1990) show that DMU_o is efficient under (1.5) or (1.6) if and only if DMU_o is efficient under (5.1) or (5.2). This conclusion is due to the presence of the convexity constraint $\sum_{j=1}^{n} \lambda_j = 1$.

In general, there are three cases of invariance under data transformation in DEA. The first case is restricted to the "classification invariance" where the classifications of efficiencies and inefficiencies are invariant to the data transformation. The second case is the "ordering invariance" of the inefficient DMUs. The last case is the "solution invariance" in which the new DEA model (after data translation) must be equivalent to the old one, i.e., both mathematical programming problems must have exactly the same solution. The method of Seiford and Zhu (2002b) is concerned only with the first level of invariance – classification invariance. See Pastor (1996) and Lovell and Pastor (1995) for discussions in invariance property in DEA.

5.2   Undesirable Outputs

Let y_{rj}^g and y_{rj}^b denote the desirable (good) and undesirable (bad) outputs, respectively. Obviously, we wish to increase y_{rj}^g and to decrease

y_{rj}^b to improve the performance. However, in the output-oriented VRS envelopment model, both y_{rj}^g and y_{rj}^b are supposed to increase to improve the performance. In order to increase the desirable outputs and to decrease the undesirable outputs, we proceed as follows.

First, we multiply each undesirable output by "-1" and then find a proper value v_r to let all negative undesirable outputs be positive. That is, $\overline{y}_{rj}^b = -y_{rj}^b + v_r > 0$. This can be achieved by $v_r = \max_j \{y_{rj}^b\} + 1$, for example.

Based upon (5.2), we have

$$\max h$$
subject to
$$\sum_{j=1}^{n} \lambda_j y_{rj}^g \geq h y_{ro}^g$$
$$\sum_{j=1}^{n} \lambda_j \overline{y}_{rj}^b \geq h \overline{y}_{ro}^b \qquad (5.3)$$
$$\sum_{j=1}^{n} \lambda_j x_{ij} \leq x_{io}$$
$$\sum_{j=1}^{n} \lambda_j = 1$$
$$\lambda_j \geq 0, \quad j = 1,...,n$$

Note that (5.3) increases desirable outputs and decreases undesirable outputs. The following theorem ensures that the optimized undesirable output of y_{ro}^b $(=v_r - h^* \overline{y}_{ro}^b)$ cannot be negative.

Theorem 5.1 Given a translation vector v, suppose h^* is the optimal value to (5.3), we have $h^* \overline{y}_{ro}^b \leq v_r$.

[Proof] Note that all outputs now are non-negative. Let λ_j^* be an optimal solution associated with h^*. Since $\sum_{j=1}^{n} \lambda_j^* = 1$, $h^* \overline{y}_{ro}^b \leq \overline{y}_r^*$, where $\overline{y}_r^*$ is composed from (translated) maximum values among all bad outputs. Note that $\overline{y}_r^* = -y_r^* + v_r$, where y_r^* is composed from (original) minimum values among all bad outputs. Thus, $h^* \overline{y}_o^b \leq v_r$. ∎

We may treat the undesirable outputs as inputs. However, this does not reflect the true production process. We may also apply a monotone decreasing transformation (e.g., $1/y_{rj}^b$) to the undesirable outputs and then to use the adapted variables as outputs. The current method, in fact, applies a linear monotone decreasing transformation. Since the use of linear transformation preserves the convexity, it is a good choice for a DEA model.

Figure 5.1 illustrates the method. The five DMUs A, B, C, D and E use an equal input to produce one desirable output (g) and one undesirable output (b). GCDEF is the (output) frontier. If we treat the undesirable output as an input, then ABCD becomes the VRS frontier. Model (5.2) rotates the output frontier at EF and obtains the symmetrical frontier. In this case, DMUs A', B' and C', which are the adapted points of A, B and C, respectively, are efficient.

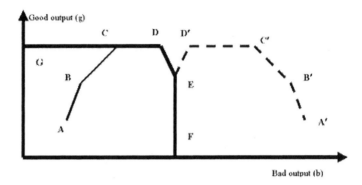

Figure 5.1. Treatment of Bad Output

The efficient target for DMU_o is

$$\begin{cases} \hat{x}_{io} = x_{io} - s_i^{-*} \\ \hat{y}_{ro}^g = h^* y_{ro}^g + s_r^{+*} \\ \hat{y}_{ro}^b = v_r - (h^* \bar{y}_{ro}^b + s_r^{+*}) \end{cases}$$

Table 5.1. Vendors

Vendors	Price ($/unit)	%Rejects	% Late deliveries
1	0.1958	1.2	5
2	0.1881	0.8	7
3	0.2204	0	0
4	0.2081	2.1	0
5	0.2118	2.3	3
6	0.2096	1.2	4

Source: Weber and Desai. (1996).

We conclude this section by applying the method to the six vendors studied in Weber and Desai (1996). Table 5.1 presents the data. The input is price per unit, and the outputs are percentage of late deliveries and percentage of rejected units. (See Weber and Desai (1996) for detailed discussion on the input and the two outputs.)

Obviously, the two outputs are bad outputs. We use an translation vector of (3.3%, 8%). (Or one could use (100%, 100%) as in Chapter 7.) Figure 5.2

shows the translated data and the spreadsheet model. This is actually a spreadsheet model for the output-oriented VRS envelopment model. Figure 5.3 shows the Solver parameters. Column G in Figure 5.2 reports the efficiency scores.

	A	B	C	D	E	F	G
1	·	Price		%Rejects	% Late deliveries	λ	Efficiency
2	Vendor 1	0.1958		2.1	3	0	1.08921
3	Vendor 2	0.1881		2.5	1	0.327059	1
4	Vendor 3	0.2204		3.3	8	0.653754	1
5	Vendor 4	0.2081		1.2	8	0.019187	1
6	Vendor 5	0.2118		1	5	0	1.6
7	Vendor 6	0.2096		2.1	4	0	1.427647
8							
9		Reference		DMU unde	6	Efficiency	
10	**Constrain**	set		Evaluation		1.427647	
11	price	0.2096	≤	0.2096			
12	Rejects	2.998059	≥	2.998059		Run	
13	Late delive	5.710589	≥	5.710589			
14	Σλ	1	=	1			

Figure 5.2. Bad Outputs Spreadsheet Model

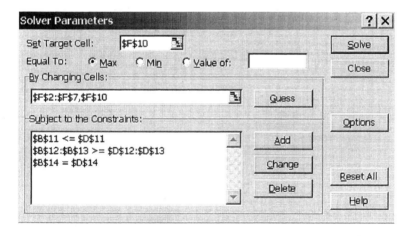

Figure 5.3. Solver Parameters for Bad Outputs Spreadsheet Model

If we do not translate the bad outputs and calculate the regular output-oriented VRS envelopment model, vendor 5 is classified as efficient, and vendor 3 is classified as inefficient. (see Figure 5.4 where 0.0001 is used to replace 0.) The same Solver parameters shown in Figure 5.3 are used.

	A	B	C	D	E	F	G
1		Price		%Rejects	% Late deliveries	λ	Efficiency
2	Vendor 1	0.1958		1.2	5	0	1.075329
3	Vendor 2	0.1881		0.8	7	0.518519	1
4	Vendor 3	0.2204		0.0001	0.0001	0	23000
5	Vendor 4	0.2081		2.1	0	0	1
6	Vendor 5	0.2118		2.3	3	0.481481	1
7	Vendor 6	0.2096		1.2	4	0	1.268519
8							
9		Reference		DMU unde	6	Efficiency	
10	**Constrain**	set		Evaluation		1.268519	
11	price	0.199511	≤	0.2096			
12	Rejects	1.522222	≥	1.522222		Run	
13	Late delive	5.074074	≥	5.074074			
14	Σλ	1	=	1			

Figure 5.4. Efficiency Scores When Bad Outputs Are Not Translated

If we treat the two bad outputs as inputs and use the input-oriented VRS envelopment model, we obtain the efficiency scores shown in Figure 5.5 (Figure 5.6 shows the Solver parameters). In this case, we do not have outputs.

	A	B	C	D	E	F	G
1		Price		%Rejects	% Late deliveries	λ	Efficiency
2	Vendor 1	0.1958		1.2	5	0	0.990548
3	Vendor 2	0.1881		0.8	7	0.541904	1
4	Vendor 3	0.2204		0	0	0.122632	1
5	Vendor 4	0.2081		2.1	0	0.335464	1
6	Vendor 5	0.2118		2.3	3	0	0.944315
7	Vendor 6	0.2096		1.2	4	0	0.948332
8							
9		Reference		DMU unde	6	Efficiency	
10	**Constrain**	set		Evaluation		0.948332	
11	price	0.19877	≤	0.19877			
12	Rejects	1.137998	≤	1.137998		Run	
13	Late delive	3.793326	≤	3.793326			
14	Σλ	1	=	1			

Figure 5.5. Efficiency Scores When Bad Outputs Are Treated As Inputs

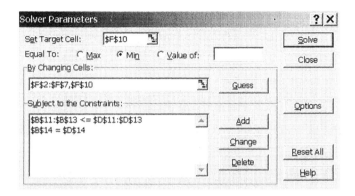

Figure 5.6. Solver Parameters When Bad Outputs Are Treated As Inputs

5.3 Undesirable Inputs

The above discussion can also be applied to situations when some inputs need to be increased rather than decreased to improve the performance. In this case, we denote x_{ij}^I and x_{ij}^D the inputs that need to be increased and decreased, respectively.

We next multiply x_{ij}^I by "-1" and then find a proper u_i to let $\overline{x}_{ij}^I = -x_{ij}^I + u_i > 0$. Based upon model (5.1), we have

$$\min \tau$$
subject to
$$\sum_{j=1}^{n} \lambda_j x_{ij}^D \leq \tau x_{io}^D$$
$$\sum_{j=1}^{n} \lambda_j \overline{x}_{ij}^I \leq \tau \overline{x}_{oi}^I \qquad (5.4)$$
$$\sum_{j=1}^{n} \lambda_j y_{rj} \geq y_{ro}$$
$$\sum_{j=1}^{n} \lambda_j = 1$$
$$\lambda_j \geq 0 \qquad j=1,...,n.$$

where x_{ij}^I is increased and x_{ij}^D is decreased for a DMU to improve the performance. The efficient target for DMU_o is

$$\begin{cases} \hat{x}_{io}^D = \tau^* x_{io}^I - s_i^{-*} \\ \hat{x}_{io}^I = u_i - (\tau^* x_{io}^I - s_i^{-*}) \\ \hat{y}_{ro} = y_{ro} + s_r^{+*} \end{cases}$$

*Part of the material in this section is adapted from European Journal of Operational Research, Vol 142, Seiford, L.M. and Zhu, J., Modeling undesirable factors in efficiency evaluation, 16-20, 2002, with permission from Elsevier Science.

Chapter 6

Context-dependent Data Envelopment Analysis

6.1   Introduction

Adding or deleting an inefficient DMU or a set of inefficient DMUs does not alter the efficiencies of the existing DMUs and the best-practice frontier. The inefficiency scores change only if the best-practice frontier is altered. i.e., the performance of DMUs depends only on the identified best-practice frontier. In contrast, researchers of the consumer choice theory point out that consumer choice is often influenced by the context. e.g., a circle appears large when surrounded by small circles and small when surrounded by larger ones. Similarly a product may appear attractive against a background of less attractive alternatives and unattractive when compared to more attractive alternatives (Simonson and Tversky, 1992).

Considering this influence within the framework of DEA, one could ask "what is the relative attractiveness of a particular DMU when compared to others?" As in Tversky and Simonson (1993), one agrees that the relative attractiveness of DMU_x compared to DMU_y depends on the presence or absence of a third option, say DMU_z (or a group of DMUs). Relative attractiveness depends on the evaluation context constructed from alternative options (or DMUs). In the original DEA methodology, each DMU is evaluated against a set of frontier DMUs. That is, the original DEA methodology can rank the performance of inefficient DMUs with respect to the best-practice frontier. However, when DMU_x and DMU_y are members of best-practice frontier, DEA cannot identify which of DMU_x and DMU_y is a better option with respect to DMU_z (or a set of inefficient DMUs). Because both DMU_x and DMU_y have an efficiency score of one. Although one may use the super-efficiency DEA models (Chapter 10) to rank the performance of efficient DMUs, the evaluation context or third option (the reference set) changes in each evaluation. i.e., DMU_x and DMU_y are not evaluated against the same third option by the super-efficiency concept.

From the above discussion, we see that DEA provides performance measures that are absolute in the sense that all DMUs are evaluated against the best-practice frontier. In order to obtain the relative attractiveness within DEA, we modify the original DEA methodology to a situation where the relative performance is defined with respect to a particular best-practice context (evaluation context).

In order to obtain the evaluation contexts, an algorithm is developed to remove the (original) best-practice frontier to allow the remaining (inefficient) DMUs to form a new second-level best-practice frontier. If we remove this new second-level best-practice frontier, a third-level best-practice frontier is formed, and so on, until no DMU is left. In this manner, we partition the set of DMUs into several levels of best-practice frontiers.

Note that each best-practice frontier provides an evaluation context for measuring the relative attractiveness. e.g., the second-level best-practice frontier serves as the evaluation context for measuring the relative attractiveness of the DMUs located on the first-level (original) best-practice frontier. It can be seen that the presence or absence (or the shape) of the second-level best-practice frontier affects the relative attractiveness of DMUs on the first-level best-practice frontier. A relative attractiveness measure is obtained when DMUs having worse performance are chosen as the evaluation context. When DMUs in a specific level are viewed as having equal performance, the attractiveness measure allows us to differentiate the "equal performance" based upon the same specific evaluation context (or third option).

On the other hand, we can measure the performance of DMUs on the third-level best-practice frontier with respect to the first or second level best-practice frontier. We define this type of measure as a progress measure where DMUs having better performance are chosen as the evaluation context. i.e., we measure the progress of DMUs with respect to best-practice frontiers at advanced levels. Note that the original DEA method provides a projection function to improve the performance of inefficient DMUs. However, it is likely that a particular inefficient DMU is unable to immediately improve its performance onto the first-level best-practice frontier because of such restrictions as management expertise, available resources, etc. Therefore intermediate (and more easily achievable) targets may be desirable for an inefficient DMU. By focusing on different levels of best-practice frontiers, the progress measure provides incremental improvements for a DMU's performance. i.e., we move the DMU step by step onto an attainable best-practice frontier. The resulting intermediate targets are *local targets*, whereas the targets on the first-level (original) best-practice frontier are *global targets*.

6.2   Stratification DEA Method

Define $\mathbf{J}^1 = \{DMU_j, j = 1,...,n\}$ (the set of all n DMUs) and interactively define $\mathbf{J}^{l+1} = \mathbf{J}^l - \mathbf{E}^l$ where $\mathbf{E}^l = \{DMU_k \in \mathbf{J}^l \mid \theta^*(l,k) = 1\}$, and $\theta^*(l,k)$ is the optimal value to the following input-oriented CRS envelopment model when DMU_k is under evaluation

$$\theta^*(l,k) = \min_{\lambda_j, \theta(l,k)} \theta(l,k)$$

subject to
$$\sum_{j \in F(\mathbf{J}^l)} \lambda_j x_{ij} \leq \theta(l,k) x_{ik} \tag{6.1}$$
$$\sum_{j \in F(\mathbf{J}^l)} \lambda_j y_{rj} \geq y_{rk}$$
$$\lambda_j \geq 0 \quad j \in F(\mathbf{J}^l).$$

where $j \in F(\mathbf{J}^l)$ means $DMU_j \in \mathbf{J}^l$, i.e., F($\cdot$) represents the correspondence from a DMU set to the corresponding subscript index set.

When $l = 1$, model (6.1) becomes the original input-oriented CRS envelopment model, and $\mathbf{E}^1$ consists of all the frontier DMUs. These DMUs in set $\mathbf{E}^1$ define the first-level best-practice frontier. When $l = 2$, model (6.1) gives the second-level best-practice frontier after the exclusion of the first-level frontier DMUs. And so on. In this manner, we identify several levels of best-practice frontiers. We call $\mathbf{E}^l$ the lth-level best practice frontier. The following algorithm accomplishes the identification of these best-practice frontiers by model (6.1).

Step 1: Set $l = 1$. Evaluate the entire set of DMUs, $\mathbf{J}^1$, by model (6.1) to obtain the first-level frontier DMUs, set $\mathbf{E}^1$ (the first-level best-practice frontier).
Step 2: Exclude the frontier DMUs from future DEA runs. $\mathbf{J}^{l+1} = \mathbf{J}^l - \mathbf{E}^l$. (If $\mathbf{J}^{l+1} = \varnothing$ then stop.)
Step 3: Evaluate the new subset of "inefficient" DMUs, $\mathbf{J}^{l+1}$, by model (6.1) to obtain a new set of efficient DMUs $\mathbf{E}^{l+1}$ (the new best-practice frontier).
Step 4: Let $l = l + 1$. Go to step 2.
Stopping rule: $\mathbf{J}^{l+1} = \varnothing$, the algorithm stops.

Thus, model (6.1) yields a stratification of the whole set of DMUs. From the algorithm, we know that l goes from 1 to L, where L is determined by the stopping rule. Consider Figure 1.2 in Chapter 1. DMUs 1, 2, 3 and 4 form the first-level CRS frontier and DMU5 forms the second-level CRS frontier $(L = 2)$.

It is easy to show that these sets of DMUs have the following properties

(i) $\mathbf{J}^1 = \bigcup_{l=1}^{L} \mathbf{E}^l$ and $\mathbf{E}^l \cap \mathbf{E}^{l'} = \varnothing$ for $l \neq l'$;

(ii) The DMUs in $\mathbf{E}^{l'}$ are dominated by the DMUs in $\mathbf{E}^l$ if $l' > l$;

(iii) Each DMU in set $\mathbf{E}^l$ is efficient with respect to the DMUs in set $\mathbf{E}^{l+l'}$ for all $0 < l' \leq l - L$.

Table 6.1. Data for the Flexible Manufacturing Systems

FMS	Inputs					Outputs		
	TC	WIP	TT	EMP	SR	VF	PF	RF
1	1.19	98	12.33	5	5.30	619	88	2
2	4.91	297	34.84	14	1.10	841	14	4
3	4.60	418	16.68	12	6.30	555	39	1
4	3.69	147	40.83	10	3.80	778	31	2
5	1.31	377	20.82	3	9.80	628	51	6
6	3.04	173	38.87	4	1.60	266	13	5
7	1.83	202	49.67	13	4.30	46	60	4
8	2.07	533	30.07	14	8.80	226	21	4
9	3.06	898	27.67	2	3.90	354	86	5
10	1.44	423	6.02	10	5.40	694	20	3
11	2.47	470	4.00	13	5.30	513	40	5
12	2.85	87	43.09	8	2.40	884	17	7
13	4.85	915	54.79	5	2.40	439	58	4
14	1.31	852	86.87	3	0.50	401	18	4
15	4.18	924	54.46	4	6.00	491	27	4
16	1.99	273	91.08	3	2.50	937	6	3
17	1.60	983	37.93	13	8.80	709	39	2
18	4.04	106	23.39	11	2.90	615	91	3
19	3.76	955	54.98	1	9.40	499	46	3
20	4.76	416	1.55	9	1.50	58	2	6
21	3.60	660	3.98	6	3.90	592	29	4
22	3.24	771	52.26	8	1.60	535	61	1
23	3.05	318	35.09	4	9.20	124	25	2
24	1.60	849	62.83	15	7.30	923	60	3

We next use a data set from the DEA Dataset Repository at http://java.emp.pdx.edu/etm/dea/dataset/ to illustrate the algorithm. Table 6.1 presents the data. The data set contains 24 flexible manufacturing systems (FMS). Each FMS has five inputs (1) total cost (TC) ($millions), (2) work in process (WIP) (units), (3) throughput (TT) (hours/unit), (4) employees

(EMP) (persons), and (5) space requirements (SR) (thousands of square feet), and three outputs (1) volume flexibility (VF) (average range of production capacity per product type), (2) production mix flexibility (PF) (product types), and (3) routing flexibility (RF) (average number of operations per machining center).

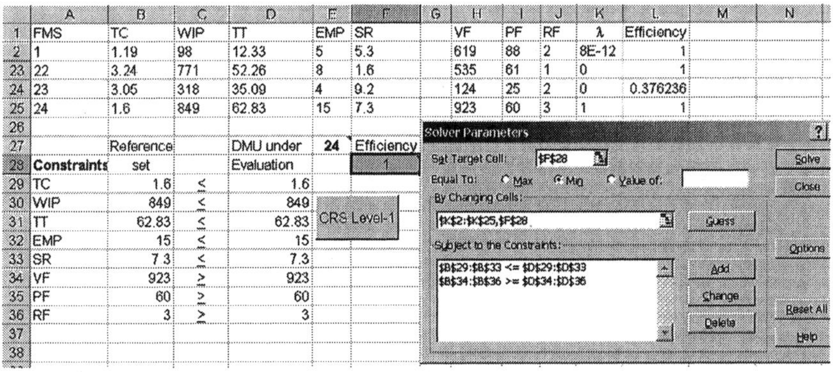

Figure 6.1. First Level CRS Frontier

Figure 6.1 shows the spreadsheet model for identifying the first level of CRS frontier. The target cell is F28, and the changing cells are K2:K25 and F28. The formulas for cells B29:B36 are

Cell B29=SUMPRODUCT(B2:B25,K2:K25)
Cell B30=SUMPRODUCT(C2:C25,K2:K25)
Cell B31=SUMPRODUCT(D2:D25,K2:K25)
Cell B32=SUMPRODUCT(E2:E25,K2:K25)
Cell B33=SUMPRODUCT(F2:F25,K2:K25)
Cell B34=SUMPRODUCT(H2:H25,K2:K25)
Cell B35=SUMPRODUCT(I2:I25,K2:K25)
Cell B36=SUMPRODUCT(J2:J25,K2:K25)

The formulas for cell D29:D36 are

Cell D29=F28*INDEX(B2:B25,E27,1)
Cell D30=F28*INDEX(C2:C25,E27,1)
Cell D31=F28*INDEX(D2:D25,E27,1)
Cell D32=F28*INDEX(E2:E25,E27,1)
Cell D33=F28*INDEX(F2:F25,E27,1)
Cell D34=INDEX(H2:H25,E27,1)
Cell D35=INDEX(I2:I25,E27,1)
Cell D36=INDEX(J2:J25,E27,1)

The button "CRS Level-1" is linked to the VBA procedure "Level1" which records the CRS efficiency scores in column L.

```
Sub Level1()
    Dim i As Integer
    For i = 1 To 24
'set the value of cell E27 equal to i (1, 2,..., 24)
    Range("E27") = i
    SolverSolve UserFinish:=True
'Place the efficiency into column L
    Range("L" & i + 1) = Range("F28")
    Next i
End Sub
```

Sixteen FMSs are on the first level CRS frontier. They are DMUs 1, 2, 5, 6, 9, 10, 11, 12, 14, 16, 18, 19, 20, 21, 22, and 24.

	A	B	C	D	E	F	G	H	I	J	K	L
1	FMS	TC	WIP	TT	EMP	SR		VF	PF	RF	λ	Efficiency
2	3	4.6	418	16.68	12	6.3		555	39	1	0	1
3	4	3.69	147	40.83	10	3.8		778	31	2	0	1
4	7	1.83	202	49.67	13	4.3		46	60	4	0.201	1
5	8	2.07	533	30.07	14	8.8		226	21	4	0	1
6	13	4.85	915	54.79	5	2.4		439	58	4	0.157	1
7	15	4.18	924	54.46	4	6		491	27	4	0.142	1
8	17	1.6	983	37.93	13	8.8		709	39	2	0	1
9	23	3.05	318	35.09	4	9.2		124	25	2	0	0.991748
10												
11			Reference		DMU under	8	Efficiency					
12	Constraints	set		Evaluation		0.991748						
13	TC	1.722457	≤	3.024832								
14	WIP	315.3759	≤	315.3759								
15	TT	26.31838	≤	34.80044	CRS Level-2							
16	EMP	3.966992	≤	3.966992								
17	SR	2.093367	≤	9.124083								
18	VF	147.8423	≥	124								
19	PF	25	≥	25								
20	RF	2	≥	2								

Figure 6.2. Second Level CRS Frontier

Next, we remove those FMSs with efficiency score of one. Because no absolute references are used in the formulas in the spreadsheet shown in Figure 6.1, the Solver automatically adjusts the parameters as we remove the rows related to the FMSs with efficiency score of one. Figure 6.2 shows the new spreadsheet.

Seven FMSs are on the second level CRS frontier. Because only one FMS, namely DMU 23, is left, this DMU forms the third level CRS frontier (L = 3).

6.3 Input-oriented Context-dependent DEA

The DEA stratification model (6.1) partitions the set of DMUs into different frontier levels characterized by $\mathbf{E}^l$ ($l = 1, ..., L$). We present the input-oriented context-dependent DEA based upon the evaluation context $\mathbf{E}^l$. The context-dependent DEA is characterized by an attractiveness measure and a progress measure.

6.3.1 Attractiveness

Consider a specific $DMU_q = (x_q, y_q)$ from a specific level $\mathbf{E}^{l_o}$, $l_o \in \{1, ..., L-1\}$. We have the following model to characterize the attractiveness.

$$H_q^*(d) = \min H_q(d) \qquad d = 1,...,L-l_o$$
subject to
$$\sum_{j \in F(\mathbf{E}^{l_o+d})} \lambda_j x_j \leq H_q(d) x_q \qquad (6.2)$$
$$\sum_{j \in F(\mathbf{E}^{l_o+d})} \lambda_j y_j \geq y_q$$
$$\lambda_j \geq 0 \quad j \in F(\mathbf{E}^{l_o+d})$$

Lemma 6.1 For a specific $DMU_q \in \mathbf{E}^{l_o}$, $l_o \in \{1, ..., L-1\}$, model (6.2) is equivalent to the following linear programming problem

$$\tilde{H}_q^*(d) = \min_{\lambda_j, \tilde{H}_q(d)} \tilde{H}_q(d) \qquad d = 1,...,L-l_o$$
subject to
$$\sum_{j \in F(\mathbf{J}^{l_o+d})} \lambda_j x_j \leq \tilde{H}_q(d) x_q \qquad (6.3)$$
$$\sum_{j \in F(\mathbf{J}^{l_o+d})} \lambda_j y_j \geq y_q$$
$$\lambda_j \geq 0 \quad j \in F(\mathbf{J}^{l_o+d})$$

[Proof]: Note that $\mathbf{J}^{l_o+d} = \bigcup_{l=\alpha}^{L-l_o} \mathbf{E}^{l_o+l}$. Therefore, (6.3) can be rewritten as
$$\tilde{H}_q^*(d) = \min_{\mu_j, \lambda_j, \tilde{H}_q(d)} \tilde{H}_q(d) \qquad d = 1,...,L-l_o$$
subject to
$$\sum_{j \in F(\mathbf{E}^{l_o+d})} \mu_j x_j + \sum_{j \in F(\mathbf{J}^{l_o+d} - \mathbf{E}^{l_o+d})} \lambda_j x_j \leq \tilde{H}_q(d) x_q \qquad (6.4)$$
$$\sum_{j \in F(\mathbf{E}^{l_o+d})} \mu_j y_j + \sum_{j \in F(\mathbf{J}^{l_o+d} - \mathbf{E}^{l_o+d})} \lambda_j y_j \geq y_q$$
$$\mu_j, \lambda_j \geq 0$$

Obviously, $\lambda_j = 0$ for all $j \in F(\mathbf{J}^{l_o+d} - \mathbf{E}^{l_o+d}) = F(\bigcup_{l=d+1}^{L-l_o} \mathbf{E}^{l_o+l})$ in any optimal solutions to (6.4). Otherwise, if some $\lambda_j \neq 0$, then $\mathbf{E}^{l_o+d} \cap$

$(\bigcup_{l=d+1}^{L-l_o} \mathbf{E}^{l_o+l}) \neq \varnothing$ (A contradiction). Therefore, $\widetilde{\Omega}_q^*(d) = \Omega_q^*(d)$ and (6.2) is equivalent to (6.3). ∎

Theorem 6.1 For a specific $DMU_q \in \mathbf{E}^{l_o}$, $l_o \in \{1, ..., L\text{-}1\}$, we have
(i) $G_q^*(g) < 1$ for each $g = 1, ..., l_o - 1$.
(ii) $H_q^*(d+1) > H_q^*(d)$.

[Proof]:
(i) Suppose $H_q^*(d) \leq 1$.
   If $H_q^*(d) = 1$, then $DMU_q \in \mathbf{E}^{l_o+d}$. This means that $\mathbf{E}^{l_o+d} \cap \mathbf{E}^{l_o} \neq \varnothing$. A contradiction.
   If $H_q^*(d) < 1$, then DMU_q is dominated by $\mathbf{E}^{l_o+d}$. However, $\mathbf{E}^{l_o+d}$ is dominated by $\mathbf{E}^{l_o}$. Thus, DMU_q is dominated by $\mathbf{E}^{l_o}$. This means that $DMU_q \notin \mathbf{E}^{l_o}$. A contradiction. Therefore, $H_q^*(d) > 1$.
(ii) $H_q^*(d+1)$ is obtained by solving the following problem

$$H_q^*(d+1) = \min_{\lambda_j, H_q(d+1)} H_q(d+1)$$
subject to
$$\sum_{j \in \mathrm{F}(\mathbf{E}^{l_o+d+1})} \lambda_j x_j \leq H_q(d+1)x_q \qquad (6.5)$$
$$\sum_{j \in \mathrm{F}(\mathbf{E}^{l_o+d+1})} \lambda_j y_j \geq y_q$$
$$\lambda_j \geq 0 \quad j \in \mathrm{F}(\mathbf{E}^{l_o+d+1})$$

$H_q^*(d)$ is obtained by solving the following problem

$$H_q^*(d) = \min_{\mu_j, H_q(d)} H_q(d)$$
subject to
$$\sum_{j \in \mathrm{F}(\mathbf{E}^{l_o+d})} \mu_j x_j \leq H_q(d)x_q$$
$$\sum_{j \in \mathrm{F}(\mathbf{E}^{l_o+d})} \mu_j y_j \geq y_q;$$
$$\mu_j \geq 0 \quad j \in \mathrm{F}(\mathbf{E}^{l_o+d})$$

which is, by Lemma 6.1, equivalent to the following linear programming problem

$$H_q^*(d) = \min_{\mu_j, \lambda_j, H_q(d)} H_q(d)$$
subject to
$$\sum_{j \in \mathrm{F}(\mathbf{E}^{l_o+d})} \mu_j x_j + \sum_{j \in \mathrm{F}(\mathbf{E}^{l_o+d+1})} \lambda_j x_j \leq H_q(d)x_q \qquad (6.6)$$
$$\sum_{j \in \mathrm{F}(\mathbf{E}^{l_o+d})} \mu_j y_j + \sum_{j \in \mathrm{F}(\mathbf{E}^{l_o+d+1})} \lambda_j y_j \geq y_q;$$
$$\mu_j, \lambda_j \geq 0$$

It can be seen that any optimal solution to (6.5) is a feasible solution to (6.6). Therefore $H_q^*(d+1) \geq H_q^*(d)$. However, if $H_q^*(d+1) = H_q^*(d)$, then $\mathbf{E}^{l_o+d} \cap \mathbf{E}^{l_o+d+1} \neq \varnothing$. Thus, $H_q^*(d+1) > H_q^*(d)$. ∎

Definition 6.1 $H_q^*(d)$ is called (input-oriented) *d-degree* attractiveness of DMU_q from a specific level $\mathbf{E}^{l_o}$.

Suppose, e.g., each DMU in the first-level best practice frontier represents an option, or product. Customers may compare a specific DMU in $\mathbf{E}^{l_o}$ with other alternatives that are currently in the same level as well as with relevant alternatives that serve as evaluation contexts. The relevant alternatives are those DMUs, say, in the second or third level best-practice frontier, etc. Given the alternatives (evaluation contexts), model (6.2) enables us to select the best option – the most attractive one.

In model (6.2), each best-practice frontier of $\mathbf{E}^{l_o+d}$ represents an evaluation context for measuring the relative attractiveness of DMUs in $\mathbf{E}^{l_o}$. The larger the value of $H_q^*(d)$, the more attractive the DMU_q is. Because this DMU_q makes itself more distinctive from the evaluation context $\mathbf{E}^{l_o+d}$. We are able to rank the DMUs in $\mathbf{E}^{l_o}$ based upon their attractiveness scores and identify the best one.

	A	B	C	D	E	F	G	H	I	J	K
1	FMS (Level1)	TC	WIP	TT	EMP	SR		VF	PF	RF	Attractiveness
2	1	1.19	98	12.33	5	5.3	16	619	88	2	5.257398
3	2	4.91	297	34.84	14	1.1		841	14	4	3.883129
4	5	1.31	377	20.82	3	9.8	Score	628	51	6	3.942397
5	6	3.04	173	38.87	4	1.6	1.594	266	13	5	3.222047
6	9	3.06	898	27.67	2	3.9		354	88	5	3.706897
7	10	1.44	423	6.02	10	5.4		694	20	3	5.347655
8	11	2.47	470	4	13	5.3		513	40	5	10.45603
9	12	2.85	87	43.09	8	2.4		884	17	7	4.625919
10	14	1.31	852	86.87	3	0.5		401	18	4	4.8
11	16	1.99	273	91.08	3	2.5		937	6	3	3.334894
12	18	4.04	108	23.39	11	2.9		615	81	3	3.528959
13	19	3.76	955	54.98	1	9.4		499	46	3	4.845534
14	20	4.76	416	1.55	9	1.5		58	2	6	29.1
15	21	3.8	860	3.98	6	3.9		592	29	4	9.24551
16	22	3.24	771	52.26	8	1.6		535	61	1	1.789802
17	24	1.6	849	62.83	15	7.3		923	60	3	1.593583
18	DMU under evaluation	2.5497	1359	100.12	23.9	11.63		923	60	3	
19		IV	IV	IV	IV	IV		AI	AI	AI	
20	Evaluation background	2.5497	1227.1	57.897	19.73	11.63		923	80	3.27	
21	FMS(Level2)	TC	WIP	TT	EMP	SR		VF	PF	RF	λ
22	3	4.6	418	16.68	12	6.3		555	38	1	0
23	4	3.69	147	40.83	10	3.8		778	31	2	0.082849
24	7	1.83	202	49.67	13	4.3		46	60	4	0.177585
25	8	2.07	533	30.07	14	8.8		228	21	4	0
26	13	4.85	915	54.78	5	2.4		439	58	4	0
27	15	4.18	924	54.48	4	8		491	27	4	0
28	17	1.6	983	37.93	13	8.8		709	39	2	1.1994

Figure 6.3. First Degree Attractiveness Spreadsheet Model

Figure 6.3 shows a spreadsheet model for the attractiveness measure – model (6.2). Cells A1:J17 and A21:J28 store the DMUs in the first and second levels, respectively. This spreadsheet model measures the first-degree attractiveness. Cell G2 is reserved to indicate the DMU under evaluation. Cell G5 represents the attractiveness score, and is the target cell and a changing cell. Cells K22:K28 are reserved for changing cells of λ_j.

Cells B20:F20, and cells H20:J20 contain formulas for the reference set (DMUs in the second level CRS frontier). The formula for cell B20 is "=SUMPRODUCT(B22:B28,$K$22:$K$28)" and is copied into cells C20:F20 and cells H20:J20.

Cells B18:F18, and cells H18:J18 contain formulas for the DMU under evaluation (DMUs in the first level CRS frontier). The formula for cell B18 is "=$G$5*INDEX(B2:B17,$G$2,1)" and is copied into cells C18:F18. The formula for cell H18 is "=INDEX(H2:H17,$G$2,1)" and is copied into cells I18:J18.

Figure 6.4 shows the Solver parameters. After solve the model for the first DMU, we use the VBA procedure "Attractiveness" to obtain the attractiveness scores for the remaining DMUs.

```
Sub Attractiveness()
 Dim i As Integer
    For i = 1 To 16
'set the value of cell G2 equal to i (1, 2,..., 16)
    Range("G2") = i
    SolverSolve UserFinish:=True
'Place the attractiveness score in cell G5 into column K
    Range("K" & i + 1) = Range("G5")
    Next
End Sub
```

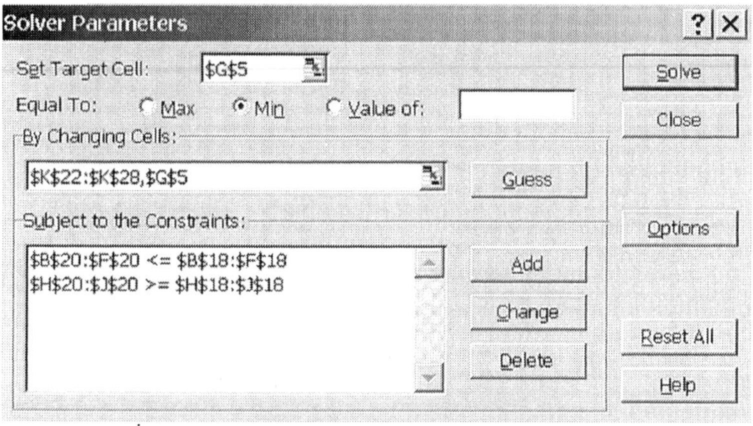

Figure 6.4. Solver Parameters for First Degree Attractiveness

	A	B	C	D	E	F	G	H	I	J	K
1	FMS (Level1)	TC	WIP	TT	EMP	SR		VF	PF	RF	Attractiveness
2	1	1.19	98	12.33	5	5.3	16	619	88	2	16.19832
3	2	4.91	297	34.84	14	1.1		841	14	4	56.72434
4	5	1.31	377	20.82	3	9.8	Score	628	51	6	11.79143
5	6	3.04	173	38.87	4	1.6	14.19	266	13	5	14.375
6	9	3.06	898	27.67	2	3.9		354	88	5	8.114872
7	10	1.44	423	6.02	10	5.4		694	20	3	32.62306
8	11	2.47	470	4	13	5.3		513	40	5	36.29268
9	12	2.85	87	43.09	8	2.4		884	17	7	27.32796
10	14	1.31	852	86.87	3	0.5		401	18	4	59.50323
11	16	1.99	273	91.08	3	2.5		937	8	3	27.80774
12	18	4.04	106	23.39	11	2.9		815	91	3	15.73415
13	19	3.76	955	54.98	1	9.4		499	46	3	16.09677
14	20	4.76	416	1.55	9	1.5		58	2	6	67.91613
15	21	3.8	680	3.98	8	3.9		592	29	4	42.09207
16	22	3.24	771	52.26	8	1.6		535	61	1	24.80847
17	24	1.6	849	62.83	15	7.3		923	60	3	14.18926
18	DMU under evaluation	22.703	12047	891.51	212.8	103.6		923	60	3	
19		Iv	Iv	Iv	Iv	Iv		ΛI	ΛI	ΛI	
20	Evaluation background	22.703	2367	261.19	29.77	68.48		923	186	14.9	
21	FMS(Level3)	TC	WIP	TT	EMP	SR		VF	PF	RF	λ
22	23	3.05	318	35.09	4	9.2		124	25	2	7.443548

Figure 6.5. Second Degree Attractiveness Spreadsheet Model

If we change the evaluation background to the third level CRS frontier (DMU23), we obtain the spreadsheet model for measuring the second degree attractiveness (see Figure 6.5). This spreadsheet can be obtained via replacing the second level CRS frontier by the DMU23 in Figure 6.3.

Based upon the attractiveness scores shown in Figure 6.3, DMU20 and DMU11 are ranked as the top two most attractive systems. However, if we change the evaluation context to the third level CRS frontier, DMU11 is ranked fifth, and DMU14 becomes the second most attractiveness system. This example illustrates that under a different evaluation context, the attractiveness of DMUs on the same level may be different. Therefore, the context-dependent DEA can differentiate the performance of efficient DMUs, or DMUs on the same performance level.

6.3.2   Progress

Consider the following linear programming problem for determining the progress measure for $DMU_q \in \mathbf{E}^{l_o}$, $l_o \in \{2, ..., L\}$.

$$G_q^*(g) = \min_{\lambda_j, G_q(g)} G_q(g) \quad g = 1, ..., l_o - 1$$

subject to

$$\sum_{j \in F(\mathbf{E}^{l_o - g})} \lambda_j x_j \leq G_q(\beta) x_q \tag{6.7}$$

$$\sum_{j \in F(\mathbf{E}^{l_o - g})} \lambda_j y_j \geq y_q$$

$$\lambda_j \geq 0 \quad j \in F(\mathbf{E}^{l_o - g})$$

Lemma 6.2 For a specific $DMU_q \in \mathbf{E}^{l_o}$, $l_o \in \{2, ..., L\}$, model (6.7) is equivalent to the following linear programming problem

$$\tilde{G}_q^*(g) = \min_{\lambda_j, \tilde{G}_q(\beta)} \tilde{G}_q(g)$$

subject to

$$\sum_{j \in F(\mathbf{J}^{l_o-g})} \lambda_j x_j \leq \tilde{G}_q(g) x_q \qquad (6.8)$$

$$\sum_{j \in F(\mathbf{J}^{l_o-g})} \lambda_j y_j \geq y_q$$

$$\lambda_j \geq 0 \quad j \in F(\mathbf{J}^{l_o-g})$$

[Proof]: Note that $\mathbf{J}^{l_o-g} = \mathbf{E}^{l_o-g} \cup \mathbf{J}^{l_o-g+1}$, since all DMUs in $\mathbf{J}^{l_o-g}$ are dominated by the frontiers constructed by the DMUs in $\mathbf{E}^{l_o-g}$. Therefore, by the nature of DEA method, we know that $\lambda_j = 0$ ($j \notin F(\mathbf{E}^{l_o-g})$) in any optimal solutions to (6.8). Thus, $\tilde{G}_q^*(g) = G_q^*(g)$ and (6.7) is equivalent to (6.8). ■

Theorem 6.2 For a specific $DMU_q \in \mathbf{E}^{l_o}$, $l_o \in \{2, ..., L\}$, we have
(i) $G_q^*(g) < 1$ for each $g = 1,...,l_o - 1$.
(ii) $G_q^*(g+1) < G_q^*(g)$.

[Proof]: The proof is similar to that of Theorem 6.1 by using Lemma 6.2 and therefore is omitted. ■

Definition 6.2: $M_q^*(g) \equiv 1/G_q^*(g)$ is called (input-oriented) *g-degree* progress of DMU_q from a specific level $\mathbf{E}^{l_o}$.

Obviously $M_q^*(g) > 1$. For a larger $M_q^*(g)$, more progress is expected. Each best-practice frontier, $\mathbf{E}^{l_o-g}$, contains a possible target for a specific DMU in $\mathbf{E}^{l_o}$ to improve its performance. The progress here is a level-by-level improvement.

Now consider the following linear programming problem

$$\max \|S^+(g)\|_1 + \|S^-(g)\|_1 \quad g = 1,...,l_o - 1$$

subject to

$$S^-(g) = G_q^*(g) x_q - \sum_{j \in F(E^{l_o-g})} \lambda_j x_j$$

$$S^+(g) = \sum_{j \in F(E^{l_o-g})} \lambda_j y_j - y_q \qquad (6.9)$$

$$S^+(g), S^-(g) \geq 0$$

$$\lambda_j \geq 0 \quad j \in F(E^{l_o-g})$$

where $\|S^+(g)\|_1$ and $\|S^-(g)\|_1$ represent L_1-*norms* for $S^+(g) = (s_1^+(g),...,s_s^+(g))$ and $S^-(g) = (s_1^-(g),...,s_m^-(g))$, respectively, i.e., $\|S^+(g)\|_1 + \|S^-(g)\|_1 = \sum_{r=1}^s s_r^+(g) + \sum_{i=1}^m s_i^-(g)$.

Definition 6.3 (Global Efficient Target and Local Efficient Target).
The following point

$$\begin{cases} \hat{y}_q = P_q^*(g)y_q + S^{+*}(g) \\ \hat{x}_q = x_q - S^{-*}(g) \end{cases}$$

is the *global efficient target* for $DMU_q \in \mathbf{E}^{l_o}$, $l_o \in \{2, ..., L\}$ if $g = l_o - 1$;
Otherwise, if $g < l_o - 1$, it represents a *local efficient target*, where $G_q^*(g)$ is
the optimal value to (6.7), and $S^{+*}(g)$ and $S^{-*}(g)$ represent the optimal
values in (6.9).

It can be seen that if the first-level best-practice frontier is chosen as the
evaluation context ($g = l_o - 1$), then we obtain the global efficient target, i.e.,
the original DEA efficient target. The local efficient targets are obtained
when other best-practice frontiers are selected. Although the local efficient
targets are not non-dominated points compared to the DMUs in $\mathbf{E}^1$, they
may represent a better alternative and an attainable target for a specific
inefficient DMU. That is, in the presence of possible external or internal
restrictions, a DMU may be unable to move itself onto the first-level best-
practice frontier (global efficient target). Thus, our progress measure extends
the original DEA projection function and enables an inefficient DMU to
improve its performance at a reasonable and desirable scale.

	A	B	C	D	E	F	G	H	I	J	K
1	FMS(Level3)	TC	WIP	TT	EMP	SR		VF	PF	RF	Progress
2		23	3.05	318	35.09	4	9.2	1	124	25	2	0.991748
3											
4	DMU under evaluation	3.0248	315.38	34.8	3.97	9.124		124	25	2	
5		IV	IV	IV	IV	IV		ΛI	ΛI	ΛI	
6	Evaluation background	1.7225	315.38	26.318	3.97	2.093		147	25	2	
7	FMS(Level2)	TC	WIP	TT	EMP	SR		VF	PF	RF	λ
8		3	4.6	418	16.68	12	6.3		555	39	1	0
9		4	3.69	147	40.83	10	3.8		778	31	2	0
10		7	1.83	202	49.67	13	4.3		46	60	4	0.201125
11		8	2.07	533	30.07	14	8.8		226	21	4	0
12		13	4.85	915	54.79	5	2.4		439	58	4	0.156867
13		15	4.18	924	54.46	4	6		491	27	4	0.142008
14		17	1.6	983	37.93	13	8.8		709	39	2	0

Figure 6.6. First Degree Progress Spreadsheet Model

Figure 6.6 shows a spreadsheet for the progress measure where the
evaluation background is the second level DMUs and the DMU under
evaluation is the DMU23.

The formula for cell B4 is "=$K$2*INDEX(B2,$G$2,1), where cell K2
is the target cell (its reciprocal represents the first-degree progress). This
formula is copied into cells C4:F4.

The formula for H4 is "=INDEX(H2,$G$2,1)" and is copied into cells I4:J4

The formula for cell B6 is "=SUMPRODUCT(B8:B14,$K$8:$K$14)" and is copied into cells C6:F6, and cells H6:J6.

Figure 6.7 shows the Solver parameters for the spreadsheet model shown in Figure 6.6. In Figure 6.6, the first degree progress score for DMU23 is 1/0.99175 = 1.0083. The optimal values in cells B6:F6 and cells H6:J6 represent the local target for DMU23.

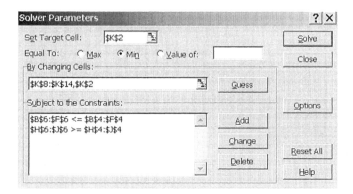

Figure 6.7. Solver Parameters for First Degree Progress

	A	B	C	D	E	F	G	H	I	J	K
1	FMS(Level3)	TC	WIP	TT	EMP	SR		VF	PF	RF	Progress
2	23	3.05	318	35.09	4	9.2	1	124	25	2	0.376236
3											
4	DMU under evaluation	1.1475	119.64	13.202	1.5	3.461		124	25	2	
5		IV	IV	IV	IV	IV		^I	^I	^I	
6	Evaluation background	0.5355	119.64	7.7206	1.5	3.434		258.6	25	2	
7	FMS(Level1)	TC	WIP	TT	EMP	SR		VF	PF	RF	λ
8		1	1.19	98	12.33	5	5.3	619	88	2	0.117385
9		2	4.91	297	34.84	14	1.1	841	14	4	0
10		5	1.31	377	20.82	3	9.8	628	51	6	0.285026
11		6	3.04	173	38.87	4	1.6	266	13	5	0
12		9	3.06	898	27.67	2	3.9	354	86	5	0
13		10	1.44	423	6.02	10	5.4	694	20	3	0
14		11	2.47	470	4	13	5.3	513	40	5	0
15		12	2.85	87	43.09	8	2.4	884	17	7	0.007867
16		14	1.31	852	86.87	3	0.5	401	18	4	0
17		16	1.99	273	91.08	3	2.5	937	6	3	0
18		18	4.04	106	23.39	11	2.9	615	91	3	0
19		19	3.76	955	54.98	1	9.4	499	46	3	0
20		20	4.76	416	1.55	9	1.5	58	2	6	0
21		21	3.6	660	3.98	6	3.9	592	29	4	0
22		22	3.24	771	52.26	8	1.6	535	61	1	0
23		24	1.6	849	62.83	15	7.3	923	60	3	0

Figure 6.8. Second Degree Progress Spreadsheet Model

If we replace the second-level DMUs with the first-level DMUs, we obtain the second-degree progress measure for DMU23. Figure 6.8 shows the spreadsheet.

This spreadsheet model is actually the input-oriented CRS envelopment model when DMU23 is under evaluation. Figure 6.9 shows the Solver parameters for the model shown in Figure 6.8. The second degree progress score for DMU23 is 1/0.37624 = 2.6579, and the optimal values in cells B6:F6 and H6:J6 represent the global target for DMU23

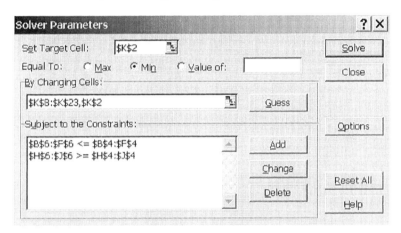

Figure 6.9. Solver Parameters for Second Degree Progress

6.4 Output-oriented Context-dependent DEA

Similar to the discussion on the input-oriented context-dependent DEA, for a specific $DMU_q = (x_q, y_q)$ from a specific level $\mathbf{E}^{l_o}$, $l_o \in \{1, ..., L\text{-}1\}$, we have the following model to characterize the output-oriented attractiveness

$$\Omega_q^*(d) = \max_{\lambda_j, \Omega_q(d)} \Omega_q(d) \qquad d = 1,...,L - l_o$$
subject to
$$\sum_{j \in F(\mathbf{E}^{l_o+d})} \lambda_j y_j \geq \Omega_q(d) y_q \qquad\qquad (6.10)$$
$$\sum_{j \in F(\mathbf{E}^{l_o+d})} \lambda_j x_j \leq x_q$$
$$\lambda_j \geq 0 \qquad j \in F(\mathbf{E}^{l_o+d})$$

Similar to Theorem 6.1, we have

Theorem 6.3 For a specific $DMU_q \in \mathbf{E}^{l_o}$, $l_o \in \{1, ..., L\text{-}1\}$, we have
(i) $\Omega_q^*(d) < 1$ for each $d = 1,..., L - l_o$.
(ii) $\Omega_q^*(d + 1) < \Omega_q^*(d)$.

Definition 6.4 $A_q^*(d) \equiv 1/\Omega_q^*(d)$ is called the (output-oriented) *d-degree* attractiveness of DMU_q from a specific level $\mathbf{E}^{l_o}$.

Note that $A_q^*(d)$ is the reciprocal of the optimal value to (6.10), therefore $A_q^*(d) > 1$. The larger the value of $A_q^*(d)$, the more attractive the DMU_q is. Because this DMU_q makes itself more distinctive from the evaluation context $\mathbf{E}^{l_o+d}$. We are able to rank the DMUs in $\mathbf{E}^{l_o}$ based upon their attractiveness scores and identify the best one.

Next, consider the following linear programming problem for determining the progress measure for $DMU_q \in \mathbf{E}^{l_o}$, $l_o \in \{2, ..., L\}$.

$$P_q^*(g) = \max_{\lambda_j, P_q(g)} P_q(g) \qquad g = 1,..., l_o - 1$$
subject to
$$\sum_{j \in F(E^{l_o-g})} \lambda_j y_j \geq P_q(g) y_q \qquad (6.11)$$
$$\sum_{j \in F(E^{l_o-g})} \lambda_j x_j \leq x_q$$
$$\lambda_j \geq 0 \quad j \in F(E^{l_o-g})$$

Similar to Theorem 6.2, we have

Theorem 6.4 For a specific $DMU_q \in \mathbf{E}^{l_o}$, $l_o \in \{2, ..., L\}$, we have
(i) $P_q^*(g) > 1$ for each $g = 1, ..., l_o\text{-}1$.
(ii) $P_q^*(g + 1) > P_q^*(g)$.

Definition 6.5 The optimal value to (6.11), i.e., $P_q^*(g)$, is called the (output-oriented) *g-degree* progress of DMU_q from a specific level $\mathbf{E}^{l_o}$.

For a larger $P_q^*(g)$, more progress is expected for DMU_q. Thus, a smaller value of $P_q^*(g)$ is preferred. To obtain the efficient target, we consider

$$\max \| S^+(g) \|_1 + \| S^-(g) \|_1 \qquad g = 1,..., l_o - 1$$
subject to
$$S^+(g) = \sum_{j \in F(E^{l_o-g})} \lambda_j y_j - P_q^*(g) y_q$$
$$S^-(g) = x_q - \sum_{j \in F(E^{l_o-g})} \lambda_j x_j \qquad (6.12)$$
$$S^+(g), S^-(g) \geq 0$$
$$\lambda_j \geq 0 \quad j \in F(E^{l_o-g})$$

Definition 6.6 (Global Efficient Target and Local Efficient Target)
The following point

$$\begin{cases} \hat{y}_q = P_q^*(g)y_q + S^{+*}(g) \\ \hat{x}_q = x_q - S^{-*}(g) \end{cases}$$

is the *global efficient target* for $DMU_q \in \mathbf{E}^{l_o}$, $l_o \in \{2, \ldots, L\}$ if $g = l_o - 1$; otherwise, if $g < l_o - 1$, it represents a *local efficient target*, where $P_q^*(g)$ is the optimal value to (6.11), and $S^{+*}(g)$ and $S^{-*}(g)$ represent the optimal values in (6.12).

The relationship between the input-oriented and output-oriented context-dependent DEA can be summarized in the following Theorem.

Theorem 6.5 $H_q^*(d) = 1/\Omega_q^*(d)$, and $G_q^*(g) = 1/P_q^*(g)$.

Theorem 6.5 indicates that the output-oriented attractiveness and progress measures can be obtained from the input-oriented context-dependent DEA. However, Theorem 6.5 is not necessarily true when the frontiers do not exhibit CRS.

	A	B	C	D	E	F	G	H	I	J	K	L
1	FMS (Level1)	TC	WIP	TT	EMP	SR		VF	PF	RF	Attractiveness	input-oriented
2	1	1.19	88	12.33	5	5.3	16	819	88	2	0.190208157	5.257398084
3	2	4.91	297	34.84	14	1.1		841	14	4	0.257524313	3.88312851
4	5	1.31	377	20.82	3	9.8	Score	628	51	8	0.253652805	3.942398767
5	6	3.04	173	38.87	4	1.6	0.828	266	13	5	0.310361728	3.222046761
6	9	3.06	898	27.67	2	3.9		354	86	5	0.269767442	3.706896552
7	10	1.44	423	6.02	10	5.4		694	20	3	0.186997849	5.347655092
8	11	2.47	470	4	13	5.3		513	40	5	0.095638588	10.45603059
9	12	2.85	87	43.09	8	2.4		884	17	7	0.216173255	4.62591916
10	14	1.31	852	86.87	3	0.5		401	18	4	0.208333333	4.8
11	16	1.99	273	91.08	3	2.5		937	8	3	0.299859601	3.334694047
12	18	4.04	108	23.39	11	2.9		815	91	3	0.283369718	3.528958618
13	19	3.76	855	54.98	1	9.4		499	46	3	0.20637561	4.845533835
14	20	4.76	416	1.55	8	1.5		58	2	8	0.034364281	29.1
15	21	3.6	680	3.98	6	3.9		592	29	4	0.108160605	9.245510401
16	22	3.24	771	52.26	8	1.8		535	61	1	0.558720872	1.789802475
17	24	1.8	849	62.83	15	7.3		923	60	3	0.627516581	1.593583388
18	DMU under evaluation	1.8	849	62.83	15	7.3		579.2	37.85	1.88		Attractiveness
19		IV	IV	IV	IV	IV		AI	AI	AI		
20	Evaluation background	1.8	770	38.208	11.75	7.3		570.2	37.85	2.08		
21	FMS(Level2)	TC	WIP	TT	EMP	SR		VF	PF	RF	λ	
22	3	4.8	418	16.68	12	6.3		555	39	1	0	
23	4	3.89	147	40.83	10	3.8		778	31	2	0.0519893	
24	7	1.83	202	49.87	13	4.3		46	80	4	0.111437381	
25	8	2.07	533	30.07	14	8.8		226	21	4	0	
26	13	4.85	915	54.79	5	2.4		439	58	4	0	
27	15	4.18	924	54.46	4	6		481	27	4	0	
28	17	1.8	983	37.93	13	8.8		709	39	2	0.752643173	

Figure 6.10. Output-oriented First Degree Attractiveness Spreadsheet Model

Figure 6.10 shows the output-oriented spreadsheet for the first-degree attractiveness for DMUs in the first-level CRS frontier. This spreadsheet is similar to the one shown in Figure 6.3. The formula for cell B18 is changed to

Cell B18 =INDEX(B2:B17,$G$2,1)

and is copied into cells C18:F18.
   The formula for cell H18 is changed to

Cell H18 =$G$5*INDEX(H2:H17,$G$2,1)

where cell G5 represents the output-oriented attractiveness measure. This formula is then copied into cells I18:J18.
   To obtain the Solver parameters for the model shown in Figure 6.10, we change the "Min" to "Max" in Figure 6.4, as shown in Figure 6.11. The results are reported in cells K2:K17. Cells L2:L17 report the input-oriented attractiveness scores. It can be seen that Theorem 6.5 is true.

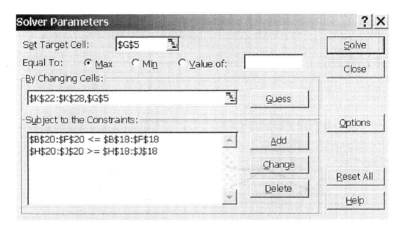

Figure 6.11. Solver Parameters for Output-oriented First Degree Attractiveness

   Finally, the discussion in this chapter is based upon CRS frontier. Similar discussion can be obtained for other RTS frontiers. However, the related context-dependent DEA may be infeasible. See Chapters 7 and 10 for the discussion on infeasibility of DEA-type models. The DEA Excel Solver discussed in Chapter 12 allows you to calculate the context-dependent DEA under non-CRS assumptions.

Chapter 7

Benchmarking Models

7.1   Introduction

Gap analysis is often used as a fundamental method in performance evaluation and benchmarking. However, gap analysis only deals one measure at a time. It is rare that one single measure can suffice for the purpose of performance evaluation (Camp, 1995). As a result, some multi-factor based gap analysis methods have been developed. e.g., Spider charts, AHP maturity index, and Z charts. Although gaps can be identified with respect to individual performance measures, it remains a challenging task to combine the multiple measures in the final stage. Therefore, benchmarking models that can deal with multiple performance measures and provide an integrated benchmarking measure are needed.

Benchmarking is a process of defining valid measures of performance comparison among peer DMUs, using them to determine the relative positions of the peer DMUs and, ultimately, establishing a standard of excellence. In that sense, DEA can be regarded as a benchmarking tool, because the frontier identified can be regarded as an empirical standard of excellence.

Once the frontier is established, we may compare a set of new DMUs to the frontier. However, when a new DMU outperforms the identified frontier, a new frontier is generated by DEA. As a result, we do not have the same benchmark (frontier) for other (new) DMUs.

In the current chapter, we present a number of DEA-based benchmarking models where each (new) DMU is evaluated against a set of given benchmarks (standards).

7.2   Variable-benchmark Model

Let E^* represent the set of benchmarks or the best-practice identified by the DEA. Based upon the input-oriented CRS envelopment model, we have

$$\min \delta^{CRS}$$
subject to
$$\sum_{j \in E^*} \lambda_j x_{ij} \le \delta^{CRS} x_i^{new} \qquad\qquad (7.1)$$
$$\sum_{j \in E^*} \lambda_j y_{rj} \ge y_r^{new}$$
$$\lambda_j \ge 0, j \in E^*$$

where a new observation is represented by DMU^{new} with inputs x_i^{new} ($i = 1$, ..., m) and outputs y_r^{new} ($r = 1$, ..., s). The superscript of CRS indicates that the benchmark frontier composed by benchmark DMUs in set E^* exhibits CRS.

Model (7.1) measures the performance of DMU^{new} with respect to benchmark DMUs in set E^* when outputs are fixed at their current levels. Similarly, based upon the output-oriented CRS envelopment model, we can have a model that measures the performance of DMU^{new} in terms of outputs when inputs are fixed at their current levels.

$$\max \tau^{CRS}$$
subject to
$$\sum_{j \in E^*} \lambda_j x_{ij} \le x_i^{new} \qquad\qquad (7.2)$$
$$\sum_{j \in E^*} \lambda_j y_{rj} \ge \tau^{CRS} y_r^{new}$$
$$\lambda_j \ge 0, j \in E^*$$

Theorem 7.1 $\delta^{CRS*} = 1/\tau^{CRS*}$, where δ^{CRS*} is the optimal value to model (7.1) and τ_o^{CRS*} is the optimal value to model (7.2).

[Proof]: Suppose λ_j^* ($j \in E^*$) is an optimal solution associated with δ^{CRS*} in model (7.1). Now, let $\tau^{CRS*} = 1/\delta^{CRS*}$, and $\lambda_j' = \lambda_j^* \delta_o^{CRS*}$. Then τ^{CRS*} and λ_j' are optimal in model (7.2). Thus, $\delta^{CRS*} = 1/\tau^{CRS*}$. ∎

Model (7.1) or (7.2) yields a benchmark for DMU^{new}. The ith input and the rth output for the benchmark can be expressed as

$$\begin{cases} \sum_{j \in E^*} \lambda_j^* x_{ij} & (ith \quad input) \\ \sum_{j \in E^*} \lambda_j^* y_{ij} & (rth \quad output) \end{cases} \qquad (7.3)$$

Note also that although the DMUs associated with set E^* are given, the resulting benchmark may be different for each new DMU under evaluation. Because for each new DMU under evaluation, (7.3) may represent a different combination of DMUs associated with set E^*. Thus, models (7.1) and (7.2) represent a variable-benchmark scenario.

Theorem 7.2
(i) $\delta^{CRS*} < 1$ or $\tau^{CRS*} > 1$ indicates that the performance of DMU_o^{new} is dominated by the benchmark in (7.3).
(ii) $\delta^{CRS*} = 1$ or $\tau^{CRS*} = 1$ indicates that DMU^{new} achieve the same performance level of the benchmark in (7.3).
(iii) $\delta^{CRS*} > 1$ or $\tau^{CRS*} < 1$ indicates that input savings or output surpluses exist in DMU_o^{new} when compared to the benchmark in (7.3).

[Proof]: (i) and (ii) are obvious results in terms of DEA efficiency concept.
Now, $\delta^{CRS*} > 1$ indicates that DMU^{new} can increase its inputs to reach the benchmark. This in turn indicates that $\delta^{CRS*} - 1$ measures the input saving achieved by DMU^{new}. Similarly, $\tau^{CRS*} < 1$ indicates that DMU^{new} can decrease its outputs to reach the benchmark. This in turn indicates that $1 - \tau^{CRS*}$ measures the output surplus achieved by DMU^{new}. ∎

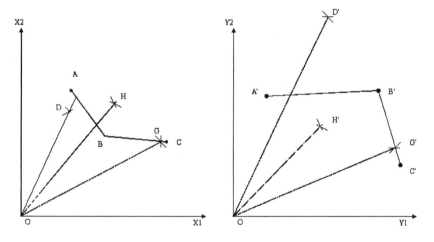

Figure 7.1. Variable-benchmark Model

Figure 7.1 illustrates the three cases described in Theorem 7.2. ABC (A'B'C') represents the input (output) benchmark frontier. D, H and G (or D', H', and G') represent the new DMUs to be benchmarked against ABC (or A'B'C'). We have $\delta_D^{CRS*} > 1$ for DMU D ($\tau_{D'}^{CRS*} < 1$ for DMU D') indicating that DMU D can increase its input values by δ_D^{CRS*} while producing the same amount of outputs generated by the benchmark (DMU D' can decrease its output levels while using the same amount of input levels consumed by the benchmark). Thus, $\delta_D^{CRS*} > 1$ is a measure of input savings achieved by DMU D and $\tau_{D'}^{CRS*} < 1$ is a measure of output surpluses achieved by DMU D'.

For DMU G and DMU G', we have $\delta_G^{CRS*} = 1$ and $\tau_{G'}^{CRS*} = 1$ indicating that they achieve the same performance level of the benchmark and no input savings or output surpluses exist. For DMU H and DMU H', we have $\delta_H^{CRS*} < 1$ and $\tau_{H'}^{CRS*} > 1$ indicating that inefficiency exists in the performance of these two DMUs.

Note that for example, in Figure 7.1, a convex combination of DMU A and DMU B is used as the benchmark for DMU D while a convex combination of DMU B and DMU C is used as the benchmark for DMU G. Thus, models (7.1) and (7.2) are called variable-benchmark models.

From Theorem 7.2, we can define $\delta^{CRS*} - 1$ or $1 - \tau^{CRS*}$ as the performance gap between DMU^{new} and the benchmark. Based upon δ^{CRS*} or τ^{CRS*}, a ranking of the benchmarking performance can be obtained.

It is likely that scale inefficiency may be allowed in the benchmarking. We therefore modify models (7.1) and (7.2) to incorporate scale inefficiency by assuming VRS.

$$\min \delta^{VRS}$$
subject to
$$\sum_{j \in E^*} \lambda_j x_{ij} \leq \delta^{VRS} x_i^{new}$$
$$\sum_{j \in E^*} \lambda_j y_{rj} \geq y_r^{new} \tag{7.4}$$
$$\sum_{j \in E^*} \lambda_j = 1$$
$$\lambda_j \geq 0, j \in E^*$$

$$\max \tau^{VRS}$$
subject to
$$\sum_{j \in E^*} \lambda_j x_{ij} \leq x_i^{new}$$
$$\sum_{j \in E^*} \lambda_j y_{rj} \geq \tau^{VRS} y_r^{new} \tag{7.5}$$
$$\sum_{j \in E^*} \lambda_j = 1$$
$$\lambda_j \geq 0, j \in E^*$$

Similar to Theorem 7.2, we have

Theorem 7.3
(i) $\delta^{VRS*} < 1$ or $\tau^{VRS*} > 1$ indicates that the performance of DMU^{new} is dominated by the benchmark in (7.3).

(ii) $\delta^{VRS*} = 1$ or $\tau^{VRS*} = 1$ indicates that DMU^{new} achieve the same performance level of the benchmark in (7.3).

(iii) $\delta^{VRS*} > 1$ or $\tau^{VRS*} < 1$ indicates that input savings or output surpluses exist in DMU^{new} when compared to the benchmark in (7.3).

Note that model (7.2) is always feasible, and model (7.1) is infeasible only if certain patterns of zero data are present (Zhu 1996b). Thus, if we assume that all the data are positive, (7.1) is always feasible. However, unlike models (7.1) and (7.2), models (7.4) and (7.5) may be infeasible.

Theorem 7.4

(i) If model (7.4) is infeasible, then the output vector of DMU^{new} dominates the output vector of the benchmark in (7.3).

(ii) If model (7.5) is infeasible, then the input vector of DMU^{new} dominates the input vector of the benchmark in (7.3).

[Proof]: The proof follows directly from the necessary and sufficient conditions for infeasibility in super-efficiency DEA model provided in Seiford and Zhu (1999c) (see also Chapter 10). ■

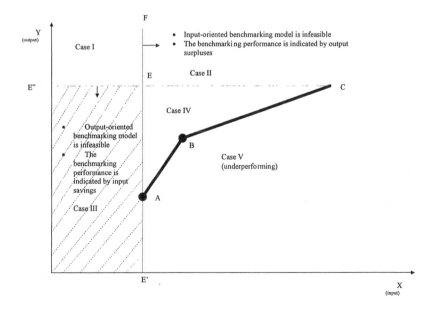

Figure 7.2. Infeasibility of VRS Variable-benchmark Model

The implication of the infeasibility associated with models (7.4) and (7.5) needs to be carefully examined. Consider Figure 7.2 where ABC represents the benchmark frontier. Models (7.4) and (7.5) yield finite optimal values for any DMU^{new} located below EC and to the right of EA. Model (7.4) is infeasible for DMU^{new} located above ray E"C and model (7.5) is infeasible for DMU^{new} located to the left of ray E'E.

Both models (7.4) and (7.5) are infeasible for DMU^{new} located above E"E and to the left of ray EF. Note that if DMU^{new} is located above E"C, its output value is greater than the output value of any convex combinations of A, B and C.

Note also that if DMU^{new} is located to the left of E'F, its input value is less than the input value of any convex combinations of A, B and C.

Based upon Theorem 7.4 and Figure 7.2, we have four cases:

Case I: When both models (7.4) and (7.5) are infeasible, this indicates that DMU^{new} has the smallest input level and the largest output level compared to the benchmark. Thus, both input savings and output surpluses exist in DMU^{new}.

Case II: When model (7.4) is infeasible and model (7.5) is feasible, the infeasibility of model (7.4) is caused by the fact that DMU^{new} has the largest output level compared to the benchmark. Thus, we use model (7.5) to characterize the output surpluses.

Case III: When model (7.5) is infeasible and model (7.4) is feasible, the infeasibility of model (7.5) is caused by the fact that DMU^{new} has the smallest input level compared to the benchmark. Thus, we use model (7.4) to characterize the input savings.

Case IV: When both models (7.4) and (7.5) are feasible, we use both of them to determine whether input savings and output surpluses exist.

If we change the constraint $\sum \lambda_j = 1$ to $\sum \lambda_j \leq 1$ and $\sum \lambda_j \geq 1$, then we obtain the NIRS and NDRS variable-benchmark models, respectively. Infeasibility may be associated with these two types of RTS frontiers, and we should apply the four cases discussed above. Table 7.1 summarizes the variable-benchmark models.

We next use 22 internet companies to illustrate the variable-benchmark models. Table 7.2 presents the data. We have four inputs: (1) number of website visitors (thousand), (2) number of employees (person), (3) marketing expenditure ($ million), and (4) development expenditure ($ million), and two outputs: (1) number of customers, and (2) revenue ($ million).

Table 7.1. Variable-benchmark Models

Frontier Type	Input-Oriented	Output-Oriented
CRS	$\min \delta^{Frontier}$ subject to $\sum_{j \in E^*} \lambda_j x_{ij} \leq \delta^{Frontier} x_i^{new}$ $\sum_{j \in E^*} \lambda_j y_{rj} \geq y_r^{new}$ $\lambda_j \geq 0, j \in E^*$	$\max \tau^{Frontier}$ subject to $\sum_{j \in E^*} \lambda_j x_{ij} \leq x_i^{new}$ $\sum_{j \in E^*} \lambda_j y_{rj} \geq \tau^{Frontier} y_r^{new}$ $\lambda_j \geq 0, j \in E^*$
VRS	Add $\sum \lambda_j = 1$	
NIRS	Add $\sum \lambda_j \leq 1$	
NDRS	Add $\sum \lambda_j \geq 1$	

Table 7.2. Data for the Internet Companies

Company	Visitors	Employee	Marketing	Development	Customers	Revenue
Barnes&Noble	64812	1237	111.55	21.01	4700000	202.57
Amazon.com	177744	7600	413.2	159.7	16900000	1640
CDnow	79848	502	89.73	23.42	3260000	147.19
eBay	168384	300	95.96	23.79	10010000	224.7
1-800-Flowers	11940	2100	92.15	8.07	7800000	52.89
Buy.com	27372	255	71.3	7.84	1950000	596.9
FTD.com	11856	75	29.93	5.29	1800000	62.6
Autobytel.com	12000	225	44.18	14.26	2065000	40.3
Beyond.com	17076	250	81.35	10.39	2000000	117.28
eToys	13896	940	120.46	43.43	1900000	151.04
E*Trade	29532	2400	301.7	78.5	1551000	621.4
Garden.com	16344	290	16	4.8	1070000	8.2
Drugstore.com	19092	408	61.5	14.9	695000	34.8
Outpost.com	7716	164	41.67	7	627000	188.6
iPrint	42132	225	8.13	3.54	380000	3.26
Furniture.com	10668	213	33.949	6.685	260000	10.904
PlanetRX.com	17124	390	55.18	12.95	254000	8.99
NextCard	46836	365	24.65	22.05	220000	26.56
PetsMart.com	18564	72	33.47	2.43	180000	10.45
Peapod	2076	1020	7.17	3.54	111900	73.13
Webvan	1680	1000	11.75	15.24	47000	13.31
CarsDirect.com	15612	702	33.43	2.14	12885	98.56

Suppose we select the first seven companies (Barnes & Noble, Amazon.com, CDnow, eBay, 1-800-Flowers, Buy.com, and FTD.com) as the benchmarks. If we apply the output-oriented CRS envelopment model to the seven companies, the top three companies (Barnes & Noble, Amazon.com, and CDnow) are not on the best-practice frontier, and therefore can be excluded. However, if we include them in the benchmark set, the benchmarking results will not be affected. Because λ_j^* related to the three companies must be equal to zero.

The spreadsheet model of the variable-benchmark models is very similar to the context-dependent DEA spreadsheet model. In fact, the evaluation background now is the selected benchmarks. Figure 7.3 shows the spreadsheet model for the output-oriented CRS variable-benchmark model where the benchmarks (evaluation background) are entered in rows 2-8.

Cell F2 is reserved to indicate the DMU under benchmarking. Cell F4 is the target cell which represent the τ_o^{CRS} in model (7.2). Cells I2:I8 represent the λ_j for the benchmarks. Cell B9 contains the formula "=SUMPRODUCT (B2:B8,$I$2:$I$8)". This formula is then copied into cells C9:E9. Cell G9 contains the formula "=SUMPRODUCT(G2:G8,$I$2:$I$8)". This formula is then copied into cell H9.

	A	B	C	D	E	F	G	H	I
1	Company	Visitors	Employee	Marketing	Development		Customers	Revenue	λ
2	Barnes&Noble	84812	1237	111.55	21.01	15	4700000	202.57	0
3	Amazon.com	177744	7800	413.2	159.7	Score	16900000	1640	0
4	Cdnow	79848	502	89.73	23.42		3260000	147.19	0
5	eBay	168384	300	95.96	23.79		10010000	224.7	0
6	1-800-Flowers	11940	2100	92.15	8.07		7800000	52.89	0
7	Buy.com	27372	255	71.3	7.84		1950000	596.9	0.272859184
8	FTD.com	11856	75	29.93	5.29		1800000	82.6	0
9	**Benchmarks**	7471.438778	69.6045918	19.46199	2.14		532270.41	162.929337	
10		I^	I^	I^	I^		V I	V I	Benchmarking
11	**DMU under evaluation**	15612	702	33.43	2.14		21300.187	162.929337	Score
12	Autobytel.com	12000	225	44.18	14.26		2065000	40.3	1.095779422
13	Beyond.com	17076	250	81.35	10.39		2000000	117.28	1.327240986
14	eToys	13896	940	120.46	43.43	Variable	1900000	151.04	1.600761668
15	E*Trade	28532	2400	301.7	78.5	Benchmark	1551000	621.4	1.036374356
16	Garden.com	16344	290	16	4.8		1070000	8.2	1.42713759
17	Drugstore.com	19092	408	61.5	14.9		885000	34.8	4.852307242
18	Outpost.com	7718	184	41.67	7		627000	188.6	0.890769639
19	iPrint	42132	225	8.13	3.54		380000	3.28	2.231776947
20	Furniture.com	10668	213	33.949	6.685		260000	10.804	7.369719663
21	PlanetRX.com	17124	390	55.18	12.95		254000	8.99	12.93451824
22	NextCard	46836	365	24.65	22.05		220000	26.58	5.917828607
23	PetsMart.com	18564	72	33.47	2.43		180000	10.45	5.549682175
24	Peapod	2076	1020	7.17	3.54		111900	73.13	0.619051581
25	Webvan	1680	1000	11.75	15.24		47000	13.31	2.732644609
26	CarsDirect.com	15612	702	33.43	2.14		12885	98.56	1.653097976

Figure 7.3. Output-oriented CRS Variable-benchmark Spreadsheet Model

Cells B11:E11, and Cells G11:H11 contain the formulas for the DMU under benchmarking – the right-hand-side of model (7.2). The formula for B11 is "=INDEX(B12:B26,$F$2,1)", and is copied into cells C11:E11. The formula for cell G11 is "=$F$4*INDEX(G12:G26,$F$2,1)", and is copied into cell H11.

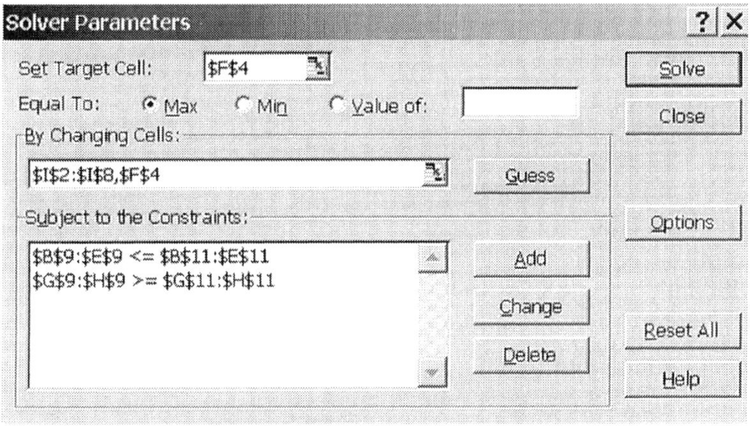

Figure 7.4. Solver Parameters for Output-oriented CRS Variable-benchmark Model

Figure 7.4 shows the Solver parameters for the spreadsheet model shown in Figure 7.3. A VBA procedure "VariableBenchmark" is used to record the benchmarking scores into cells I12:I26.

```
Sub VariableBenchmark()
Dim i As Integer
For i = 1 To 15
Range("F2") = i
SolverSolve UserFinish:=True
Range("I" & i + 11) = Range("F4")
Next
End Sub
```

Because the model in Figure 7.3 is an output-oriented model, a smaller score (τ^{CRS*}) indicates a better performance. Thus, Peapod is the best company with respective to the specified benchmarks. The non-zero optimal λ_j^* indicates the actual benchmark for a company under benchmarking. For example, Buy.com is used as the actual benchmark for CarsDirect.com (see cell I7 in Figure 7.3).

If we use the input-oriented CRS variable-benchmark model, we need change the formula for cell B11 in Figure 7.3 to "=$F$4*INDEX (B12:B26,$F$2,1)". This formula is then copied into cells C11:E11. The formula for cell G11 is changed to "=INDEX(G12:G26,$F$2,1)" and is copied into cell H11. All the other formulas in Figure 7.3 remain unchanged.

We also need to change the Solver parameters shown in Figure 7.4 by selecting "Min", as shown in Figure 7.5. Figure 7.6 shows the spreadsheet model for the input-oriented CRS variable-benchmark model and the benchmarking scores. It can be seen that Theorem 7.1 is true.

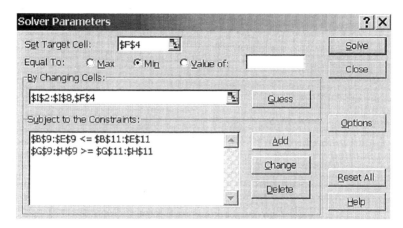

Figure 7.5. Solver Parameters for Input-oriented CRS Variable-benchmark Model

	A	B	C	D	E	F	G	H	I
1	Company	Visitors	Employee	Marketing	Development		Customers	Revenue	λ
2	Barnes&Noble	84812	1237	111.55	21.01	15	4700000	202.57	0
3	Amazon.com	177744	7800	413.2	159.7	Score	16900000	1840	0
4	Cdnow	79848	502	89.73	23.42		3260000	147.19	0
5	eBay	168394	300	95.96	23.79		10010000	224.7	0
6	1-800-Flowers	11940	2100	92.15	8.07		7800000	52.89	0
7	Buy.com	27372	255	71.3	7.84		1950000	598.6	0.165119786
8	FTD.com	11858	75	29.93	5.29		1800000	82.8	0
9	Benchmarks	4519.65877	42.1055453	11.77304	1.294539118		321983.58	98.58	input-oriented
10		≥	≥	≥	≥		≤	≤	Benchmarking
11	DMU under evaluation	9444.088318	424.657225	20.22284	1.294539119		12885	98.56	Score
12	Autobytel.com	12000	225	44.18	14.26		2065000	40.3	0.912592425
13	Beyond.com	17076	250	81.35	10.39		2000000	117.28	0.753442678
14	eToys	13898	940	120.48	43.43	Variable	1900000	151.04	0.624702615
15	E*Trade	29532	2400	301.7	78.5	Benchmark	1551000	821.4	0.9849023
16	Garden.com	18344	290	18	4.8		1070000	8.2	0.700703287
17	Drugstore.com	18092	408	81.5	14.8		885000	34.8	0.206087527
18	Outpost.com	7716	184	41.67	7		627000	188.6	1.122624702
19	iPrint	42132	225	8.13	3.54		380000	3.26	0.448073452
20	Furniture.com	10868	213	33.848	6.685		260000	10.904	0.135690371
21	PlanetRX.com	17124	380	55.18	12.95		254000	8.99	0.077312505
22	NextCard	46836	365	24.65	22.05		220000	26.56	0.168980899
23	PetsMart.com	18564	72	33.47	2.43		180000	10.45	0.180163681
24	Peapod	2076	1020	7.17	3.54		111900	73.13	1.615374328
25	Webvan	1880	1000	11.75	15.24		47000	13.31	0.365819085
26	CarsDirect.com	15812	702	33.43	2.14		12885	98.56	0.604924822

Figure 7.6. Input-oriented CRS Variable-benchmark Spreadsheet Model

We now consider the input-oriented VRS variable-benchmark model. We need to add a cell representing $\sum \lambda_j$ in the spreadsheet shown in Figure 7.6. We select cell I9, and enter the formula "=SUM(I2:I8)". We also need to add an additional constraint on $\sum \lambda_j = 1$ in the Solver parameters shown in Figure 7.5. This constraint is "$I$9 = 1", as shown in Figure 7.7.

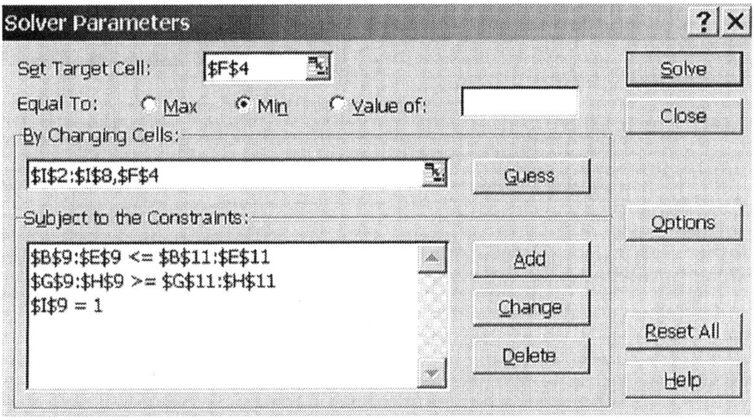

Figure 7.7. Solver Parameters for Input-oriented VRS Variable-benchmark Model

Figure 7.8. Input-oriented VRS Variable-benchmark Spreadsheet Model

Figure 7.8 shows the spreadsheet for the input-oriented VRS variable-benchmark model and the benchmarking scores in cells I12:I26. The button "VRS Variable Benchmark" is linked to the VBA procedure "VRSVariableBenchmark".

```
Sub VRSVariableBenchmark()
Dim i As Integer
For i = 1 To 15
```

```
Range("F2") = i
SolverSolve UserFinish:=True
If SolverSolve(UserFinish:=True) = 5 Then
Range("I" & i + 11) = "Infeasible"
Else
Range("I" & i + 11) = Range("F4")
End If
Next
End Sub
```

Because of the VRS frontier, the model may be infeasible. The SolverSolve function returns an integer value that indicates Solver's "success". If this value is 5, it means that there are no feasible solutions. This is represented by the statement "SolverSolve(UserFinish:=True) = 5". In the procedure, if the Solver returns a value of 5, then the procedure records "infeasible". Otherwise, the procedure records the optimal value in cell F4 of Figure 7.8.

7.3   Fixed-benchmark Model

Although the benchmark frontier is given in the variable-benchmark models, a DMU^{new} under benchmarking has the freedom to choose a subset of benchmarks so that the performance of DMU^{new} can be characterized in the most favorable light. Situations when the same benchmark should be fixed are likely to occur. For example, the management may indicate that DMUs A and B in Figure 7.1 should be used as the fixed benchmark. i.e., DMU C in Figure 7.1 may not be used in constructing the benchmark.

To couple with this situation, we turn to the multiplier models. For example, the input-oriented CRS multiplier model determines a set of referent best-practice DMUs represented by a set of binding constraints in optimality. Let set $B = \{DMU_j : j \in I_B\}$ be the selected subset of benchmark set E^*. i.e., $I_B \subset E^*$. Based upon the input-oriented CRS multiplier model, we have

$$\tilde{\sigma}^{CRS^*} = \max \sum_{r=1}^{s} \mu_r y_r^{new}$$

subject to

$$\sum_{r=1}^{s} \mu_r y_{rj} - \sum_{i=1}^{s} v_i x_{ij} = 0 \quad j \in I_B$$

$$\sum_{r=1}^{s} \mu_r y_{rj} - \sum_{i=1}^{s} v_i x_{ij} \leq 0 \quad j \notin I_B \qquad (7.6)$$

$$\sum_{i=1}^{m} v_i x_i^{new} = 1$$

$$\mu_r, v_i \geq 0.$$

By applying equalities in the constraints associated with benchmark DMUs, model (7.6) measures DMU^{new}'s performance against the benchmark constructed by set **B**. At optimality, some $DMU_j \, j \notin \mathbf{I}_B$, may join the fixed-benchmark set if the associated constraints are binding.

Note that model (7.6) may be infeasible. For example, the DMUs in set **B** may not be fit into the same facet when they number greater than m+s-1, where m is the number of inputs and s is the number of outputs. In this case, we need to adjust the set **B**.

Three possible cases are associated with model (7.6). $\widetilde{\sigma}^{CRS*} > 1$ indicating that DMU^{new} outperforms the benchmark. $\widetilde{\sigma}^{CRS*} = 1$ indicating that DMU^{new} achieves the same performance level of the benchmark. $\widetilde{\sigma}^{CRS*} < 1$ indicating that the benchmark outperforms DMU^{new}.

By applying RTS frontier type and model orientation, we obtain the fixed-benchmark models in Table 7.3

Table 7.3. Fixed-benchmark Models

Frontier Type	Input-Oriented	Output-Oriented
	$\max \sum_{r=1}^{s} \mu_r y_r^{new} + \mu$ subject to $\sum_{r=1}^{s} \mu_r y_{rj} - \sum_{i=1}^{s} v_i x_{ij} + \mu = 0 \quad j \in \mathbf{I}_B$ $\sum_{r=1}^{s} \mu_r y_{rj} - \sum_{i=1}^{s} v_i x_{ij} + \mu \le 0 \quad j \notin \mathbf{I}_B$ $\sum_{i=1}^{m} v_i x_i^{new} = 1$ $\mu_r, v_i \ge 0$	$\min \sum_{i=1}^{m} v_i x_i^{new} + v$ subject to $\sum_{i=1}^{s} v_i x_{ij} - \sum_{r=1}^{s} \mu_r y_{rj} + v = 0 \quad j \in \mathbf{I}_B$ $\sum_{i=1}^{s} v_i x_{ij} - \sum_{r=1}^{s} \mu_r y_{rj} + v \ge 0 \quad j \notin \mathbf{I}_B$ $\sum_{r=1}^{s} \mu_r y_r^{new} = 1$ $\mu_r, v_i \ge 0$
CRS	where $\mu = 0$	where $v = 0$
VRS	where μ free	where v free
NIRS	where $\mu \le 0$	where $v \ge 0$
NDRS	where $\mu \ge 0$	where $v \le 0$

DMU^{new} is not included in the constraints of $\sum_{r=1}^{s} \mu_r y_{rj} - \sum_{i=1}^{m} v_i x_{ij} + \mu \le 0$ ($j \notin \mathbf{I}_B$) ($\sum_{i=1}^{m} v_i x_{ij} - \sum_{r=1}^{s} \mu_r y_{rj} + v \ge 0$ ($j \notin \mathbf{I}_B$)). However, other peer DMUs (($j \notin \mathbf{I}_B$) are included.

Figure 7.9 shows the output-oriented CRS fixed-benchmark spreadsheet model where 1-800-Flowers and Buy.com are two fixed benchmarks. Cells B5:E5 and G5:H5 are reserved for input and output multipliers, respectively. They are the changing cells in the Solver parameters.

Cell C7 is the target cell and contains the formula "=SUMPRODUCT (B5:E5,INDEX(B10:E24,C6,0))", where cell C6 indicates the DMU under evaluation – Autobytel.com.

Cell C8 contains the formula representing $\sum_{r=1}^{s} \mu_r y_r^{new}$

Cell C8=SUMPRODUCT(G5:H5,INDEX (G10:H24,C6,0))

The formula for cell I2 is "=SUMPRODUCT(B2:E2,$B$5:$E$5)-SUMPRODUCT(G2:H2,$G$5:$H$5)", and is copied into cells I3 and I10:I24.

	A	B	C	D	E	F	G	H	I
1	Company	Visitors	Employee	Marketing	Development		Customers	Revenue	**Constraints**
2	1-800-Flowers	11940	2100	92.15	8.07		7800000	52.89	4.885E-15
3	Buy.com	27372	255	71.3	7.84		1950000	596.9	4.5519E-15
4									Equality
5	Multipliers	3.4E-06	0.001489	0.008619	0		4.843E-07	0	constraint
6	DMU under evaluation		1	Weighted Input					on benchmark
7	Score		0.688082	Target cell Min					Constraint not
8	Weighted output		1	Weighted Output = 1					included
9									
10	Autobytel.com	12000	225	44.18	14.28		2085000	40.3	-0.3319178
11	Beyond.com	17078	250	81.35	10.39		2000000	117.29	9.5479E-15
12	eToys	13896	940	120.46	43.43		1900000	Constraints for other	.32392744
13	E*Trade	29532	2400	301.7	78.5		1551000	DMUs	.91942618
14	Garden.com	16344	280	18	4.8		1070000	8.2	0.07489194
15	Drugstore.com	19092	408	61.5	14.9		695000	34.8	0.74285995
16	Outpost.com	7716	164	41.67	7		627000	188.6	0.24250252
17	iPrint	42132	225	8.13	3.54		380000	3.26	0.34747683
18	Furniture.com	10668	213	33.949	6.685		260000	10.904	0.45207708
19	PlanetRX.com	17124	390	55.18	12.95		254000	8.99	0.88092163
20	NextCard	46836	385	24.65	22.05		220000	26.56	0.75869065
21	PetsMart.com	18564	72	33.47	2.43		180000	10.45	0.30443708
22	Peapod	2076	1020	7.17	3.54		111900	73.13	1.51906364
23	Webvan	1680	1000	11.75	15.24		47000	13.31	1.54988667
24	CarsDirect.com	15612	702	33.43	2.14		12885	98.56	1.31316454

Figure 7.9. Output-oriented CRS Fixed-benchmark Spreadsheet Model

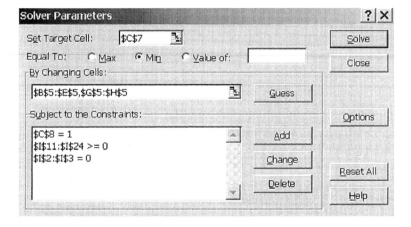

Figure 7.10. Solver Parameters for Output-oriented CRS Fixed-benchmark Model

Figure 7.10 shows the Solver parameters for Autobytel.com. Note that we have "$I$2:$I$3 = 0" for the two benchmarks. Note also that "$I$11:$I$24 >=0" does not include the DMU under evaluation, Autobytel.com.

To solve the remaining DMUs, we need to set up different Solver parameters. Because the constraints change for each DMU under evaluation. For example, if we change the value of cell C6 to 15, i.e., we benchmark CarsDirect.com, we obtain a set of new Solver parameters by removing "$I$24>=0" from the Solver parameters shown in Figure 7.10 and then adding "$I$10>=0", as shown in Figure 7.11.

Because different Solver parameters are used for different DMUs under benchmarking, a set of sophisticated VBA codes is required to automate the calculation. We here do not discuss it, and suggest using the "DEA Excel Solver" – a DEA Add-In for Microsoft® Excel described in Chapter 12 to obtain the scores (see cells J10:J24 in Figure 7.11).

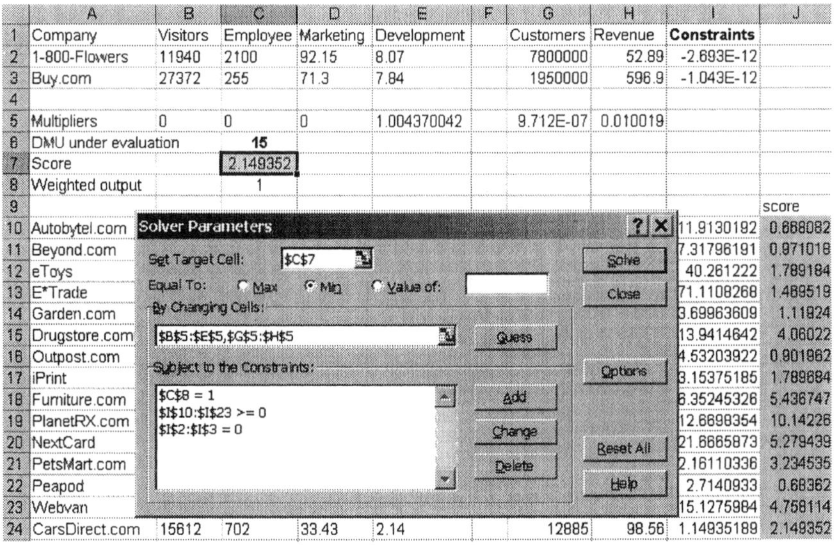

Figure 7.11. Output-oriented CRS Fixed-benchmark Scores for Internet Companies

7.4 Fixed-benchmark Model and Efficiency Ratio

A commonly used measure of efficiency is the ratio of output to input. For example, profit per employee measures the labor productivity. When multiple inputs and outputs are present, we may define the following efficiency ratio

$$\frac{\sum_{r=1}^{s} u_r y_{ro}}{\sum_{i=1}^{m} v_i x_{io}}$$

where v_i and u_r represent the input and output weights, respectively.

DEA calculate the ratio efficiency without the information on the weights. In fact, the multiplier DEA models can be transformed into linear fractional programming problems. For example, if we define $v_i = t v_i$ and $\mu_r = t u_r$, where $t = 1/\sum v_i x_{io}$, the input-oriented CRS multiplier model can be transformed into

$$\max \frac{\sum_{r=1}^{s} u_r y_{ro}}{\sum_{i=1}^{m} v_i x_{io}}$$

subject to   (7.7)

$$\frac{\sum_{r=1}^{s} u_r y_{rj}}{\sum_{i=1}^{m} v_i x_{ij}} \le 1 \quad j = 1,2,\ldots,n$$

$$u_r, v_i \ge 0 \qquad \forall r,i$$

The objective function in (7.7) represents the efficiency ratio of a DMU under evaluation. Because of the constraints in (7.7), the (maximum) efficiency cannot exceed one. Consequently, a DMU with an efficiency score of one is on the frontier. It can be seen that no additional information on the weights or tradeoffs are incorporated into the model (7.7).

If we apply the input-oriented CRS fixed-benchmark model to (7.7), we obtain

$$\max \frac{\sum_{r=1}^{s} u_r y_r^{new}}{\sum_{i=1}^{m} v_i x_i^{new}}$$

subject to   (7.8)

$$\frac{\sum_{r=1}^{s} u_r y_{rj}}{\sum_{i=1}^{m} v_i x_{ij}} = 1 \quad j \in \mathbf{I}_B$$

$$\frac{\sum_{r=1}^{s} u_r y_{rj}}{\sum_{i=1}^{m} v_i x_{ij}} \le 1 \quad j \notin \mathbf{I}_B$$

$$u_r, v_i \ge 0 \qquad \forall r,i$$

It can be seen from (7.8) that the fixed benchmarks incorporate implicit tradeoff information into the efficiency evaluation. i.e., the constraints associated with $\mathbf{I}_B$ can be viewed as incorporation of tradeoffs or weight restrictions in DEA. Model (7.8) yields the (maximum) efficiency under the implicit tradeoff information represented by the benchmarks.

As more DMUs are selected as fixed benchmarks, more complete information on the weights becomes available. For example, if we add FTD.com to the fixed-benchmark set, the benchmarking score for Autobytel.com becomes 1.1395, as shown in Figure 7.12. As expected, the performance of those internet companies becomes worse when the set of fixed benchmarks expands.

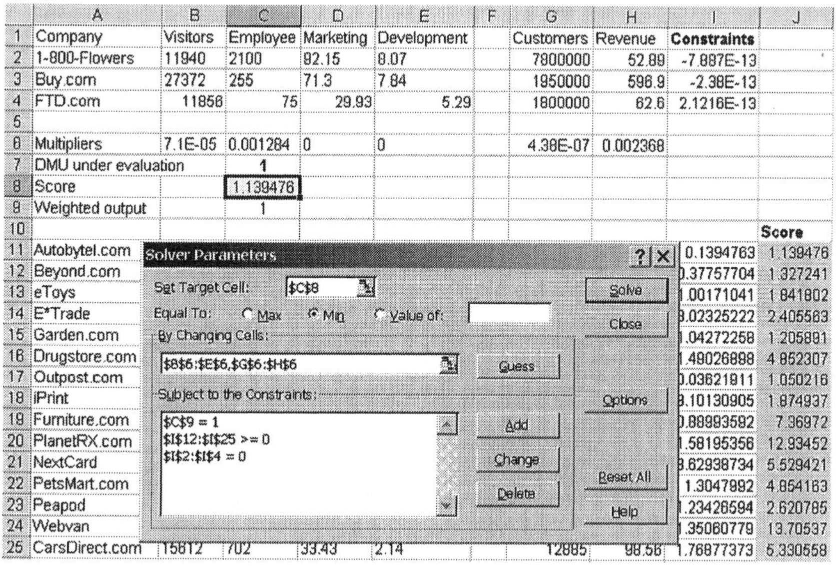

	A	B	C	D	E	F	G	H	I	J
1	Company	Visitors	Employee	Marketing	Development		Customers	Revenue	**Constraints**	
2	1-800-Flowers	11940	2100	82.15	8.07		7800000	52.89	-7.887E-13	
3	Buy.com	27372	255	71.3	7.84		1950000	596.9	-2.38E-13	
4	FTD.com	11856	75	29.93	5.29		1800000	62.6	2.1216E-13	
5										
6	Multipliers	7.1E-05	0.001284	0	0		4.38E-07	0.002368		
7	DMU under evaluation		1							
8	Score		1.139476							
9	Weighted output		1							
10										Score
11	Autobytel.com								0.1394763	1.139476
12	Beyond.com								0.37757704	1.327241
13	eToys								1.00171041	1.841802
14	E*Trade								3.02325222	2.405563
15	Garden.com								1.04272258	1.205891
16	Drugstore.com								1.49026898	4.852307
17	Outpost.com								0.03621911	1.050216
18	iPrint								3.10130905	1.874937
19	Furniture.com								0.88993582	7.36972
20	PlanetRX.com								1.58195356	12.93452
21	NextCard								3.62938734	5.529421
22	PetsMart.com								1.3047882	4.854163
23	Peapod								1.23426594	2.620785
24	Webvan								1.35060779	13.70537
25	CarsDirect.com	15812	702	33.43	2.14		12885	98.56	1.76877373	5.330558

Solver Parameters:
- Set Target Cell: $C$8
- Equal To: Min
- By Changing Cells: $B$6:$E$6,$G$6:$H$6
- Subject to the Constraints:
  - $C$9 = 1
  - $I$12:$I$25 >= 0
  - $I$2:$I$4 = 0

Figure 7.12. Spreadsheet Model and Solver Parameters for Fixed-benchmark Model

Similarly, the output-oriented CRS fixed-benchmark model is equivalent to

$$\min \frac{\sum_{i=1}^{m} v_i x_i^{new}}{\sum_{r=1}^{s} u_r y_r^{new}}$$

subject to

$$\frac{\sum_{i=1}^{m} v_i x_{ij}}{\sum_{r=1}^{s} u_r y_{rj}} = 1 \quad j \in \mathbf{I}_B$$

$$\frac{\sum_{i=1}^{m} v_i x_{ij}}{\sum_{r=1}^{s} u_r y_{rj}} \geq 1 \quad j \notin \mathbf{I}_B$$

$$u_r, v_i \geq 0 \qquad \forall r, i$$

Note that we may define an ideal benchmark whose rth output y_r^{ideal} is the maximum output value across all DMUs, and ith input x_i^{ideal} the minimum input value across all DMUs. If we replace the fixed-benchmark set by the ideal benchmark, we have

$$\max \frac{\sum_{r=1}^{s} u_r y_r^{new}}{\sum_{i=1}^{m} v_i x_i^{new}}$$

subject to

$$\frac{\sum_{r=1}^{s} u_r y_r^{ideal}}{\sum_{i=1}^{m} v_i x_i^{ideal}} = 1 \qquad\qquad\qquad (7.9)$$

$$\frac{\sum_{r=1}^{s} u_r y_{rj}}{\sum_{i=1}^{m} v_i x_{ij}} \leq 1$$

$$u_r, v_i \geq 0 \qquad \forall r, i$$

Because the ideal benchmark dominates all DMUs (unless DMU$_j$ is one of the ideal benchmark), the optimal value to (7.9) must not be greater than one. Further, $\sum u_r y_{rj} / \sum v_i x_{ij} \leq 1$ are redundant, and model (7.9) can be simplified as

$$\max \frac{\sum_{r=1}^{s} u_r y_r^{new}}{\sum_{i=1}^{m} v_i x_i^{new}}$$

subject to   (7.10)

$$\frac{\sum_{r=1}^{s} u_r y_r^{ideal}}{\sum_{i=1}^{m} v_i x_i^{ideal}} = 1$$

$$u_r, v_i \geq 0 \qquad \forall r, i$$

Model (7.10) is equivalent to the following linear programming problem

$$\max \sum_{r=1}^{s} \mu_r y_r^{new}$$
subject to
$$\sum_{r=1}^{s} \mu_r y_r^{ideal} - \sum_{i=1}^{s} v_i x_i^{ideal} = 0 \qquad (7.11)$$
$$\sum_{i=1}^{m} v_i x_i^{new} = 1$$
$$\mu_r, v_i \geq 0.$$

Model (7.10) or (7.11) calculate the maximum efficiency of a specific DMU under evaluation given that the efficiency of the ideal benchmark is set equal to one. If we introduce RTS frontier type and model orientation into (7.10), we obtain other ideal-benchmark models, as shown in Table 7.4.

Table 7.4. Ideal-benchmark Models

Frontier Type	Input-Oriented	Output-Oriented
	$\max \sum_{r=1}^{s} \mu_r y_r^{new} + \mu$ subject to $\sum_{r=1}^{s} \mu_r y_r^{ideal} - \sum_{i=1}^{s} v_i x_i^{ideal} + \mu = 0$ $\sum_{i=1}^{m} v_i x_i^{new} = 1$ $\mu_r, v_i \geq 0.$	$\min \sum_{i=1}^{m} v_i x_i^{new} + v$ subject to $\sum_{i=1}^{s} v_i x_i^{ideal} - \sum_{r=1}^{s} \mu_r y_r^{ideal} + v = 0$ $\sum_{r=1}^{s} \mu_r y_r^{new} = 1$ $\mu_r, v_i \geq 0$
CRS	where $\mu = 0$	where $v = 0$
VRS	where μ free	where v free
NIRS	where $\mu \leq 0$	where $v \geq 0$
NDRS	where $\mu \geq 0$	where $v \leq 0$

7.5 Minimum Efficiency Model

Note that the fixed-benchmark models yield the maximum efficiency scores when the tradeoffs are implicitly defined by the benchmarks. If we change the objective function of model (7.8) into minimization, we have

$$\min \frac{\sum_{r=1}^{s} u_r y_r^{new}}{\sum_{i=1}^{m} v_i x_i^{new}}$$
subject to
$$\frac{\sum_{r=1}^{s} u_r y_{rj}}{\sum_{i=1}^{m} v_i x_{ij}} = 1 \quad j \in \mathbf{I}_B \qquad (7.12)$$

$$\frac{\sum\limits_{r=1}^{s} u_r y_{rj}}{\sum\limits_{i=1}^{m} v_i x_{ij}} \le 1 \quad j \notin \mathbf{I}_B$$

$$u_r, v_i \ge 0 \qquad \forall r, i$$

We refer to (7.12) as the input-oriented CRS minimum efficiency model. Although the benchmarks implicitly define the tradeoffs amongst inputs and outputs, the exact tradeoffs are still unavailable to us. Thus, the optimal value to (7.12) gives the lower efficiency bound for DMU^{new}. The optimal value to (7.8) yields the upper efficiency bound. The true efficiency of DMU^{new} lies in-between the bounds.

In fact, model (7.12) describes the worst efficiency scenario whereas model (7.8) describe the best efficiency scenario. The minimum efficiency for the original input-oriented DEA models (e.g., model (7.7)) is zero, and for the original output-oriented DEA models is infinite.

Similarly, we can obtain the output-oriented CRS minimum efficiency model,

$$\max \frac{\sum\limits_{i=1}^{m} v_i x_i^{new}}{\sum\limits_{r=1}^{s} u_r y_r^{new}}$$

subject to   (7.13)

$$\frac{\sum\limits_{i=1}^{m} v_i x_{ij}}{\sum\limits_{r=1}^{s} u_r y_{rj}} = 1 \quad j \in \mathbf{I}_B$$

$$u_r, v_i \ge 0 \qquad \forall r, i$$

Recall that a smaller score indicates a better performance in the output-oriented DEA models. Therefore, the output-oriented CRS minimum efficiency score (optimal value to model (7.13) is greater than or equal to the efficiency score obtained from the output-oriented CRS fixed-benchmark model.

The linear program equivalents to (7.12) and (7.13) are presented in Table 7.5 which summarizes the minimum efficiency models.

The spreadsheet models for the minimum efficiency models are similar to the fixed-benchmark spreadsheet models. We only need to change the "Max" to "Min" in the Solver parameters for the input-oriented models, and change the "Min" to "Max" for the output-oriented models. For example, consider the output-oriented CRS fixed-benchmark model shown in Figure 7.9. Figure 7.13 shows the corresponding minimum efficiency spreadsheet model.

Cell F2 contains the formula for the ideal benchmark, that is

Cell F2=SUMPRODUCT(D2:E2,D4:E4)-B2*B4+G3

Cell C5 is reserved to indicate the vendor under evaluation. The (maximum) efficiency is presented in cell C6 which contains the formula

Cell C6=SUMPRODUCT(D4:E4,INDEX(D9:E14,C5,0))+G3

Cell C7 is the weighted input and contains the formula

Cell C7=B4*INDEX(B9:B14,C5,1)

The Solver parameters shown in Figure 7.15 remain the same for all the vendors, and the calculation is performed by the VBA procedure "IdealBenchmark".

```
Sub IdealBenchmark()
Dim i As Integer
For i = 1 To 6
Range("C5") = i
SolverSolve UserFinish:=True
Range("F" & i + 8) = Range("C6")
Next
End Sub
```

Based upon the scores in cells F9:F14 in Figure 7.14, vendor 2 has the best performance.

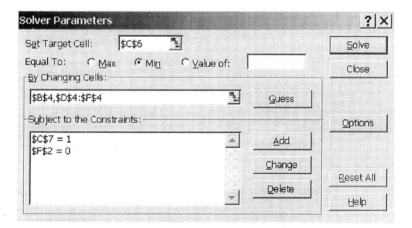

Figure 7.16. Solver Parameters for VRS Ideal-benchmark Minimum Efficiency Model

Next, we turn to the ideal-benchmark minimum efficiency model (7.14). The spreadsheet is the same as the one shown in Figure 7.14. However, we need to change "Max" to "Min" in the Solver parameters shown in Figure 7.15. Figure 7.16 shows the result. Figure 7.17 shows the minimum efficiency scores in cells F9:F14. The minimum efficiency model also indicates that vendor 2 is the best one.

	A	B	C	D	E	F	G
1		Price ($/units)		% accepted units	% on-time deliveries	constraint	
2	Ideal target	0.1881		100	100	-1.11E-16	
3						free variable	0
4	multipliers	4.770992		0	0.008974	0	0
5	DMU under evaluation		6				
6	Score		0.8615				
7	Weighted input		1			Minimum	
8						Efficiency	
9	Vendor 1	0.1958		98.8	95	0.9126404	
10	Vendor 2	0.1881		99.2	93	0.93	Min
11	Vendor 3	0.2204		100	100	0.8534483	
12	Vendor 4	0.2081		97.9	100	0.8849106	
13	Vendor 5	0.2118		97.7	97	0.8614589	
14	Vendor 6	0.2096		98.8	96	0.8615267	

Figure 7.17. Minimum Efficiency Scores for the Six Vendors

Chapter 8

Models for Evaluating Value Chains

8.1   Value Chain Efficiency

So far, the value-added processes or systems have been treated as a "black-box". We examine the resources available to the processes or systems and monitor the "conversions" of these resources (inputs) into the desired outputs. However, each process or system can include many subprocesses. For example, if the process is to make a car, then important subprocesses include assembling and painting. If we evaluate the efficiency of a supply chain system, then we need to measure the performance of each individual supply chain components, including suppliers, manufacturers, retailers, and customers.

In a fast-changing competitive environment, the business operations must be efficient both individually and as a collective group. This makes performance evaluation of value chains a challenging task. Two hurdles are present in measuring the performance of value chains. One is the existence of multiple measures that characterize the performance of each subprocess in the value chain. The other is the existence of conflicts between value chain members with respect to specific measures.

Consider three supplier-manufacturer supply chains presented in Table 8.1 where the supplier has two inputs (shipping cost and labor) and one output (revenue from selling the raw materials to the manufacturer), and the manufacture has one input (raw material cost which is the supplier's revenue) and one output (profit).

Applying the input-oriented VRS envelopment model to the suppliers and the manufacturers indicate that the suppliers in supply chains A and B, and the manufacturer in supply chain C are efficient. Now, if we ignore the intermediate measure of revenue (raw material cost) and apply the input-oriented VRS envelopment model, the last column of Table 8.1 indicates that all supply chains are efficient.

Table 8.1. Simple Supplier-Manufacturer Example

Supply Chain	Supplier Shipping Costs	Labor	Manufacturer Revenue	Profit	Supplier efficiency	Manufacturer efficiency	Overall efficiency
			Material costs				
A	7	9	4	16	1	0.75	1
B	9	4	6	14	1	0.5	1
C	11	6	3	23	0.791	1	1

This simple numerical example indicates that the conventional DEA fails to correctly characterize the performance of value chain. Since an overall DEA efficient performance does not necessarily indicate efficient performance in individual components in the value chain. Consequently, improvement to the best-practice can be distorted. i.e., the performance improvement of one subprocess affects the efficiency status of the other, because of the presence of intermediate measures. Seiford and Zhu (1999d) develop a procedure for value chain performance improvement by using RTS sensitivity analysis (see Chapter 3). In this chapter, we present models that can directly evaluate the performance of value chains, and set value chain performance target.

8.2   Measuring Information Technology's Indirect Impact

Information technology (IT) has become a key enabler of business process reengineering if an organization is to survive and continues to prosper in a rapidly changing business environment while facing competition in a global marketplace. As a result, IT investments have grown annually in a relatively large rate (Keen, 1991). The increasing use of IT has resulted in a need for evaluating the impact of IT investment on firm performance and productivity. Although increases in IT spending are expected to increase productivity and improve performance, research examining these effects has yielded mixed results and labeled this "the productivity paradox" (Brynjolfsson, 1993). There are still relatively few means of measuring the exact impact of IT investments on productivity. Examining the impact of IT investment on firm performance remains an important topic for IT research. Here we present a DEA-based model to measure the indirect impact of IT investments on productivity.

The impact of IT on performance has been studies within firms, industry, and individual information systems (see, e.g., Bakos and Kemerer, 1992, and Kauffman and Weill, 1989). It has been recognized that it is difficult to empirically link investment in IT with firm performance due to a number of measurement, model specification and data availability problems. This is partly due to the fact that IT is indirectly linked with the firm performance. In this regard, Kauffman and Weill (1989) suggest using a two-stage model to explicitly incorporate the intermediate variables that link the IT with the firm performance. Chen and Zhu (2001) develop a methodology that (i) captures IT's impact on firm performance via intermediate variables; (ii) views firm performance as a result of a series of value added IT related activities; and (iii) identifies the best practice when intermediate measures are present.

8.2.1   IT Performance Model

Consider the indirect impact of IT on firm performance where IT directly impacts certain intermediate measures which in turn are transformed to realize firm performance. Figure 8.1 describes the indirect impact of IT on firm performance where the first stage uses inputs x_i ($i = 1, ..., m$) to produce outputs z_d ($d = 1, ..., D$), and then these z_d are used as inputs in the second stage to produce outputs y_r ($r = 1, ..., s$). It can be seen that z_d (intermediate measures) are outputs in stage 1 and inputs in stage 2. The first stage is viewed as an IT-related value-added activity where deposit is generated and then used as the input to the second stage where revenue is generated (Chen and Zhu, 2001).

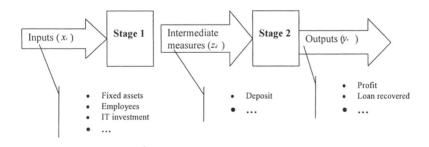

Figure 8.1. IT Impact on Firm Performance

We have

$$\min_{\alpha,\beta,\lambda_j,\mu_j,\tilde{z}} w_1\alpha - w_2\beta$$

subject to

(stage 1)

$$\sum_{j=1}^{n} \lambda_j x_{ij} \leq \alpha x_{ij_o} \qquad i = 1,...,m$$

$$\sum_{j=1}^{n} \lambda_j z_{dj} \geq \tilde{z}_{dj_o} \qquad d = 1,...,D$$

$$\sum_{j=1}^{n} \lambda_j = 1$$

$$\lambda_j \geq 0, \quad j = 1,...,n$$

$$\alpha \leq 1$$

(stage 2)   (8.1)

$$\sum_{j=1}^{n} \mu_j z_{dj} \leq \tilde{z}_{dj_o} \qquad d = 1,...,D$$

$$\sum_{j=1}^{n} \mu_j y_{rj} \geq \beta y_{rj_o} \qquad r = 1,...,s$$

$$\sum_{j=1}^{n} \mu_j = 1$$

$$\mu_j \geq 0, \quad j = 1,...,n$$

$$\beta \geq 1$$

where w_1 and w_2 are user-specified weights reflecting the preference over the two stages' performance, and symbol "~" represents unknown decision variables.

The rationale of model (8.1) is as follows: (i) when we evaluate the impact of IT investment on the intermediate measures, we want to minimize the input usage given the intermediate measures. For example, given the deposits generated, our objective is to examine whether a bank can reduce its input consumption (including IT investment) compared to the best practice, and (ii) when we evaluate the firm performance as a result of the intermediate measures, we want to maximize the performance given the intermediate measures. For example, given the deposits it generated, our objective is to examine whether a bank can increase its profit. Model (8.1) characterizes the indirect impact of IT on firm performance in a single linear programming problem.

Theorem 8.1 If $\alpha^* = \beta^* = 1$, then there must exist an optimal solution such that $\lambda_{j_o}^* = \mu_{j_o}^* = 1$, where (*) represents optimal value in model (8.1).

[Proof]: Note that $\lambda_{j_o}^* = \mu_{j_o}^* = 1$, $\alpha^* = \beta^* = 1$, and $\tilde{z}_{dj_o}^* = z_{dj_o}$ are feasible solutions in model (8.1). This completes the proof. ∎

Theorem 8.2 If $\alpha^* = \beta^* = 1$, then $\theta^* = 1$ and $\phi^* = 1$, where θ^* and ϕ^* are the optimal values to the input-oriented and output-oriented VRS envelopment models, respectively.

[Proof]: Suppose $\alpha^* = \beta^* = 1$ in model (8.1). By Theorem 8.1, we know that $\lambda^*_{j_o} = \mu^*_{j_o} = 1$, $\alpha^* = \beta^* = 1$, and $\tilde{z}^*_{dj_o} = z_{dj_o}$. Now, if $\theta^* < 1$ and $\phi^* > 1$, then this indicates that $\alpha^* = \beta^* = 1$ is not optimal in model (8.1). A contradiction. ∎

Theorem 8.2 indicates if $\alpha^* = \beta^* = 1$, the value chain achieves efficient performance when the two-stage process is viewed as a whole.

If $\alpha^* = 1$ and $\beta^* > 1$ (or $\alpha^* < 1$ and $\beta^* = 1$), then model (8.1) indicates that one of the stages can achieve 100% efficiency given a set of optimal intermediate measures. In this case, the original envelopment DEA models can be used to provide additional information.

From Theorem 8.2, we immediately have the following result

Corollary 8.1 A firm must be a frontier point in both stages with respect to $\alpha^* x_{ij_o}$ ($i = 1, \ldots, m$), $\tilde{z}^*_{dj_o}$ ($d = 1, \ldots, D$), and $\beta^* y_{rj_o}$ ($r = 1, \ldots, s$), where (*) represents optimal value in model (8.1).

Based upon Corollary 8.1, model (8.1) yields directions for achieving the best practice of this two-stage process. Consequently, we can study the (marginal) impact of IT investment on firm performance by using RTS estimation discussed in Chapter 3 (see Chen and Zhu (2001) for such a study).

In model (8.1), the intermediate measures for a specific DMU_o under evaluation are set as unknown decision variables, $\tilde{z}_{dj_o}$. As a result, additional constraints can be imposed on the intermediate measures. This can further help in correctly characterizing the indirect impact of IT on firm performance.

To illustrate model (8.1), Figure 8.2 shows the spreadsheet model of (8.1) with the data in Table 8.1. Since the intermediate measures are set as decision variables, cell E6 is reserved to represent the Revenue variable. Cell D7 indicates the DMU under evaluation. Cells E8 and F8 represent α and β, respectively. Cell G8 is the objective function and contains the formula "=E8-F8".

The changing cells are cells H2:H4, cells I2:I4, cells E8:F8, ,and cell E6. The formulas for cells B9:B15 are

Cell B9 =SUMPRODUCT(B2:B4,H2:H4)
Cell B10 =SUMPRODUCT(C2:C4,H2:H4)

Cell B11 =SUMPRODUCT(E2:E4,H2:H4)
Cell B12 =SUMPRODUCT(E2:E4,I2:I4)
Cell B13 =SUMPRODUCT(G2:G4,I2:I4)
Cell B14 =SUM(H2:H4)
Cell B15 =SUM(I2:I4)

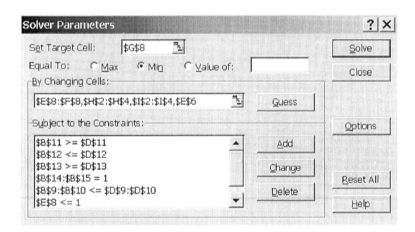

	A	B	C	D	E	F	G	H	I	J	K	L
1	Supply Chain	Shipping costs	Labor		Revenue		Profit	λ	μ	α	β	Optimal Revenue
2	A	7	9		4		16	0.14925	0	1	1.4375	4
3	B	9	4		6		14	0.85075	0	1	1.6429	6
4	C	11	6		3		23	0	1	0.79104	1	3
5												
6					3							
7				3	α	β						
8	Constraints				0.79104	1	-0.20896					
9	Shipping costs	8.701492537	≤	8.70149								
10	Labor	4.746268657	≤	4.74627								
11	Revenue	5.701492537	≥	3								
12	Revenue	3	≤	3			Run					
13	Profit	23	≥	23								
14	Σλ	1	=	1								
15	Σμ	1	=	1								

Figure 8.2. Spreadsheet Model for Model (8.1)

Solver Parameters   ? ✕

Set Target Cell: $G$8   [Solve]

Equal To: ○ Max ● Min ○ Value of: [   ]   [Close]

By Changing Cells:

$E$8:$F$8,$H$2:$H$4,$I$2:$I$4,$E$6   [Guess]

Subject to the Constraints:

$B$11 >= $D$11   [Add]
$B$12 <= $D$12
$B$13 >= $D$13   [Change]
$B$14:$B$15 = 1
$B$9:$B$10 <= $D$9:$D$10   [Delete]   [Reset All]
$E$8 <= 1   [Help]

Figure 8.3. Solver Parameters for Model (8.1)

The formulas for cells D9:D13 are

Cell D9 =E8*INDEX(B2:B4,D7,1)
Cell D10 =E8*INDEX(C2:C4,D7,1)
Cell D11 =E6
Cell D12 =E6
Cell D13 =F8*INDEX(G2:G4,D7,1)

Figure 8.3 shows the Solver parameters for the spreadsheet model shown in Figure 8.2. We have "$E$8 <=1" and "$F$8 >=1" in the Constraints, representing $\alpha \leq 1$ and $\beta \geq 1$, respectively.

In Figure 8.2, cells J2:K4 record the efficiency scores. Cells L2:L4 report the optimal values on Revenue. Since optimal Revenue values are equal to the original values, α^* and β^* must be equal to the θ^* and ϕ^* of the VRS envelopment models, respectively. In this case, multiple optimal solutions on Revenue exist. (Click the "Run" button several time, you may get a set of different optimal values on Revenue.)

8.2.2 Efficiency of IT Utilization

We demonstrate how model (8.1) can be used to measure the indirect impact of IT on firm performance. Consider a set of 15 banks obtained from the Functional Cost and Profit Analysis data set collected by the Federal Reserve Bank under its Functional Cost Analysis (FCA) program. The data for this study is based on the FCA Plus data set from 1997. Figure 8.4 presents the spreadsheet version of model (8.1). In the first stage, we have three inputs: (i) Transactional IT investment, (ii) Strategic IT investment, and (iii) Labor expenses, and two outputs: (i) number of Accounts and (ii) number of Transactions. In the second stage, we have two outputs: (i) Revenue and (ii) Equity. (see also Mistry (1999) and Mistry and Zhu (2001).)

	A	B	C	D	E	F	G	H	I	J	K	L	M	N
1	Bank	Tran IT	Strategic IT	Labor		Accounts	Transactions		Revenue	Equity	λ	μ	α	β
2	1	68374862.88	27207295.82	98644431		28430.63	109486141		4561844525	507245000	0	0.00737	0.594086	1
3	2	43674295.91	20728716.45	82211383		4020.105	149772606		819640950	1697263000	0	0.02239	1	1
4	3	36240479.82	22876333.28	41677506		1417653	42281949		705076794	740666344	-8E-17	0	0.624362	1
5	4	10974089.39	3604030.058	23366094		4801.735	41624391		252167755	250842739	0	0	0.749539	2.417864
6	5	8165838.45	4598047.449	11074813		5777.526	14023708		137014849	120597000	0	0	1	3.716476
7	6	5826343.93	1383431.384	10723845		9335	1982414		160695007	218540000	0	0.34852	0.856766	1.840422
8	7	3039890	2701361.5	17225000		16539.81	45748993		353726000	451221000	0	0	1	1.395902
9	8	2631636.49	891139.9067	7585518		4245.225	10054751		50543312	81451129	0	0	1	4.433396
10	9	2445674.33	531648.2537	7537537		1668.805	8294216		59544335	55444711	0	0	1	4.981338
11	10	1481996.55	459703.0989	370169		3801	433717		28100210	23699857	0	0	1	1
12	11	1471033.14	1070595.245	6378768		2230.61	5915536		70210212	65192518	0	0.62171	1	4.821728
13	12	1321121.35	863879.5153	3718510		16935.8	7093301		37509806	37123165	0	0	1	7.50955
14	13	1287557	687890.0796	5609930		3121.808	6223975		41187111	36704000	0	0	1	7.495762
15	14	1164952.09	762892.2893	3449934		3822.564	4476600		28526966	25739404	0	0	1	8.17228
16	15	1121467.92	391687.7105	3185637		4939.944	8530050		41220844	43067174	1	0	1	3.67904
17														
18						4939.944	8530050							
19					15	α	β							
20	Constraints					1	3.679039724		2.672039724					
21	Tran IT	1121467.92	≤	1121467.9										
22	Strategic IT	391687.7105	≤	391687.71										
23	Labor	3185637	≤	3185637										
24	Accounts	4939.944444	≥	4939.9444					IT					
25	Transactions	8530050	≥	8530050										
26	Accounts	4939.944444	≤	4939.9444										
27	Transactions	8530050	≤	8530050										
28	Revenue	151653122.6	≥	151653123										
29	Equity	158446844	≥	158446844										
30	Σλ	1	=	1										
31	Σμ	1	=	1										

Figure 8.4. Evaluating IT Utilization Spreadsheet Model

Based upon Mistry (1999), the IT investment measures are obtained using data from the following FCA defined expense categories: (i) Vendor Data Processing (all expenses for data processing performed by outside firms, e.g., check processing centers); (ii) Telephone and Electronic Access (total expense for communications, e.g., fees for telephone lines, on-line charges, software installation and modification); (iii) Network Expense Fees (ATM) (all membership and participation fees charged by ATM networks); EFT/ACH Cost Center expense (all expenses related to electronic banking delivery systems other than ATMs; (iv) ATM Cost Center expenses (all expenses related to maintenance and support of all ATM transactions on ATMs either owned or leased by the bank); (v) Proof & Transit Cost Center expense (all expenses related to check processing, such as encoding, check sorting, and generating account balances); and (vi) Data processing Cost Center expense (all expenses related to internal data processing, i.e., services provided by the bank's own data processing staff, maintenance and support of institution's software, operating systems, PCs, mainframes, etc.).

In Mistry (1999), Transactional IT refers to IT investment aimed at automation of routine and repetitive tasks to reduce processing costs. The Transactional IT measure is obtained by adding the total expenses for Vendor Data Processing, the Proof & Transit Cost Center, and the Data Processing Cost Center. Strategic IT refers to IT investment aimed at increasing market share or generating revenues. The Strategic IT measure is constructed by adding all expenses related to electronic access and automation of customer interface, total expenses for telephone and electronic access, ATM Network Fees, the EFT/ACH Cost Center, and the ATM Cost Center. The labor input is the sum of the salary plus benefits costs of full time equivalent personnel.

Range names are used in the spreadsheet shown in Figure 8.4. Cells B2:D16 are named as "Stage1Input". Cells F2:G16 are named as "Intermediate". Cells I2:J16 are named as "Stage2Output". These cells represent the performance measures for the 15 banks.

Cells K2:K16 are named as "Lambdas" and cells L2:L16 are named as "Mus". These cells are changing cells in the Solver parameters. Other changing cells include cell F19 – "Accounts", cell G18 – "Transactions", representing the decision variables for the intermediate measures, cell F20 – "Efficiency1", and cell G20 – "Efficiency2", representing α and β in model (8.1).

Cell I20 is the objective function of model (8.1). It contains the formula "=Efficiency1-Efficiency2", i.e., "=F20-G20". Cell I20 is named as "Efficiency".

Based upon these range names and the related cells, we have the formulas for the constraints

Cell B21 =SUMPRODUCT(Lambdas,INDEX(Stage1Inputs,0,1))
Cell B22 =SUMPRODUCT(Lambdas,INDEX(Stage1Inputs,0,2))
Cell B23 =SUMPRODUCT(Lambdas,INDEX(Stage1Inputs,0,3))
Cell B24 =SUMPRODUCT(Lambdas,INDEX(Intermediate,0,1))
Cell B25 =SUMPRODUCT(Lambdas,INDEX(Intermediate,0,2))
Cell B26 =SUMPRODUCT(Mus,INDEX(Intermediate,0,1))
Cell B27 =SUMPRODUCT(Mus,INDEX(Intermediate,0,2))
Cell B28 =SUMPRODUCT(Mus,INDEX(Stage2Outputs,0,1))
Cell B29 =SUMPRODUCT(Mus,INDEX(Stage2Outputs,0,2))
Cell B30 =SUM(Lambdas)
Cell B31 =SUM(Mus)

Cell D21 =Efficiency1*INDEX(Stage1Inputs,E19,1)
Cell D22 =Efficiency1*INDEX(Stage1Inputs,E19,2)
Cell D23 =Efficiency1*INDEX(Stage1Inputs,E19,3)
Cell D24 =Accounts
Cell D25 =Transactions
Cell D26 =Accounts
Cell D27 =Transactions
Cell D28 =Efficiency2*INDEX(Stage2Outputs,E19,1)
Cell D29 =Efficiency2*INDEX(Stage2Outputs,E19,2)

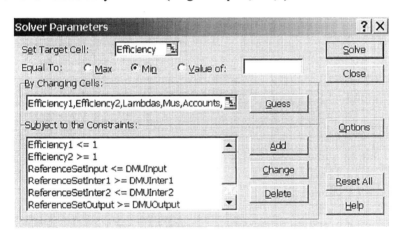

Figure 8.5. Solver Parameters for Evaluating IT Utilization

We then apply the following range names to the constraints

Cells B21:B23 – ReferenceSetInput
Cells B24:B25 – ReferenceSetInter1
Cells B26:B27 – ReferenceSetInter2

Cells B28:B29 – ReferenceSetOutput
Cell B30 – SumLambda
Cell B31 – SumMu
Cells D21:D23 – DMUInput
Cells D24:D25 – DMUInter1
Cells B26:B27 – DMUInter2
Cells D28:D29 – DMUOutput

Figure 8.5 shows the Solver Parameters. ("SumLambda=1" and "SumMu=1" are not shown in Figure 8.5.) The calculation is performed by the following VBA procedure

```
Sub IT()
Dim i As Integer
For i = 1 To 15
Range("E19") = i
SolverSolve UserFinish:=True
'Place the efficiency into column J and column K
Range("M" & i + 1) = Range("Efficiency1")
Range("N" & i + 1) = Range("Efficiency2")
Next i
End Sub
```

The last three columns of Table 8.2 report the efficiency based upon the VRS envelopment models in stage 1, stage 2, and overall, respectively. The overall efficiency is calculated using the input-oriented VRS envelopment model with Transactional IT, Strategic IT and Labor as the inputs, and Revenue and Equity as the outputs. (i.e., we ignore the intermediate measures.) It can be seen that overall efficient banks do not necessarily indicate efficient performance in the two stages (see, e.g., banks 1, 7, 17, and 15).

The second and third columns of Table 8.2 report the efficiency based upon model (8.1) with $w_1 = w_2 = 1$. We have, given the optimal intermediate measures of Accounts and Transactions, (i) 2 banks (2 and 10) achieve 100% efficiency in both stage 1 and stage 2; (ii) 10 banks achieve 100% efficiency in the IT-related activity (stage 1) without achieving 100% efficiency in stage 2; (iii) 2 banks (1 and 3) do not achieve 100% efficiency in the IT-related activity while achieving 100% efficiency in stage 2; and (iv) 2 banks (4 and 6) do not achieve 100% efficiency in both stages.

Model (8.1) provides optimized values on the intermediate measures of Accounts and Transactions. Consider bank 3. Model (8.1) indicates that bank 3 should increase its values on Accounts and Transactions (see Figure 8.6).

Table 8.2. IT Efficiency

Bank	Model (8.1)		DEA		
	α*	β*	θ*	φ*	Overall
1	0.59	1.00	0.59	1.00	1.00
2	1.00	1.00	1.00	1.00	1.00
3	0.62	1.00	1.00	1.00	0.88
4	0.75	2.42	0.68	1.83	0.52
5	1.00	3.72	0.47	1.82	0.44
6	0.86	1.84	0.33	1.00	1.00
7	1.00	1.40	1.00	1.40	1.00
8	1.00	4.43	0.55	2.04	0.68
9	1.00	4.98	0.74	1.00	0.97
10	1.00	1.00	1.00	1.00	1.00
11	1.00	4.82	0.76	1.00	0.88
12	1.00	7.51	1.00	6.89	0.85
13	1.00	7.50	0.87	2.40	0.87
14	1.00	8.17	0.96	3.23	0.96
15	1.00	3.68	1.00	3.68	1.00

	A	B	C	D	E	F	G	H	I	J	K	L
1	Bank	Tran IT	Strategic IT	Labor		Accounts	Transactions		Revenue	Equity	λ	μ
2	1	6837488.88	27207295.82	96644431		28430.63	109496141		4561844525	507245000	0	0.07265
3	2	43674295.91	20728716.45	82211383		4020.105	149772606		819640950	1697263000	0.1354	0.33743
4	3	36240479.82	22876333.28	41677506		1417653	42281949		705076794	740666344	0	0.0042
5	4	10974089.39	3604030.058	23386094		4801.735	41624391		252167755	250842739	0	0
6	5	8185838.45	4598047.449	11074813		5777.526	14023708		137014849	120597000	0	0
7	6	5826343.93	1383431.384	10723845		9335	1982414		160695007	218540000	0	0.58572
8	7	3039890	2701361.5	17225000		16539.81	45748993		353726000	451221000	0.8646	0
9	8	2631636.49	891139.9067	7585518		4245.225	10054751		50543312	81451129	0	0
10	9	2445674.33	531648.2537	7537537		1668.805	8294216		59544335	55444711	0	0
11	10	1481996.55	459703.0989	370169		3801	433717		28100210	23699857	0	0
12	11	1471033.14	1070595.245	6378768		2230.61	5915536		70210212	65192518	0	0
13	12	1321121.35	863879.5153	3718510		16935.8	7093301		37509806	37123155	0	0
14	13	1287557	687890.0796	5609930		3121.808	6223975		41187111	36704000	0	0
15	14	1164952.09	762892.2893	3449934		3822.564	4476600		28526966	25739404	0	0
16	15	1121467.92	391687.7105	3185637		4939.944	8530050		41220844	43067174	0	0
17												
18						14845.08	59830119.19					
19					3	α	β					
20	Constraints					0.624362	1		0.376637215			
21	Tran IT	8540354.565	≤	22627189								
22	Strategic IT	5141629.172	≤	14283120								
23	Labor	26021862.88	≤	26021863								
24	Accounts	14845.08331	≥	14845.083			IT					
25	Transactions	59830119.19	≥	59830119								
26	Accounts	14845.08331	≤	14845.083								
27	Transactions	59830119.19	≤	59830119								
28	Revenue	705076794	≥	705076794								
29	Equity	740666344	≥	740666344								
30	Σλ	1	=	1								
31	Σμ	1	=	1								

Figure 8.6. Optimal Intermediate Measures

This indicates that (i) optimal solutions in the VRS envelopment models are only feasible solutions to model (8.1), and (ii) model (8.1) is not just a simple unification of the VRS envelopment models

Finally, we should point out that the results of model (8.1) depend on the choice of weights w_i.

8.3   Supply Chain Efficiency

Supply chain management has been proven a very effective tool to provide prompt and reliable delivery of high-quality products and services at the least cost. To achieve this, performance evaluation of entire supply chain is extremely important, since it means utilizing the combined resources of the entire supply chain in the most efficient way possible to provide market-wining and cost-effective products and services. However, a lack of appropriate performance measurement systems has been a major obstacle to an effective supply chain management (Lee and Billington, 1992).

This is due to the fact that the concept of supply chain management requires the performance of overall supply chain rather than only the performance of the individual supply chain members. Each supply chain member has is own strategy to achieve 100% efficiency. One supply chain member's 100% efficiency does not necessarily mean another's 100% efficiency. Sometimes, because of the possible conflicts between supply chain members, one member's inefficiency may be caused by another's efficient operations. For example, the supplier may increase its raw material price to increase its revenue and to achieve an efficient performance. This increased revenue means increased cost to the manufacturer. Consequently, the manufacturer may become inefficient unless the manufacturer adjusts it current operating policy.

As demonstrated in Table 8.1, some measures linked to related supply chain members cannot be simply classified as "outputs" or "inputs" of the supply chain. For example, the supplier's revenue is not only an output of the supplier (the supplier wishes to maximize it), but also an input to the manufacturer (the manufacturer wishes to minimize it). Simply minimizing the total supply chain cost or maximizing the total supply chain revenue (profit) does not model and solve the conflicts. Therefore, the meaning of supply chain efficiency needs to be carefully defined and studied, and we need models that can both define and measure the efficiency of supply chain as well as supply chain members.

Methods have been developed to estimate the exact performance of supply chain members based upon single performance measures (e.g., Cheung and Hausman, 2000). However, no attempts have been made to identify the best practice of the supply chain. No solid mathematical models have been developed to simultaneously (i) define and measure the whole supply chain performance with possible conflicts on specific measures, (ii) evaluate the performance of supply chain members, and (iii) identify the best practice and provide directions to achieve the supply chain best practice.

We here generalize model (8.1) to charactering and measuring supply chain performance and achieving the best practice when multiple supply chain performance measures related to individual supply chain members are present. The new DEA methodology measures the efficiency of supply chain system as a whole as well as each supply chain member, and provides directions for supply chain improvement to reach the best practice. This eliminates the needs for unrealistic assumptions in typical supply chain optimization models and probabilistic models, e.g., a typical EOQ model assumes constant and known demand rate and lead-time for delivery.

8.3.1   Supply Chain as an Input-Output System

A typical supply chain can be presented in Figure 8.7 with four echelons – suppliers, manufacturers, distributors, and retailers. The traditional objective of supply chain management is to minimize the total supply chain cost to meet the customer needs through coordination efforts among supply chain members. To achieve this objective, timely and accurate assessment of the supply chain system and individual member performance is of extreme importance. Because an effective performance evaluation system (i) provides the basis to understand the supply chain operations, (ii) monitors and manages supply chain performance through identifying the best-practice supply chain operations, and (iii) provides directions for further supply chain improvement.

Supply chain systems can be viewed as an integrated input-output system where each supply chain member uses inputs to produce. Consequently, we may classify supply chain member's performance measures into inputs and outputs. Caution should be paid when we classify the performance measures into inputs and outputs based upon specific supply chain members, since incorrect classification may lead to false conclusion on the efficiency of supply chain members as well as supply chain. The classification can be based upon the material and information flows in a supply chain system.

Let I^Δ and R^Δ represent the input and output subscript sets for a supply chain member Δ, respectively. We denote x_i^Δ $(i \in I^\Delta)$ and y_r^Δ $(r \in R^\Delta)$ the inputs and outputs associated with each supply chain member, respectively. Now, let $\bar{x}_\Delta$ and $\bar{y}_\Delta$ be the vectors consisting of x_i^Δ $(i \in I^\Delta)$ and y_r^Δ $(r \in R^\Delta)$, respectively. The following Pareto-Koopmans efficiency is used to define an efficient supply chain member.

Definition 8.1 (Efficient Supply Chain Member) A supply chain member Δ is efficient *if* $(\bar{x}_\Delta, \bar{y}_\Delta)$ is not dominated.

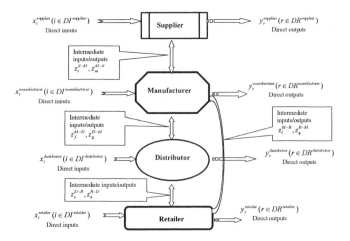

Figure 8.7. Supply Chain

Some measures are associated with a specific supply chain member only. We call these measures the "direct" inputs and outputs. For example, labor and manufacturing lead time are two direct inputs to the manufacturer. These direct inputs and outputs of supply chain members can be viewed as the inputs and outputs of the supply chain.

We also have "intermediate" inputs/outputs associated with two supply chain members. For example, the number of finished products shipped from the manufacturer to the retailer and the distributor represent outputs of the manufacturer. These outputs then become inputs to the distributor and the retailer (see Figure 8.7). These intermediate measures cannot be simply treated as inputs or outputs of the supply chain, although they are inputs/outputs of specific supply chain members.

In supply chain management, it is believed that values of intermediate measures should be determined through coordination among related supply chain members (Parlar and Weng, 1997; Thomas and Griffin, 1996). Because such intermediate measures are usually cost to one supply chain member and benefit to the other. Simply minimizing the total supply chain cost or maximizing the supply chain revenue does not model situations with intermediate measures. This poses a challenge to defining and measuring the supply chain efficiency.

To facilitate our discussion, let DI^{Δ} and DR^{Δ} represent the direct input and direct output subscript sets for a supply chain member Δ, respectively. We then use the following notions to represent intermediate inputs and outputs, x_i^{Δ} ($i \notin DI^{\Delta} \subseteq I^{\Delta}$) and y_r^{Δ} ($r \notin DR^{\Delta} \subseteq R^{\Delta}$),

z_t^{S-M} = tth intermediate output from the supplier to manufacturer, t = 1, ..., T;

z_m^{M-S} = mth intermediate output from the manufacturer to the supplier, m = 1, ..., M;

z_f^{M-D} = fth intermediate output from the manufacturer to the distributor, f = 1, ..., F;

z_g^{D-M} = gth intermediate output from the distributor to the manufacturer, g = 1, ..., G;

z_l^{M-R} = lth intermediate output from the manufacturer to the retailer, l = 1, ..., L;

z_q^{R-M} = qth intermediate output from the retailer to the manufacturer, q = 1, ..., Q;

z_e^{D-R} = eth intermediate output from the distributor to the retailer, e = 1, ..., E;

z_n^{R-D} = nth intermediate output from the retailer to the distributor, n = 1, ..., N.

Note that only intermediate outputs are defined, since each such output also represents an input to an associated supply chain member. For example, z_t^{S-M} (output of the supplier) also represents an input to the manufacturer.

8.3.2   Supply Chain Efficiency Model

Suppose we have J observations associated with each supply chain member. i.e., we have observed input and output values of x_{ij}^{Δ} ($i \in I^{\Delta}$) and y_{rj}^{Δ} ($r \in R^{\Delta}$), where j = 1, ..., J. The efficiency of supply chain member Δ can be measured by the following DEA model – input-oriented CRS envelopment model

$$\theta^{\Delta*} = \min_{\phi_j^{\Delta}, \theta^{\Delta}} \theta^{\Delta}$$

subject to

$$\sum_{j=1}^{J} \phi_j^{\Delta} x_{ij}^{\Delta} \leq \theta^{\Delta} x_{ij_o}^{\Delta} \qquad i \in I^{\Delta} \qquad\qquad (8.2)$$

$$\sum_{j=1}^{J} \phi_j^{\Delta} y_{rj}^{\Delta} \geq y_{rj_o}^{\Delta} \qquad r \in R^{\Delta}$$

$$\phi_j^{\Delta} \geq 0, \quad j = 1, ..., J$$

If $\theta^{\Delta*} = 1$, then a supply chain member Δ is efficient (including weakly efficient). Also, for inefficient performance, model (8.2) provides projection paths onto the efficient frontier via the optimal values of $\sum_{j=1}^{J} \phi_j^{\Delta*} x_{ij}^{\Delta}$ and $\sum_{j=1}^{J} \phi_j^{\Delta*} y_{rj}^{\Delta}$.

Because of the possible conflicts represented by the intermediate measures between associated supply chain members, the supply chain's performance cannot be simply defined and characterized by non-dominancy through using model (8.2). Let w_i be the user-specified weights reflecting the preference over supply chain member's performance (operation). Based upon (8.1), we establish the following liner programming problem for the supply chain

$$\Omega^* = \min_{\Omega_i, \lambda_j, \beta_j, \delta_j, \gamma_j, \tilde{z}} \frac{\sum_{i=1}^{4} w_i \Omega_i}{\sum_{i=1}^{4} w_i}$$

subject to

(supplier)

$$\sum_{j=1}^{J} \lambda_j x_{ij}^{\text{supplier}} \leq \Omega_1 x_{ij_o}^{\text{supplier}} \qquad i \in DI^{\text{supplier}}$$

$$\sum_{j=1}^{J} \lambda_j y_{rj}^{\text{supplier}} \geq y_{rj_o}^{\text{supplier}} \qquad r \in DR^{\text{supplier}}$$

$$\sum_{j=1}^{J} \lambda_j z_{tj}^{\text{S-M}} \geq \tilde{z}_{tj_o}^{\text{S-M}} \qquad t = 1,\dots, T$$

$$\sum_{j=1}^{J} \lambda_j z_{mj}^{\text{M-S}} \leq \tilde{z}_{mj_o}^{\text{M-S}} \qquad m = 1,\dots, M$$

$$\lambda_j \geq 0, \quad j = 1,\dots, J$$

(manufacturer)

$$\sum_{j=1}^{J} \beta_j x_{ij}^{\text{manufacturer}} \leq \Omega_2 x_{ij_o}^{\text{manufacturer}} \qquad i \in DI^{\text{manufacturer}}$$

$$\sum_{j=1}^{J} \beta_j y_{rj}^{\text{manufacturer}} \geq y_{rj_o}^{\text{manufacturer}} \qquad r \in DR^{\text{manufacturer}}$$

$$\sum_{j=1}^{J} \beta_j z_{tj}^{\text{S-M}} \leq \tilde{z}_{tj_o}^{\text{S-M}} \qquad t = 1,\dots, T$$

$$\sum_{j=1}^{J} \beta_j z_{mj}^{\text{M-S}} \geq \tilde{z}_{mj_o}^{\text{M-S}} \qquad m = 1,\dots, M$$

$$\sum_{j=1}^{J} \beta_j z_{fj}^{\text{M-D}} \geq \tilde{z}_{fj_o}^{\text{M-D}} \qquad f = 1,\dots, F \qquad\qquad (8.3)$$

$$\sum_{j=1}^{J} \beta_j z_{gj}^{\text{D-M}} \leq \tilde{z}_{gj_o}^{\text{D-M}} \qquad g = 1,\dots, G$$

$$\sum_{j=1}^{J} \beta_j z_{lj}^{\text{M-R}} \geq \tilde{z}_{lj_o}^{\text{M-R}} \qquad l = 1,\dots, L$$

$$\sum_{j=1}^{J} \beta_j z_{qj}^{\text{R-M}} \leq \tilde{z}_{qj_o}^{\text{R-M}} \qquad q = 1,\dots, Q$$

$$\beta_j \geq 0, \quad j = 1,\dots, J$$

(distributor)

$$\sum_{j=1}^{J} \delta_j x_{ij}^{distributor} \le \Omega_3 x_{ij_o}^{distributor} \qquad i \in DI^{distributor}$$

$$\sum_{j=1}^{J} \delta_j y_{rj}^{distributor} \ge y_{rj_o}^{distributor} \qquad r \in DR^{distributor}$$

$$\sum_{j=1}^{J} \delta_j z_{fj}^{M\text{-}D} \le \widetilde{z}_{fj_o}^{M\text{-}D} \qquad f = 1,...,F$$

$$\sum_{j=1}^{J} \delta_j z_{gj}^{D\text{-}M} \ge \widetilde{z}_{gj_o}^{D\text{-}M} \qquad g = 1,...,G$$

$$\sum_{j=1}^{J} \delta_j z_{ej}^{D\text{-}R} \ge \widetilde{z}_{ej_o}^{D\text{-}R} \qquad e = 1,...,E$$

$$\sum_{j=1}^{J} \delta_j z_{nj}^{D\text{-}R} \le \widetilde{z}_{nj_o}^{D\text{-}R} \qquad n = 1,...,N$$

$$\delta_j \ge 0, \quad j = 1,...,J$$

(retailer)

$$\sum_{j=1}^{J} \gamma_j x_{ij}^{retailer} \le \Omega_4 x_{ij_o}^{retailer} \qquad i \in DI^{retailer}$$

$$\sum_{j=1}^{J} \gamma_j y_{rj}^{retailer} \ge y_{rj_o}^{retailer} \qquad r \in DR^{retailer}$$

$$\sum_{j=1}^{J} \gamma_j z_{lj}^{M\text{-}R} \le \widetilde{z}_{lj_o}^{M\text{-}R} \qquad l = 1,...,L$$

$$\sum_{j=1}^{J} \gamma_j z_{qj}^{R\text{-}M} \ge \widetilde{z}_{qj_o}^{R\text{-}M} \qquad q = 1,...,Q$$

$$\sum_{j=1}^{J} \gamma_j z_{ej}^{D\text{-}R} \le \widetilde{z}_{ej_o}^{D\text{-}R} \qquad e = 1,...,E$$

$$\sum_{j=1}^{J} \gamma_j z_{nj}^{R\text{-}D} \ge \widetilde{z}_{nj_o}^{R\text{-}D} \qquad n = 1,...,N$$

$$\gamma_j \ge 0, \quad j = 1,...,J$$

Additional constraints can be added into model (8.3). For example, if $z_f^{M\text{-}D}$ represents the number of product f shipped from the manufacturer to the distributor, and if the capacity of this manufacturer in producing product f is C_f, then we may add $\widetilde{z}_f^{M\text{-}D} \le C_f$.

Obviously, if $\Omega^* = 1$, then there must exists an optimal solution such that $\lambda_{j_o}^* = \beta_{j_o}^* = \delta_{j_o}^* = \gamma_{j_o}^* = 1$, where (*) represents optimal value in model (8.3). Further, if $\Omega^* = 1$, then $\theta^{\Delta*} = 1$, where $\theta^{\Delta*}$ is the optimal value to model (8.2). i.e., when $\Omega^* = 1$, all supply chain members are efficient.

If $\Omega^* \ne 1$, then we immediately have the following result

All supply chain members are efficient with respect to $\Omega_1^* x_{ij_o}^{supplier}$ ($i \in DI^{supplier}$), $\Omega_2^* x_{ij_o}^{manufacturer}$ ($i \in DI^{manufacturer}$), $\Omega_3^* x_{ij_o}^{distributor}$ ($i \in DI^{distributor}$), $\Omega_4^* x_{ij_o}^{retailer}$ ($i \in DI^{retailer}$), $y_{rj_o}^{supplier}$ ($r \in DR^{supplier}$), $y_{rj_o}^{manufacturer}$ ($r \in DR^{manufacturer}$), $y_{rj_o}^{distributor}$ ($r \in DR^{distributor}$), $y_{rj_o}^{retailer}$ ($r \in DR^{retailer}$), $\widetilde{z}_{tj_o}^{S\text{-}M*}$ ($t = 1, ..., T$), $\widetilde{z}_{mj_o}^{M\text{-}S*}$ ($m = 1,..., M$), $\widetilde{z}_{fj_o}^{M\text{-}D*}$ ($f = 1, ... ,F$), $\widetilde{z}_{gj_o}^{D\text{-}M*}$ ($g = 1, ..., G$), $\widetilde{z}_{lj_o}^{M\text{-}R*}$ ($l = 1, ...,$

L), $\widetilde{z}_{q_{i_o}}^{R-M^*}$ $(q = 1, ..., Q)$, $\widetilde{z}_{e_{j_o}}^{D-R^*}$ $(e = 1, ..., E)$, where (*) represents optimal value in model (8.3).

Definition 8.2 (Efficient Supply Chain) A supply chain is efficient if $\Omega^* = 1$, where Ω^* is the optimal value to model (8.3).

θ^{Δ^*} measures the efficiency of supply chain member Δ under the context of supply chain member best practice. Ω_i^* can actually be used as a new efficiency measure for a specific supply chain member under the context of supply chain best practice. We have

Definition 8.3 Ω_i^* is called supply-chain-best-practice-dependent efficiency score for a specific supply chain member.

Note that Ω^* can be viewed as an index for input or cost savings for (inefficient) supply chains. The smaller the Ω^*, more savings could be achieved to reach the best practice. The same observation can also be applied to θ^{Δ^*} in the context of supply chain member best practice. Let $(w_1\theta^{supplier^*} + w_2\theta^{manufacturer^*} + w_3\theta^{distributor^*} + w_4\theta^{retailer^*})/\sum_{i=1}^{4} w_i$ represent the index for input savings achievable by all supply chain members combined. The following Theorem indicates that supply chain as a whole has potential to achieve more input savings and a better performance

Theorem 8.3 $\Omega^* \le (w_1\theta^{supplier^*} + w_2\theta^{manufacturer^*} + w_3\theta^{distributor^*} + w_4\theta^{retailer^*})/\sum_{i=1}^{4} w_i$.

8.3.3 Measuring Supply Chain Performance

We establish a spreadsheet model for a numerical example constructed as follows. For the supplier, we use labor and operating cost as two direct inputs, and revenue as the intermediate output. This revenue becomes an intermediate input of the manufacturer.

For the manufacturer, we use manufacturing cost and manufacturing lead time as two direct inputs, in addition to the intermediate input – supplier's revenue. We also have three intermediate manufacturer outputs: number of products shipped to the distributor, number of products shipped to the retailer, and distributor's fill rate. These outputs then become inputs to the distributor and the retailer. Note that the distributor's fill rate is actually a cost measure to the distributor, since the fill rate is associated with inventory holding cost and the amount of products required from the manufacturer. The distributor's fill rate implies benefit to the manufacturer, since more products are needed from the manufacturer (meaning more revenue to the manufacturer) if the distributor wishes to maintain a higher fill rate. Thus, the distributor's fill rate is treated as an output from the manufacturer and an input to the distributor. From a distributor's point of view, the distributor always tries to meet the needs of its customer while maintaining a fill rate as low as possible, because unnecessary high fill rate incurs additional cost to the distributor.

For the distributor, we use inventory cost and distribution cost as two direct inputs in addition to the above intermediate inputs linked with the manufacturer. Two intermediate outputs from the distributor are the number of products shipped from the distributor to the retailer, and the percentage of on-time delivery.

For the retailer, in addition to the intermediate inputs from the manufacturer and the distributor, we have one direct input of number of backorders, and one direct output of profit. Figure 8.8 presents the data with ten observations, i.e., $J = 10$.

	A	B	C	D	E	F	G	H	I	J	K	L	M
1			Observation	1	2	3	4	5	6	7	8	9	10
2			Supplier-labor	150	140	130	165	170	145	155	175	160	125
3			Supplier-cost	130	150	165	170	200	185	135	190	185	190
4			Supplier-revenue	20	21	23	24	27	25	24	30	28	25
5			mfg cost	125	120	110	150	146	115	105	100	135	120
6			mfg time	3	2	3	4	2	3	2	2	4	3
7			DC cost	90	100	80	70	85	77	78	90	78	68
8			customer res time	3	3	2	4	2	2	1	3	2	1
9			fill rate	70%	90%	78%	88%	73%	95%	89%	87%	95%	90%
10			product DC-retailer	1800	2000	2400	2300	2500	2500	2000	2000	2500	2300
11			on-time	96%	95%	97%	89%	99%	89%	93%	88%	99%	83%
12			product mfg-retaile	2000	2100	2500	1900	2600	2300	2200	2300	2500	2500
13			product mfg-DC	500	300	450	200	300	250	350	450	300	400
14			Retailer cost	100	110	130	125	140	135	125	155	135	130
15			Retailer revenue	310	220	300	230	320	240	350	370	325	355
16													
17													
18			λ	0	0	0	0	0	0	0.884	0	0	0
19			β	0	1.011	0	0	0	0	0	0	0	0
20			δ	0	0	0.07784	0	0	0	0	0	0.893	0
21			γ	1	0	0	0	0	0	0	0	0	3E-12
22													
23				0.92									
24				0.97			Supply Chain						
25		1	0.932955109	0.84									
26				1		Efficienc	supplier		mfg		DC		Retailer
27	Supplier-labor	150	S-labor	138	137.733	137.05							
28	Supplier-cost	130	S-cost	119	119.368	119.37							
29	Supplier-revenue	20	S-revenue	21.2		21.221		21.2					
30	mfg cost	125	mfg cost	121	121.263			121					
31	mfg time	3	mfg time	2.91	2.91032			2.02					
32	DC cost	90	DC cost	75.9	75.9147					75.91			
33	customer res time	3	customer res time	2.53	2.53049					1.943			
34	fill rate	0.7	fill rate	0.91				0.91		0.909			
35	product DC-retailer	1800	product DC-retailer	2420						2420		1800	
36	on-time	0.96	on-time	0.96				0.96		0.96		0.96	
37	product mfg-retaile	2000	product mfg-retaile	2122				2122				2000	
38	product mfg-DC	500	product mfg-DC	303				303		303.1			
39	Retailer cost	100	Retailer cost	100	100							100	
40	Retailer revenue	310	Retailer revenue									310	

Figure 8.8. Supply Chain Efficiency Spreadsheet Model

In Figure 8.8, cells D18:M21 represents λ_j, β_j, δ_j, and γ_j. Cell B25 indicates the observation under evaluation. Cells D23:D26 represents Ω_i (i = 1, 2, 3, 4). Cell C25 is the objective function of model (8.3), and contains the formula "= (D23+D24+D25+D26)/4".

Cells B27:B40 record the performance measures for a specific observation under evaluation. Cell B27 contains the formula "=INDEX (D2:M2,1,$B$25) which is copied into cell B28:B40.

Cells D27:D39 are used to represent the decision variables. The formulas used in the rest of the spreadsheet model shown in Figure 8.8 are

Cell F27=$D$23*B27
Cell F28=$D$23*B28
Cell F30=$D$24*B30
Cell F31 =$D$24*B31
Cell F32 =$D$25*B32
Cell F33 =$D$25*B33
Cell F39 =$D$26*B39

Cell G27=SUMPRODUCT($D$18:$M$18,D2:M2)
Cell G28 =SUMPRODUCT($D$18:$M$18,D3:M3)
Cell G29 =SUMPRODUCT($D$18:$M$18,D4:M4)

Cell I29=SUMPRODUCT($D$19:$M$19,D4:M4)
Cell I30=SUMPRODUCT($D$19:$M$19,D5:M5)
Cell I31 =SUMPRODUCT($D$19:$M$19,D6:M6)
Cell I34 =SUMPRODUCT($D$19:$M$19,D9:M9)
Cell I36 =SUMPRODUCT($D$19:$M$19,D11:M11)
Cell I37 =SUMPRODUCT($D$19:$M$19,D12:M12)
Cell I38 =SUMPRODUCT($D$19:$M$19,D13:M13)

Cell K32 =SUMPRODUCT($D$20:$M$20,D7:M7)
Cell K33=SUMPRODUCT($D$20:$M$20,D8:M8)
Cell K34 =SUMPRODUCT($D$20:$M$20,D9:M9)
Cell K35 =SUMPRODUCT($D$20:$M$20,D10:M10)
Cell K36 =SUMPRODUCT($D$20:$M$20,D11:M11)
Cell K38 =SUMPRODUCT($D$20:$M$20,D13:M13)

Cell M35 =SUMPRODUCT($D$21:$M$21,D10:M10)
Cell M36 =SUMPRODUCT($D$21:$M$21,D11:M11)
Cell M37 =SUMPRODUCT($D$21:$M$21,D12:M12)
Cell M39 =SUMPRODUCT($D$21:$M$21,D14:M14)
Cell M40 =SUMPRODUCT($D$21:$M$21,D15:M15)

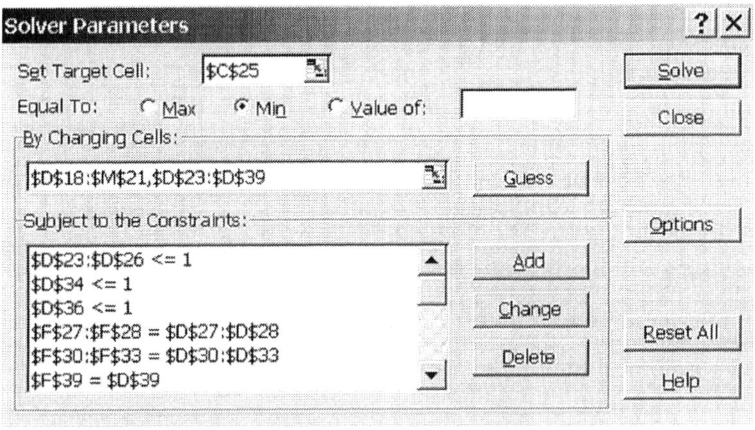

Figure 8.9. Solver Parameters for Supply Chain Efficiency

Figure 8.9 shows the Solver parameters for the spreadsheet shown in Figure 8.8 where cells D18:M21 and cells D23:D39 are changing cells. In this case, two additional constraints are added into model (8.3). One is "fill rate ≤ 100%", and the other "percentage of on-time delivery ≤ 100%". The constraints include

```
$D$23:$D$26 <= 1
$D$34 <= 1
$D$36 <= 1
$F$27:$F$28 = $D$27:$D$28
$F$30:$F$33 = $D$30:$D$33
$F$39 = $D$39
$G$27:$G$28 <= $D$27:$D$28
$G$29 >= $D$29
$I$29:$I$31 <= $D$29:$D$31
$I$34 >= $D$34
$I$36:$I$38 >= $D$36:$D$38
$K$32:$K$34 <= $D$32:$D$34
$K$35:$K$36 >= $D$35:$D$36
$K$38 <= $D$38
$M$35:$M$37 <= $D$35:$D$37
$M$39 <= $D$39
$M$40 >= $B$40
```

Table 8.3 reports the efficiency scores, optimal values to models (8.2) and (8.3) with $w_i = 1$ ($i = 1, ..., 4$).

Columns 2-5 characterize the performance of supply chain members based upon model (8.2). The sixth column reports the average efficiency score of the supply chain members. The supply chain performance is reported in the seventh column with Ω_i^* reported in the last four columns.

Although a number of observations on supply chain members are efficient, only one supply chain performance (observation 7) is efficient. i.e., the observation 7 represents the best practice of the supply chain system. Note that in this case, all supply chain members are efficient.

We observe that the average supply chain member efficiency score (column 6) is greater than the supply chain efficiency score (Ω^*). For example, consider observation 5 where two supply chain members (manufacturer and distributor) are efficiently operating. The average supply chain member efficiency score is 0.79456 and the supply chain efficiency score is 0.79456, indicating that the supply chain system could achieve more input savings.

Table 8.3. Supply Chain Efficiency

	Member Efficiency					Supply Chain Efficiency				
	Supplier	Manufacturer	Distributor	Retailer	Average	Supply Chain	Supplier	Manufacturer	Distributor	Retailer
Observation	$\theta^{supplier*}$	$\theta^{manufacturer*}$	$\theta^{distributor*}$	$\theta^{retailer*}$		Ω^*	Ω_1^*	Ω_2^*	Ω_3^*	Ω_4^*
1	0.865	1	1	1	0.966	0.933	0.918	0.970	0.843	1
2	0.881	1	0.880	0.673	0.859	0.669	0.599	0.624	0.465	0.714
3	0.964	1	1	0.810	0.944	0.791	0.720	0.747	0.747	0.948
4	0.870	0.856	1	0.754	0.870	0.576	0.518	0.460	0.658	0.667
5	0.895	1	1	0.820	0.929	0.795	0.688	0.768	0.768	0.954
6	0.937	0.999	1	0.673	0.902	0.613	0.529	0.579	0.625	0.717
7	1	1	1	1	1	1	1	1	1	1
8	1	1	0.811	1	0.953	0.943	1	1	0.770	1
9	0.994	0.904	1	0.856	0.938	0.783	0.696	0.694	0.874	0.868
10	1	0.986	1	1	0.997	0.992	1	0.968	1	1

Model (8.3) yields optimal values on the performance measures for (an inefficient) supply chain to reach the best practice. Consider observation 1 in Figure 8.8 where a set of optimal solutions is shown in cells D27:D39. Since $\Omega_4^* = 1$ indicating the retailer is efficient, no adjustments for measures related to the retailer are required. However, in order to reach the best practice, the supplier, the manufacturer and the distributor should reduce their "direct inputs" based upon Ω_i^* ($i = 1, 2, 3$). In addition, the supplier and the manufacturer should reach an agreement on the selling price of raw materials to increase the supplier's revenue by 6%. The distributor's fill rate should be increased to 90.95% (from the current rate of 70%). The products shipped from the manufacturer to the distributor should be reduced by 39%. This solution indicates that based upon the best practice, the distributor should be able to maintain the fill rate of 90.95% while the manufacturer reduces its shipment to the distributor.

Additional managerial information is available from the optimal values of λ_j^*, β_j^*, δ_j^*, and γ_j^*, since they provide information on which observations of supply chain members are used as benchmarks. For example, when the observation 1 is under evaluation by model (8.3), we have (i) $\lambda_7^* = 0.884$, indicating that the supplier in observation 7 is used as the benchmark; (ii) $\beta_2^* = 1.011$, indicating that the manufacturer in observation 2 is used as the benchmark; (iii) $\delta_3^* = 0.08$ and $\delta_9^* = 0.893$, indicating that the distributor in observations 3 and 9 is used as the benchmark; and (iv) $\gamma_1^* = 1$, indicating that the retailer in observation 1 is efficient and itself is used as the benchmark.

Some supply chains may choose to operate with high cost and high availability while others are lean with lower levels of service. The notion of DEA efficiency (i) provides an approach for characterizing and measuring the efficiency of supply chain as well as supply chain members, and (ii) makes it clear that two supply chains may have different input-output mix yet both may be efficient. Model (8.3) enables supply chain members to collectively improve the supply chain performance. Through the use of model (8.3), any supply chains can find ways to achieve best-practice performance and to gain a competitive edge. The approach also provides information on which supply chain members are used as a benchmark when a specific supply chain observation is under evaluation.

Chapter 9

Congestion

9.1 Congestion Measure

Congestion, as used in economics, refers to situations where reductions in one or more inputs generate an increase in one or more outputs. Examples can be found in underground mining and agriculture. For example, too much fertilizer applied to a given plot could reduce the overall output. We here adopt the following definition of congestion from Cooper, Thompson and Thrall (1996).

Definition 9.1 (Congestion) Evidence of congestion is present when reductions in one or more inputs can be associated with increases in one or more outputs – or, proceeding in reverse, when increases in one or more inputs can be associated with decreases in one or more outputs – without worsening any other input or output.

Färe and Grosskopf (1983) apply this concept to DEA using strong and weak input disposabilities. The envelopment DEA models discussed in Chapter 1 are strong input/output disposability models. We re-write the VRS envelopment models as

$$\theta^* = \min \theta$$
subject to
$$\sum_{j=1}^{n} \lambda_j x_{ij} \leq \theta x_{io} \qquad i = 1,2,...,m; \tag{9.1}$$
$$\sum_{j=1}^{n} \lambda_j y_{rj} \geq y_{ro} \qquad r = 1,2,...,s;$$

$$\sum_{j=1}^{n} \lambda_j = 1$$

$$\lambda_j \geq 0 \qquad\qquad j = 1, ..., n.$$

$$\phi^* = \max \phi$$
subject to
$$\sum_{j=1}^{n} \lambda_j x_{ij} \leq x_{io} \qquad i = 1,2,...,m;$$
$$\sum_{j=1}^{n} \lambda_j y_{rj} \geq \phi y_{ro} \qquad r = 1,2,...,s; \qquad\qquad (9.2)$$
$$\sum_{j=1}^{n} \lambda_j = 1$$
$$\lambda_j \geq 0 \qquad\qquad j = 1, ..., n.$$

If we assume weak disposability of inputs and outputs in models (9.1) and (9.2), respectively, we obtain

$$\widetilde{\theta}^* = \min \widetilde{\theta}$$
subject to
$$\sum_{j=1}^{n} \lambda_j x_{ij} = \widetilde{\theta} x_{io} \qquad i = 1,2,...,m;$$
$$\sum_{j=1}^{n} \lambda_j y_{rj} \geq y_{ro} \qquad r = 1,2,...,s; \qquad\qquad (9.3)$$
$$\sum_{j=1}^{n} \lambda_j = 1$$
$$\lambda_j \geq 0 \qquad\qquad j = 1, ..., n.$$

$$\widetilde{\phi}^* = \max \widetilde{\phi}$$
subject to
$$\sum_{j=1}^{n} \lambda_j x_{ij} \leq x_{io} \qquad i = 1,2,...,m;$$
$$\sum_{j=1}^{n} \lambda_j y_{rj} = \widetilde{\phi} y_{ro} \qquad r = 1,2,...,s; \qquad\qquad (9.4)$$
$$\sum_{j=1}^{n} \lambda_j = 1$$
$$\lambda_j \geq 0 \qquad\qquad j = 1, ..., n.$$

Note that, for example, the difference between models (9.1) and (9.3) is that input inequalities are changed into input equalities. If we apply weak disposability to other envelopment models, we obtain the weak disposability DEA models shown in Table 9.1.

The input and output congestion measures are then defined as $C(\theta^*, \widetilde{\theta}^*)$ = $\theta^* / \widetilde{\theta}^*$, and $C(\phi^*, \widetilde{\phi}^*) = \phi^* / \widetilde{\phi}^*$, respectively. Note that we must have $\theta^* \leq \widetilde{\theta}^*$ because the latter is associated with equalities. As shown by Färe, Grosskopf and Lovell (1994), we can use $C(\theta^*, \widetilde{\theta}^*)$ (or $C(\phi^*, \widetilde{\phi}^*)$) as a measure of congestion with the following properties. If $C(\theta^*, \tilde{\theta}^*) = 1$ $(C(\phi^*, \tilde{\phi}^*) = 1)$, then input (output) is not congested; alternatively, if $C(\theta^*, \tilde{\theta}^*) < 1$ $(C(\phi^*, \tilde{\phi}^*) > 1)$, then input (output) congestion is present.

Table 9.1. Weak Disposability DEA Models

Frontier Type	Weak Input Disposability	Weak Output Disposability
CRS	$\min \tilde{\theta}$ subject to $\sum_{j=1}^{n} \lambda_j x_{ij} = \tilde{\theta} x_{io} \quad i = 1,2,...,m;$ $\sum_{j=1}^{n} \lambda_j y_{rj} \geq y_{ro} \quad r = 1,2,...,s;$ $\lambda_j \geq 0 \qquad j = 1,2,...,n.$	$\max \tilde{\phi}$ subject to $\sum_{j=1}^{n} \lambda_j x_{ij} \leq x_{io} \quad i = 1,2,...,m;$ $\sum_{j=1}^{n} \lambda_j y_{rj} = \tilde{\phi} y_{ro} \quad r = 1,2,...,s;$ $\lambda_j \geq 0 \qquad j = 1,2,...,n.$
VRS		Add $\sum_{j=1}^{n} \lambda_j = 1$
NIRS		Add $\sum_{j=1}^{n} \lambda_j \leq 1$
NDRS		Add $\sum_{j=1}^{n} \lambda_j \geq 1$

	A	B	C	D	E	F	G	H	I	J
1	Mines	Labor	K1	K2	T1	1/D1		Output	λ	Weak
2	1	98.5	142	245	8	0.016		3264	0	1
3	2	96.5	30	215	6	0.016		3065	0	1
4	3	57.6	18	105	5.6	0.026		2275	0	1
5	4	59.2	160	0	5.9	0.025		1978	0	1
6	5	57.6	200	0	8	0.022		1833	0	1
7	6	49.9	27	85	4.5	0.019		1218	0	1
8	7	53.5	143	65	8	0.01		928	0	1
9	8	34	70	65	8	0.02		919	0	1
10	9	39.6	67.5	40	6.5	0.013		777	0	1
11	10	51.3	0	145	3.2	0.019		745	0	1
12	11	74.2	110	85	2.1	0.014		742	0	1
13	12	24	25	85	4.4	0.012		488	0	1
14	13	26.5	58	0	3	0.014		407	0	1
15	14	43.1	70	0	8.5	0.012		402	0	1
16	15	20.7	236	0	5.7	0.01		396	1	1
17										
18		Reference		DMU under	**15**	Efficiency				
19	**Constraints**	set		Evaluation		1				
20	Labor	20.7	=	20.7						
21	K1	236	=	236						
22	K2	0	=	0		Weak				
23	T1	5.7	=	5.7						
24	1/D1	0.01	=	0.01						
25	output	396	≥	396						
26	Σλ	1	=	1						

Figure 9.1. VRS Weak Input Disposability Spreadsheet Model

Byrnes, Färe and Grosskopf (1984) study the congestion of 15 Illinois coal mines. Figure 9.1 presents the 15 mines with one output (thousands tons) and five inputs, namely, labor (thousand miner-days), dragline capacity (K1) (cubic yards), power-shovel capacity (K2) (cubic yards), thickness of first-seam mined (T1) (feet), and reciprocal of depth to first-seam mined (1/D1) (D1 in feet).

In Figure 9.1, cells B20:B26 contain the formulas

Cell B20 =SUMPRODUCT(B2:B16,$I$2:$I$16)
Cell B21 =SUMPRODUCT(C2:C16,$I$2:$I$16)
Cell B22 =SUMPRODUCT(D2:D16,$I$2:$I$16)
Cell B23 =SUMPRODUCT(E2:E16,$I$2:$I$16)
Cell B24 =SUMPRODUCT(F2:F16,$I$2:$I$16)
Cell B25 =SUMPRODUCT(H2:H16,$I$2:$I$16)
Cell B26 =SUM(I2:I16)

where cells I2:I16 represent the changing cells, λ_j (j = 1, ..., 15).

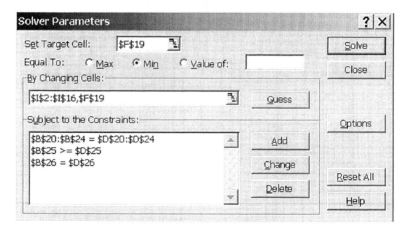

Figure 9.2. Solver Parameters for VRS Weak Input Disposability Model

Cells D20:D25 contain the formulas

D20 =$F$19*INDEX($B$2:$F$16,$E$18,1)
D21 =$F$19*INDEX($B$2:$F$16,$E$18,2)
D22 =$F$19*INDEX($B$2:$F$16,$E$18,3)
D23 =$F$19*INDEX($B$2:$F$16,$E$18,4)
D24 =$F$19*INDEX($B$2:$F$16,$E$18,5)
D25 =INDEX(H2:H16,$E$18,1)

where F19 is the target cell ($\widetilde{\theta}$), and cell E18 indicates the DMU under evaluation.

Figure 9.2 shows the Solver parameters for model (9.3) shown in Figure 9.1.

The optimal value to model (9.3) in this case is equal to one across all DMUs. i.e., each mine is on the frontier. To obtain the congestion measure, we also need to calculate model (9.1). Figure 9.3 shows the results. Figure 9.3 is the input-oriented VRS envelopment model where the inputs are strongly disposable. The related Solver parameters can be obtained by changing the equalities to inequalities in Figure 9.2, as shown in Figure 9.4. The efficiency scores are reported in cells J2:J16. The efficiency scores for weak input disposability are reported in cells K2:K16. It can be seen that congestion is present at DMUs 6 and 8.

	A	B	C	D	E	F	G	H	I	J	K
1	Mines	Labor	K1	K2	T1	1/D1		Output	λ	Strong	Weak
2	1	98.5	142	245	8	0.018		3264	0	1	1
3	2	86.5	30	215	8	0.018		3085	0	1	1
4	3	57.8	18	105	5.8	0.026		2275	0	1	1
5	4	59.2	160	0	5.9	0.025		1978	0	1	1
6	5	57.8	200	0	8	0.022		1833	0	1	1
7	6	48.9	27	85	4.5	0.019		1218	0	0.97128	1
8	7	53.5	143	85	8	0.01		828	0	1	1
9	8	34	70	85	8	0.02		918	0	0.93747	1
10	9	39.6	67.5	40	6.5	0.013		777	0	1	1
11	10	51.3	0	145	3.2	0.019		745	0	1	1
12	11	74.2	110	65	2.1	0.014		742	0	1	1
13	12	24	25	85	4.4	0.012		488	0	1	1
14	13	26.5	58	0	3	0.014		407	0	1	1
15	14	43.1	70	0	8.5	0.012		402	0	1	1
16	15	20.7	236	0	5.7	0.01		396	1	1	1
17											
18		Reference		DMU under	15	Efficiency					
19	**Constr**	set		Evaluation		1					
20	Labor	20.7	≤	20.7							
21	K1	236	≤	236							
22	K2	0	≤	0		Strong					
23	T1	5.7	≤	5.7							
24	1/D1	0.01	≤	0.01							
25	output	396	≥	396							
26	Σλ	1	=	1							

Figure 9.3. Congestion Measure For 15 Mines

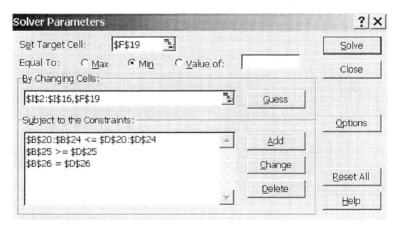

Figure 9.4. Solver Parameters for Input-oriented VRS Strong Input Disposability Model

When input congestion is present, we need to identify sources and amounts of congestion. Färe, Grosskopf and Lovell (1994) suggest a procedure for identifying input measure responsible for the input congestion.

$$\alpha^* = \min \alpha$$
subject to
$$\sum_{j=1}^{n} \lambda_j x_{ij} = \alpha x_{io} \quad i \in A;$$
$$\sum_{j=1}^{n} \lambda_j x_{ij} \leq \alpha x_{io} \quad i \in \overline{A}; \quad (9.5)$$
$$\sum_{j=1}^{n} \lambda_j y_{rj} \geq y_{ro} \quad r = 1,...,s;$$
$$\sum_{j=1}^{n} \lambda_j = 1$$
$$\lambda_j \geq 0 \quad j = 1,...,n.$$

where $A \subseteq \{1, 2, ..., m\}$ and $\overline{A}$ is the complement. Using $\tilde{\theta}^*$ and α^* for each $A \subseteq \{1, 2, ..., m\}$, if $C(\theta^*, \tilde{\theta}^*) < 1$, and $\theta^* = \alpha^*$, as obtained from (9.1) and (9.5), the components of the subvectors associated with $\overline{A}$ (= $\{i \mid i \notin A\}$) then identify sources and amounts of congestion. Similar models can be established for different RTS frontier and orientation assumptions. For example, if we remove $\sum \lambda_j = 1$, we obtain the model under VRS.

The suggested route requires additional computation which can be onerous because it involves obtaining solutions over all possible partitions of A. In fact, the route followed by Färe, Grosskopf and Lovell (1994) emphasizes efficiency measurements with identification of sources and amounts of inefficiencies to be undertaken as an additional job.

9.2 Congestion and Slacks

We first provide the following definition.

Definition 9.2 (DEA Slacks) An optimal value of s_i^- and s_r^+ in (1.4) (or (1.7), which we represent by s_i^{-*} and s_r^{+*}, are respectively called DEA input and output slack values. i.e., we refer to the slacks obtained in the second stage of DEA calculation as DEA slacks.

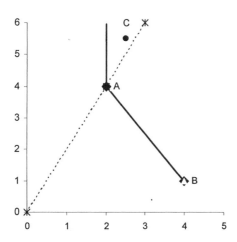

Figure 9.5. Congestion at point C

To illustrate the nature of congestion. Figures 9.5 and 9.6 plot an input isoquant. The input isoquant bends at point A in Figure 9.5 because of the weak input disposability. As a result, AC is part the frontier, and for C, the optimal value to model (9.3) is one. However, for C, the optimal value to model (9.1) is less than one. Thus, input congestion is presented at C in Figure 9.5.

In Figure 9.6, the isoquant bends at point D. Because of the existence of D, the optimal values to models (9.1) and (9.3) are equal. Thus, input congestion is absent at C in Figure 9.6.

Furthermore, note that if the efficient reference set consists of A, point C will have a positive DEA slack value for the second input x2. Because of the presence of the weakly efficient point D (a frontier point with non-zero DEA slacks), if the efficient reference set consists of points A and D, point C will not have slack values. (The (input) slacks do not necessarily represent DEA slack values.)

However, if all frontier DMUs are extreme efficient, e.g., A and B, in Figure 9.5, then the input slacks are the same as the DEA slack values. In Figure 9.6, because C can be compared to a convex combination of D (weakly efficient) and A, no input slack is detected.

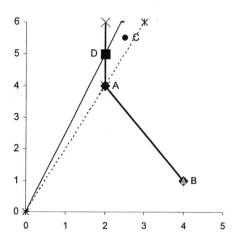

Figure 9.6. No Congestion at Point C

Theorem 9.1 Input congestion as defined by C(θ^*, $\tilde{\theta}^*$) is not present in the performance of DMU_o *if and only if* an optimal solution is associated with referent frontier DMUs such that non-zero input slack values are <u>not</u> detected in model (9.1).

[Proof]: Recall that the only difference between (9.1) and (9.3) is that the input inequalities are changed to equalities. The referent frontier DMUs are those in the basis when calculating the strong disposability model (9.1). If we have some referent DMUs such that no non-zero input slack values are detected for DMU_o, then we have, at optimality,

$$\sum_{j \in B} \lambda_j^* x_{ij} = \theta^* x_{io} \text{ for } i = 1, \ldots, m$$

where B represents the set of referent DMUs, $B=\{j|\ \lambda_j^*>0\}$. Obviously, λ_j^* and θ^* are also optimal for (9.3). Therefore $\theta^* = \beta^*$. Thus, no input congestion occurs. This completes the *if* part.

To establish the *only if* part, we note that if no input congestion is identified when an optimum is associated with a basis B' such that $\sum_{j\in B'}\lambda_j^* x_{ij} = \beta^* x_{io} = \theta^* x_{io}$, then this same optimum provides referent DMUs such that the input constraints are binding in (9.1). Therefore no non-zero input slack values are detected by reference to those DMUs in B'. ∎

It is well know that in the single input and the single output situation, no input or output slack will occur for CRS envelopment models, whereas non-zero slack values may occur for VRS models. That is to say, in the single input and the single output situation, congestion will never occur with CRS but can possibly happen with VRS.

Based upon Theorem 9.1, we have

Corollary 9.1 If the observed values on the efficient frontier are composed only of extreme efficient DMUs, then congestion can occur *if and only if* non-zero DEA slack values are detected. Furthermore, the sources of congestion can then only be found in these non-zero DEA slack values.

Corollary 9.1 can be important in real world applications, since the frontiers in most real world data sets contain only the extreme efficient DMUs. Consequently, the congestion and its amount can simply be represented by the DEA slacks (see Ray, Seiford and Zhu, 1998).

The discussion here is based upon the VRS envelopment model and input congestion measure. The discussion for output congestion measures is the same.

9.3   Slack-based Congestion Measure

The previous section indicates that there is a strong relationship between (input) slacks and the measure of (input) congestion. In fact, Brockett, Cooper, Shin and Wang (1998) develop a new slack-based approach to capture input congestion and identify its sources and amounts. Cooper, Seiford and Zhu (2000) study the relationship between these two DEA congestion approaches, and show that the work of Brockett, Cooper, Shin and Wang (1998) improves upon the work of Färe, Grosskopf and Lovell (1994) in that it not only (i) detects congestion but also (ii) determines the amount of congestion, and simultaneously, (iii) identifies factors responsible for congestion and distinguishes congestion amounts from other components of inefficiency.

The following model is employed by Brockett, Cooper, Shin and Wang (1998) after solving the input-oriented VRS envelopment model

$$max \sum_{i=1}^{m} \delta_i^+$$

subject to

$$\sum_{j=1}^{n} \lambda_j x_{ij} - \delta_i^+ = \theta^* x_{io} - s_i^{-*} = \hat{x}_{io} \quad i = 1,2,...,m;$$

$$\sum_{j=1}^{n} \lambda_j y_{rj} = y_{ro} + s_r^{+*} = \hat{y}_{ro} \quad r = 1,2,...,s; \qquad (9.6)$$

$$\sum_{j=1}^{n} \lambda_j = 1$$

$$\lambda_j \geq 0, \ s_i^{-*} \geq \delta_i^+$$

where θ^* is obtained from (9.1) while s_i^{-*} and s_r^{+*} are obtained from (1.4). The amount of congestion in each input can then be determined by the difference between each pair of s_i^{-*} and δ_i^{+*}, where δ_i^{+*} are optimal values in (9.6). That is,

$$s_i^c = s_i^{-*} - \delta_i^{+*}, i = 1, 2, \ldots m \qquad (9.7)$$

Definition 9.3 (Congestion Slacks) s_i^c defined in (9.7) are called input congestion slacks.

Similarly, we can calculate the output congestion slacks by

$$max \sum_{r=1}^{s} \delta_r^-$$

subject to

$$\sum_{j=1}^{n} \lambda_j x_{ij} = x_{io} - s_i^{-*} = \hat{x}_{io} \quad i = 1,2,...,m;$$

$$\sum_{j=1}^{n} \lambda_j y_{rj} + \delta_r^- = \phi^* y_{ro} + s_r^{+*} = \hat{y}_{ro} \quad r = 1,2,...,s;$$

$$\sum_{j=1}^{n} \lambda_j = 1$$

$$\lambda_j \geq 0, \ s_r^{+*} \geq \delta_r^-$$

where ϕ^* is obtained from (9.2) while s_i^{-*} and s_r^{+*} are obtained from (1.7).

To establish the relationship between model (9.6) and C(θ^*, $\tilde{\theta}^*$), we proceed as follows. Let x (s_i^c) be an input subvector in which its *i*th component corresponds to $s_i^c \neq 0$, i.e., x (s_i^c) is a congesting subvector. Next, let $\mathbf{X}^C$ be the set of all congesting subvectors obtained via (9.5). We have

Theorem 9.2 $x(s_i^c) \in \mathbf{X}^{\mathbf{C}}$. Furthermore, if (9.6) yields a unique optimal solution, then $\mathbf{X}^{\mathbf{C}} = \{x(s_i^c)\}$.

[Proof]: Let $A = \{i \mid s_i^c = 0\}$ and $\overline{A} = \{i \mid s_i^c \neq 0\}$. Then the constraints of (9.6) become

$$\sum_{j=1}^{n} \lambda_j x_{ij} = \theta^* x_{io} \quad i \in A;$$

$$\sum_{j=1}^{n} \lambda_j x_{ij} \leq \theta^* x_{io} \quad i \in \overline{A};$$

$$\sum_{j=1}^{n} \lambda_j y_{rj} = y_{ro} + s_r^{+*} \quad r = 1,2,...,s; \tag{9.8}$$

$$\sum_{j=1}^{n} \lambda_j = 1$$

$$\lambda_j \geq 0, s_i^{-*} \geq \delta_i.$$

where θ^* is the optimal value to (9.1). This implies that θ^* is a feasible solution to (9.5). Thus, $\alpha^* \leq \theta^*$, where α^* is the optimal value to (9.5) associated with A and $\overline{A}$. On the other hand, any optimal solution to (9.5) is a feasible solution (1), therefore $\alpha^* \geq \theta^*$. Thus, $\theta^* = \alpha^*$ indicating that the input subvector associated with $\overline{A}$, $x(s_i^c)$, is a source of congestion. Therefore, $x(s_i^c) \in \mathbf{X}^{\mathbf{C}}$.

Moreover, if (9.6) yields a unique optimal solution, then the solution in (9.8) is also unique. This means that $\theta^* = \alpha^*$ does not hold for other input subvectors. Thus, $\mathbf{X}^{\mathbf{C}} = \{x(s_i^c)\}$. ■

Theorem 9.2 indicates that under the condition of uniqueness, congestion will occur in the Brockett, Cooper, Shin and Wang (1998) approach if and only if it appears in Färe, Grosskopf and Lovell (1994) approach. However, the Brockett, Cooper, Shin and Wang (1998) approach identifies technical or mix inefficiencies and distinguishes these from congestion components via (9.7).

We observe that the use of (9.5) may result in different congestion factors because of possible multiple optimal solutions. Theorem 9.2 indicates that the results from (9.6) then yield one of the congesting subvectors obtained from (9.5). As a result, the procedure by Färe, Grosskopf and Lovell (1994) for detecting the factors responsible for the congestion may be replaced by model (9.6) and one can more easily find and identify congestion and its sources without having to conduct a series of solutions as required for (9.5).

Consider the mine example again. Before we solve model (9.6), ,we need to determine the DEA slacks for the spreadsheet shown in Figure 9.3. i.e., we need to perform the second stage calculation for the input-oriented VRS envelopment model.

Figure 9.7 shows the spreadsheet for calculating the DEA slacks. Cells F20:F25 and F26 represent the input slacks and output slack, respectively. Cell F19 represent the sum of slacks and is the target cell in the Solver parameters shown in Figure 9.8.

	A	B	C	D	E	F	G	H	I	J	K	L	M	N	O	P	Q
1	Mines	Labor	K1	K2	T1	1/D1		Output	λ	Strong		Labor	K1	K2	T1	1/D1	Output
2	1	98.5	142	245	6	0.016		3264	0	1		0.000	0.000	0.000	0.000	0.000	0.000
3	2	98.5	30	215	6	0.015		3085	0	1		0.000	0.000	0.000	0.000	0.000	0.000
4	3	57.6	18	105	5.6	0.026		2275	0	1		0.000	0.000	0.000	0.000	0.000	0.000
5	4	59.2	160	0	5.9	0.025		1978	0	1		0.000	0.000	0.000	0.000	0.000	0.000
6	5	57.6	200	0	8	0.022		1833	1E-15	1		0.000	0.000	0.000	0.000	0.000	0.000
7	6	49.9	27	85	4.5	0.019		1218	0	0.97129		5.384	0.000	0.000	0.000	0.000	0.000
8	7	53.5	143	65	6	0.01		928	0	1		0.000	0.000	0.000	0.000	0.000	0.000
9	8	34	70	65	8	0.02		919	0	0.93747		0.000	0.000	0.000	0.693	0.004	0.000
10	9	39.6	87.5	40	6.5	0.013		777	0	1		0.000	0.000	0.000	0.000	0.000	0.000
11	10	51.3	0	145	3.2	0.019		745	0	1		0.000	0.000	0.000	0.000	0.000	0.000
12	11	74.2	110	65	2.1	0.014		742	0	1		0.000	0.000	0.000	0.000	0.000	0.000
13	12	24	25	65	4.4	0.012		488	0	1		0.000	0.000	0.000	0.000	0.000	0.000
14	13	26.5	58	0	3	0.014		407	0	1		0.000	0.000	0.000	0.000	0.000	0.000
15	14	43.1	70	0	8.5	0.012		402	0	1		0.000	0.000	0.000	0.000	0.000	0.000
16	15	20.7	236	0	5.7	0.01		398	1	1		0.000	0.000	0.000	0.000	0.000	0.000
17																	
18			Reference		DMU under	15	Sum of Slacks										
19	Constraints	set		Evaluation		0.0000		DEA Slack									
20	Labor	20.7	=	20.7		0.0000											
21	K1	236	=	236		0.0000											
22	K2	0	=	0		0.0000											
23	T1	5.7	=	5.7		0.0000											
24	1/D1	0.01	=	0.01		0.0000											
25	output	398	=	398		0.0000											
26	Σλ	1	=	1													

Figure 9.7. DEA Slacks for 15 Mines

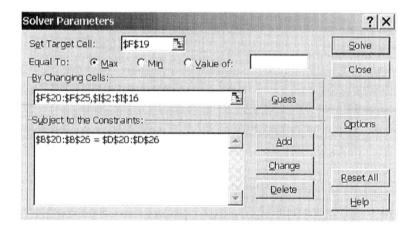

Figure 9.8. Solver Parameters for Calculating DEA Slacks for 15 Mines

The formulas for cells B20:B25 are

Cell B20 =SUMPRODUCT(B2:B16,$I$2:$I$16)+F20

Cell B21 =SUMPRODUCT(C2:C16,$I$2:$I$16)+F21
Cell B22 =SUMPRODUCT(D2:D16,$I$2:$I$16)+F22
Cell B23 =SUMPRODUCT(E2:E16,$I$2:$I$16)+F23
Cell B24 =SUMPRODUCT(F2:F16,$I$2:$I$16)+F24
Cell B25 =SUMPRODUCT(H2:H16,$I$2:$I$16)-F25

Cell F26 represents the sum of λ_j (=SUM(I2:I16)). Cells D20:D25 contains

D20 =INDEX(J2:J16,E18,1)*INDEX($B$2:$F$16,$E$18,1)
D21 =INDEX(J2:J16,E18,1)*INDEX($B$2:$F$16,$E$18,2)
D22 =INDEX(J2:J16,E18,1)*INDEX($B$2:$F$16,$E$18,3)
D23 =INDEX(J2:J16,E18,1)*INDEX($B$2:$F$16,$E$18,4)
D24 =INDEX(J2:J16,E18,1)*INDEX($B$2:$F$16,$E$18,5)
D25 =INDEX(H2:H16,$E$18,1)

The DEA slack calculation is performed by the VBA procedure "DEASlack"

```
Sub DEASlack()
Dim i As Integer
For i = 1 To 15
Range("E18") = i
SolverSolve UserFinish:=True
Range("F20:F25").Copy
Range("L" & i + 1).Select
Selection.PasteSpecial Paste:=xlPasteValues, Transpose:=True
Next i
End Sub
```

We next calculate model (9.6) for DMUs 6 and 8. Based upon the DEA slacks in cells L2:Q16, Figure 9.9 shows the spreadsheet for calculating the congestion slacks.

Cells F20:F24 now represent δ_i^+. Cell F19 contains the formula "=SUM (F20:F24)", and is the target cell. We change the formulas for cells B20:B25 and D20:D25 to

Cell B20 =SUMPRODUCT(B2:B16,$I$2:$I$16)-F20
Cell B21 =SUMPRODUCT(C2:C16,$I$2:$I$16)-F21
Cell B22 =SUMPRODUCT(D2:D16,$I$2:$I$16)-F22
Cell B23 =SUMPRODUCT(E2:E16,$I$2:$I$16)-F23
Cell B24 =SUMPRODUCT(F2:F16,$I$2:$I$16)-F24

Cell B25 =SUMPRODUCT(H2:H16,$I$2:$I$16)

D20 =INDEX(J2:J16,E18,1)*INDEX($B$2:$F$16,$E$18,1)-
INDEX(L2:L16,E18,1)

D21 =INDEX(J2:J16,E18,1)*INDEX($B$2:$F$16,$E$18,2)-
INDEX(M2:M16,E18,1)

D22 =INDEX(J2:J16,E18,1)*INDEX($B$2:$F$16,$E$18,3)-
INDEX(N2:N16,E18,1)

D23 =INDEX(J2:J16,E18,1)*INDEX($B$2:$F$16,$E$18,4)-
INDEX(O2:O16,E18,1)

D24 =INDEX(J2:J16,E18,1)*INDEX($B$2:$F$16,$E$18,5)-
INDEX(P2:P16,E18,1)

D25 =INDEX(H2:H16,$E$18,1)+INDEX(Q2:Q16,E18,1)

	A	B	C	D	E	F	G H	I	J	K	L	M	N	O	P	Q
1	Mines	Labor	K1	K2	T1	1/D1	Output	λ	Strong	Labor	K1	K2	T1	1/D1	Output	
2	1	98.5	142	245	8	0.016	3264	0	1	0.000	0.000	0.000	0.000	0.000	0.000	
3	2	96.5	30	215	8	0.016	3065	0	1	0.000	0.000	0.000	0.000	0.000	0.000	
4	3	57.8	18	105	5.8	0.026	2275	0.2522751	1	0.000	0.000	0.000	0.000	0.000	0.000	
5	4	59.2	180	0	5.9	0.025	1978	0	1	0.000	0.000	0.000	0.000	0.000	0.000	
6	5	57.8	200	0	8	0.022	1833	7.9E-17	1	0.000	0.000	0.000	0.000	0.000	0.000	
7	6	49.9	27	85	4.5	0.019	1218	0	0.97128	5.384	0.000	0.000	0.000	0.000	0.000	
8	7	53.5	143	85	8	0.01	928	0	1	0.000	0.000	0.000	0.000	0.000	0.000	
9	8	34	70	85	8	0.02	919	0	0.93747	0.000	0.000	0.000	0.693	0.004	0.000	
10	9	39.6	67.5	40	6.5	0.013	777	0	1	0.000	0.000	0.000	0.000	0.000	0.000	
11	10	51.3	0	145	3.2	0.019	745	0	1	0.000	0.000	0.000	0.000	0.000	0.000	
12	11	74.2	110	85	2.1	0.014	742	0	1	0.000	0.000	0.000	0.000	0.000	0.000	
13	12	24	25	85	4.4	0.012	488	0.5299453	1	0.000	0.000	0.000	0.000	0.000	0.000	
14	13	26.5	58	0	3	0.014	407	0.0200163	1	0.000	0.000	0.000	0.000	0.000	0.000	
15	14	43.1	70	0	6.5	0.012	402	0	1	0.000	0.000	0.000	0.000	0.000	0.000	
16	15	20.7	236	0	5.7	0.01	396	0.1977633	1	0.000	0.000	0.000	0.000	0.000	0.000	
17																
18			Reference		DMU under	8	Sum of δi		DEA	Congestion						
19	Constraints		set		Evaluation		0.0000		Slacks	Slacks						
20		Labor	31.8739	=	31.873884		0.0000	<	0	0.0000						
21		K1	85.6227	=	85.622662		0.0000	<	0	0.0000						
22		K2	60.9353	=	60.935329		0.0000	<	0	0.0000						
23		T1	4.9318	=	4.9317994		0.0000	<	0.693	0.6930						
24		1/D1	0.0152	=	0.0151764		0.0000	<	0.004	0.0038						
25		output	919	=	919.000											
26		Σλ	1	=	1											

Figure 9.9. Congestion Slack Spreadsheet Model

Cells H20:H24 represent the DEA slacks for a DMU under evaluation and return the DEA slacks reported in cells L2:Q16. The formulas are

Cells H20 =INDEX(L2:L16,E18,1)
Cells H21 =INDEX(M2:M16,E18,1)
Cells H22 =INDEX(N2:N16,E18,1)
Cells H23 =INDEX(O2:O16,E18,1)
Cells H24 =INDEX(P2:P16,E18,1)

Figure 9.10 shows the Solver parameters for calculating the congestion slacks. The congestion slacks are reported in cells I20:I24. In this example, the congestion slacks are equal to the DEA slacks for DMUs 6 and 8, because $\delta_i^+ = 0$ in optimality. For example, for DMU 6, the congestion factor is labor with a congestion slack of 5.384.

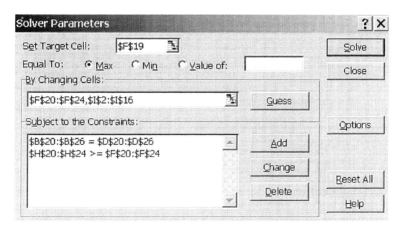

Figure 9.10. Solver Parameters for Calculating Congestion Slacks

Chapter 10

Super Efficiency

10.1 Super-efficiency DEA Models

When a DMU under evaluation is not included in the reference set of the envelopment models, the resulting DEA models are called super-efficiency DEA models. Charnes, Haag, Jaska and Semple (1992) use a super-efficiency model to study the sensitivity of the efficiency classifications. Zhu (1996b) and Seiford and Zhu (1998d) develop a number of new super-efficiency models to determine the efficiency stability regions (see Chapter 11). Andersen and Petersen (1993) propose using the CRS super-efficiency model in ranking the efficient DMUs. Also, the super-efficiency DEA models can be used in detecting influential observations (Wilson, 1995) and in identifying the extreme efficient DMUs (Thrall, 1996). Seiford and Zhu (1999c) study the infeasibility of various super-efficiency models developed from the envelopment models in Table 1.2. Chapter 11 presents other super-efficiency models that are used in sensitivity analysis.

Table 10.1 presents the basic super-efficiency DEA models based upon the envelopment DEA models. Based upon Table 10.1, we see that the difference between the super-efficiency and the envelopment models is that the DMU_o under evaluation is excluded from the reference set in the super-efficiency models. i.e., the super-efficiency DEA models are based on a reference technology constructed from all other DMUs.

Consider the example in Table 1.1. If we measure the (CRS) super efficiency of DMU2, then DMU2 is evaluated against point A on the new facet determined by DMUs 1 and 3 (see Figure 10.1). To calculate the (CRS) super efficiency score for DMU2, we use the spreadsheet model shown in Figure 10.2.

Table 10.1. Super-efficiency DEA Models

Frontier Type	Input-Oriented		Output-Oriented	
CRS	$\min \theta^{super}$ subject to $\sum_{\substack{j=1 \\ j \neq o}}^{n} \lambda_j x_{ij} \leq \theta^{super} x_{io}$ $\sum_{\substack{j=1 \\ j \neq o}}^{n} \lambda_j y_{rj} \geq y_{ro}$ $\lambda_j \geq 0$	$i = 1,2,...,m;$ $r = 1,2,...,s;$ $j \neq o.$	$\max \phi^{super}$ subject to $\sum_{\substack{j=1 \\ j \neq o}}^{n} \lambda_j x_{ij} \leq x_{io}$ $\sum_{\substack{j=1 \\ j \neq o}}^{n} \lambda_j y_{rj} \geq \phi^{super} y_{ro}$ $\lambda_j \geq 0$	$i = 1,2,...,m;$ $r = 1,2,...,s;$ $j \neq o.$
VRS	Add $\sum_{j \neq o} \lambda_j = 1$			
NIRS	Add $\sum_{j \neq o} \lambda_j \leq 1$			
NDRS	Add $\sum_{j \neq o} \lambda_j \geq 1$			

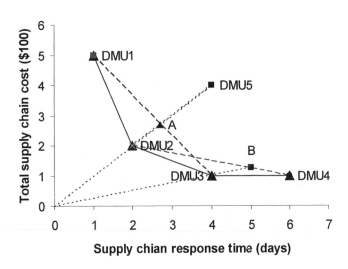

Figure 10.1. Super-efficiency

Cell E9 indicates the DMU under evaluation which is excluded from the reference set. Cells F2:F6 are reserved for λ_j ($j = 1, 2, 3, 4, 5$), and cell F10 is reserved for the super-efficiency score (θ^{super}).

Cells B11:B13 contain the following formulas

Cell B11 =SUMPRODUCT(B2:B6,F2:F6)
Cell B12 =SUMPRODUCT(C2:C6,F2:F6)

Cell B13 =SUMPRODUCT(E2:E6,F2:F6)

	A	B	C	D	E	F	G	H
1	DMU	Cost	Time		Profit	λ		
2	1	1	5		2	0.428571		
3	2	2	2		2	0		
4	3	4	1		2	0.571429		
5	4	6	1		2	0		
6	5	4	4		2	0		
7				Reserved to indicate				
8				the DMU under		Super		
9		Reference		evaluation.		Efficiency		
10	**Constraints**	set		DMU under	2		Super Efficiency;	
				Evaluation		1.357143	θsuper;	
11	Cost	2.7142857	≤	2.7142857			A changing cell;	
12	Time	2.7142857	≤	2.7142857			Target cell in Solver	
13	Profit	2	≥	2				
14	λo	0	=	0				
15	Represent the DMU							
16	under evaluation;							
17	Set this λ = 0 in the							
18	Solver parameters							

Figure 10.2. Input-oriented CRS Super-efficiency Spreadsheet Model

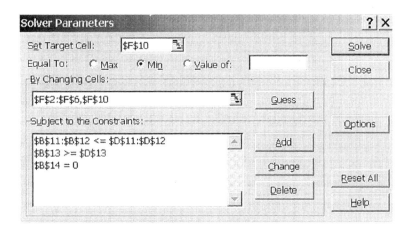

Figure 10.3. Solver Parameters for Input-oriented CRS Super-efficiency

Note that in the above formulas, the DMU under evaluation is included in the reference set. In order to exclude the DMU under evaluation from the reference set, we introduce the following formula into cell B14

Cell B14 =INDEX(F2:F6,E9,1)

which returns the λ_j for the DMU$_j$ under evaluation. In the Solver parameters shown in Figure 10.3, we set cell B14 equal to zero.

Cells D11:D13 contain the following formulas

Cell D11 =$F$10*INDEX(B2:B6,E9,1)
Cell D12 =$F$10*INDEX(C2:C6,E9,1)
Cell D13 =INDEX(E2:E6,E9,1)

Based upon Figure 10.2 and Figure 10.3, the super-efficiency score for DMU2 is 1.357, and the non-zero λ_j in cells F2 and F4 indicate that DMU1 and DMU3 form a new efficient facet.

DMU3 is evaluated against B on the new facet determined by DMUs 2 and 4. If we change the value of cell E9 to 3, we obtain the super-efficiency score for DMU3 using the Solver parameters shown in Figure 10.3. The score is 1.25 (see cell G4 in Figure 10.4).

	A	B	C	D	E	F	G
1	DMU	Cost	Time		Profit	λ	Super Efficiency
2	1	1	5		2	5.55E-17	2
3	2	2	2		2	1	1.357142857
4	3	4	1		2	0	1.25
5	4	6	1		2	0	1
6	5	4	4		2	0	0.5
7							
8						Super	
9		Reference		DMU under	5	Efficiency	
10	**Constraints**	set		Evaluation		0.5	
11	Cost	2	≤	2			
12	Time	2	≤	2		CRS Super-efficiency	
13	Profit	2	≥	2			
14	λo	0	=	0			

Figure 10.4. Super-efficiency·Scores

If we remove DMU4 or DMU 5 from the reference set, the frontier remains the same. Therefore, the super-efficiency score for DMU4 (DMU5) equals to the input-oriented CRS efficiency score (see Figure 10.4).

If we measure the super-efficiency of DMU1, DMU1 is evaluated against C on the frontier extended from DMU2 (see Figure 10.5). It can be seen that C is a weakly efficient DMU in the remaining four DMUs 2, 3, 4 and 5. In fact, we may want to adjust such a super-efficiency score (see Zhu (2001b) and Chen and Sherman (2002)).

Although the super-efficiency models can differentiate the performance of the efficient DMUs, the efficient DMUs are not compared to the same "standard". Because the frontier constructed from the remaining DMUs changes for each efficient DMU under evaluation. In fact, the super-efficiency should be regarded the potential input savings or output surpluses (see Chen (2002)).

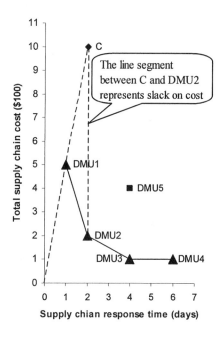

Figure 10.5. Super-efficiency and Slacks

10.2 Infeasibility of Super-efficiency DEA Models

Consider the input-oriented VRS super-efficiency model shown Figure 10.6. In fact, this is the spreadsheet model for the input-oriented VRS envelopment model except that we introduce the formula "=INDEX(I2:I16, E18,1)" into cell B26. This formula is used to exclude the DMU under evaluation from the reference set. That is, one needs to add an additional constraint of "$B$26=0" into the Solver parameters for the input-oriented VRS envelopment spreadsheet model, as shown in Figure 10.7.

Once we set up the Solver parameters, the calculation is performed by the VBA procedure "SuperEfficiency".

```
Sub SuperEfficiency()
Dim i As Integer
```

```
For i = 1 To 15
Range("E18") = i
SolverSolve UserFinish:=True
If SolverSolve(UserFinish:=True) = 5 Then
Range("J" & i + 1) = "Infeasible"
Else
Range("J" & i + 1) = Range("F19")
End If
Next
End Sub
```

	A	B	C	D	E	F	G	H	I	J
1	Company	Assets	Equity	Employees		Revenue	Profit		λ	Super efficiency
2	Mitsubishi	91920.6	10950	36000		184365.2	346.2		0	Infeasible
3	Mitsui	68770.9	5553.9	80000		181518.7	314.8		0	1.751885253
4	Itochu	65708.9	4271.1	7182		169164.6	121.2		0	1.606521649
5	General Motors	217123.4	23345.5	709000		168828.6	6880.7		0	Infeasible
6	Sumitomo	50268.9	6881	6193		167530.7	210.5		0.77	1.320957592
7	Marubeni	71439.3	5239.1	6702		161057.4	156.6		0	1.009347188
8	Ford Motor	243283	24547	346990		137137	4139		0	0.737555958
9	Toyota Motor	106004.2	49691.6	146855		111052	2662.4		0	0.603245345
10	Exxon	91296	40436	82000		110009	6470		0	1.344388672
11	Royal Dutch/Shell Group	118011.6	58986.4	104000		109833.7	6904.6		0	Infeasible
12	Wal-Mart	37871	14762	675000		93627	2740		0.23	1.765155063
13	Hitachi	91620.9	29907.2	331852		84167.1	1468.8		0	0.557595838
14	Nippon Life Insurance	364762.5	2241.9	89690		83206.7	2426.6		0	4.806917893
15	Nippon Telegraph & Telephone	127077.3	42240.1	231400		81937.2	2209.1		0	0.470810997
16	AT&T	88884	17274	299300		79609	139		0	0.533543522
17						Super				
18		Reference		DMU under	15	Efficiency				
19	**Constraints**	set		Evaluation		0.5335435				
20	Assets	47423.482	≤	47423.4824						
21	Equity	8535.6544	≤	9216.4308						
22	Employees	159689.58	≤	159689.576		VRS Super-efficiency				
23	Revenue	150569.21	≥	79609						
24	Profit	791.04056	≥	139						
25	Σλ	1	=	1						
26	λo	0	=	0						

Figure 10.6. Input-oriented VRS Super-efficiency Spreadsheet Model

It can be seen that the input-oriented VRS super-efficiency model is infeasible for three VRS efficient companies (Mitsubishi, General Motors, and Royal Dutch/Shell Group). Note that in the VBA procedure "SuperEfficiency", a VBA statement on infeasibility check is added.

If we consider the output-oriented VRS super-efficiency model, we have the spreadsheet shown in Figure 10.8. Figure 10.8 is based upon the output-oriented VRS envelopment with an additional formula in cell B26 "=INDEX (I2:I16,E18,1)". To calculate the output-oriented super-efficiency scores, we need to change the "Min" to "Max" in the Solver parameters shown in Figure 10.7.

Based upon Figure 10.8, the output-oriented VRS super-efficiency model is infeasible for five output-oriented VRS efficient companies (Itochu, Sumitomo, Marubeni, Wal-Mart, and Nippon Life Insurance).

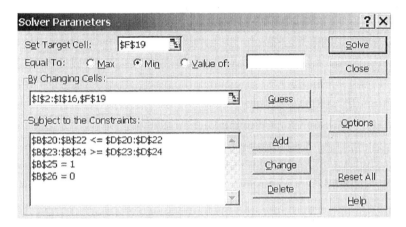

Figure 10.7. Solver Parameters for Input-oriented VRS Super-efficiency

	A	B	C	D	E	F	G	H	I	J
1	Company	Assets	Equity	Employees		Revenue	Profit		λ	Super efficiency
2	Mitsubishi	91820.8	10850	36000		184365.2	346.2		0.869	0.938120353
3	Mitsui	68770.9	5553.9	80000		181518.7	314.8		0.131	0.937264375
4	Itochu	65708.9	4271.1	7182		169164.6	121.2		0	Infeasible
5	General Motors	217123.4	23345.5	709000		168828.6	6880.7		0	0.647119111
6	Sumitomo	50268.9	6881	6193		167530.7	210.5		0	Infeasible
7	Marubeni	71439.3	5239.1	6702		161057.4	156.6		0	Infeasible
8	Ford Motor	243283	24547	346990		137137	4139		0	1.158414974
9	Toyota Motor	106004.2	49691.6	146855		111052	2662.4		0	1.371588284
10	Exxon	91296	40436	82000		110009	6470		0	0.873147631
11	Royal Dutch/Shell Group	118011.6	58986.4	104000		109833.7	6904.6		0	0.939143546
12	Wal-Mart	37871	14762	675000		93627	2740		0	Infeasible
13	Hitachi	91620.9	29907.2	331852		84167.1	1468.8		0	1.898938938
14	Nippon Life Insurance	364762.5	2241.9	89690		83206.7	2426.6		0	Infeasible
15	Nippon Telegraph & Telephone	127077.3	42240.1	231400		81937.2	2209.1		0	1.892916538
16	AT&T	88884	17274	299300		79609	139		0	2.311193684
17						Super				
18		Reference		DMU under	16	Efficiency				
19	Constraints	set		Evaluation		2.3111837				
20	Assets	88884	≤	88884						
21	Equity	10242.181	≤	17274		Output-oriented				
22	Employees	41771.582	≤	299300		VRS Super-efficiency				
23	Revenue	183991.82	≥	183991.818						
24	Profit	342.08119	≥	321.255922						
25	ΣΛ	1	=	1						
26	λ0	0	=	0						

Figure 10.8. Output-oriented VRS Super-efficiency Spreadsheet Model

Thrall (1996) shows that the super-efficiency CRS model can be infeasible. However, Thrall (1996) fails to recognize that the output-oriented CRS super-efficiency model is always feasible for the trivial solution which has all variables set equal to zero. Moreover, Zhu (1996b) shows that the input-oriented CRS super-efficiency model is infeasible if and only if a certain pattern of zero data occurs in the inputs and outputs.

Figure 10.9 illustrates how the VRS super-efficiency model works and the infeasibility for the case of a single output and a single input case. We have three VRS frontier DMUs, A, B and C. AB exhibits IRS and BC exhibits DRS. The VRS super-efficiency model evaluates point B by reference to B′ and B″ on section AC through output-reduction and input-increment, respectively. In an input-oriented VRS super-efficiency model, point A is evaluated against A′. However, there is no referent DMU for point C for input variations. Therefore, the input-oriented VRS super-efficiency model is infeasible at point C. Similarly, in an output-oriented VRS super-efficiency model, point C is evaluated against C′. However, there is no referent DMU for point A for output variations. Therefore, the output-oriented VRS super-efficiency model is infeasible at point A. Note that point A is the left most end point and point B is the right most end point on this frontier.

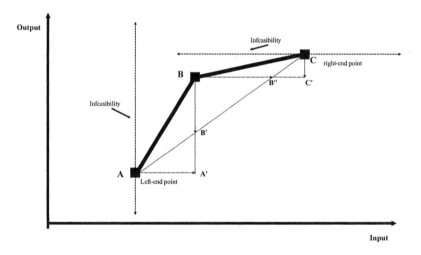

Figure 10.9. Infeasibility of Super-efficiency Model

As in Charnes, Cooper and Thrall (1991), the DMUs can be partitioned into four classes E, E′, F and N described as follows. First, E is the set of extreme efficient DMUs. Second, E′ is the set of efficient DMUs that are not extreme points. The DMUs in set E′ can be expressed as linear combinations of the DMUs in set E. Third, F is the set of frontier points (DMUs) with non-zero slack(s). The DMUs in set F are usually called weakly efficient. Fourth, N is the set of inefficient DMUs.

For example, DMUs 1, 2, and 3 in Figure 10.1 are extreme efficient (in set E), DMU4 is in set F, and DMU5 is in set N.

Thrall (1996) shows that if the CRS super-efficiency model is infeasible, or if the super-efficiency score is greater than one for input-oriented model (less than one for output-oriented model), then $DMU_o \in E$. This result can also be applied to other super-efficiency models. i.e., the extreme efficient DMUs can be identified by the super-efficiency models. This finding is important in empirical applications. For example, in the slack-based congestion measures discussed in Chapter 9, if we can know that the data set consists of only extreme efficient DMUs, then the congestion slacks are equal to the DEA slacks.

Note that if a specific $DMU_o \in E'$, F or N and is not included in the reference set, then the efficient frontiers (constructed by the DMUs in set E) remain unchanged. As a result, the super-efficiency DEA models are always feasible and equivalent to the original DEA models when $DMU_o \in E'$, F or N. Thus we only need to consider the infeasibility when $DMU_o \in E$.

We next study the infeasibility of the VRS, NIRS and NDRS super-efficiency models, where we assume that all data are positive.

From the convexity constraint ($\sum_{j \neq o} \lambda_j = 1$) on the intensity lambda variables, we immediately have

Proposition 10.1 $DMU_o \in E$ under the VRS model *if and only if* $DMU_o \in E$ under the NIRS model or NDRS model.

Thus in the discussion to follow, we limit our consideration to $DMU_o \in E$ under the VRS model. We have

Proposition 10.2 Let θ^{super*} and ϕ^{super*} denote, respectively, optimal values to the input-oriented and output-oriented super-efficiency DEA models when evaluating an extreme efficient DMU_o, then
(i) Either $\theta^{super*} > 1$ or the specific input-oriented super-efficiency DEA model is infeasible.
(ii) Either $\phi^{super*} < 1$ or the specific output-oriented super-efficiency DEA model is infeasible.

Based upon Seiford and Zhu (1999c), we next (i) present the necessary and sufficient conditions for the infeasibility of various super-efficiency DEA models in a multiple inputs and multiple outputs situation, and (ii) reveal the relationship between infeasibility and RTS classification. (Note that, in Figure 10.9, point A is associated with IRS and point C is associated with DRS.)

10.2.1   Output-oriented VRS Super-efficiency Model

Suppose each DMU_j $(j = 1, 2, ..., n)$ consumes a vector of inputs, x_j, to produce a vector of outputs, y_j. We have

Theorem 10.1 For a specific extreme efficient $DMU_o = (x_o, y_o)$, the output-oriented VRS super-efficiency model is infeasible *if and only if* $(x_o, \delta y_o)$ is efficient under the VRS envelopment model for any $0 < \delta \le 1$.

[Proof]: Suppose that the output-oriented VRS super-efficiency model is infeasible and that $(x_o, \delta^o y_o)$ is inefficient, where $0 < \delta^o \le 1$. Then

$$\phi_o^{super*} = \max \phi_o^{super}$$
subject to
$$\sum_{j=1}^{n} \lambda_j x_j \le x_o \tag{10.1}$$
$$\sum_{j=1}^{n} \lambda_j y_j \ge \phi_o^{super}(\delta^o y_o)$$
$$\sum_{j=1}^{n} \lambda_j = 1$$

has a solution of $\lambda_j^*(j \ne o)$, $\lambda_o^* = 0$, $\phi_o^{super*} > 1$. Since $\lambda_o^* = 0$, we have that model (10.1) is equivalent to an output-oriented VRS super-efficiency model and thus the output-oriented VRS super-efficiency model is feasible. A contradiction. This completes the proof of the *only if* part.

To establish the *if* part, we note that if the output-oriented VRS super-efficiency model is feasible, then $\phi^{super*} < 1$ is the maximum radial reduction of all outputs preserving the efficiency of DMU_o. Therefore, δ cannot be less than ϕ^{super*}. Otherwise, DMU_o will be inefficient under the output-oriented VRS envelopment model. Thus, the output-oriented VRS super-efficiency model is infeasible. ∎

Theorem 10.2 The output-oriented VRS super-efficiency model is infeasible *if and only if* $\hbar^*$, where $\hbar^* > 1$ is the optimal value to (10.2).

$$\hbar^* = \min \hbar$$
subject to
$$\sum_{\substack{j=1 \\ j \ne o}}^{n} \lambda_j x_j \le \hbar x_o \tag{10.2}$$
$$\sum_{\substack{j=1 \\ j \ne o}}^{n} \lambda_j = 1$$
$$\lambda_j \ge 0, j \ne o$$

[Proof]: We note that for any $\lambda_j (j \neq o)$ with $\sum_{j \neq o} \lambda_j = 1$, the constraint $\sum_{j \neq o} \lambda_j y_j \geq \phi^{super} y_o$ always holds. Thus the output-oriented super-efficiency-VRS is infeasible if and only if there exists no $\lambda_j (j \neq o)$ with $\sum_{j \neq o} \lambda_j = 1$ such that $\sum_{j \neq o} \lambda_j x_j \leq x_o$ holds. This means that the optimal value to (10.2) is greater than one, i.e., $\hbar^* > 1$. ∎

	A	B	C	D	E	F	G	H	I
1	Company	Assets	Equity	Employees			λ	h	Super efficiency
2	Mitsubishi	91920.6	10950	36000			0	0.57426	0.936120353
3	Mitsui	68770.9	5553.9	80000			0	0.8919	0.937264375
4	Itochu	65708.9	4271.1	7182			0	1.20984	Infeasible
5	General Motors	217123.4	23345.5	709000			0	0.25382	0.647119111
6	Sumitomo	50268.9	6681	6193			0.77	1.30639	Infeasible
7	Marubeni	71439.3	5239.1	6702			0	1.00935	Infeasible
8	Ford Motor	243283	24547	346990			0	0.23236	1.158414974
9	Toyota Motor	106004.2	49691.6	146855			0	0.4634	1.371588284
10	Exxon	91296	40436	82000			0	0.54283	0.673147631
11	Royal Dutch/Shell Group	118011.6	58986.4	104000			0	0.42008	0.939143546
12	Wal-Mart	37871	14762	675000			0.23	1.32737	Infeasible
13	Hitachi	91620.9	29907.2	331852			0	0.51532	1.898938938
14	Nippon Life Insurance	364762.5	2241.9	89690			0	1.90513	Infeasible
15	Nippon Telegraph & Telephone	127077.3	42240.1	231400			0	0.38353	1.892916538
16	AT&T	88884	17274	299300			0	0.53354	2.311193684
17									
18		Reference		DMU under	15	h			
19	Constraints	set		Evaluation		0.533544			
20	Assets	47423.482	<	47423.482					
21	Equity	8535.6544	<	9216.4308		Infeasibility			
22	Employees	159689.58	<	159689.58					
23	Σλ	1	=	1					
24	λo	0	=	0					

Figure 10.10. Spreadsheet for Infeasibility Test (Output-oriented VRS Super-efficiency)

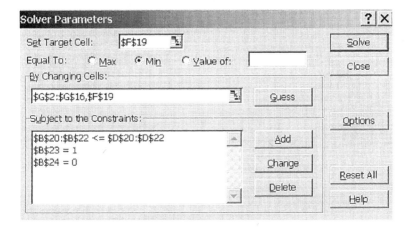

Figure 10.11. Solver Parameters for Infeasibility Test (Output-oriented)

Figure 10.10 shows the spreadsheet model for model (10.2) where the output-oriented VRS super-efficiency scores are reported in cells I2:I16.

The spreadsheet shown in Figure 10.10 is obtained by removing the output constraints from the spreadsheet shown in Figure 10.6. Figure 10.11 shows the Solver parameters. It can be seen that $\hbar^* > 1$ if and only if model (10.2) is infeasible for a company.

Further, note that the DMU_o is also CRS efficient if and only if CRS prevail . Therefore, if IRS or DRS prevail, then DMU_o must be CRS inefficient. Thus, in this situation, the CRS super-efficiency model is identical to the CRS envelopment model. Based upon Chapter 3, IRS or DRS on DMU_o can be determined by

Lemma 10.1 The RTS for DMU_o can be identified as IRS *if and only if* $\sum_{j \neq o} \lambda_j^* < 1$ in all optima for the CRS super-efficiency model and DRS *if and only if* $\sum_{j \neq o} \lambda_j^*$ in all optima for the CRS super-efficiency model.

Lemma 10.2 If DMU_o exhibits DRS, then the output-oriented VRS super-efficiency model is feasible and $\phi^{super*} < 1$, where ϕ^{super*} is the optimal value to the output-oriented VRS super-efficiency model.

[Proof]: The output-oriented VRS super-efficiency model is as follows

$$\phi^{super*} = \max \phi^{super}$$
$$\text{subject to}$$
$$\sum_{\substack{j=1 \\ j \neq o}}^{n} \lambda_j x_j \leq x_o$$
$$\sum_{\substack{j=1 \\ j \neq 0}}^{n} \lambda_j y_j \geq \phi^{super} y_o \qquad\qquad (10.3)$$
$$\sum_{\substack{j=1 \\ j \neq 0}}^{n} \lambda_j = 1;$$
$$\phi^{super}, \lambda_j \geq 0, j \neq o$$

Let $\theta = 1/\phi^{super}$. Multiplying all constraints in (10.3) by θ yields

$$\min \theta$$
$$\text{subject to}$$
$$\sum_{\substack{j=1 \\ j \neq o}}^{n} \tilde{\lambda}_j x_j \leq \theta x_o$$
$$\sum_{\substack{j=1 \\ j \neq o}}^{n} \tilde{\lambda}_j y_j \geq y_o \qquad\qquad (10.4)$$

$$\sum_{\substack{j=1 \\ j \neq o}}^{n} \widetilde{\lambda}_j = \theta = \frac{1}{\phi^{\text{super}}}$$

$$\phi^{\text{super}}, \theta, \widetilde{\lambda}_j \geq 0, j \neq o$$

where $\widetilde{\lambda}_j = \theta \lambda_j \, (j \neq o)$.

Since DMU_o exhibits DRS, then by Lemma 10.1, $\sum_{j \neq 0} \lambda_j^* > 1$ in all optima to the following CRS super-efficiency model

$$\min \theta^{\text{super}}$$

$$\sum_{\substack{j=1 \\ j \neq o}}^{n} \lambda_j x_j \leq \theta^{\text{super}} x_o$$

$$\sum_{\substack{j=1 \\ j \neq o}}^{n} \lambda_j y_j \geq y_o \tag{10.5}$$

$$\lambda_j \geq 0.$$

Let $\sum_{j \neq 0} \lambda_j^* = \theta$. Obviously $\theta > \theta^{\text{super}}$ is a feasible solution to (10.5). This in turn indicates that $\lambda_j^* \, (j \neq o)$ and θ is a feasible solution to (10.4). Therefore, (10.3) is feasible. Furthermore by Proposition 10.2, we have that $\phi^{\text{super}*} < 1$, where $\phi^{\text{super}*}$ is the optimal value to (10.3). ■

Theorem 10.3 If the output-oriented VRS super-efficiency model is infeasible, then DMU_o exhibits IRS or CRS.

[Proof]: Suppose that DMU_o exhibits DRS. By Lemma 10.2, the output-oriented VRS super-efficiency model is feasible. A contradiction. ■

Theorems 10.1 and 10.2 indicate that if the output-oriented VRS super-efficiency model is infeasible, then DMU_o is one of the *endpoints*. Moreover, if IRS prevail, then DMU_o is a *left endpoint* (see Figure 10.9).

10.2.2   Other Output-oriented Super-efficiency Models

Now, consider the output-oriented NIRS and NDRS super-efficiency models. Obviously, we have a feasible solution of $\lambda_j = 0 \, (j \neq o)$ and $\phi^{\text{super}} = 0$ in the output-oriented NIRS super-efficiency model. Therefore, we have

Theorem 10.4 The output-oriented NIRS super-efficiency model is always feasible.

Lemma 10.3 The output-oriented NDRS super-efficiency model is infeasible *if and only if* the output-oriented VRS super-efficiency model is infeasible.

[Proof]: The *only if* part is obvious and hence is omitted. To establish the *if* part, we suppose that the output-oriented NDRS super-efficiency model is feasible. i.e., we have a feasible solution with $\sum_{j\neq o}\lambda_j \geq 1$ for the output-oriented NDRS super-efficiency model. If $\sum_{j\neq o}\lambda_j = 1$, then this solution is also feasible for the output-oriented VRS super-efficiency. If $\sum_{j\neq o}\lambda_j > 1$, let $\sum_{j\neq o}\lambda_j = d > 1$. Then $\sum_{j\neq o}\tilde{\lambda}_j x_j \leq \sum_{j\neq o}\lambda_j x \leq x_o$, where $\tilde{\lambda}_j = \lambda_j/d$ ($j\neq o$) and $\sum_{j\neq o}\tilde{\lambda}_j = 1$. Therefore $\tilde{\lambda}_j$ ($j\neq o$) is a feasible solution to the output-oriented VRS super-efficiency model. Both possible cases lead to a contradiction. Thus, the output-oriented NDRS super-efficiency model is infeasible if the output-oriented VRS super-efficiency model is infeasible. ∎

On the basis of Lemma 10.3, we have

Theorem 10.5 For a specific extreme efficient $DMU_o = (x_o, y_o)$, we have
(i) The output-oriented NDRS super-efficiency model is infeasible *if and only if* $(x_o, \delta y_o)$ is efficient under the VRS envelopment model for any $0 < \delta \leq 1$.
(ii) The output-oriented NDRS super-efficiency model is infeasible *if and only if* $\hbar^* > 1$, where $\hbar^*$ is the optimal value to (10.2).

If $DMU_o \in E$ for the NDRS model, then DMU_o exhibits IRS or CRS. By Proposition 10.1, DMU_o also lies on the VRS frontier that satisfies IRS or CRS. i.e., the VRS and NDRS envelopment models are identical for DMU_o. Thus, $(x_o, \delta y_o)$ is also efficient under the NDRS envelopment model for any $0 < \delta \leq 1$.

10.2.3   Input-oriented VRS Super-efficiency Model

Theorem 10.6 For a specific extreme efficient $DMU_o = (x_o, y_o)$, the input-oriented VRS super-efficiency model is infeasible *if and only if* $(\chi x_o, y_o)$ is efficient under the VRS envelopment model for any $1 \leq \chi < +\infty$.

[Proof]: Suppose the input-oriented VRS super-efficiency model is infeasible and assume that $(\chi^o x_o, y_o)$ is inefficient, where $1 \leq \chi^o < +\infty$. Then

$$\theta_o^{super*} = \min \theta_o^{super}$$
subject to
$$\sum_{j=1}^{n} \lambda_j x_j \leq \theta_o^{super}(\chi^o x_o) \qquad (10.6)$$
$$\sum_{j=1}^{n} \lambda_j y_j \geq y_o$$
$$\sum_{j=1}^{n} \lambda_j = 1$$

has a solution of $\lambda_j^*(j \neq o)$, $\lambda_o^* = 0$, θ_o^{super*}. Since $\lambda_o^* = 0$, model (10.6) is equivalent to the input-oriented VRS super-efficiency model. Thus, the input-oriented VRS super-efficiency model is feasible. This completes the proof of *only if* part.

To establish the *if* part, we note that if the input-oriented VRS super-efficiency model is feasible, then $\theta^{super*} > 1$ is the maximum radial increase of all inputs preserving the efficiency of DMU_o. Therefore, χ cannot be bigger than θ^{super*}. Otherwise, DMU_o will be inefficient under the input-oriented VRS envelopment model. Thus, the input-oriented VRS super-efficiency model is infeasible. ■

Theorem 10.7 The input-oriented super-efficiency-VRS model is infeasible *if and only if* $g^* < 1$, where g^* is the optimal value to (10.7).

$$g^* = \max g$$
subject to
$$\sum_{\substack{j=1 \\ j \neq o}}^{n} \lambda_j y_j \geq gy_o \qquad (10.7)$$
$$\sum_{\substack{j=1 \\ j \neq o}}^{n} \lambda_j = 1$$
$$\lambda_j \geq 0, j \neq o$$

[Proof]: We note that for any $\lambda_j(j \neq o)$ with $\sum_{j \neq o} \lambda_j = 1$, the constraint $\sum_{j \neq o} \lambda_j x_j \leq \theta^{super} x_o$ always holds. Thus, the input-oriented VRS super-efficiency model is infeasible if and only if $\sum_{j \neq o} \lambda_j y_j \geq y_o$ does not hold for any $\lambda_j (j \neq o)$ with $\sum_{j \neq o} \lambda_j = 1$. This means that the optimal value to (10.7) is less than one, i.e., $g^* < 1$.■

Figure 10.12 shows the spreadsheet model for model (10.7) where the input-oriented VRS super-efficiency scores are reported in cells I2:I16. This spreadsheet is obtained from the output-oriented VRS super-efficiency model shown in Figure 10.8. Figure 10.13 shows the Solver parameters. It can be seen that $g^* < 1$ if and only if model (10.7) is infeasible for a company.

	A	B	C	D	E	F	G	H	I
1	Company	Revenue	Profit	λ				g	Super efficiency
2	Mitsubishi	184365.2	346.2	1				0.9843	Infeasible
3	Mitsui	181518.7	314.8	0				1.0157	1.751885253
4	Itochu	169164.6	121.2	0				1.0899	1.606521649
5	General Motors	168828.6	6880.7	0				0.7623	Infeasible
6	Sumitomo	167530.7	210.5	0				1.1005	1.320957592
7	Marubeni	161057.4	156.6	0				1.1447	1.009347188
8	Ford Motor	137137	4139	0				1.26	0.737555958
9	Toyota Motor	111052	2662.4	0				1.5777	0.603245345
10	Exxon	110009	6470	0				1.0667	1.344368672
11	Royal Dutch/Shell Group	109833.7	6904.6	0				0.9965	Infeasible
12	Wal-Mart	93627	2740	0				1.8493	1.765155063
13	Hitachi	84167.1	1468.8	0				2.1126	0.557595838
14	Nippon Life Insurance	83206.7	2426.6	0				2.0813	4.806917693
15	Nippon Telegraph & Telephone	81937.2	2209.1	0				2.124	0.470610997
16	AT&T	79609	139	0				2.3159	0.533543522
17						Super			
18		Reference		DMU under	15	Efficiency			
19	**Constraints**	set		Evaluation		2.315884			
20	Revenue	184365.2	≥	184365.2					
21	Profit	346.2	≥	321.90786		Infeasibility			
22	Σλ	1	=	1					
23	λo	0	=	0					

Figure 10.12. Spreadsheet for Infeasibility Test (Input-oriented VRS Super-efficiency)

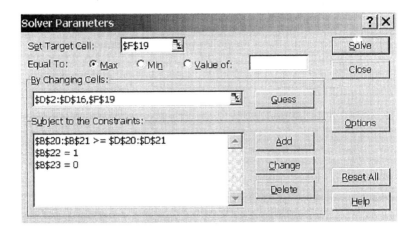

Figure 10.13. Solver Parameters for Infeasibility Test (Input-oriented)

Lemma 10.4 If DMU_o exhibits IRS, then the input-oriented VRS super-efficiency model is feasible and $\theta^{super*} > 1$, where θ^{super*} is the optimal value to the input-oriented VRS super-efficiency model.

[Proof]: Let $\vartheta = 1/\theta^{super}$, then the input-oriented VRS super-efficiency model becomes

$$\max \vartheta$$

subject to

$$\sum_{\substack{j=1 \\ j\neq 0}}^{n} \hat{\lambda}_j x_j \leq x_o;$$

$$\sum_{\substack{j=1 \\ j\neq 0}}^{n} \hat{\lambda}_j y_j \geq \vartheta y_o; \tag{10.8}$$

$$\sum_{\substack{j=1 \\ j\neq 0}}^{n} \hat{\lambda}_j = \vartheta = \frac{1}{\theta^{super}};$$

$$\theta^{super}, \vartheta, \hat{\lambda}_j \geq 0.$$

where $\hat{\lambda}_j = \vartheta \lambda_j \ (j \neq o)$.

Since DMU_o exhibits IRS, then by Lemma 10.1, $\sum_{j\neq0} \lambda_j^* < 1$ in all optima to the following output-oriented CRS super-efficiency model

$$\max \phi^{super}$$

$$\sum_{\substack{j=1 \\ j\neq 0}}^{n} \lambda_j x_j \leq x_o$$

$$\sum_{\substack{j=1 \\ j\neq 0}}^{n} \lambda_j y_j \geq \phi^{super} y_o \tag{10.9}$$

$$\phi^{super}, \lambda_j \geq 0.$$

Let $\sum_{j\neq0} \lambda_j^* = \vartheta < 1$. Since DMU_o is CRS inefficient, therefore $\phi^{super} > 1$ and hence $\phi^{super} > \vartheta$ is a feasible solution to (10.9). This in turn indicates that ϑ and $\lambda_j^*(j \neq o)$ with $\sum_{j\neq0} \lambda_j^* = \vartheta$ is a feasible solution to (10.8). Therefore, the input-oriented VRS super-efficiency model is feasible. Furthermore, by Proposition 10.2, we have that $\phi^{super*} > 1$, where ϕ^{super*} is the optimal value to the input-oriented VRS super-efficiency model. ∎

Theorem 10.8 If the input-oriented VRS super-efficiency model is infeasible, then DMU_o exhibits DRS or CRS.

[Proof]: If DMU_o exhibits IRS, then by Lemma 10.4, the input-oriented VRS super-efficiency model is feasible. A contradiction.∎

Theorems 10.6 and 10.7 indicate that if the input-oriented VRS super-efficiency model is infeasible, then DMU_o is one of the *endpoints*. Furthermore, if DRS prevail, then DMU_o is an *right endpoint* (see Figure 10.9).

10.2.4   Other Input-oriented Super-efficiency Models

Now, consider the input-oriented NIRS and NDRS super-efficiency models.

Theorem 10.9 The input-oriented NDRS super-efficiency model is always feasible.

[Proof]: Since $\sum_{j\neq o}\lambda_j \geq 1$ in the input-oriented DNRS super-efficiency model, there must exist some $\tilde{\lambda}_j$ with $\sum_{j\neq o}\tilde{\lambda}_j > 1$ such that $\sum_{j\neq o}\tilde{\lambda}_j y_j \geq y_o$ holds. Note that $\sum_{j\neq o}\tilde{\lambda}_j x_j \leq \theta^{super}x_o$ can always be satisfied by a proper θ^{super}. Thus, the input-oriented NDRS super-efficiency model is always feasible. ∎

Lemma 10.5 The input-oriented NIRS super-efficiency model is infeasible *if and only if* the input-oriented VRS super-efficiency model is infeasible.

[Proof]: The *only if* part is obvious and hence is omitted. To establish the *if* part, we suppose that the input-oriented NIRS super-efficiency model is feasible. i.e., we have a feasible solution with $\sum_{j\neq o}\lambda_j \leq 1$ for the input-oriented NIRS super-efficiency model. If $\sum_{j\neq o}\lambda_j = 1$, then this solution is also feasible for the output-oriented VRS super-efficiency model. If $\sum_{j\neq o}\lambda_j < 1$, let $\sum_{j\neq o}\lambda_j = e < 1$. Then $\sum_{j\neq o}\hat{\lambda}_j y_j \geq \sum_{j\neq o}\lambda_j y_j \geq y_o$, where $\hat{\lambda}_j = \lambda_j/e$ ($j\neq o$) and $\sum_{j\neq o}\hat{\lambda}_j = 1$. Therefore $\hat{\lambda}_j(j\neq o)$ is a feasible solution to the output-oriented VRS super-efficiency model. Both possible cases lead to a contradiction. Thus, the output-oriented NIRS super-efficiency model is infeasible if the output-oriented VRS super-efficiency model is infeasible. ∎

On the basis of this Lemma 10.5, we have

Theorem 10.10 For a specific extreme efficient $DMU_o = (x_o, y_o)$, we have
(i) The input-oriented NIRS super-efficiency model is infeasible *if and only if* $(\chi x_o, y_o)$ is efficient under the VRS envelopment model for any $1 \leq \chi < +\infty$.
(ii) The input-oriented NIRS super-efficiency model is feasible *if and only if* $g^* < 1$, where g^* is the optimal value to (10.7).

If $DMU_o \in E$ under the NIRS model, then DMU_o exhibits DRS or CRS. By Proposition 10.1, the DMU_o also lies on the VRS frontier that satisfies DRS or CRS. i.e., the VRS and NIRS envelopment models are identical for DMU_o. Thus $(\chi x_o, y_o)$ is also efficient under the NIRS envelopment model for any $1 \leq \chi < +\infty$.

Furthermore, Theorems 10.3 and 10.8 demonstrate that the possible infeasibility of the output-oriented and input-oriented VRS super-efficiency models can only occur at those extreme efficient DMUs exhibiting IRS (or CRS) and DRS (or CRS), respectively. Note that IRS and DRS are not allowed in the NIRS and NDRS models, respectively. Therefore, we have the following corollary.

Corollary 10.1

(i) If $DMU_o \in E$ exhibits DRS, then all output-oriented super-efficiency DEA models are feasible.

(ii) If $DMU_o \in E$ exhibits IRS, then all input-oriented super-efficiency DEA models are feasible.

By Theorems 10.1 and 10.6, we know that infeasibility indicates that the inputs of an extreme efficient DMU_o can be proportionally increased without limit or that the outputs can be decreased in any positive proportion, while preserving the efficiency of DMU_o. This indicates that the efficiency of DMU_o is always stable under the proportional data changes.

Models (10.2) and (10.7) are useful in the determination of infeasibility while Theorems 10.1 and 10.6 are useful in the sensitivity analysis of efficiency classifications. Table 10.2 summarizes the relationship between infeasibility and the super-efficiency DEA models.

Table 10.2. Super-efficiency DEA Models and Infeasibility

Super-efficiency Models		Infeasibility	RTS
Output-oriented	VRS	Theorem 10.2 (Model (10.2))	DRS
	NIRS	always feasible	always feasible
Input-oriented	NDRS	Lemma 10.3, Theorem 10.2	Corollary 10.1 (i)
	VRS	Theorem 10.7 (Model (10.7))	IRS
	NIRS	Lemma 10.5, Theorem 7	always feasible
	NDRS	always feasible	Corollary 10.1 (ii)

Finally, we note that the super-efficiency VRS models can also be used to estimate RTS. This is a possible new usage of the super-efficiency DEA models.

Chapter 11

Sensitivty Analysis and Its Uses

11.1   Efficiency Sensitivity Analysis

One important issue in DEA which has been studied by many DEA researchers is the efficiency sensitivity to perturbations in the data. Some DEA sensitivity studies focus on the sensitivity of DEA results to the variable and model selection, e.g., Ahn and Seiford (1993). Most of the DEA sensitivity analysis studies focus on the misspecification of efficiency classification of a test DMU. However, note that DEA is an extremal method in the sense that all extreme points are characterized as efficient. If data entry errors occur for various DMUs, the resulting isoquant may vary substantially. We say that the calculated frontiers of DEA models are stable if the frontier DMUs that determine the DEA frontier remain on the frontier after particular data perturbations are made.

By updating the inverse of the basis matrix associated with a specific efficient DMU in a DEA linear programming problem, Charnes, Cooper, Lewin, Morey and Rousseau (1985) study the sensitivity of DEA model to a single output change. This is followed by a series of sensitivity analysis articles by Charnes and Neralic in which sufficient conditions preserving efficiency are determined (see, e.g. Charnes and Neralic (1990)).

Another type of DEA sensitivity analysis is based on super-efficiency DEA models. Charnes, Haag, Jaska and Semple (1992), Rousseau and Semple (1995) and Charnes, Rousseau and Semple (1996) develop a super-efficiency DEA sensitivity analysis technique for the situation where simultaneous proportional change is assumed in all inputs and outputs for a specific DMU under consideration. This data variation condition is relaxed in Zhu (1996b) and Seiford and Zhu (1998d) to a situation where inputs or outputs can be changed individually and the entire (largest) stability region which encompasses that of Charnes, Haag, Jaska and Semple (1992) is obtained. As a result, the condition for preserving efficiency of a test DMU is necessary and sufficient.

The DEA sensitivity analysis methods we have just reviewed are all developed for the situation where data variations are only applied to the test efficient DMU and the data for the remaining DMUs are assumed fixed. Obviously, this assumption may not be realistic, since possible data errors may occur in each DMU. Seiford and Zhu (1998f) generalize the technique in Zhu (1996b) and Seiford and Zhu (1998d) to the worst-case scenario where the efficiency of the test DMU is deteriorating while the efficiencies of the other DMUs are improving. In their method, same maximum percentage data change of a test DMU and the remaining DMUs is assumed and sufficient conditions for preserving an extreme efficient DMU's efficiency are determined. Note that Thompson, Dharmapala and Thrall (1994) use the SCSC (strong complementary slackness condition) multipliers to analyze the stability of the CRS model when the data for all efficient and all inefficient DMUs are simultaneously changed in opposite directions and in same percentages. Although the data variation condition is more restrictive in Seiford and Zhu (1998f) than that in Thompson, Dharmapala and Thrall, (1994), the super-efficiency based approach generates a larger stability region than the SCSC method. Also, the SCSC method is dependent upon a particular SCSC solution, among others, and therefore the resulting analysis may vary (see Cooper, Li, Seiford, Thrall and Zhu, 2001).

Seiford and Zhu (1999c) (Chapter 10) develop the necessary and sufficient conditions for infeasibility of various super-efficiency DEA models. Although the super-efficiency DEA models employed in Charnes, Haag, Jaska and Semple (1992) and Charnes, Rousseau and Semple (1996) do not encounter the infeasibility problem, the models used in Seiford and Zhu (1998b) do. Seiford and Zhu (1998b) discover the relationship between infeasibility and stability of efficiency classification. That is, infeasibility means that the efficiency of the test DMU remains stable to data changes in the test DMU. Furthermore, Seiford and Zhu (1998f) show that this relationship is also true for the simultaneous data change case and other DEA models, such as the VRS model and the additive model of Charnes, Cooper, Golany, Seiford and Stutz (1985). This finding is critical since super-efficiency DEA models in Seiford and Zhu (1998f) are frequently infeasible for real-world data sets, indicating efficiency stability with respective to data variations in inputs/outputs associated with infeasibility.

Zhu (2001a) extends the results in Seiford and Zhu (1998d; f) to a situation when different data variations are applied to the test DMU and the remaining DMUs, respectively.

In this chapter, we focus on the DEA sensitivity analysis methods based upon super-efficiency DEA models that are developed by Zhu (1996b; 2001a) and Seiford and Zhu (1998d;f). For the DEA sensitivity analysis based upon the inverse of basis matrix, the reader is referred to Neralic (1994).

Since an increase of any output or a decrease of any input cannot worsen the efficiency of DMU_o, we restrict our attention to decreases in outputs and increases in inputs for DMU_o. We consider proportional increases of inputs or proportional decreases of outputs of the form

$$\hat{x}_{io} = \beta_i x_{io} \quad \beta_i \geq 1, i = 1, ..., m \tag{11.1}$$
$$\hat{y}_{ro} = \alpha_r y_{ro} \quad 0 < \alpha_r \leq 1, r = 1, ..., s \tag{11.2}$$

where x_{io} $(i = 1, 2,..., m)$ and y_{ro} $(r = 1, ..., s)$ are respectively, the inputs and outputs for a specific extreme efficient $DMU_o = DMU_{j_o}$ among n DMUs.

Zhu (1996b) provides a super-efficiency model to compute a stability region in which DMU_o remains efficient. Specifically, for an increase in inputs of form (11.1), this model is given by

$$\min \beta_k^o \quad \text{for each } k=1,...,m$$
subject to
$$\sum_{\substack{j=1 \\ j \neq o}}^{n} \lambda_j x_{kj} \leq \beta_k^o x_{ko}$$
$$\sum_{\substack{j=1 \\ j \neq o}}^{n} \lambda_j x_{ij} \leq x_{io} \quad i \neq k \tag{11.3}$$
$$\sum_{\substack{j=1 \\ j \neq o}}^{n} \lambda_j y_{rj} \geq y_{ro} \quad r = 1,...,s$$
$$\lambda_j, \beta_k^o \geq 0$$

where x_{ij} and y_{rj} are the ith input and rth output of DMU_j $(j =1, ..., n)$, respectively. It can be seen that model (11.3) is developed from the input-oriented measure-specific model – CRS kth input-specific model.

Zhu's (1996b) approach requires two assumptions: (i) the hyperplane constructed by the m hypothetical observations obtained from model (11.3) is not dominated by other DMUs and (ii) model (11.3) is feasible. However, in real word situations, these two assumptions may not be satisfied.

Note that any increase of input or any decrease of output will cause the DMUs in set E' (efficient but not extreme efficient) to become inefficient.

For those DMUs in set F (weakly efficient with non-zero slacks), the amount of inputs (or outputs) which have non-zero slacks can be increased (or decreased) without limit, and these DMUs will remain in the set F. However, for inputs and outputs which have no slack, any input increase of (11.1) or any output decrease of (11.2) will cause these DMUs to become inefficient. Therefore, the sensitivity issue of DMUs in set E' or F is straightforward if not trivial. Thus, we first focus on the efficiency of the DMUs in set E, i.e., the extreme efficient DMUs.

11.2   Stability Region[1]

11.2.1   Input Stability Region

For $DMU_o \in E$, we first suppose that (11.3) is feasible for each input and consider input changes of form (11.1). As shown in Zhu (1996b), the optimal value to (11.3), β_k^{o*}, gives the maximum possible increase for each individual input which allows DMU_o to remain efficient with the other inputs and all outputs held constant. Also, (11.3) provides m hypothetical frontier points   (efficient DMUs) when DMU_o is excluded from the reference set. The kth point is generated by increasing the kth input from x_{ko} to $\beta_k^{o*} x_{ko}$ and holding all other inputs and outputs constant. We denote these k hypothetical observations by

$$DMU(\beta_k^{o*}) = (x_{1o},...,\beta_k^{o*} x_{ko},...,x_{mo},y_{1o},...,y_{so}) \tag{11.4}$$

Consider the following linear programming problem

$$\min \sum_{i=1}^{m} \rho_i^o$$
subject to
$$\sum_{\substack{j=1 \\ j \neq o}}^{n} \lambda_j x_{ij} \leq \rho_i^o x_{io} \qquad i=1,...,m \tag{11.5}$$
$$\sum_{\substack{j=1 \\ j \neq o}}^{n} \lambda_j y_{rj} \geq y_{ro} \qquad r=1,...,s$$
$$\rho_i^o \geq 1, \lambda_j \geq 0.$$

This model determines the smallest summation of the proportions to move DMU_o to the boundary of the convex hull of the other DMUs.

Lemma 11.1 Denote the optimal solution for (11.5) by ρ_i^{o*} ($i = 1, 2,..., m$). For $i = 1, 2,..., m$, we have $\beta_i^{o*} \geq \rho_i^{o*} \geq 1$.

[Proof]: Suppose for some i_o, $\beta_{i_o}^{o*} < \rho_{i_o}^{o*}$, then $\sum_{j \neq o} \lambda_j x_{ij} \leq \beta_{i_o}^{o*} x_{i_o o} < \rho_{i_o}^{o*} x_{i_o o}$. Therefore, any optimal solution to (11.3) is a feasible solution to (11.5). Thus, m-1+ $\beta_{i_o}^{o*} \geq \sum_{i=1}^{m} \rho_i^{o*} > m - 1 + \beta_{i_o}^{o*}$. A contradiction. ∎

Associated with ρ_i^{o*} ($i = 1, 2,..., m$), m additional points (or DMUs) can be generated as

$$DMU(\rho_k^{o*}) = (x_{1o},..., \rho_k^{o*} x_{ko},..., x_{mo}, y_{1o},..., y_{so}) \tag{11.6}$$

Theorem 11.1 For $DMU_o = (x_{1o},..., x_{mo}, y_{1o},..., y_{so})$, denote an increase of inputs of form (11.1) by $DMU_o(\beta_1,..., \beta_m) = (\beta_1 x_{1o},..., \beta_m x_{mo}, y_{1o},..., y_{so})$ and define $\Omega^o = \{(\beta_1,..., \beta_m) \mid 1 \leq \beta_i \leq \rho_i^{o*}, i = 1,..., m\}$. If $(\beta_1,..., \beta_m) \in \Omega^o$, then $DMU_o(\beta_1,..., \beta_m)$ remains efficient.

[Proof]: Suppose $(\widetilde{\beta}_1,..., \widetilde{\beta}_m) \in \Omega^o$ and DMU_o with inputs of $\widetilde{\beta}_i x_{io}$ ($I = 1,..., m$) is inefficient. In fact, (11.5) is equivalent to the following linear programming problem where $\rho_i^o x_{io} = x_{io} + \delta_i^o$ (and $\widetilde{\beta}_i x_{io} = x_{io} + \widetilde{\delta}_i$ in which $0 \leq \widetilde{\delta}_i \leq \delta_i^{o*}$)

$$\min \sum_{i=1}^{m} \delta_i^o$$

subject to

$$\sum_{\substack{j=1 \\ j \neq o}}^{n} \lambda_j x_{ij} - \delta_i^o \leq x_{io} \quad i = 1,..., m$$

$$\sum_{\substack{j=1 \\ j \neq o}}^{n} \lambda_j y_{rj} \geq y_{ro} \quad r = 1,..., s$$

$$\delta_i^o, \lambda_j \geq 0.$$

$\sum_{i=1}^{m} \delta_i^o$ is $\sum_{i=1}^{m} \delta_i^{o*}$ at optimality when $\sum_{i=1}^{m} \rho_i^o = \sum_{i=1}^{m} \rho_i^{o*}$, and there exist λ_j ($j \neq 0$), s_i^-, $s_r^+ \geq 0$ that satisfy

$$\sum_{\substack{j=1 \\ j \neq o}}^{n} \lambda_j x_{ij} + s_i^- = x_{io} + \widetilde{\delta}_i \quad i = 1,..., m$$

$$\sum_{\substack{j=1 \\ j \neq o}}^{n} \lambda_j y_{rj} - s_r^+ = y_{ro} \quad r = 1,..., s$$

$$\lambda_j, s_i^-, s_r^+ \geq 0 \quad j = 1,..., n$$

violating the optimality of $\sum_{i=1}^{m} \delta_i^{o*}$. Thus, $DMU_o(\beta_1,..., \beta_m)$ with inputs of $\widetilde{\beta}_i x_{io}$ ($i = 1,..., m$) is efficient. ∎

Definition 11.1 A region of allowable input increases is called an **Input Stability Region** *if and only if* DMU_o remains efficient after such increases occur.

The input stability region (ISR) determines by how much all of DMU_o's inputs can be increased before DMU_o is within the convex hull of the other DMUs. From Lemma 11.1 and Theorem 11.1 we know that (i) Ω^o is only a subset of ISR and (ii) the sets $\{\beta_i \mid 1 \le \beta_i \le \beta_i^{o*}\}$ $i = 1, ..., m$, form part of the boundary of ISR.

If the input hyperplane constructed by the m points, $DMU(\beta_k^{o*})$, associated with the optimal values to (11.3), is not dominated by other DMUs except DMU_o, i.e., that input hyperplane is a new efficient facet when excluding DMU_o, then the following set Γ^o is precisely the ISR (Zhu, 1996b)

$$\Gamma^o = \{(\beta_1,..., \beta_m) \mid 1 \le \beta_i \le \beta_i^{o*}, i = 1,..., m \text{ and } B_1^o \beta_1 +...+ B_m^o \beta_m \le 1\}$$

where B_1^o, ..., B_m^o are parameters determined by the following system of equations

$$\begin{cases} \beta_1^{o*} B_1^o + B_2^o +...+ B_m^o = 1 \\ B_1^o + \beta_2^{o*} B_2^o +...+ B_m^o = 1 \\ ... \quad ... \quad ... \quad ... \quad ... \\ B_1^o + B_2^0 +...+ \beta_m^{o*} B_m^o = 1 \end{cases}$$

Zhu (1996b) shows the following result

Theorem 11.2 In the case of input increases of form (11.1), for any extreme efficient DMU_o, if the m points, $DMU(\beta_k^{o*})$, which are associated with the optimal β values to (11.3), determine an efficient input hyperplane, then DMU_o remains efficient *if and only if* $(\beta_1,..., \beta_m) \in \Gamma^o$.

Next, suppose that the hyperplane constructed by the m points in (11.4) is dominated by some other DMUs which are inefficient when including DMU_o. In this case, the ISR is no longer the set of Γ^o. Thus, we develop the following procedure.

Initiation (t = 0). Solve model (11.3) for each k, k =1, ..., m. If the input hyperplane, which is determined by the m points of $DMU(\beta_k^{o*})$ in (11.4), is not dominated by other DMUs, then we obtain the ISR defined by Γ^o. Otherwise solve model (11.5). Associated with the optimal solutions to (11.5), ρ_i^{o*}, we obtain m new points, $DMU(\rho_i^{o*})$ ($i = 1, 2,..., m$) as given in (11.6) and Ω^o.

Iteration $t = 1, 2, ..., $ T. At iteration t, for each point of iteration t-1, say point p, which is associated with the optimal ρ values to (11.5), we solve model (11.3) at each new kth input, $k = 1, 2, ..., m$ and apply the *Stopping Rule*. (a) If the rule is satisfied for a particular point p, then we have a similar set Γ'_p determined by the optimal β values, say β_k^{p*}, $k = 1, ..., m$. We continue for the remaining points. (b) Otherwise solve model (11.5) for point p to obtain m new points and a similar set Ω'_p determined by the optimal ρ values, say ρ_k^{p*}. Apply iteration t+1 to each of these m new points.

Stopping Rule. If the input hyperplane determined by the m points that are associated with the m optimal β values is not dominated by other DMUs, then iteration stops.

From the above procedure, we see that if a Γ-like set is obtained, then the iteration stops at a specific point. i.e., the Γ-like set indicates the termination of the iteration.

Theorem 11.3 The input stability region is a union of Ω^o and some Ω'_p and some Γ'_p.

[Proof]: Obviously, DMU_o remains efficient when its input increases $(\beta_1, ..., \beta_m)$ belong to Ω^o or any of the Ω'_p or Γ'_p. Conversely, from the iterations we know that the ISR is connected. Since the input increases occurred in Ω-like sets, DMU_o is first moved to a particular point p which is used to construct a Γ-like set. By Theorem 11.2, we know that the sets of Γ'_p are the boundary sets of the ISR. This means that if further input increases are not in this kind of set, then DMU_o will become inefficient. Therefore, if DMU_o remains efficient, then the input increase of form (11.1) must be in Ω^o or any of the Ω'_p or Γ'_p. ∎

11.2.2 Output Stability Region

Similarly, Seiford and Zhu (1998d) develop a sensitivity analysis procedure for output decreases of (11.2). For a specific extreme efficient DMU_o, we consider the following linear program (Zhu, 1996b)

$\min \alpha_k^o \quad$ for each $k=1,...,s$
subject to

$$\sum_{\substack{j=1 \\ j \neq o}}^{n} \lambda_j y_{kj} \geq \alpha_k^o y_{ro}$$

$$\sum_{\substack{j=1 \\ j \neq o}}^{n} \lambda_j y_{rj} \geq y_{ro} \qquad r \neq k \tag{11.7}$$

$$\sum_{\substack{j=1 \\ j\neq o}}^{n} \lambda_j x_{ij} \leq x_{io} \qquad i = 1,...,m$$

$$\lambda_j, \alpha_k^o \geq 0$$

Model (11.7) is a super-efficiency model based upon the CRS kth output specific model. The optimal values to (11.7), α_k^{o*}, $k = 1, ..., s$, give s hypothetical frontier points (or DMUs) and a set Λ^o defined as follows

$$DMU(\alpha_k^{o*}) = (x_{10},...,x_{mo}, y_{10},....,\alpha_k^{o*} y_{ko},...y_{so})$$

and

$$\Lambda^o = \{(\alpha_1,...,\alpha_m) \mid \alpha_r^{o*} \leq \alpha_r \leq 1, r = 1,...,s \text{ and } A_1^o \alpha_1 + ... + A_s^o \alpha_s \geq 1\}$$

in which the parameters of A_r^o are determined by the following system of equations

$$\begin{cases} \alpha_1^{o*} A_1^o + A_2^o + ... + A_s^o = 1 \\ A_1^o + \alpha_2^{o*} A_2^o + ... + A_s^o = 1 \\ ... \quad ... \quad ... \quad ... \quad ... \\ A_1^o + A_2^o + ... + \alpha_s^{o*} A_s^o = 1 \end{cases}$$

Here, we rewrite the result of Zhu (1996b) as the following theorem

Theorem 11.4 In the case of output decreases of form (11.2), for any extreme efficient DMU_o, if the s points, $DMU(\alpha_k^{o*})$, which are associated with the optimal α values to (11.7), determine an efficient output hyperplane, then DMU_o remains efficient *if and only if* $(\alpha_1,...,\alpha_s) \in \Lambda^o$.

Definition 11.2 A region of allowable output decreases is called an **Output Stability Region** *if and only if* DMU_o remains efficient after such decreases occur.

Now, suppose that the output hyperplane constructed by the s points, $DMU(\alpha_k^{o*})$, is dominated by some other DMUs which are originally inefficient, then the output stability region (OSR) is not the set Λ^o. We consider the following linear programming problem

$$\max \sum_{r=1}^{s} \varphi_r^o$$

subject to

$$\sum_{\substack{j=1 \\ j\neq o}}^{n} \lambda_j y_{rj} \geq \varphi_r^o y_{ro} \quad r=1,...,s \qquad\qquad (11.8)$$

$$\sum_{\substack{j=1 \\ j\neq o}}^{n} \lambda_j x_{ij} \leq x_{io} \qquad i = 1,...,m$$

$$\lambda_j \geq 0, \varphi_r^o \leq 1.$$

Similar to Theorem 11.1, we have

Theorem 11.5 For a decrease in outputs of form (11.2), if

$$(\alpha_1,...,\alpha_s) \in \Psi^o = \{(\alpha_1,...,\alpha_m) \mid \varphi_r^{o*} \le \alpha_r \le 1, r = 1,...,s\}$$

then DMU_o remains efficient.

We also have the following s new points that associated with the optimal solutions, φ_r^{o*}, of (11.8)

$$DMU(\varphi_k^{o*}) = (x_{10},..., x_{mo}, y_{10},...., \varphi_k^{o*} y_{ko},...y_{so})$$

To obtain the output stability region, we apply model (11.7) and model (11.8) at each iteration in the procedure for input stability region until no Λ-like sets can be obtained. Similarly, we have

Theorem 11.6 The output stability region is a union of Λ-like sets and Ψ-like sets.

11.2.3   Geometrical Presentation of Input Stability Region

We now illustrate the sensitivity analysis procedure geometrically for the following five DMUs with a single output and two inputs. For convenience, we suppose the five DMUs produce an equal amount of output and thus omit the output quantities in the following discussion. With the help of Figure 11.1, we will see how to keep track of newly generated points (DMUs) by the procedure.

Table 11.1. DMUs for Illustration of Input Stability Region

DMU	1 (X_1)	2 (X_2)	3 (X_3)	4 (X_4)	5 (X_5)
input 1 x_1	5	2	1	5/2	9/4
input 2 x_2	1	2	5	5/2	11/4

It is obvious that DMUs 1, 2, and 3 are extreme efficient, and DMUs 4 and 5 are inefficient. Let DMU_o = DMU2 ($x_{10} = 2, x_{20} = 2$), i.e., we consider the robustness of the efficiency of DMU2 when the two inputs increase.
Initiation (t=0). First we solve model (11.3) for DMU_o (point X_2), that is

$$\beta_1^{o*} = \min \beta_1^o$$
$$\text{subject to}$$

$$5\lambda_1 + \lambda_3 + \frac{5}{2}\lambda_4 + \frac{9}{4}\lambda_5 \le 2\beta_1^o$$
$$\lambda_1 + 5\lambda_3 + \frac{5}{2}\lambda_4 + \frac{11}{4}\lambda_5 \le 2$$
$$\lambda_1 + \lambda_3 + \lambda_4 + \lambda_5 \ge 1$$
$$\lambda_1, \lambda_3, \lambda_4, \lambda_5, \beta_1^o \ge 0$$

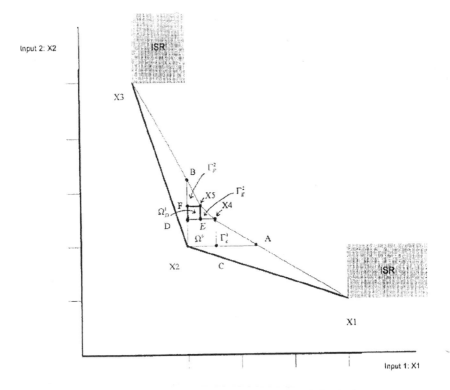

Figure 11.1. Geometrical Presentation of Input Stability Region

Figure 11.2 shows the spreadsheet model. Cell D8 is reserved to indicate the DMU under consideration, and is equal to 2 now, indicating DMU2. Cells F2:F6 are reserved to indicate λ_j. Cell E9 represents β_1. This spreadsheet model is developed from the spreadsheet model for measure-specific models. The formulas for the spreadsheet shown in Figure 11.2 are

Cell B10=SUMPRODUCT(B2:B6,F2:F6)
Cell B11=SUMPRODUCT(C2:C6,F2:F6)
Cell B12=SUMPRODUCT(E2:E6,F2:F6)
Cell B13=INDEX(F2:F6,D8,1)

Cell D10=E9*INDEX(B2:B6,D8,1)
Cell D11=INDEX(C2:C6,D8,1)
Cell D12=INDEX(E2:E6,D8,1)
Cell D13=0

	A	B	C	D	E	F
1	DMUs	input 1	input 2		output	λ
2	1	5	1		1	0.333333
3	2	2	2		1	0
4	3	1	5		1	0
5	4	2 1/2	2 1/2		1	0.666667
6	5	2 1/4	2 3/4		1	0
7		DMU under				
8		consideration		2	β	
9	Constraints				1 2/3	
10	input1	3.333333	≤	3 1/3		
11	input2	2	≤	2	point A	
12	output	1	≥	1		
13	DMUo	0	=	0		

Figure 11.2. Spreadsheet for Input Stability Region (Input 1)

Figure 11.3 shows the Solver parameters for the spreadsheet shown in
Figure 11.2. We have β_1^{o*} = 5/3 (see cell E9 in Figure 11.2). For k = 2, we
have the spreadsheet model shown in Figure 11.4. The formulas for cells
B10:B13 and cells D12:D13 remain the same. We need to change the
formulas in cells D10:D11 to

Cell D10=INDEX(B2:B6,D8,1)
Cell D11=E9*INDEX(C2:C6,D8,1)

Using the Solver parameters shown in Figure 11.3, we obtain β_2^{o*} = 8/5
(see cell F9 in Figure 11.4). Furthermore, we have the following two newly
generated points associated with the optimal β values (cells D10:D11 in
Figures 11.2 and 11.4)

$$\begin{cases} A = (\beta_1^{o*} x_{10}, x_{20}) = (\frac{10}{3}, 2) \\ B = (x_{10}, \beta_2^{o*} x_{20}) = (2, \frac{16}{5}) \end{cases}$$

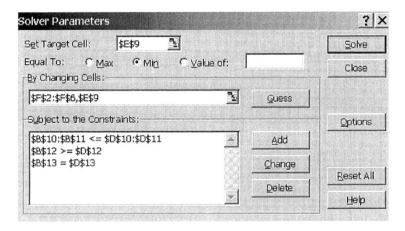

Figure 11.3. Solver Parameters for Input Stability Region

	A	B	C	D	E	F
1	DMUs	input 1	input 2		output	λ
2	1	5	1		1	0
3	2	2	2		1	0
4	3	1	5		1	0.2
5	4	2 1/2	2 1/2		1	0
6	5	2 1/4	2 3/4		1	0.8
7		DMU under				
8		consideration		2	β	
9	Constraints				1 3/5	
10	input1	2	≤	2		
11	input2	3.2	≤	3 1/5	Point B	
12	output	1	≥	1		
13	DMUo	0	=	0		

Figure 11.4. Spreadsheet for Input Stability Region (Input 2)

Obviously, the input hyperplane (line segment AB) constructed by A and B is dominated by DMU4 and DMU5. Thus, we solve model (11.5) for DMU_o, that is

$$\min \rho_1^o + \rho_2^o$$
subject to
$$5\lambda_1 + \lambda_3 + \frac{5}{2}\lambda_4 + \frac{9}{4}\lambda_5 \leq 2\rho_1^o$$

$$\lambda_1 + 5\lambda_3 + \frac{5}{2}\lambda_4 + \frac{11}{4}\lambda_5 \leq 2\rho_2^o$$
$$\lambda_1 + \lambda_3 + \lambda_4 + \lambda_5 \geq 1$$
$$\lambda_1, \lambda_3, \lambda_4, \lambda_5 \geq 0, \rho_1^o, \rho_2^o \geq 1$$

Figure 11.5 shows the spreadsheet model for model (11.5). Cell E9 and Cell F9 represent ρ_1 and ρ_2, respectively. The target cell G9 (=E9+F9) represents the objective function of model (11.5). We change the formulas of cells D10:D11 to

Cell D10=E9*INDEX(B2:B6,D8,1)
Cell D11=F9*INDEX(C2:C6,D8,1)

	A	B	C	D	E	F	G
1	DMUs	input 1	input 2		output	λ	
2	1	5	1		1	0	
3	2	2	2		1	0	
4	3	1	5		1	0	
5	4	2 1/2	2 1/2		1	1	
6	5	2 1/4	2 3/4		1	0	
7		DMU under					
8		consideration		2	ρ1	ρ2	
9	Constraints				1 1/4	1 1/4	2 1/2
10	input1	2.5	≤	2 1/2			
11	input2	2.5	≤	2 1/2		Target cell	
12	output	1	≥	1			
13	DMUo	0	=	0			

Figure 11.5. Spreadsheet for Input Stability Region (Model (11.5))

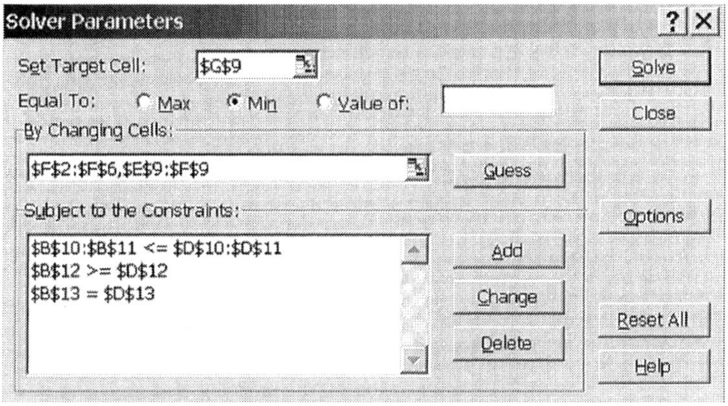

Figure 11.6. Solver Parameters for Model (11.5)

Figure 11.6 shows the Solver parameters for model (11.5). We obtain $\rho_1^{o*} = \rho_2^{o*} = 5/4$. Moreover, we have $\Omega^o = \{(\beta_1, \beta_2) \mid 1 \le \beta_1 \le 5/4,$ $1 \le \beta_2 \le 5/4\}$ as shown in Figure 11.1 and obtain the following two additional points associated with optimal ρ values

$$\begin{cases} C = (\rho_1^{o*} x_{10}, x_{20}) = (x_{10}^C, x_{20}^C) = (5/2, 2) \\ D = (x_{10}, \rho_2^{o*} x_{20}) = (x_{10}^D, x_{20}^D) = (2, 5/2) \end{cases}$$

Iteration: t=1. For the first point C, we solve model (11.3)

$$\min \beta_1^C$$
subject to
$$5\lambda_1 + \lambda_3 + \frac{5}{2}\lambda_4 + \frac{9}{4}\lambda_5 \le \beta_1^C x_{10}^C = \frac{5}{2}\beta_1^C$$
$$\lambda_1 + 5\lambda_3 + \frac{5}{2}\lambda_4 + \frac{11}{4}\lambda_5 \le x_{20}^C = 2$$
$$\lambda_1 + \lambda_3 + \lambda_4 + \lambda_5 \ge 1$$
$$\lambda_1, \lambda_3, \lambda_4, \lambda_5, \beta_1^C \ge 0$$

We have $\beta_1^{C*} = 4/3$. Similarly, $\beta_2^{C*} = 5/4$. The two corresponding new points are as follows

$$\begin{cases} A = (\beta_1^{C*} x_{10}^C, x_{20}^C) = (\frac{10}{3}, 2) \\ X_4 = (x_{10}^C, \beta_2^{C*} x_{20}^C) = (\frac{5}{2}, \frac{5}{2}) \end{cases}$$

The input hyperplane constructed by these two points (line segment $A X_4$) is not dominated by other DMUs, therefore the iteration for point C stops and we have the following results.

Let $\hat{x}_{10} = c_1 x_{10}^C = c_1 \beta_1^{o*} x_{10}$ and $\hat{x}_{20} = c_2 x_{20}^C = c_2 x_{20}$. By Zhu (1996b), we have

$$\Gamma_c^1 = \{(c_1, c_2) \mid 1 \le c_k \le \beta_k^{C*}, k = 1,2 \text{ and } B_1^C c_1 + B_2^C c_2 \le 1\}$$

where B_1^C and B_2^C are determined as follows

$$\begin{cases} B_1^C \beta_1^{C*} + B_2^C = 1 \\ B_1^C + B_2^C \beta_2^{C*} = 1 \end{cases} \Rightarrow \begin{cases} \frac{4}{3}B_1^C + B_2^C = 1 \\ B_1^C + \frac{5}{4}B_2^C = 1 \end{cases} \Rightarrow \begin{cases} B_1^C = \frac{3}{8} \\ B_2^C = \frac{1}{2} \end{cases}$$

Hence,

$$\Gamma_c^1 = \{(c_1\rho_1^{o*}, c_2) \mid \rho_1^{o*} \le c_1\rho_1^{o*} \le \rho_1^{o*}\beta_1^{C*} = \beta_1^{o*}, 1 \le c_2 \le \beta_2^{C*}, \text{and } \frac{3}{8}\rho_1^{o*}c_1 + \frac{1}{2}\rho_1^{o*}c_2 \le \rho_1^{o*}\}$$

Let $\beta_1 = c_1\rho_1^{o*}$ and $\beta_2 = c_2$. Then $\Gamma_c^1 = \{(\beta_1, \beta_2) \mid 5/4 \le \beta_1 \le 5/3,$ $1 \le \beta_2 \le 5/4, 3\beta_1 + 5\beta_2 \le 10\}$.

Next, for the second point D, solving model (11.3) when k = 1 and k = 2 yields $\beta_1^{D^*} = 5/4$ and $\beta_2^{D^*} = 32/25$, respectively. Associated with these two optimal β values, we have two new points

$$\begin{cases} X_4 = (\beta_1^{D^*} x_{10}^D, x_{20}^D) = (\dfrac{5}{2}, \dfrac{5}{2}) \\ B = (x_{10}^D, \beta_2^{D^*} x_{20}^D) = (2, \dfrac{16}{5}) \end{cases}$$

The input hyperplane determined by these two points (X_4 and B) is dominated by DMU5, therefore we compute model (11.5) for point D,

$$\min \rho_1^D + \rho_2^D$$
subject to
$$5\lambda_1 + \lambda_3 + \frac{5}{2}\lambda_4 + \frac{9}{4}\lambda_5 \le \rho_1^D x_{10}^D = 2\rho_1^D$$
$$\lambda_1 + 5\lambda_3 + \frac{5}{2}\lambda_4 + \frac{11}{4}\lambda_5 \le \rho_2^D x_{20}^D = \frac{5}{2}\rho_2^D$$
$$\lambda_1 + \lambda_3 + \lambda_4 + \lambda_5 \ge 1$$
$$\lambda_1, \lambda_3, \lambda_4, \lambda_5 \ge 0, \rho_1^D, \rho_2^D \ge 1$$

We have $\rho_1^{D^*} = 9/8$ and $\rho_2^{D^*} = 11/10$. Next we compute Ω_D^1.

First, let $\hat{x}_{10} = d_1 x_{10}^D = d_1 x_{10}$ and $\hat{x}_{20} = d_2 x_{20}^D = d_2 \rho_2^{o^*} x_{20}$. By Theorem 11.1, we have

$$\Omega_D^1 = \{(d_1, d_2) \mid 1 \le d_k \le \rho_k^{D^*}, k = 1, 2\}$$

and

$$\Omega_D^1 = \{(d_1, \rho_2^{o^*} d_2) \mid 1 \le d_1 \le \rho_1^{D^*}, \rho_2^{o^*} \le \rho_2^{o^*} d_2 \le \rho_2^{o^*} \rho_1^{D^*}\}$$

and further $\Omega_D^1 = \{(\beta_1, \beta_2) \mid 1 \le \beta_1 \le 9/8, 5/4 \le \beta_2 \le 11/8\}$.

Associated with the two optimal values of $\rho_1^{D^*}$ and $\rho_2^{D^*}$, we now have the following two points

$$\begin{cases} E = (\rho_1^{D^*} x_{10}^D, x_{20}^D) = (x_{10}^E, x_{20}^E) = (\dfrac{9}{4}, \dfrac{5}{2}) \\ F = (x_{10}^D, \rho_2^{D^*} x_{20}^D) = (x_{10}^F, x_{20}^F) = (2, \dfrac{11}{4}) \end{cases}$$

Iteration t = 2. For the point E generated from the point D in the first iteration, we obtain, by solving model (11.3), $\beta_1^{E^*} = 10/9$, $\beta_2^{E^*} = 11/10$, and two corresponding points

$$\begin{cases} X_4 = (\beta_1^{E^*} x_{10}^E, x_{20}^E) = (\dfrac{5}{2}, \dfrac{5}{2}) \\ X_5 = (x_{10}^E, \beta_2^{E^*} x_{20}^E) = (\dfrac{9}{4}, \dfrac{11}{4}) \end{cases}$$

The input hyperplane constructed by the two points of X_4 and X_5 is not dominated by other DMUs, therefore the iteration stops.

Let $\hat{x}_{10} = e_1 x_{10}^E = e_1 \rho_1^{D*} x_{10}^D = e_1 \rho_1^{D*} x_{10}$ and $\hat{x}_{20} = e_2 x_{20}^E = e_2 x_{20}^D = e_2 \rho_2^{o*} x_{20}$. Similar to Γ^o, we have $\Gamma_E^2 = \{(e_1, e_2) | 1 \le e_k \le \beta_k^{E*}, \ k = 1, 2 \ \text{and} \ B_1^E e_1 + B_2^E e_2 \le 1\}$ in which B_1^E and B_2^E are determined by

$$\begin{cases} B_1^E \beta_1^{E*} + B_2^E = 1 \\ B_1^E + B_2^E \beta_2^{E*} = 1 \end{cases} \Rightarrow \begin{cases} \dfrac{10}{9} B_1^E + B_2^E = 1 \\ B_1^E + \dfrac{11}{10} B_2^E = 1 \end{cases} \Rightarrow \begin{cases} B_1^E = \dfrac{9}{20} \\ B_2^E = \dfrac{1}{2} \end{cases}$$

Thus, $\Gamma_E^2 = \{(e_1 \rho_1^{D*}, e_2 \rho_2^{o*}) | \rho_1^{D*} \le e_1 \rho_1^{D*} \le \rho_1^{D*} \beta_1^{E*} = \rho_1^{o*}, \rho_2^{o*} \le e_2 \rho_2^{o*} \le \beta_2^{E*} \rho_2^{o*}$, and $(9/20)\rho_1^{D*} \rho_2^{o*} e_1 + (1/2)\rho_1^{D*} \rho_2^{o*} e_2 \le \rho_1^{D*} \rho_2^{o*}\} = \{(\beta_1, \beta_2) | 9/8 \le \beta_1 \le 5/4, 5/4 \le \beta_2 \le 11/8, 18\beta_1 + 2\beta_2 \le 45\}$, where $\beta_1 = e_1 \rho_1^{D*}$ and $\beta_2 = e_2 \rho_2^{o*}$.

For the point F, we have $\beta_1^{F*} = 9/8$ and $\beta_2^{F*} = 64/55$, and two corresponding points

$$\begin{cases} X_5 = (\beta_1^{F*} x_{10}^F, x_{20}^F) = (\dfrac{9}{4}, \dfrac{11}{4}) \\ B = (x_{10}^F, \beta_2^{F*} x_{20}^F) = (2, \dfrac{16}{5}) \end{cases}$$

The input hyperplane constructed by these two points of X_5 and B is not dominated by other DMUs, therefore the iteration stops.

Let $\hat{x}_{10} = f_1 x_{10}^F = f_1 x_{10}$ and $\hat{x}_{20} = f_2 x_{20}^F = f_2 \rho_2^{D*} x_{20}^D = f_2 \rho_2^{D*} \rho_2^{o*} x_{20}$. Similar to Γ^o, we have $\Gamma_F^2 = \{(f_1, f_2) | 1 \le f_k \le \beta_k^{F*}, k = 1, 2 \ \text{and} \ B_1^F f_1 + B_2^F f_2 \le 1\}$ in which B_1^F and B_2^F are the solutions to the following system of equations

$$\begin{cases} B_1^F \beta_1^{F*} + B_2^F = 1 \\ B_1^F + B_2^F \beta_2^{F*} = 1 \end{cases} \Rightarrow \begin{cases} \dfrac{9}{8} B_1^F + B_2^F = 1 \\ B_1^F + \dfrac{64}{55} B_2^F = 1 \end{cases} \Rightarrow \begin{cases} B_1^F = \dfrac{9}{17} \\ B_2^F = \dfrac{55}{136} \end{cases}$$

Thus, $\Gamma_F^2 = \{(\beta_1, \beta_2) | 1 \le \beta_1 \le 9/8, \ 11/8 \le \beta_2 \le 8/5, \ 9\beta_1 + 5\beta_2 \le 17\}$. Finally, we obtain the following input stability region for DMU2 (point X_2) as shown in Figure 11.1.

$$\text{ISR} = \Omega^o \bigcup \Omega_D^1 \bigcup \Gamma_C^1 \bigcup \Gamma_E^2 \bigcup \Gamma_F^2$$

11.3   Infeasibility and Stability

The previous sensitivity analysis procedure is developed under the assumption that model (11.3) (or model (11.7)) is feasible. However, this may not be always the case. For example, if we calculate (11.3) for DMU3 in Table 11.1, then we have $\beta_1^* = 2$ for the first input but infeasibility for the second input. If we calculate (11.3) for DMU1, then we have infeasibility for the first input. Figure 11.7 presents the results for the three efficient DMUs 1, 2, and 3. The calculation is performed by a VBA procedure "InputStabilityRegion".

```
Sub InputStabilityRegion()
Dim i As Integer
For i = 1 To 3
Range("D8") = i
SolverSolve UserFinish:=True
If SolverSolve(UserFinish:=True) = 5 Then
Range("G" & i + 1) = "Infeasible"
Else
Range("G" & i + 1) = Range("E9")
End If
Next
End Sub
```

Note that, in fact, we can increase infinitely the amount of DMU3's second input (DMU1's first input) while maintaining the efficiency of DMU3.

	A	B	C	D	E	F	G
1	DMUs	input 1	input 2		output	λ	ISR
2	1	5	1		1	0	Infeasible
3	2	2	2		1	1	1 2/3
4	3	1	5		1	0	2
5	4	2 1/2	2 1/2		1	0	
6	5	2 1/4	2 3/4		1	0	
7							
8				3	β		
9	Constraints				2		
10	input1	2		≤	2		
11	input2	2		≤	5	Input1	
12	output	1		≥	1		
13	DMUo	0		=	0		

	A	B	C	D	E	F	G
1		input 1	input 2		output	λ	ISR
2	1	5	1		1	0	2
3	2	2	2		1	0.5	1 3/5
4	3	1	5		1	0	Infeasible
5	4	2 1/2	2 1/2		1	0	
6	5	2 1/4	2 3/4		1	0	
7							
8				3	β		
9	Constraints				1/5		
10	input1	1		≤	1		
11	input2	1		≤	1	Input2	
12	output	0.5		≥	1		
13	DMUo	0		=	0		

Figure 11.7. Optimal β

Theorem 11.7 For an efficient DMU_o, an increase of the kth input only, model (11.3) is infeasible, *if and only if,* the amount of kth input of DMU_o can be increased without limitation while maintaining the efficiency of DMU_o.

[Proof]: The *if* part is obvious from the fact that if (11.3) is feasible, then the optimal value to (11.3) gives the maximum increase proportion of the kth input. Therefore, the amount of kth input cannot be infinitely increased.

To establish the *only if* part we suppose that the kth input is increased by $M \geq 1$ and DMU_o is inefficient. By substituting DMU_o into CRS envelopment model, we obtain an optimal solution $\theta^* \leq 1$, $\lambda_o^* = 0, \lambda_j^*(j \neq o)$, in which $\theta^* \leq 1$ implies $DMU_o \in F$. Therefore,

$$
\begin{cases}
\displaystyle\sum_{\substack{j=1 \\ j \neq o}}^{n} \lambda_j^* x_{kj} \leq \theta^* M x_{ko} \\
\displaystyle\sum_{\substack{j=1 \\ j \neq o}}^{n} \lambda_j^* x_{ij} \leq \theta^* x_{io} \leq x_{io} \qquad i \neq k
\end{cases}
$$

This means that $\lambda_j^*(j \neq o), \beta_k = \theta^* M$ is a feasible solution to (11.3) and leads to a contradiction. Since M is arbitrary, the amount of the kth input can be infinitely increased while maintaining DMU_o's efficiency. ∎

As the Theorem 11.7 indicates, if (11.3) is infeasible, then $\beta_k^{o^*} = +\infty$. Thus, in this situation, we must modify the sensitivity analysis procedure. Because we are unable to express the new frontier point associated with $\beta_k^{o^*} = +\infty$, and further, to apply the stopping rule. Note that if we here assume that all data are positive, then model (11.5) is always feasible. But in the case of infeasibility, (11.5) does not perform well. For example, if we apply (11.5) to DMU3, we obtain $\rho_1^* = 2$ and $\rho_2^* = 1$. i.e., $\rho_i^* = 1$ relative to the unbounded input i. Consequently, we are unable to determine the stability region. Thus, from a computational point of view, in this situation, we apply model (11.5) with $\rho_i^o = \theta_o$ $(i = 1,...,m)$. That is,

$$\min \theta_o$$
subject to
$$\sum_{\substack{j=1 \\ j \neq o}}^{n} \lambda_j x_{ij} \leq \theta_o x_{io} \qquad i = 1,...,m \tag{11.9}$$
$$\sum_{\substack{j=1 \\ j \neq o}}^{n} \lambda_j y_{rj} \geq y_{ro} \qquad r = 1,...,s$$
$$\lambda_j \geq 0 \qquad j = 1,...,n.$$

At each point, in each iteration, we first apply (11.9) when (11.3) is infeasible, and then, for the newly generated points, we apply (11.3). If (11.3) is feasible, we use the procedure suggested previously. If (11.3) is still infeasible, then apply (11.9) again (go to next iteration). We can, in fact, regard infeasibility as the rejection of the stopping rule, and then we calculate model (11.9) instead of (11.5) to generate new frontier DMUs for the next iteration. In this situation, the set Ω^o obtained from (11.9) corresponds to the $\infty-norm$ in Charnes, Haag, Jaska and Semple (1992).

This general procedure for the infeasibility case is stated below

Step 1: Solve model (11.9).
Step 2: Solve (11.3) for the newly generated points by (11.9):
$DMU(\theta_o^*) = (x_{1o},...,\theta_o^* x_{ko},...,x_{mo}, y_{1o},..., y_{so})$, $k=1,...,m$.
(a) If (11.3) is feasible, then go to the procedure given in section 11.2.1;
(b) If (11.3) is infeasible, then go to step 1.

Note that infeasibility often occurs in real world situations. In theory, one can always use this general procedure to determine the ISR. However, in practice one may use this procedure to approximate the ISR due to the fact that some inputs' amount can be infinitely increased. For example, it is obvious that the IRS for DMU3 in Table 11.1 is

$$ISR = \{(\beta_1, \beta_2) \mid 1 \le \beta_1 < 2,\ 1 \le \beta_2 < +\infty\} \qquad (11.10)$$

which is the shaded region shown in Figure 11.1. Furthermore, we have

Theorem 11.8 For the two-input case, one of the two optimal β values in (11.3) is equal to the corresponding optimal value to (11.9), *if and only if*, $ISR = \{(\beta_1, \beta_2) \mid 1 \le \beta_i < \beta_i^{o^*}, i = 1,2\}$, where one of the $\beta_i^{o^*}$ is finite and the other is $+\infty$.

[Proof]: Without loss of generality, assume that $\beta_1^{o^*}$ is finite and $\beta_2^{o^*} = +\infty$.

Suppose that $ISR = \{(\beta_1, \beta_2) \mid 1 \le \beta_1 < \beta_1^{o^*},\ 1 \le \beta_2 < +\infty\}$. Let $\beta_1 = \beta_1^{o^*}$, then DMU_o with $(\beta_1^{o^*} x_{1o}, \beta_1^{o^*} x_{2o})$ is a frontier point. Therefore $\theta_o^* = \beta_1^{o^*}$. This completes the proof of the *if* part.

Suppose $\theta_o^* = \beta_1^{o^*}$. Obviously, if DMU_o with inputs of $(\beta_1 x_{1o}, \beta_2 x_{2o})$ is in set E, then $(\beta_1, \beta_2) \in ISR = \{(\beta_1, \beta_2) \mid 1 \le \beta_1 < \beta_1^{o^*} = \theta_o^*,\ 1 \le \beta_2 < +\infty\}$. Next, note that the original DMU_o belongs to set E, therefore $\theta_o^* > 1$. By θ_o^* and $\beta_1^{o^*}$, we obtain two frontier points $A = (\theta_o^* x_{1o}, \theta_o^* x_{2o})$ and $B = (\beta_1^{o^*} x_{1o}, x_{2o}) = (\theta_o^* x_{1o}, x_{2o})$. Thus,
$\theta_o^* = \beta_1^{o^*} \Rightarrow A \in F$ with nonzero slack on the second input $\Rightarrow$ $(\beta_1^{o^*} x_{1o}, \beta_2 x_{2o}) \in F$, where $1 \le \beta_2 < +\infty \Rightarrow (\beta_1 x_{1o}, \beta_2 x_{2o}) \in E$, where $1 \le \beta_1 < \beta_1^{o^*},\ 1 \le \beta_2 < +\infty$.

Therefore, if $(\beta_1, \beta_2) \in ISR$, then DMU_o preserves its efficiency. This completes the *only if* part. ∎

By the proof of Theorem 11.8 and the result of Theorem 11.7, we can easily obtain

Corollary 11.1 For the two-input case, if one of the two optimal β values in (11.3) is equal to the corresponding optimal value to (11.9), then (11.3) is infeasible for the other input.

Note that equality is not held in the right hand side of the inequalities in (11.10) of β_i. Otherwise, DMU_o will be in set F. For instance, if $\beta_1 = 2$ in (11.10), then DMU3 (X3) is moved into set F. However, if we only consider weak efficiency, then the equality can be imposed. Because the efficiency ratings are equal to one for the DMUs in set F.

Finally, the above discussion and development holds for the output case when (11.7) is infeasible. That is,

Theorem 11.9 For an efficient DMU_o, an increase of the kth output only, model (11.7) is infeasible, *if and only if*, the amount of kth output of DMU_o can be increased without limitation while maintaining the efficiency of DMU_o.

Theorems 11.7 and 11.9 indicate that if model (11.3) or (11.7) is infeasible, then the test DMU remains efficient when data variations are applied to the specific input or output. This conclusion is also true when the data variations are applied to both the test DMU and the remaining DMUs.

11.4   Simultaneous Data Change[2]

Zhu (2001a) shows that a particular super-efficiency score can be decomposed into two data perturbation components of a particular test DMU and the remaining DMUs. Also, necessary and sufficient conditions for preserving a DMU's efficiency classification are developed when various data changes are applied to all DMUs. As a result, DEA sensitivity analysis can be easily applied if we employ various super-efficiency DEA models.

We rewrite the input-oriented CRS envelopment model and its dual as

$$\theta_{CRS}^{o*} = \min \theta_{CRS}^{o}$$
subject to
$$\sum_{j=1}^{n} \lambda_j x_{ij} + s_i^- = \theta_{CRS}^o x_{io} \quad i = 1,2,\dots,m; \qquad (11.10)$$
$$\sum_{j=1}^{n} \lambda_j y_{rj} - s_r^+ = y_{ro} \quad r = 1,2,\dots,s;$$
$$\theta_{CRS}^o, \lambda_j, s_i^-, s_r^+ \ge 0.$$

$$\max \sum_{r=1}^{s} u_r y_{ro}$$
subject to
$$\sum_{r=1}^{s} u_r y_{rj} - \sum_{i=1}^{m} v_i x_{ij} \leq 0, \quad j = 1,...,n \tag{11.11}$$
$$\sum_{i=1}^{m} v_i x_{io} = 1$$
$$u_r, v_i \geq 0.$$

We also present the input-oriented and output-oriented CRS super-efficiency models

$$\theta_o^{super*} = \min \theta_o^{super}$$
subject to
$$\sum_{\substack{j=1 \\ j \neq o}}^{n} \lambda_j x_{ij} \leq \theta_o^{super} x_{io} \qquad i = 1,2,...,m \tag{11.12}$$
$$\sum_{\substack{j=1 \\ j \neq o}}^{n} \lambda_j y_{rj} \geq y_{ro} \qquad r = 1,2,...,s$$
$$\theta_o^{super}, \lambda_j (j \neq o) \geq 0.$$

$$\phi_o^{super*} = \max \phi_o^{super}$$
subject to
$$\sum_{\substack{j=1 \\ j \neq o}}^{n} \lambda_j y_{rj} \geq \phi_o^{super} y_{ro} \quad r = 1,...,s \tag{11.13}$$
$$\sum_{\substack{j=1 \\ j \neq o}}^{n} \lambda_j x_{ij} \leq x_{io} \qquad i = 1,...,m$$
$$\phi_o^{super}, \lambda_j (j \neq o) \geq 0.$$

In order to simultaneously consider the data changes for other DMUs, we suppose increased output and decreased input for all other DMUs. i.e., our discussion is based on a worst-case scenario in which efficiency of DMU_o declines and the efficiencies of all other DMU_j ($j \neq o$) improve.

Let **I** and **O** denote respectively the input and output subsets in which we are interested. i.e., we consider the data changes in set **I** and set **O**. Then the simultaneous data perturbations in input/output of all DMU_j ($j \neq o$) and DMU_o can be written as

Percentage data perturbation (variation)

For DMU_o

$$\begin{cases} \hat{x}_{io} = \delta_i x_{io} & \delta_i \geq 1, i \in \mathbf{I} \\ \hat{x}_{io} = x_{io} & i \notin \mathbf{I} \end{cases} \text{ and } \begin{cases} \hat{y}_{ro} = \tau_r y_{ro} & 0 < \tau_r \leq 1, r \in \mathbf{O} \\ \hat{y}_{ro} = y_{ro} & r \notin \mathbf{O} \end{cases}$$

For DMU_j $(j \neq o)$

$$\begin{cases} \hat{x}_{ij} = x_{ij} / \tilde{\delta}_i & \tilde{\delta}_i \geq 1, i \in \mathbf{I} \\ \hat{x}_{ij} = x_{ij} & i \notin \mathbf{I} \end{cases} \text{ and } \begin{cases} \hat{y}_{rj} = y_{rj} / \tilde{\tau}_r & 0 < \tilde{\tau}_r \leq 1, r \in \mathbf{O} \\ \hat{y}_{rj} = y_{rj} & r \notin \mathbf{O} \end{cases}$$

where ($\wedge$) represents adjusted data. Note that the data perturbations represented by δ_i and $\tilde{\delta}_i$ (or τ_r and $\tilde{\tau}_r$) can be different for each $i \in \mathbf{I}$ (or $r \in \mathbf{O}$).

Lemma 11.2 Suppose $DMU_o \in$ set F with non-zero input/output slack values associated with set $\mathbf{I}$/set $\mathbf{O}$. Then DMU_o with inputs of $\hat{x}_{io}$ and outputs of $\hat{y}_{ro}$ as defined above still belongs to set F when other DMUs are fixed.

[Proof]: Applying the complementary slackness theorem for models (11.10) and (11.11), we have $s_i^{-*} v_i^* = s_r^{+*} u_r^* = 0$. Since $s_i^{-*} \neq 0$ for $i \in \mathbf{I}$ and $s_r^{+*} \neq 0$ for $r \in \mathbf{O}$, we have $v_i^* = 0$ for $i \in \mathbf{I}$ and $u_r^* = 0$ for $r \in \mathbf{O}$. Therefore, v_i^* and u_r^* is a feasible solution to (11.11) for DMU_o with inputs of $\hat{x}_{io}$ and outputs of $\hat{y}_{ro}$. Note that $\sum_{r=1}^{s} u_r^* \hat{y}_{ro} = \sum_{r \in \mathbf{O}} u_r^* \hat{y}_{ro} = \sum_{r \in \mathbf{O}} u_r^* y_{ro} = 1$ indicating that the maximum value of 1 is achieved. Therefore, DMU_o still belongs to set F. ∎

11.4.1   Sensitivity Analysis Under CRS

We first modify models (11.12) and (11.13) to the following two super-efficiency DEA models that are based upon the measure-specific models

$$\theta_{\mathbf{I}}^{o*} = \min \theta_{\mathbf{I}}^{o}$$
subject to
$$\sum_{\substack{j=1 \\ j \neq o}}^{n} \lambda_j x_{ij} \leq \theta_{\mathbf{I}}^{o} x_{io} \qquad i \in \mathbf{I}$$

$$\sum_{\substack{j=1 \\ j \neq o}}^{n} \lambda_j x_{ij} \leq x_{io} \qquad i \notin \mathbf{I} \tag{11.14}$$

$$\sum_{\substack{j=1 \\ j \neq o}}^{n} \lambda_j y_{rj} \geq y_{ro} \qquad r = 1, 2, ..., s$$

$$\theta_{\mathbf{I}}^{o}, \lambda_j (j \neq o) \geq 0.$$

and

$$\phi_0^{o*} = \max \phi_0^o$$
subject to

$$\sum_{\substack{j=1 \\ j \neq o}}^{n} \lambda_j \, y_{rj} \geq \phi_0^o \, y_{ro} \qquad r \in \mathbf{O}$$

$$\sum_{\substack{j=1 \\ j \neq o}}^{n} \lambda_j \, y_{rj} \geq y_{ro} \qquad r \notin \mathbf{O} \qquad\qquad (11.15)$$

$$\sum_{\substack{j=1 \\ j \neq o}}^{n} \lambda_j \, x_{ij} \leq x_{io} \qquad i = 1,...,m$$

$$\phi_0^o, \ \lambda_j (j \neq o) \geq 0.$$

If $\mathbf{I} = \{k\}$, $k \in \{1, ..., m\}$ and $\mathbf{O} = \{l\}$, $l \in \{1, ..., s\}$, then optimal values of $\theta_{\mathbf{I}}^{o*} = (\theta_k^{o*})$ ($k = 1, ..., m$) and $\phi_{\mathbf{O}}^{o*} = (\phi_l^{o*})$ ($l = 1, ..., s$) are the optimal values to models (11.3) and (11.7), respectively.

Table 11.2. Sample DMUs

DMU	y	x_1	x_2	$\theta_o^{super*} = \theta_{\mathbf{I}=\{1,2\}}^{o*}$	$\theta_{\mathbf{I}=\{1\}}^{o*}$	$\theta_{\mathbf{I}=\{2\}}^{o*}$
A	1	2	5	15/13	5/4	7/5
B	1	3	3	26/21	14/9	17/12
C	1	6	2	3/2	infeasible	3/2
D	1	2	7	1	1	5/7

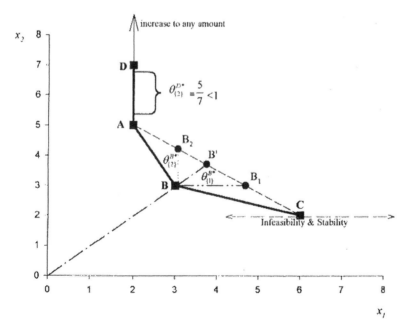

Figure 11.8. Super-efficiency and Sensitivity Analysis

Models (11.14) and (11.15) measure the maximum increase rate of inputs associated with **I** and the maximum decrease rate of outputs associated with **O**, respectively, required for DMU_o to reach the frontier of DMU_j ($j \neq o$) when other inputs and outputs are kept at their current levels. For example, consider B in Table 11.2 (Figure 11.8) and model (11.14). If $\mathbf{I} = \{1\}$, $\theta_{\{1\}}^{B*} = 14/9$ indicates that B reaches B_1 by changing its x_1 to $(14/9) \times 3 = 14/3$. If **I** $= \{2\}$, $\theta_{\{2\}}^{B*} = 17/12$ indicates that B reaches B_2 by changing its x_2 to $(17/12) \times 3 = 17/14$. If **I** $= \{1, 2\}$, $\theta_{\{1,2\}}^{B*} = \theta_B^{super*} = 26/21$ gives the input increase rate for B in order to reach B'.

Associated with the optimal values in models (11.12), (11.13), (11.14) and (11.15), we have

Lemma 11.3
(i) If $\theta_o^{super} = 1$, then $\theta_I^{o*} \leq 1$.
(ii) If $\phi_o^{super*} = 1$, then $\phi_O^{o*} \geq 1$.

[Proof]: The proof is obvious from the fact that $\theta_o^{super} = 1$ is a feasible solution to (11.4) and $\phi_o^{super*} = 1$ is a feasible solution to (11.5). ∎

Lemma 11.4
(i) If $\theta_o^{super} = 1$ and $\theta_I^{o*} < 1$, then $DMU_o \in$ F.
(ii) If $\phi_o^{super*} = 1$ and $\phi_O^{o*} > 1$, then $DMU_o \in$ F.

[Proof]: (i) $\theta_o^{super} = 1$ indicates that $DMU_o \in$ E'∪F. $\theta_I^{o*} < 1$ further indicates that there are non-zero slack values in x_{io} for $i \in \mathbf{I}$. Thus, $DMU_o \in$ F.
(ii) The proof is similar to that of (i). ∎

Theorem 11.10
(i) If $\theta_o^{super} = 1$ and $\theta_I^{o*} < 1$, then for any $\delta_i \geq 1$ and $\tilde{\delta}_i \geq 1$ ($i \in \mathbf{I}$), DMU_o remains in set F.
(ii) If $\phi_o^{super*} = 1$ and $\phi_O^{o*} > 1$, then for any $0 < \tau_r \leq 1$ and $0 < \tilde{\tau}_r \leq 1$ ($r \in \mathbf{O}$), DMU_o remains in set F.

[Proof]: (i) From Lemma 11.4, we know that $DMU_o \in$ F with non-zero slack values in x_{io} for $i \in \mathbf{I}$. Based upon Lemma 11.2 and the proof of Lemma 11.2, we know that for any $\delta_i \geq 1$ and $\tilde{\delta}_i \geq 1$, with an objective function value of 1, v_i^* and u_r^* is a feasible solution to (11.11) in which inputs are replaced by $\hat{x}_{ij}$ for $i \in \mathbf{I}$ and x_{ij} for $i \notin \mathbf{I}$. Thus, DMU_o remains in set F after input data changes set **I** in all DMUs.
(ii) The proof is similar to that of (i). ∎

In fact, Lemma 11.2 and Theorem 11.10 indicate that the classification of DMUs in set F is stable under any data perturbations in all DMUs occurred in inputs (outputs) which have non-zero slack values in DMU_o. For example, if $\mathbf{I} = \{2\}$, then model (11.14) yields $\theta_{\{2\}}^{D*} = 5/7 < 1$ for D indicating that D has non-zero slack value in its second input. From Figure 11.8, it is clear that D can increase its x_2 to any amount and still belongs to set F while other DMUs, A, B and C decrease their amount of x_2. This finding is very useful for the sensitivity analysis of the DMUs in set F.

Theorem 11.10 gives the sufficient condition for $DMU_o \in$ set F to preserve its efficiency classification. By Lemma 11.3, we immediately have

Corollary 11.2
(i) If for any $\delta_i \geq 1$ and $\widetilde{\delta}_i \geq 1$ ($i \in \mathbf{I}$), DMU_o remains in set F, then (a) $\theta_o^{\text{super}} = 1$ and $\theta_{\mathbf{I}}^{o*} < 1$, or (b) $\theta_o^{\text{super}} = 1$ and $\theta_{\mathbf{I}}^{o*} = 1$.
(ii) If for any $0 < \tau_r \leq 1$ and $0 < \widetilde{\tau}_r \leq 1$ ($r \in \mathbf{O}$), DMU_o remains in set F, then (a) $\phi_o^{\text{super}*} = 1$ and $\phi_{\mathbf{O}}^{o*} > 1$, or (b) $\phi_o^{\text{super}*} = 1$ and $\phi_{\mathbf{O}}^{o*} = 1$.

Corollary 11.2 implies that for $DMU_o \in$ set F, some inputs without slack values may also be increased while preserving the efficiency of DMU_o. For example, consider two DMUs: $DMU_1 = (y, x_1, x_2, x_3)$ and $DMU_2 = (y, x_1, x_2, \pi x_3)$, where $\pi > 1$, a constant. Obviously, $DMU_1 \in$ set E and $DMU_2 \in$ set F with non-zero slack value on the third input. Now, let $\mathbf{I} = \{2, 3\}$. We have that DMU_2 with $(y, x_1, \delta x_2, \delta \pi x_3)$ ($\delta > 1$) remains in set F while DMU_1 is changed to $(y, x_1, x_2/\widetilde{\delta}, x_3/\widetilde{\delta}) \in$ set E ($\widetilde{\delta} > 1$). In this situation, $\theta_{\{2,3\}}^{2*} = 1$ in (11.14).

From Lemma 11.3, we know that $\theta_{\mathbf{I}}^{o*}$ or $\phi_{\mathbf{O}}^{o*}$ may also be equal to one. Obviously, in this situation, $DMU_o \in$ set E' or set F and our approach indicates that no data variations are allowed in DMU_o and other DMUs. In fact, any data perturbation defined above will change the efficiency classification of DMUs in set E'. Note also that $\theta_{\{1\}}^{D*} = 1$ for D in Table 11.2. Thus, any data variation in the first input will let D become non-frontier point (see Figure 11.8).

Furthermore, from Lemma 11.3, we have

Corollary 11.3 Infeasibility of model (11.14) or model (11.15) can only be associated with extreme efficient DMUs in set E.

[Proof]: Lemma 11.3 implies that models (11.14) and (11.15) are always feasible for DMUs in set E' or set F. Also, models (11.14) and (11.15) are always feasible for non-frontier DMUs. Therefore, infeasibility of models (11.14) and (11.15) may only occur for extreme efficient DMUs in set E.∎

Seiford and Zhu (1998f) show that infeasibility of a super-efficiency DEA model means stability of the efficiency classification of DMU_o with respect to the changes of corresponding inputs and (or) outputs in all DMUs. We summarize Seiford and Zhu's (1998f) finding as the following theorem.

Theorem 11.11
(i) If a specific super-efficiency DEA model associated with set **I** is infeasible, *if and only if* for any $\delta_i \geq 1$ and $\tilde{\delta}_i \geq 1$ ($i \in$ **I**), DMU_o remains extreme efficient.
(ii) If a specific super-efficiency DEA model associated with set **O** is infeasible, *if and only if* for any $0 < \tau_r \leq 1$ and $0 < \tilde{\tau}_r \leq 1$ ($r \in$ **O**), DMU_o remains extreme efficient.

Theorem 11.11 indicates that, for example, if mode (11.14) is infeasible, then DMU_o will still be extreme efficient no matter how much its inputs associated with set **I** are increased while the corresponding inputs of other DMUs are decreased. Consider C in Table 11.2. If **I** = {1}, then model (11.14) is infeasible. (Note that model (11.12) is feasible for C.) From Figure 11.8, it is clear that C will remain extreme efficient if its first input is increased to any amount while DMUs A, C, and D decrease their amount of x_1.

In the discussion to follow, we assume that super-efficiency DEA models (11.14) and (11.15) are feasible. Otherwise, the efficiency classification of DMU_o is stable to data perturbations in all DMUs by Theorem 11.11.

Lemma 11.5
(i) If model (11.14) is feasible and $\theta_o^{super} > 1$ then $\theta_I^{o*} > 1$.
(ii) If model (11.15) is feasible and $\phi_o^{super*} < 1$ then $\phi_0^{o*} < 1$.

[Proof]: (i) Suppose $\theta_I^{o*} \leq 1$. Then the input constraints of (11.14) turn into

$$\begin{cases} \sum_{\substack{j=1 \\ j \neq o}}^{n} \lambda_j x_{ij} \leq \theta_I^{o*} x_{io} \leq x_{io} & i \in \mathbf{I} \\ \sum_{\substack{j=1 \\ j \neq o}}^{n} \lambda_j x_{ij} \leq x_{io} & i \notin \mathbf{I} \end{cases}$$

which indicates that $\theta_o^{super} = 1$ is a feasible solution to (11.12). Therefore, $\theta_o^{super*} \leq 1$. A contradiction. Thus, $\theta_I^{o*} > 1$.
(ii) The proof is similar to that of (i). ∎

Lemma 11.5 indicates that if $DMU_o \in$ set E and model (11.14) (or model (11.15)) is feasible, then θ_I^{o*} must be greater than one (or ϕ_0^{o*} must be less than one). We next study the efficiency stability of extreme efficient DMUs and we relax the assumption that same percentage change holds for data variation of DMU_o and DMU_j ($j \neq o$) and generalize the results in Seiford and Zhu (1998f).

Theorem 11.12 Suppose $\theta_o^{super*} > 1$ and $\phi_o^{super*} < 1$, then
(i) If $1 \leq \delta_i \tilde{\delta}_i < \theta_1^{o*}$ for $i \in \mathbf{I}$, then DMU_o remains extreme efficient. Furthermore, if equality holds for $\delta_i \tilde{\delta}_i = \theta_1^{o*}$, i.e., $1 \leq \delta_i \tilde{\delta}_i \leq \theta_1^{o*}$, then DMU_o remains on the frontier, where θ_1^{o*} is the optimal value to (11.14).
(ii) If $\phi_o^{o*} < \tau_r \tilde{\tau}_r \leq 1$ for $r \in \mathbf{O}$, then DMU_o remains extreme efficient. Furthermore, if equality holds for $\tau_r \tilde{\tau}_r = \phi_o^{o*}$, i.e., $\phi_o^{o*} \leq \tau_r \tilde{\tau}_r \leq 1$, then DMU_o remains on the frontier, where ϕ_o^{o*} is the optimal value to (11.15).

[Proof]: (i) Note that from Lemma 11.5, $\theta_1^{o*} > 1$. Now suppose $1 \leq \delta_i^o \tilde{\delta}_i^o < \theta_1^{o*}$, and DMU_o is not extreme efficient when $\hat{x}_{io} = \delta_i^o x_{io}$ and $\hat{x}_{ij} = x_{ij} / \tilde{\delta}_i^o$, $i \in \mathbf{I}$. Then, there exist λ_j ($j \neq o$) ≥ 0 and $\theta_o^{super*} \leq 1$ in (11.12) such that

$$\sum_{\substack{j=1 \\ j \neq o}}^{n} \lambda_j \frac{x_{ij}}{\tilde{\delta}_i^o} \leq \theta_o^{super*} \delta_i^o x_{io} \qquad i \in \mathbf{I}$$

$$\sum_{\substack{j=1 \\ j \neq o}}^{n} \lambda_j x_{ij} \leq \theta_o^{super*} x_{io} \leq x_{io} \qquad i \notin \mathbf{I}$$

$$\sum_{\substack{j=1 \\ j \neq o}}^{n} \lambda_j y_{rj} \geq y_{ro} \qquad r = 1, 2, \ldots, s.$$

This means that $\lambda_j (j \neq o) \geq 0$ and $\theta_o^{super*} \delta_i^o \tilde{\delta}_i^o$ is a feasible solution to (11.14). But $\theta_o^{super*} \delta_i^o \tilde{\delta}_i^o < \theta_o^{super*} \theta_1^{o*} \leq \theta_1^{o*}$ violating the optimality of θ_1^{o*}. Thus, if $1 \leq \delta_i^o \tilde{\delta}_i^o < \theta_1^{o*}$, then DMU_o remains extreme efficient.
Next, if $\delta_i^o \tilde{\delta}_i^o = \theta_1^{o*}$, then we assume DMU_o is not a frontier when $\hat{x}_{io} = \delta_i^o x_{io}$ and $\hat{x}_{ij} = x_{ij} / \tilde{\delta}_i^o$, $i \in \mathbf{I}$. Thus, we have $\theta_o^{super*} < 1$ in (11.12). Now we have $\theta_o^{super*} \delta_i^o \tilde{\delta}_i^o \leq \theta_o^{super*} \theta_1^{o*} < \theta_1^{o*}$ violating the optimality of θ_1^{o*}. Thus, if $1 \leq \delta_i^o \tilde{\delta}_i^o \leq \theta_1^{o*}$, then DMU_o remains on the frontier.
(ii) The proof is similar to (i), but is based upon (11.13) and (11.15). ∎

Theorem 11.12 indicates that the optimal value to a super-efficiency DEA model can actually be decomposed into a data perturbation component (e) for DMU_o and a data perturbation component ($\tilde{e}$) for the remaining DMUs, DMU_j ($j \neq o$). Define

$$\Omega^o = \begin{cases} \theta_1^{o*} & \text{if } e = \delta \text{ and } \tilde{e} = \tilde{\delta} \\ \phi_o^{o*} & \text{if } e = \tau \text{ and } \tilde{e} = \tilde{\tau} \end{cases}$$

Then, the data perturbation can be expressed in a quadratic function,

$$e \, \widetilde{e} \; = \; \Omega^{o} \qquad\qquad\qquad\qquad\qquad\qquad\qquad\qquad (11.16)$$

Function (11.16) gives an upper boundary for input changes and a lower boundary for output changes. Figures 11.9 and 11.10 illustrate the admissible regions for e and $\widetilde{e}$. For example, in Figure 11.9, since $\delta \geq 1$ and $\widetilde{\delta} \geq 1$, only part of the function $\delta \, \widetilde{\delta} \; = \; \theta_1^{o*}$ forms the upper boundary of a admissible region for δ and $\widetilde{\delta}$. Any data variations fall below MN and above lines $\delta = 1$ and $\widetilde{\delta} = 1$ will preserve the frontier status of DMU_o. The bigger the θ_1^{o*} (or the smaller the ϕ_0^{o*}), the larger the input (output) variation regions will be. In fact, the function given by (11.16) defines the maximum percentage change rates for DMU_o and DMU_j ($j \neq o$).

Theorem 11.12 gives sufficient conditions for preserving efficiency. The following theorem implies necessary conditions for preserving efficiency of an extreme efficient DMU_o.

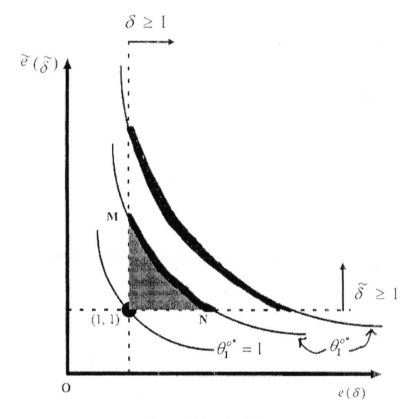

Figure 11.9. Input Variations

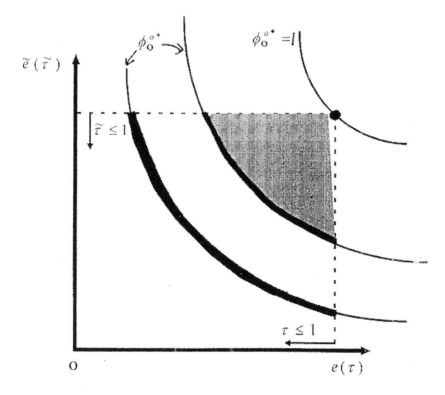

Figure 11.10. Output Variations

Theorem 11.13 Suppose $\theta_o^{super*} > 1$ and $\phi_o^{super*} < 1$, then
(i) If $\delta_i \, \tilde{\delta}_i > \theta_{\mathbf{I}}^{o*}$ for $i \in \mathbf{I}$, then DMU_o will not be extreme efficient, where $\theta_{\mathbf{I}}^{o*}$ is the optimal value to (11.14).
(ii) If $\tau_r \, \tilde{\tau}_r < \phi_{\mathbf{O}}^{o*}$ for $r \in \mathbf{O}$, then DMU_o will not be extreme efficient, where $\phi_{\mathbf{O}}^{o*}$ is the optimal value to (11.15).

[Proof]: (i) We assume that DMU_o remains extreme efficient after the data changes in all DMUs with $\delta_i \, \tilde{\delta}_i > \theta_{\mathbf{I}}^{o*}$. Consider the input constraints associated with set $\mathbf{I}$ in (11.14),

$$\sum_{\substack{j=1 \\ j \neq o}}^{n} \lambda_j \frac{x_{ij}}{\tilde{\delta}_i} \leq \hat{\theta}_{\mathbf{I}}^o \delta_i \, x_{io}, \ i \in \mathbf{I} \tag{11.17}$$

where $\hat{\theta}_{\mathbf{I}}^o$ is the objective function in (11.14).
    Equation (11.17) is equivalent to

$$\sum_{\substack{j=1 \\ j \neq o}}^{n} \lambda_j x_{ij} \leq \hat{\theta}_{\mathbf{I}}^o \delta_i \, \tilde{\delta}_i \, x_{io}, \ i \in \mathbf{I}$$

Let $\hat{\theta}_1^{o*}$ be the optimal value. Obviously, $\hat{\theta}_1^{o*} = \theta_1^{o*}/\delta_i\tilde{\delta}_i < 1$ where θ_1^{o*} is the optimal value to (11.14). On the basis of Lemma 11.5 (i), $\hat{\theta}_1^{o*}$ must be greater than one in (11.14) with input constraints of (11.17). A contradiction. (ii) The proof is similar to (i), but is based upon (11.17). ∎

Theorem 11.13 indicates that input (output) data perturbations in all DMUs beyond the variation regions prescribed by function (11.16) will change the efficiency classification of extreme efficient DMUs.

Note that $\delta_i \tilde{\delta}_i = \theta_1^{o*}$ (or $\tau_r \tilde{\tau}_r = \phi_0^{o*}$) may or may not keep the efficiency classification of an extreme efficient DMU_o. For example, in Figure 11.8, A remains extreme efficient if $\delta_2 \tilde{\delta}_2 = \theta_{\{2\}}^{A*} = 7/5$. (In this situation, A coincides D and both become extreme efficient.) However, if we consider C and if C's second input is increased to $\theta_{\{2\}}^{C*} x_{2C} = (3/2) \times 2 = 3$, then C becomes a member of set F along the ray BB_1 in Figure 11.8. (In this situation, we assume $\delta_2 = \theta_{\{2\}}^{C*} = 3/2$ for C and $\tilde{\delta}_2 = 1$ for the remaining DMUs of A, B and D.)

Turning to point A again. If we are only interested in whether a DMU remains on the frontier, rather than in its original efficiency classification, then we may still increase A's second input after A coincides D. We can find this "extra" data perturbation by applying a very small data perturbation to the changed DMU_o and then applying model (11.14) or (11.15). For example, we apply a data perturbation of ε to $\hat{x}_{2A}$ which is the new input value when $\delta_2 \tilde{\delta}_2 = \theta_{\{2\}}^{A*} = 7/5$. If we use models (11.12) and (11.14), then we know that this changed DMU A with it second input equal to $\hat{x}_{2A} + \varepsilon$ is now in set F, and therefore A can still increase it x_2 to any amount larger than 7 and remains on the frontier. Note that, in this case, A may no longer be extreme efficient. In fact, $\delta_2 \tilde{\delta}_2 = \theta_{\{2\}}^{A*} = 7/5$ prescribes a point on line segment AB including A and B. If $\delta_2 \tilde{\delta}_2 > 7/5$, then A and D switch their positions. Namely, A becomes a weakly efficient DMU and D becomes an extreme efficient DMU.

Above developments consider the input changes or output changes in all DMUs. Next we consider the following modified DEA model for simultaneous variations of inputs and outputs

$$\Gamma^* = \min \Gamma$$
subject to
$$\sum_{\substack{j=1 \\ j \neq o}}^{n} \lambda_j x_{ij} \leq (1 + \Gamma)x_{io} \qquad i \in \mathbf{I} \qquad\qquad (11.18)$$

$$\sum_{\substack{j=1 \\ j \neq o}}^{n} \lambda_j x_{ij} \leq x_{io} \qquad i \notin \mathbf{I}$$

$$\sum_{\substack{j=1 \\ j \neq o}}^{n} \lambda_j y_{rj} \geq (1 - \Gamma)y_{ro} \qquad r \in \mathbf{O}$$

$$\sum_{\substack{j=1 \\ j\neq o}}^{n} \lambda_j y_{rj} \geq y_{ro} \qquad r \notin \mathbf{O}$$

$$\lambda_j (j \neq o) \geq 0, \ \Gamma \ unrestricted$$

If $\mathbf{I} = \{1, 2, ..., m\}$ and $\mathbf{O} = \{1, 2, ..., s\}$, then (11.18) is identical to the model of Charnes, Rousseau and Semple (1996) when variations in the data are only applied to DMU_o. Note that if DMU_o is a frontier point, then $\Gamma \geq 0$.

Theorem 11.14 Suppose DMU_o is a frontier point. If $1 \leq \delta_i, \tilde{\delta}_i \leq \sqrt{1+\Gamma^*}$ and $\sqrt{1-\Gamma^*} \leq \tau_r, \tilde{\tau}_r \leq 1$, then DMU_o remains as a frontier point, where Γ^* is the optimal value to (11.18).

[Proof]: Equivalently we prove that if $\delta_i, \tilde{\delta}_i = \sqrt{1+\Gamma^*}$ and $\tau_r, \tilde{\tau}_r = \sqrt{1-\Gamma^*}$, then DMU_o still remains on the frontier. We assume that after the data changes, DMU_o is a nonfrontier point, and therefore can be enveloped by the adjusted DMU_o ($j \neq o$). Thus,

$$\sum_{\substack{j=1 \\ j\neq o}}^{n} \lambda_j \frac{x_{ij}}{\tilde{\delta}_i} \leq \delta_i x_{io} \qquad i \in \mathbf{I}$$

$$\sum_{\substack{j=1 \\ j\neq o}}^{n} \lambda_j x_{ij} \leq x_{io} \qquad i \notin \mathbf{I}$$

$$\sum_{\substack{j=1 \\ j\neq o}}^{n} \lambda_j \frac{y_{rj}}{\tilde{\tau}_r} \geq \tau_r y_{ro} \qquad r \in \mathbf{O}$$

$$\sum_{\substack{j=1 \\ j\neq o}}^{n} \lambda_j y_{rj} \geq y_{ro} \qquad r \notin \mathbf{O}$$

That is

$$\sum_{\substack{j=1 \\ j\neq o}}^{n} \lambda_j x_{ij} \leq (1+\Gamma^*) x_{io} \qquad i \in \mathbf{I}$$

$$\sum_{\substack{j=1 \\ j\neq o}}^{n} \lambda_j x_{ij} \leq x_{io} \qquad i \notin \mathbf{I}$$

$$\sum_{\substack{j=1 \\ j\neq o}}^{n} \lambda_j y_{rj} \geq (1-\Gamma^*) y_{ro} \qquad r \in \mathbf{O}$$

$$\sum_{\substack{j=1 \\ j\neq o}}^{n} \lambda_j y_{rj} \geq y_{ro} \qquad r \notin \mathbf{O}$$

This means that the adjusted DMU_o with $(1+\Gamma^*)x_{io}$ ($i \in \mathbf{I}$), x_{io} ($i \notin \mathbf{I}$), $(1-\Gamma^*)y_{ro}$ ($r \in \mathbf{O}$) and y_{ro} ($r \notin \mathbf{O}$) can be enveloped by the original $DMU_j (j \neq o)$. However, by Charnes, Rousseau and Semple (1996), we know that proportional changes to inputs and outputs respectively within the computed values of $(1+\Gamma^*)$ and $(1-\Gamma^*)$ cannot change the efficiency of DMU_o when the remaining DMU_j ($j \neq o$) are fixed. Therefore, this leads to a contradiction and completes the proof. ∎

The result in Theorem 11.14 generalizes the finding of Charnes, Rousseau and Semple (1996) to the situation where variations in the data are applied to all DMUs. Similar to Theorem 11.13, for an extreme efficient DMU_o, if $\delta_i \, \tilde{\delta}_i > \sqrt{1+\Gamma^*}$ and $\tau_r \, \tilde{\tau}_r < \sqrt{1-\Gamma^*}$, then DMU_o will not remain extreme efficient.

11.4.2   Sensitivity Analysis under VRS

It is obvious that the results in the previous section hold for the VRS frontier DMUs if we add the additional constraint of $\sum_{j\neq o} \lambda_j = 1$ into models (11.12), (11.13), (11.14) and (11.15), respectively.

Because of the translation invariance property resulted from the convex constraint of $\sum_{j\neq o} \lambda_j = 1$ in the VRS models, we are able to discuss the simultaneous absolute data changes in all DMUs. That is,

<u>Absolute Data Perturbations (Variations)</u>

For DMU_o

$$\begin{cases} \hat{x}_{io} = x_{io} + \alpha_i & \alpha_i \geq 0, i \in \mathbf{I} \\ \hat{x}_{io} = x_{io} & i \notin \mathbf{I} \end{cases} \text{ and } \begin{cases} \hat{y}_{ro} = y_{ro} - \beta_r & \beta_r \geq 0, r \in \mathbf{O} \\ \hat{y}_{ro} = y_{ro} & r \notin \mathbf{O} \end{cases}$$

For DMU_j ($j \neq o$)

$$\begin{cases} \hat{x}_{ij} = x_{ij} - \tilde{\alpha}_i & \tilde{\alpha}_i \geq 0, i \in \mathbf{I} \\ \hat{x}_{ij} = x_{ij} & i \notin \mathbf{I} \end{cases} \text{ and } \begin{cases} \hat{y}_{rj} = y_{rj} + \tilde{\beta}_r & \tilde{\beta}_r \geq 0, r \in \mathbf{O} \\ \hat{y}_{rj} = y_{rj} & r \notin \mathbf{O} \end{cases}$$

where (^) represents adjusted data. Note that the data changes defined above are not only applied to all DMUs, but also different in various inputs and outputs. In this case the sensitivity analysis results are also suitable to the slack-based models.

We modify model (11.18) to the following linear programming problem

$\gamma^* = \min \gamma$
subject to
$$\sum_{\substack{j=1 \\ j\neq o}}^{n} \lambda_j x_{ij} \leq x_{io} + \gamma \qquad i \in \mathbf{I}$$

$$\sum_{\substack{j=1 \\ j\neq o}}^{n} \lambda_j x_{ij} \leq x_{io} \qquad i \notin \mathbf{I} \qquad\qquad (11.19)$$

$$\sum_{\substack{j=1 \\ j \neq o}}^{n} \lambda_j y_{rj} \geq y_{ro} - \gamma \qquad r \in \mathbf{O}$$

$$\sum_{\substack{j=1 \\ j \neq o}}^{n} \lambda_j y_{rj} \geq y_{ro} \qquad r \notin \mathbf{O}$$

$$\sum_{\substack{j=1 \\ j \neq o}}^{n} \lambda_j = 1$$

$$\gamma, \lambda_j (j \neq o) \geq 0.$$

If $\mathbf{I} = \{1, 2, ..., m\}$ and $\mathbf{O} = \{1, 2, ..., s\}$, then model (11.19) is used by Charnes, Haag, Jaska and Semple (1992) to study the sensitivity of efficiency classifications in the additive model via L_{∞} norm when variations in the data are only applied to DMU_o.

Theorem 11.5 Suppose DMU_o is a frontier point. If $0 \leq \alpha_i + \tilde{\alpha}_i \leq \gamma^*$ ($i \in \mathbf{I}$), $0 \leq \beta_r + \tilde{\beta}_r \leq \gamma^*$ ($r \in \mathbf{O}$), then DMU_o remains as a frontier point, where γ^* is the optimal value to (11.19).

[Proof]: The proof is similar to that of Theorem 11.13 by noting that $\sum_{j \neq o} \lambda_j = 1$. ∎

If $\mathbf{O} = \varnothing$, then (11.19) only considers absolute changes in inputs. If $\mathbf{I} = \varnothing$, then (10) only considers absolute changes in output. For different choices of subsets $\mathbf{I}$ and $\mathbf{O}$, we can determine the sensitivity of DMU_o to the absolute changes of different sets of inputs or (and) outputs when DMU_o's efficiency is deteriorating and DMU_j's ($j \neq o$) efficiencies are improving.

We may change the objective function of (11.19) to "minimize $\sum_{i \in \mathbf{I}} \gamma_i^- + \sum_{r \in \mathbf{O}} \gamma_r^+$" and obtain the following super-efficiency DEA model

$$\min \sum_{i \in \mathbf{I}} \gamma_i^- + \sum_{r \in \mathbf{O}} \gamma_r^+$$

subject to

$$\sum_{\substack{j=1 \\ j \neq o}}^{n} \lambda_j x_{ij} \leq x_{io} + \gamma_i^- \qquad i \in \mathbf{I}$$

$$\sum_{\substack{j=1 \\ j \neq o}}^{n} \lambda_j x_{ij} \leq x_{io} \qquad i \notin \mathbf{I}$$

$$\sum_{\substack{j=1 \\ j \neq o}}^{n} \lambda_j y_{rj} \geq y_{ro} - \gamma_r^+ \qquad r \in \mathbf{O} \qquad\qquad (11.20)$$

$$\sum_{\substack{j=1 \\ j \neq o}}^{n} \lambda_j y_{rj} \geq y_{ro} \qquad r \notin \mathbf{O}$$

$$\sum_{\substack{j=1 \\ j \neq o}}^{n} \lambda_j = 1$$

$$\gamma_i^-, \gamma_r^+, \lambda_j (j \neq o) \geq 0$$

We then obtain a generalized model under L_1 norm. The results in Charnes, Haag, Jaska and Semple (1992) are generalized to the situation of data changes in all DMUs by the following Theorem.

Theorem 11.16 Suppose DMU_o is a frontier point. If $0 \leq \alpha_i + \tilde{\alpha}_i \leq \gamma_i^{-*}$ ($i \in \mathbf{I}$), $0 \leq \beta_r + \tilde{\beta}_r \leq \gamma_r^{+*}$ ($r \in \mathbf{O}$), then DMU_o remains as a frontier point, where γ_i^{-*} ($i \in \mathbf{I}$) and γ_r^{+*} ($r \in \mathbf{O}$) are optimal values in (11.20).

[Proof]: The proof is similar to that of Theorem 11.13 and is omitted. ∎

Similar to Theorem 11.13, for an extreme efficient DMU_o, if $\alpha_i + \tilde{\alpha}_i > \gamma_i^{-*}$ and $\beta_r + \tilde{\beta}_r > \gamma_r^{+*}$ then DMU_o will not remain extreme efficient.

11.4.3   Spreadsheet Models for Sensitivity Analysis

The current chapter presents a new approach for the sensitivity analysis of DEA models by using various super-efficiency DEA models. The sensitivity analysis approach simultaneously considers the data perturbations in all DMUs, namely, the change of the test DMU and the changes of the remaining DMUs. The data perturbations in the test DMU and the remaining DMUs can be different when all remaining DMUs work at improving their efficiencies against the deteriorating of the efficiency of the test efficient DMU. It is obvious that larger (smaller) optimal values to the input-oriented (output-oriented) super-efficiency DEA models presented in the current study correspond to greater stability of the test DMU in preserving efficiency when the inputs and outputs of all DMUs are changed simultaneously and unequally.

By using super-efficiency DEA models based upon the measure-specific models, the sensitivity analysis of DEA efficiency classification can be easily achieved. Since the approach uses optimal values to various super-efficiency DEA models, the results are stable and unique. By the additional constraint on $\sum_{j \neq o} \lambda_j$, the approach can easily be modified to study the sensitivity of other DEA models. Table 11.3 presents the measure-specific super-efficiency DEA models.

The stability measure is actually the optimal value to a specific measure-specific super-efficiency DEA model. Thus, the sensitivity analysis can be performed based upon the spreadsheets for related measure-specific models discussed in Chapter 2.

Figure 11.11 shows an input-oriented VRS measure-specific super-efficiency model where $\mathbf{I} = \{$Assets, ,Equity$\}$. i.e., we are interested in the sensitivity of VRS efficiency to the (proportional) data changes in Assets and Equity.

Table 11.3. Measure-specific Super-efficiency DEA Models

Frontier Type	Input-Oriented	Output-Oriented
	$\theta_I^{o*} = \min \theta_I^o$ subject to	$\phi_O^{o*} = \max \phi_O^o$ subject to
CRS	$\sum_{\substack{j=1 \\ j \neq o}}^{n} \lambda_j x_{ij} \leq \theta_I^o x_{io} \qquad i \in \mathbf{I}$ $\sum_{\substack{j=1 \\ j \neq o}}^{n} \lambda_j x_{ij} \leq x_{io} \qquad i \notin \mathbf{I}$ $\sum_{\substack{j=1 \\ j \neq o}}^{n} \lambda_j y_{rj} \geq y_{ro} \qquad r = 1,2,...,s$ $\theta_I^o, \lambda_j (j \neq o) \geq 0.$	$\sum_{\substack{j=1 \\ j \neq o}}^{n} \lambda_j y_{rj} \geq \phi_O^o y_{ro} \qquad r \in \mathbf{O}$ $\sum_{\substack{j=1 \\ j \neq o}}^{n} \lambda_j y_{rj} \geq y_{ro} \qquad r \notin \mathbf{O}$ $\sum_{\substack{j=1 \\ j \neq o}}^{n} \lambda_j x_{ij} \leq x_{io} \qquad i = 1,...,m$ $\phi_O^o, \lambda_j (j \neq o) \geq 0.$
VRS		Add $\sum_{j \neq o} \lambda_j = 1$
NIRS		Add $\sum_{j \neq o} \lambda_j \leq 1$
NDRS		Add $\sum_{j \neq o} \lambda_j \geq 1$

	A	B	C	D	E	F	G	H	I	J
1	Company	Assets	Equity	Employees		Revenue	Profit		λ	Stability
2	Mitsubishi	91920.6	10950	36000		184365.2	346.2		0	Infeasible
3	Mitsui	68770.9	5553.9	80000		181518.7	314.8		0	1.75189
4	Itochu	65708.9	4271.1	7182		169164.6	121.2		0	Infeasible
5	General Motors	217123.4	23345.5	709000		168828.6	6880.7		0	Infeasible
6	Sumitomo	50268.9	6681	6193		167530.7	210.5		0.71	Infeasible
7	Marubeni	71439.3	5239.1	6702		161057.4	156.6		0	Infeasible
8	Ford Motor	243283	24547	346990		137137	4139		0	0.70463
9	Toyota Motor	106004.2	49691.6	146855		111052	2662.4		0	0.76929
10	Exxon	91296	40436	82000		110009	6470		0	Infeasible
11	Royal Dutch/Shell Group	118011.6	58986.4	104000		109833.7	6904.6		0	Infeasible
12	Wal-Mart	37871	14762	675000		93627	2740		0.29	1.76516
13	Hitachi	91620.9	29907.2	331852		84167.1	1468.8		0	0.48484
14	Nippon Life Insurance	364762.5	2241.9	89690		83206.7	2426.6		0	Infeasible
15	Nippon Telegraph & Telephone	127077.3	42240.1	231400		81937.2	2209.1		0	Infeasible
16	AT&T	88884	17274	299300		79609	139		0	0.52449
17										
18		Reference		DMU under	15	Stability				
19	**Constraints**	set		Evaluation		0.524492				
20	Assets	46618.92	≤	46618.922						
21	Equity	9060.07	≤	9060.07						
22	Employees	203091.7	≤	299300		Input				
23	Revenue	145773.2	≥	79609						
24	Profit	955.1922	≥	139						
25	Σλ	1								
26	λo	0								

Figure 11.11. Input Sensitivity Analysis Spreadsheet Model

In Figure 11.11, cell F19 represents θ_I^o. The formulas for this spreadsheet are

Cell B20 =SUMPRODUCT(B2:B16,$I$2:$I$16)
Cell B21 =SUMPRODUCT(C2:C16,$I$2:$I$16)

Cell B22 =SUMPRODUCT(D2:D16,$I$2:$I$16)
Cell B23 =SUMPRODUCT(F2:F16,$I$2:$I$16)
Cell B24 =SUMPRODUCT(G2:G16,$I$2:$I$16)
Cell B25 =SUM(I2:I16)
Cell B26 =INDEX(I2:I16,E18,1)

Cell D20 =$F$19*INDEX(B2:B16,E18,1)
Cell D21 =$F$19*INDEX(C2:C16,E18,1)
Cell D22 =INDEX(D2:D16,E18,1)
Cell D23 =INDEX(F2:F16,E18,1)
Cell D24 =INDEX(G2:G16,E18,1)

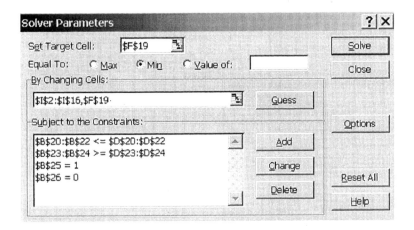

Figure 11.12. Solver Parameters for Input Sensitivity Analysis

Figure 11.12 shows the Solver parameters for the spreadsheet shown in Figure 11.11. If the optimal value in cell F19 is less than one, then this means that the associated company is VRS inefficient. The infeasibility in cells J2, J4:J7, J10:J11, and J14:J15 indicates that the corresponding companies remain VRS efficient to any simultaneous data changes in Assets and Equity across all DMUs. For DMU2 (Mitsui), we have the super-efficiency score of 1.75, indicating this DMU remains VRS efficient as long as the data variations satisfying $e\,\tilde{e} = 1.75$.

Next, we consider output changes. Figure 11.13 shows the spreadsheet for output-oriented VRS measure-specific super-efficiency model where $\mathbf{O}$ = {Revenue}. In this spreadsheet, range names are used. They are, cells B2:D16 – "InputUsed", cells F2:G16 – "OutputProduced", cells I2:I16 – "Lambdas", cells B20:B22 – "ReferenceSetInput", cells B23:B24 – "ReferenceeSetOutput", cell B25 – "SumLambdas", cell B26 – "DMUo", cells D20:D22 – "DMUInput", cells D23:D24 – "DMUOutput", cell E18 – "DMU", and cell F19 – "SuperEfficiency".

	A	B	C	D	E	F	G	H	I	J
1	Company	Assets	Equity	Employees		Revenue	Profit		λ	Stability
2	Mitsubishi	91920.6	10950	36000		184365.2	1		0.8	0.94407
3	Mitsui	68770.9	5553.9	80000		181518.7	314.8		0.19	0.93499
4	Itochu	65708.9	4271.1	7182		169164.6	121.2		0	Infeasible
5	General Motors	217123.4	23345.5	709000		168828.6	6880.7		0.01	Infeasible
6	Sumitomo	50268.9	6681	6193		167530.7	210.5		0	Infeasible
7	Marubeni	71439.3	5239.1	6702		161057.4	156.6		0	Infeasible
8	Ford Motor	243283	24547	346990		137137	4139		0	1.20986
9	Toyota Motor	106004.2	49691.6	146855		111052	2662.4		0	1.46561
10	Exxon	91296	40436	82000		110009	6470		0	Infeasible
11	Royal Dutch/Shell Group	118011.6	58986.4	104000		109833.7	6904.6		0	Infeasible
12	Wal-Mart	37871	14762	675000		93627	2740		0	Infeasible
13	Hitachi	91620.9	29907.2	331852		84167.1	1468.8		0	2.11056
14	Nippon Life Insurance	364762.5	2241.9	89690		83206.7	2426.6		0	Infeasible
15	Nippon Telegraph & Telephone	127077.3	42240.1	231400		81937.2	2209.1		0	2.16259
16	AT&T	88884	17274	299300		79609	139		0	2.30681
17										
18		Reference		DMU under	15	Stability				
19	**Constraints**	set		Evaluation		2.306807				
20	Assets	88884	≤	88884						
21	Equity	10052.63	≤	17274						
22	Employees	52057	≤	299300		Output				
23	Revenue	183642.6	≥	183642.58						
24	Profit	139	≥	139						
25	Σλ	1								
26	λo	0								

Figure 11.13. Output Sensitivity Analysis Spreadsheet Model

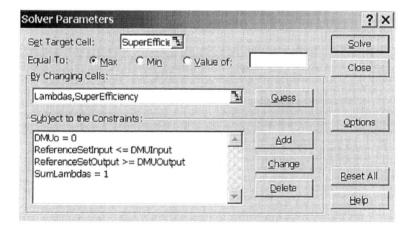

Figure 11.14. Solver Parameters for Output Sensitivity Analysis

Based upon these range names, we have the following formulas for the spreadsheet shown in Figure 11.13.

Cell B20 =SUMPRODUCT(INDEX(InputUsed,0,1),Lambdas)
Cell B21 =SUMPRODUCT(INDEX(InputUsed,0,2),Lambdas)
Cell B22 =SUMPRODUCT(INDEX(InputUsed,0,3),Lambdas)
Cell B23 =SUMPRODUCT(INDEX(OutputProduced,0,1),Lambdas)
Cell B24 =SUMPRODUCT(INDEX(OutputProduced, 0,2),Lambdas)
Cell B25 =SUM(Lambdas)
Cell B26 =INDEX(Lambdas,DMU,1)

Cell D20 =INDEX(InputUsed,DMU,1)
Cell D21 =INDEX(InputUsed,DMU,2)
Cell D22 =INDEX(InputUsed,DMU,3)
Cell D23 =SuperEfficiency*INDEX(OutputProduced,DMU,1)
Cell D24 =INDEX(OutputProduced,DMU,2)

Figure 11.14 shows the Solver parameters for the spreadsheet shown in Figure 11.13. The calculation is performed by the following VBA procedure that can be applied to other data sets once the proper range names are defined.

```
Sub SensitivityGeneral()
Dim NDMUs As Integer, NInputs As Integer, NOutputs As Integer
NDMUs = 15
NInputs = 3
NOutputs = 2
Dim i As Integer
For i = 1 To NDMUs
Range("DMU") = i
SolverSolve UserFinish:=True
If SolverSolve(UserFinish:=True) = 5 Then
Range("A1").Offset(i, NInputs + NOutputs + 4) = "Infeasible"
Else
Range("A1").Offset(i,NInputs+NOutputs+4)=Range("SuperEfficiency")
End If
Next i
End Sub
```

11.5   Identifying Critical Performance Measures

Since each DMU has its own inherent tradeoffs among the multiple measures that significantly influence the performance, it is extremely important for the management to know the critical measures. The current study takes a different and new perspective to identifying the critical measures to DMUs' performance. Note that once the DEA evaluation is done, the management needs to either (i) maintain the best practice for the efficient DMUs or (ii) achieve the best practice for the inefficient DMUs. Thus, when a set of multiple performance measures is determined, measures that are influential to maintaining and achieving the best practice should be regarded as critical to the performance of DMUs. Also, it is believed that a critical measure is signaled by whether changes in its value affect the performance, not by whether inclusion or exclusion of the measure affects the performance. Under the framework of DEA sensitivity analysis, we develop an alternative approach, which is independent of identifying DEA weights or DEA multipliers, to identify such critical measures.

Regression-based methods can be used in evaluating performance of a set of DMUs. However, they are limited to only one dependent variable. For example,

$$y = \beta_o + \sum_{i=1}^{m} \beta_i x_i + \varepsilon \tag{11.21}$$

where β_i are estimated coefficients which can be used to determine whether an independent variable has a positive effect on the dependent variable or makes an important contribution. i.e., by estimating the coefficients, we may identify the critical performance measures under the context of average behavior. Also, the estimated regression line can be served as the benchmark in performance evaluation.

In fact, formula (11.21) can be viewed as a performance frontier or tradeoff curve where x_i are inputs and y is the output. However, we are very likely to have multiple outputs y_r ($r = 1, ..., s$). We may rewrite (11.21) as (Wilkens and Zhu, 2001)

$$\sum_{r=1}^{s} u_r y_r = \alpha + \sum_{i=1}^{m} v_i x_i \tag{11.22}$$

where u_r and v_i are unknown weights representing the relative importance or tradeoffs among y_r and x_i.

Suppose we can estimate u_r and v_i, then for each DMU_j, we can define

$$h_j = \frac{\alpha + \sum_{i=1}^{m} v_i x_{ij}}{\sum_{r=1}^{s} u_r y_{rj}} \tag{11.23}$$

as a performance index, where x_{ij}, ($i = 1, 2, ..., m$) are multiple inputs, y_{rj}, ($r = 1, 2, ..., s$) are multiple outputs for DMU_j ($j = 1, 2, ..., n$).

In order to estimate u_r and v_i, and further evaluate the performance of j_oth DMU, (denoted as DMU_o) by (11.22), DEA uses the following linear fractional programming problem

$$\min_{\alpha, v_i, u_r} \frac{\alpha + \sum\limits_{i=1}^{m} v_i x_{io}}{\sum\limits_{r=1}^{s} u_r y_{ro}}$$

subject to   (11.24)

$$\frac{\alpha + \sum\limits_{i=1}^{m} v_i x_{ij}}{\sum\limits_{r=1}^{s} u_r y_{rj}} \geq 1, j = 1, \ldots, n$$

$$u_r, v_i \geq 0 \quad \forall \; r, i$$

where, x_{io} and y_{ro} are respectively the ith input and rth output for DMU_o under evaluation.

When $h_o^* = 1$, DMU_o is efficient or on the performance frontier. Otherwise, if $h_o^* > 1$, then DMU_o is inefficient. All the efficient DMUs constitute the performance frontier.

Note that when $h_o^* = 1$, we have

$$\sum_{r=1}^{s} u_r^* y_{ro} = \alpha^* + \sum_{i=1}^{m} v_i^* x_{io} \qquad (11.25)$$

where (*) represents the optimal values in model (11.24). That is, DEA estimates the "coefficients" in (11.22). It can be seen that while (1) estimates one set of coefficients, DEA model (11.24) estimates one set of coefficients for each DMU, resulting a piecewise linear tradeoff curve represented by several (11.25)-like equations associated with efficient DMUs. Equation (11.25) is theoretically available, but very difficult to obtain empirically.

Obviously, u_r^* and v_i^* represent the tradeoffs among various outputs and inputs. If we can obtain the exact information on u_r^* and v_i^*, the critical performance measures can be easily identified. However, the exact information on u_r^* and v_i^* cannot be obtained because of multiple optimal solutions in the multiplier models.

Suppose that we obtain the performance frontier. $v_k^* > v_i^*$ indicates that the kth input measure is more influential in order for DMU_o to achieve the best practice. i.e., the kth input is more important to DMU_o's performance which is characterized by the efficiency score (h_o^*). Note that the DEA model (11.24) always tries to assign larger v_i and u_r to smaller x_{io} and larger y_{ro} respectively in order to achieve the optimality. This indicates that when a set of multiple performance measures (inputs and outputs) is determined, the relative importance or tradeoffs is determined by the magnitudes of the inputs and outputs.

Consider the frontier represented by ABC in Figure 11.15 with two inputs and a single output. DMU A has the smallest value on the first input

(x_1) and DMU C has the smallest value on the second input (x_2). We have (i) $v_1 > v_2$ when DMU A is under evaluation by model (11.24), indicating that x_1 is the critical measure for DMU A and (ii) $v_2 > v_1$ when DMU C is under evaluation by model (11.24), indicating x_2 is the critical measure for DMU C.

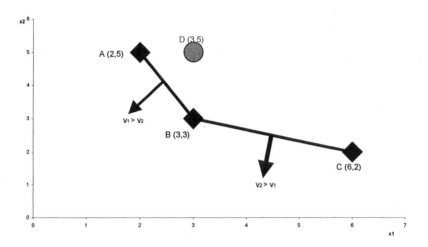

Figure 11.15. Critical Measures and Tradeoffs

It can also be seen from model (11.24) that for a specific DMU under evaluation, when a specific input increases, the associated input weight will not increase and when a specific output decreases, the associated output weight will not increase. Note that in Figure 11.15, $v_1 > v_2$ remains true for facet AB if DMU A's x_2 (uncritical one) changes its value, and $v_2 > v_1$ remains true for facet BC if DMU C's x_1 (uncritical one) changes its value. Meanwhile, DMUs A and C remain efficient when the uncritical inputs changes their value, respectively. (Note that for example, if the second input of DMU A decreases its current level to 3, the level used by DMU B, then we no longer have the efficient facet AB. Since DMU B becomes inefficient.) However, if we increase the x_1 of DMU A or x_2 of DMU C to a certain level, DMU A or DMU C becomes inefficient.

The above discussion shows that since a set of multiple performance measures is determined before the evaluation, a critical measure is signaled by whether changes in its value affect the performance, not by whether inclusion or exclusion of the measure affects the performance.

Definition 11.3 When a set of multiple performance measures is given, a specific measure is said to be critical if changes in its value are critical to the performance of a specific DMU.

For efficient DMUs, the performance is determined and characterized by the best practice status. For inefficient DMUs, the performance is determined and characterized by the distance to the frontier. Thus, a measure that is critical to the performance should be characterized by whether the measure is critical to (i) maintaining the best practice for efficient DMUs and (ii) achieving the best practice for inefficient DMUs.

11.5.1   Identifying Critical Output Measures

Consider the following super-efficiency model where the dth output is given the pre-emptive priority to change

$$\max \sigma_d$$
subject to
$$\sum_{\substack{j=1\\j\neq o}}^{n} \lambda_j y_{dj} \geq \sigma_d y_{do}$$
$$\sum_{\substack{j=1\\j\neq o}}^{n} \lambda_j y_{rj} \geq y_{ro} \qquad r \neq d \qquad\qquad (11.26)$$
$$\sum_{\substack{j=1\\j\neq o}}^{n} \lambda_j x_{ij} \leq x_{io} \qquad i = 1,...,m$$
$$\sum_{\substack{j=1\\j\neq o}}^{n} \lambda_j = 1$$

Four possible cases are associated with (11.26): (i) $\sigma_d^* > 1$, (ii) $\sigma_d^* = 1$, (iii) $\sigma_d^* < 1$ and (iv) model (11.26) is infeasible. When $\sigma_d^* > 1$, DMU_o has inefficiency in its dth output, since potential output increase can be achieved by DMU_o. Cases (ii), (iii) and (iv) indicate that no inefficiency exists in dth output.

Now, we consider the efficient DMUs and assume that DMU_o is efficient. Based upon model (11.26) the set of s outputs can be grouped into two subsets: set $O = \{d: \sigma_d^* \leq 1\}$ and set $\overline{O} = \{d:$ model (11.26) is infeasible for dth output$\}$.

Based upon Theorem 11.11, we have

Theorem 11.17 When model (11.26) is infeasible, the magnitude of the dth output across all DMUs has nothing to do with the efficiency status of DMU_o.

Theorem 11.17 indicates that the outputs in set $\overline{O}$ are not critical to the efficiency status of DMU_o, since changes in the outputs in set $\overline{O}$ do not change the efficiency classification of DMU_o. The efficiency classification of DMU_o is stable to any changes in the dth output across all DMUs when d belongs to set $\overline{O}$.

However, decreases in outputs in set O to certain magnitudes result in a change of efficiency status (performance) of DMU_o. For example, when the dth output of DMU_o is decreased from the current level y_{do} to a level which is less than $\sigma_d^* y_{do}$ ($\sigma_d^* < 1$), then DMU_o becomes inefficient. This in turn indicates that the outputs in set O are critical to the performance of DMU_o.

Now, let $P_{d^*} = \max\{\sigma_d^*\}$ for the outputs in set O. From the above discussion, we conclude that the d^*th output is the most critical output measure to the efficiency of DMU_o. Because, DMU_o's efficiency status is most sensitive to changes in the d^*th output.

Next, we consider inefficient DMUs and assume that DMU_o is inefficient. For inefficient DMUs, the issue is how to improve the inefficiency to achieve the best practice. Since the focus here is how each individual output measure contributes to the performance of DMU_o, we solve model (11.26) for each d and obtain $\sigma_d^* > 1$ ($d = 1, ..., d$), where σ_d^* measures how far DMU_o is from the frontier in terms of dth output.

As a matter of fact, model (11.26) provides an alternative way to characterize the inefficiency of DMU_o. Each σ_d^* indicates possible inefficiency existing in each associated output when other outputs and inputs are fixed at their current levels. We then can rank the inefficiency by each optimal σ_d^*. Let $G_{d^*} = \min\{\sigma_d^*\}$. That is, the d^*th output indicates the least inefficiency. If the DMU_o is to improve its performance through single output improvement, the d^*th output will yield the most effective way. Because G_{d^*} represents the shortest path onto the best practice frontier when each output is given the pre-emptive priority to improve. We therefore define that the d^*th output is the most critical output to reach the performance frontier and to DMU_o's performance.

In summary, the critical output is identified as the output associated with $\max\{\sigma_d^*\}$ for efficient DMUs and $\min\{\sigma_d^*\}$ for inefficient DMUs.

11.5.2 Identifying Critical Input Measures

Consider the following super-efficiency model when the kth input measure is of interest.

$$\min \tau_k$$

subject to

$$\sum_{\substack{j=1 \\ j \ne o}}^{n} \lambda_j x_{kj} \le \tau_k x_{ko}$$

$$\sum_{\substack{j=1 \\ j \ne o}}^{n} \lambda_j x_{ij} \le x_{io} \qquad i \ne k$$

$$\sum_{\substack{j=1 \\ j \ne o}}^{n} \lambda_j y_{rj} \ge y_{ro} \qquad r = 1,...,s \qquad\qquad (11.27)$$

$$\sum_{\substack{j=1 \\ j \ne o}}^{n} \lambda_j = 1$$

Based upon model (11.27), we have (i) $\tau_k^* < 1$, (ii) $\tau_k^* = 1$, (iii) $\tau_k^* > 1$, and (iv) (11.27) is infeasible. Case (i) indicates that inefficiency exists in DMU_o's kth input, since DMU_o needs to decrease its kth input to $\tau_k^* x_{ko}$ in order to reach the performance frontier. Cases (ii), (iii) and (iv) indicate that no inefficiency exists in DMU_o's kth input.

Now, suppose DMU_o is efficient. Based upon model (11.27), the set of m inputs can be grouped into two subsets: set $I = \{k: \tau_k^* \ge 1\}$ and set $\bar{I} = \{k:$ model (11.27) is infeasible for kth input$\}$. Similar to Theorem 11.17, we have

Theorem 11.18 When model (11.27) is infeasible, the magnitude of the kth input across all DMUs has nothing to do with the efficiency status of DMU_o.

Theorem 11.18 indicates that the inputs in set $\bar{I}$ are not critical to the efficiency status of DMU_o, since changes in the inputs in set $\bar{I}$ do not change the efficiency classification of DMU_o. Let $T_{k*} = \min\{\tau_k^*\}$ for inputs in set I. We conclude that the k^*th input is the most critical input measure to the efficiency of DMU_o. Because, DMU_o's efficiency status is most sensitive to changes in the k^*th input.

Next, suppose DMU_o is inefficient. We solve model (11.27) for each k and obtain $\tau_k^* < 1$ ($k = 1, ..., m$), where τ_k^* measures how far DMU_o is from the frontier in terms of kth input. Each τ_k^* indicates possible inefficiency existing in each associated input when other inputs and outputs are fixed at their current levels. We then can rank the inefficiency by each optimal τ_k^*. Let $H_{k*} = \max_{k} \{\tau_k^*\}$. Similar to the discussion on identifying the critical output measure, we say that the k^*th input is the most critical input to reach the performance frontier and to DMU_o's performance, since the k^*th input indicates the least inefficiency.

In summary, the critical input is identified as the input associated with $\min\{\tau_k^*\}$ for efficient DMUs and $\max\{\tau_k^*\}$ for inefficient DMUs.

Note that the above discussion is based upon the assumption that the DEA frontier exhibits VRS. The development can be applied to other DEA models with non-VRS frontiers (see Table 11.3).

To further illustrate the rationale of the current approach, consider again the four DMUs shown in Figure 11.8. Table 11.4 reports the optimal value to model (11.27). It can be seen that for DMU D, the first input is the critical measure since DMU D's efficiency can be easily improved if the first input is given the pre-emptive priority to change. For DMU A, the infeasibility associated with the second input indicates that the first input is the critical measure. Note that the efficient facet AB shows that the first input is more important than the second one, since $v_1 > v_2$. Our approach also indicates that the second input is the critical measure to DMU C's performance. This finding is confirmed by the fact that $v_2 > v_1$ in BC. As for DMU B, since it is located at the intersect of AB and BC, it is very difficult to determine which input is the critical factor by looking at the coefficients of efficient facets. Our approach indicates that the second input is the critical one for DMU B, since $\tau_2^* < \tau_1^*$ (17/12 < 14/9).

Table 11.4. Critical Measures for the Numerical Example

DMU	τ_1^*	τ_2^*
A	3/2	infeasible
B	14/9	17/12
C	infeasible	2
D	2/3	3/5

Finally, we should point out that the measure-specific super-efficiency DEA models in Table 11.3 can be used in either sensitivity analysis or critical measure identification. Zhu (2001b) provides an application.

[1] Part of the material in this section is adapted from European Journal of Operational Research, Vol 108, Seiford, L.M. and Zhu, J., Stability regions for Maintaining Efficiency in DEA, 127-139, 1998, with permission from Elsevier Science.

[2] Part of the material in this section is adapted from European Journal of Operational Research, Vol 129, Zhu, J., Super-efficiency and DEA Sensitivity Analysis, 443-455, 2001, with permission from Elsevier Science.

Chapter 12

DEA Excel Solver
Microsoft® Excel DEA Add-In

12.1 DEA Excel Solver

The CD-ROM that you find in the back of this book contains the DEA Excel Solver which is a DEA Add-In for Microsoft® Excel. This software "DEA Excel Solver.xla" requires Excel 97 or later versions. The DEA Excel Solver provides you with the ability to perform the DEA models presented in the Chapters 1-11 and additional DEA methods discussed in the current chapter.

To use the file "DEA Excel Solver.xla" in the CD-ROM using Windows, you may follow these steps:

Step 1. Insert the CD-ROM into your computer's CD-ROM drive.

Step 2. Launch Windows Explore.

Step 3. Click Browse to browse the CD and find the file *"DEA Excel Solver.xla"*. Copy this file to your hard drive.

DEA Excel Solver uses Excel Solver, and does not set any limit on the number of DMUs, inputs or outputs. However, please check www.solver.com for problem sizes that various versions of Solver can handle (see Table 12.1).

Before launching the DEA Excel Solver, the Excel Solver Parameters dialog box must at least be displayed once in your Excel session. Otherwise, an error may occur when you run the DEA Excel Solver. i.e., **you must invoke the Solver first, and then load the DEA Excel Solver by opening the file "DEA Excel Solver.xla"**

A new Menu item "DEA" will be added at the end of Excel Menu, as shown in Figure 12.1. Now, the software is ready to run after the data sheet for DMUs is properly set up.

Each DEA model reports the results in specific sheets. Rename these sheets if you want to keep the results. Otherwise, some result sheets will be over written. Also, do not use "Model", "Slack Model", and "Lambda Model" for your worksheets.

Table 12.1. Excel Solver Problem Size

	Standard Excel Solver	Premium Solver	Premium Solver Platform
Problem Size:			
Variables x Constraints	200 x 200	1000 x 8000	2000 x 8000

Source: www.solver.com

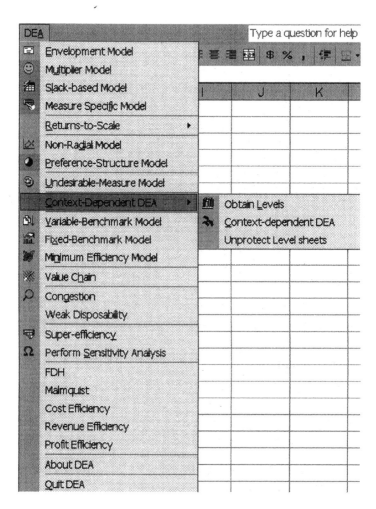

Figure 12.1. DEA Excel Solver Menu

12.2 Data Sheet Format

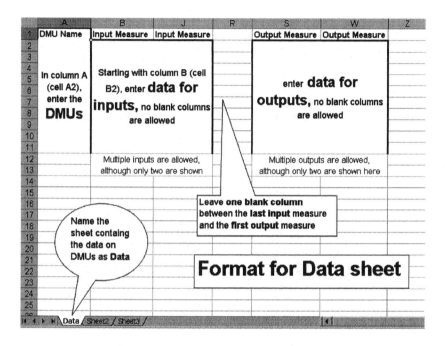

Figure 12.2. Data Sheet Format

	A	B	C	D	E	F	G
1	Company	Assets	Equity	Employees		Revenue	Profit
2	Mitsubishi	91920.6	10950	36000		184365.2	346.2
3	Mitsui	68770.9	5553.9	80000		181518.7	314.8
4	Itochu	65708.9	4271.1	7182		169164.6	121.2
5	General Motors	217123.4	23345.5	709000		168828.6	6880.7
6	Sumitomo	50268.9	6681	6193		167530.7	210.5
7	Marubeni	71439.3	5239.1	6702		161057.4	156.6
8	Ford Motor	243283	24547	346990		137137	4139
9	Totota Motor	106004.2	49691.6	146855		111052	2662.4
10	Exxon	91296	40436	82000		110009	6470
11	Royal Dutch/Shell Group	118011.6	58986.4	104000		109833.7	6904.6
12	Wal-Mart	37871	14762	675000		93627	2740
13	Hitachi	91620.9	29907.2	331852		84167.1	1468.8
14	Nippon Life Insurance	364762.5	2241.9	89690		83206.7	2426.6
15	Nippon Telegraph & Telephone	127077.3	42240.1	231400		81937.2	2209.1
16	AT&T	88884	17274	299300		79609	139

DMUs   Inputs   Outputs

Figure 12.3. Example Data Sheet

In most of the cases, the data sheet containing the data for DMUs under evaluations must be named as "Data". Other names for the data sheet will be used for the Variable-benchmark models, Fixed-benchmark models, Minimum Efficiency models, Malmquist index model, Cost Efficiency, Revenue Efficiency and Profit Efficiency. However, all the data sheets have the same format as shown in Figure 12.2 and Figure 12.3.

Leave one blank column between the input and output data. No blank columns and rows are allowed within the input and output data.

Negative or non-numerical data are deemed as invalid data. The software checks if the data are in valid form before the calculation. If the data sheet contains negative or non-numerical data, the software will quit and locate the invalid data (see Figure 12.4).

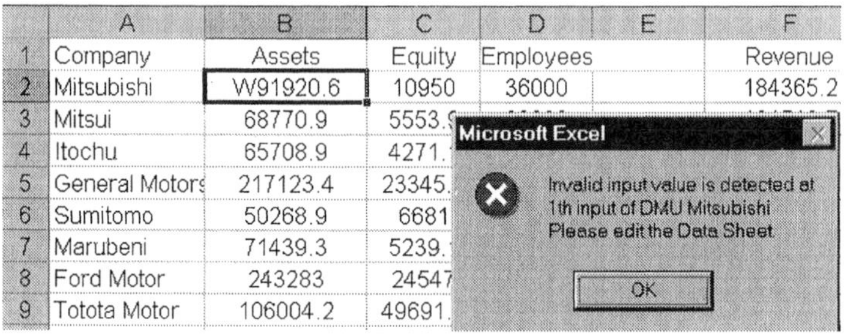

Figure 12.4. Invalid Data

12.3   Envelopment Models

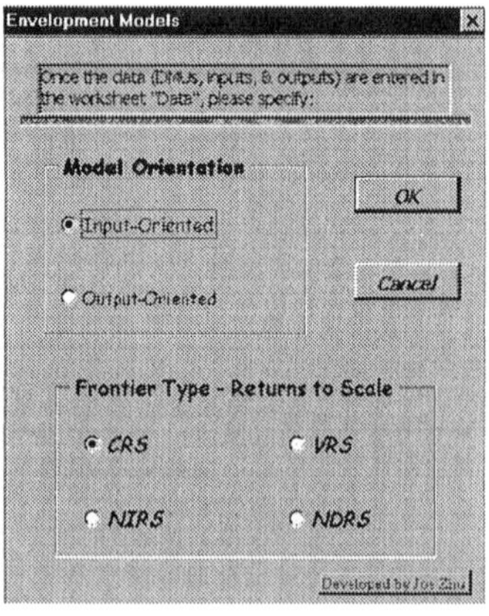

Figure 12.5. Envelopment Models

To run the envelopment models, select the "Envelopment Model" menu item. You will be prompted with a form for selecting the models presented in Table 1.2, as shown in Figure 12.4.

The software performs a two-stage DEA calculation. First, the efficiency scores are calculated, and the efficiency scores and benchmarks (λ_j^*) are reported in the "Efficiency" sheet. At the same time, a "Slack" sheet and a "Target" sheet are generated based upon the efficiency scores and the λ_j^*.

Then you will be asked whether you want to perform the second-stage calculation, i.e., fixing the efficiency scores and calculating the DEA slacks (see Figure 12.6). If Yes, then the slack and target sheets will be replaced by new ones which report the DEA slacks and the efficient targets defined in Table 1.2.

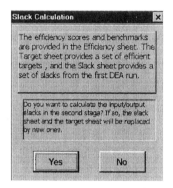

Figure 12.6. Second Stage DEA Slack Calculation

12.4 Multiplier Models

To run the multiplier models, select the "Multiplier Model" menu item. You will be prompted with a form for selecting the models presented in Table 1.4. The form is similar to the one shown in Figure 12.5. The results are reported in a sheet named "Efficiency Report".

12.5 Slack-based Models

To run the slack-based models, select the "Slack-based Model" menu item. You will be prompted with a form for selecting the models presented in Table 1.5, as shown in Figure 12.7.

If you select "Yes" under the "Weights on Slacks", you will be asked to provide the weights, as shown in Figure 12.8. If you select "No", then all the weights are set equal to one.

The results are reported in a sheet named "Slack Report" along with a sheet named "Efficient Target".

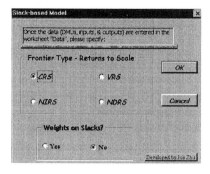

Figure 12.7. Slack-based Models

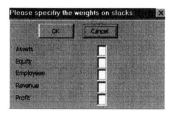

Figure 12.8. Weights on Slacks

12.6   Measure-specific Models

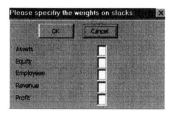

Figure 12.9. Measure-specific Models

To run the measure-specific models, select the "Measure Specific Model" menu item. You will be prompted with a form for selecting the models presented in Table 2.1, as shown in Figure 12.9.

Select the measures that are of interest. If you select all the input or all the output measures, then you have the envelopment models.

The results are reported in the "Efficiency", "Slack" and "Target" sheets.

12.7 Returns-to-Scale

The Returns-to-Scale menu item contains two submenu items (a) RTS Estimation and (b) Perform RTS Sensitivity, as shown in Figure 12.10.

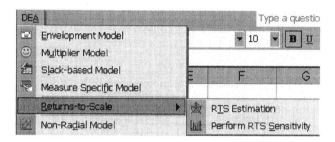

Figure 12.10. Returns-to-Scale Menu

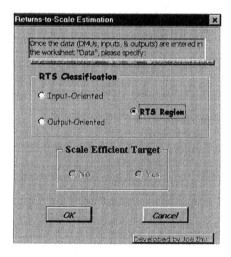

Figure 12.11. RTS Estimation

The RTS Estimation menu will provide (i) the RTS classifications, (ii) RTS regions as shown in Figure 3.2 and (iii) scale efficient targets using models (3.1) and (3.3) (see Figure 12.11).

If RTS Region is selected, then the function of Scale Efficient Target will be disabled (see Figure 12.11). The software will run both the input-oriented and output-oriented envelopment models. The results are reported in the "RTS Region" sheet.

If Input-Oriented is selected, then the software will generate the RTS classification based upon the input-oriented envelopment models and report the results in the sheet "RTS Report". If Output-Oriented is selected, then the software will generate the RTS classification based upon the output-oriented envelopment models. The "RTS Report" is protected for use in the RTS sensitivity analysis.

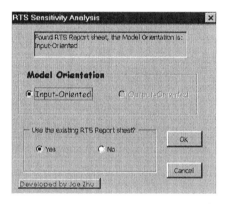

Figure 12.12. RTS Sensitivity Analysis with RTS Report Sheet

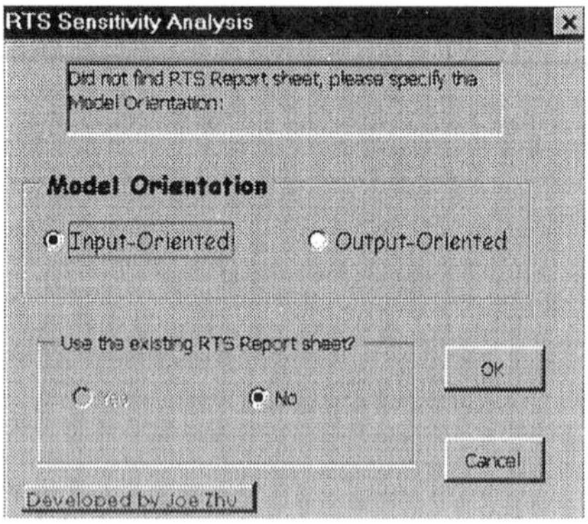

Figure 12.13. kTS Sensitivity Analysis without RTS Report Sheet

The Scale Efficient Target function will generate the smallest and largest MPSS targets in "Smallest MPSS" and "Largest MPSS" sheets, respectively.

The Perform RTS Sensitivity menu will first check the existence of the "RTS Report" sheet. If the "RTS Report" sheet is found, then the software will show the model orientation and ask if you want to perform the RTS sensitivity analysis based upon the found "RTS Report" sheet (see Figure 12.12). The results are reported in the "RTS Sensitivity" sheet.

If there does not exist the "RTS Report" sheet, the software will ask you to specify the model orientation (see Figure 12.13). The software will generate the "RTS Report" sheet first, and then generate the "RTS Sensitivity" sheet. The same procedure will be followed if you select "No" in Figure 12.12, i.e., you want to study the RTS sensitivity under a different model orientation.

12.8   Non-radial Models

To run the non-radial models, select the "Non-radial Model" menu item. You will be prompted with a form similar to the one shown in Figure 12.5 for selecting the models presented in Table 4.1. The Results are reported in "Efficiency", "Slack", and "Target" sheets.

12.9   Preference Structure Models

To run the preference structure models, select the "Preference Structure Model" menu item. Figure 12.14 shows the form for specifying the models.

If "Yes" is selected under "Restrict Input/Output Change?", then we have weighted non-radial models (see page 93). If "No" is selected, then we have the DEA/PS models presented in Table 4.2 in Chapter 4. The software will then ask you to specify the weights for the inputs or outputs, depending on the model orientation. The Results are reported in "Efficiency", "Slack", and "Target" sheets.

12.10   Undesirable Measure Models

To run the models for treating undesirable measures discussed in Chapter 5, select the Undesirable-Measure Model menu item. Figure 12.15 shows the form for specifying the models. The results are reported in "Efficiency", "Slack", and "Target" sheets.

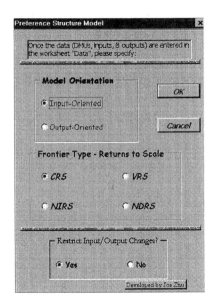

Figure 12.14. Preference Structure Models

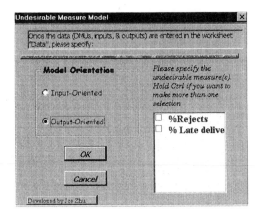

Figure 12.15. Undesirable Measure Models

12.11   Context-dependent DEA

The context-dependent DEA consists of three functions: (i) Obtain levels, (ii) Calculate context-depend DEA models, and (iii) Unprotect the sheets containing the levels (see Figure 16.16).

Figure 16.16. Context-dependent DEA Menu

The first function is the stratification model (6.1). It generates all the efficient frontiers – levels (Figure 12.17). This function will first delete any sheet with a name starting with "Level" and then generate a set of new sheets named as "Level*i*(*Frontier*)" where *i* indicates the level and *Frontier* represents the frontier type. For example, Level1(CRS) means the first level CRS frontier. The "level" sheets are protected for use in the context-dependent DEA. However, they can be unprotected by using the "Unprotect the sheets" menu item. *The format of these level sheets must not be modified. Otherwise, the context-dependent DEA will not run properly and accurately.*

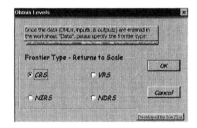

Figure 12.17. Obtain Levels

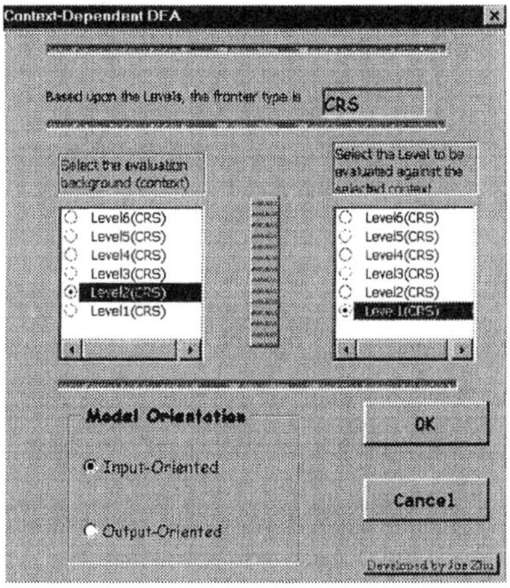

Figure 12.18. Context-dependent DEA

Once the efficient frontiers are obtained, the context-dependent DEA can be calculated using the "Context-dependent DEA" submenu item (Figure 12.18).

The results are reported in the "Context Dependent Result" sheet. In this sheet, the context-dependent scores are the optimal values to model (6.2) (or model (6.7), model (6.10), model (6.11)). To obtain the attractiveness or progress scores, one has to adjust the context-dependent scores based upon Definitions 6.1, 6.2, 6.4, and 6.5.

12.12   Variable-benchmark Models

To run the variable-benchmark models presented in Table 7.1, we need set up the data sheets. *Store the benchmarks in a sheet named "Benchmarks" and the DMUs under evaluation in a sheet named "DMUs".* The format for these two sheets is the same as that shown in Figure 12.3. Then select the Variable Benchmark Model menu item. You will be prompted a form for selecting the model orientation and the frontier type as shown in Figure 12.19. Note that if you select a frontier type other than CRS, the results may be infeasible. The benchmarking results are reported in the sheet "Benchmarking Results".

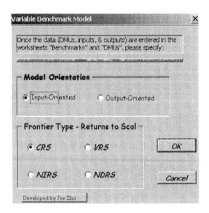

Figure 12.19. Variable Benchmark Models

12.13   Fixed-benchmark Models

To run the fixed-benchmark models presented in Table 7.3, we *store the benchmarks in a sheet named "Benchmarks" and the DMUs under evaluation in a sheet named "DMUs".* Then select the Fixed-Benchmark Model menu item. You will be prompted a form for selecting the model orientation and the frontier type. The results are reported in the "Efficiency Report" sheet. If the benchmarks are not properly selected, you will have infeasible results and need to adjust the benchmarks.

The Ideal-benchmark Models in Table 7.4 should be calculated using the Fixed-Benchmark Model menu item. The data for the ideal benchmark is stored in the "Benchmarks" sheet.

12.14 Minimum Efficiency Models

To run the minimum efficiency models presented in Table 7.5, we *store the benchmarks in a sheet named "Benchmarks" and the DMUs under evaluation in a sheet named "DMUs"*. Then select the Minimum Efficiency Model menu item. You will be prompted a form for selecting the model orientation and the frontier type. The results are reported in the "Minimum Efficiency" sheet.

The Ideal-benchmark Minimum Efficiency Models in Table 7.6 should be calculated using the Minimum Efficiency menu item. The data for the ideal benchmark is stored in the "Benchmarks" sheet.

12.15 Value Chain Efficiency

Since intermediate measures are present, the DMUs in the data sheet are set in a format shown in Figure 12.20. The inputs are entered first and followed by a blank column, and then the intermediate measures are entered followed by a blank column and the outputs.

Select the "Value Chain Efficiency" menu item to calculate the model (8.1) in Chapter 8. The results are reported in the "Efficiency1" (for stage 1), "Efficiency2" (for stage 2) and "Intermediate" (for optimal intermediate measures) sheets.

	A	B	C	D	E	F	G	H	I	J	K
1	Bank	Tran IT	Strategic IT	Labor		Accounts	Transactions		Revenue	Equity	
2	1	68374883	27207295.82	96644431		28430.63	109486141		4.56E+09	5.07E+08	
3	2	43674296	20728716.45	82211383		4020.105	149772606		8.2E+08	1.7E+09	
4	3	36240480	22876333.28	41677506		1417653	42281949		7.05E+08	7.41E+08	
5	4	10974089	3604030.058	23386094		4801.735	41624391		2.52E+08	2.51E+08	
6	5	8165838	4598047.449	11074813		5777.526	14023708		1.37E+08	1.21E+08	
7	6	5826344	1383431.384	10723845		9335	1982414		1.61E+08	2.19E+08	
8	7	3039890	2701361.5	17225000		16539.81	46748993		3.54E+08	4.51E+08	
9	8	2631636	891139.9067	7585518		4245.225	10054751		50543312	81451129	
10	9	2445874	531648.2537	7537537		1668.805	8294216		59544335	55444711	
11	10	1481997	459703.0989	370169		3801	433717		28100210	23699857	
12	11	1471033	1070595.245	6378768		2230.61	5915536		70210212	85192518	
13	12	1321121	863879.5153	3718510		16935.8	7093301		37509806	37123155	
14	13	1287557	687890.0796	5609930		3121.808	6223975		41187111	36704000	
15	14	1164952	762892.2893	3449934		3822.564	4476600		28526966	25739404	
16	15	1121468	391687.7105	3185637		4939.844	8530050		41220844	43087174	

Figure 12.20. Data Sheet For Value Chain

12.16   Congestion

To calculate the congestion slacks, select the "Congestion" menu item. The Congestion will use the Slack and Target sheets. If there exist a slack sheet and a target sheet that are generated by the same envelopment model, you will be prompted a form shown in Figure 12.21.

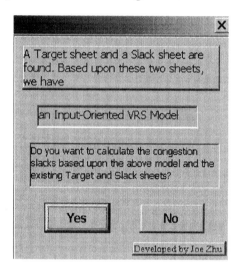

Figure 12.21. Congestion

If you choose Yes, then the software will calculate the congestion slacks based upon the information stored in the "Slack", "Target" and "Data" sheets.

If you choose No, then the software will ask you to select an envelopment model. Then, the software will calculate the specified envelopment model, generate the "Slack" and "Target" sheets, and report the congestion slacks in "Congestion Slacks" sheet. The same procedure will be applied if there do not exist the "Slack" sheet and the "Target" sheet, or the "Slack" and "Target" sheets are generated by different envelopment models.

12.17   Weak Disposability Models

To run the weak disposability models presented in Table 9.1, select the "Weak Disposability" menu item. The results are reported in the "Efficiency" sheet.

12.18 Super Efficiency Models

To run the super-efficiency models presented in Table 10.1, select the "Super-efficiency" menu item. You will be prompted a form similar to the one shown in Figure 12.5 for specifying the super-efficiency models. The results are reported in the "Super-efficiency" sheet.

12.19 Sensitivity Analysis

To perform the sensitivity analysis, select the "Perform Sensitivity Analysis" menu item. You will be prompted a form similar to the one shown in Figure 12.9. (You will select a model from Table 11.3.) The measures that are selected will be studied for sensitivity analysis. The results are reported in the "Sensitivity Report" sheet which records the optimal values to the related measure-specific super-efficiency model.

Based upon the discussion in Chapter 11, we can convert these super-efficiency scores into measures for efficiency stability.

12.20 Free Disposal Hull (FDH) Models

The free disposal hull (FDH) models are first formulated by Deprins, Simar and Tulkens (1984). The input-oriented FDH model can be written as

$$\min \theta^{FDH}$$
$$\text{subject to}$$
$$\sum_{j=1}^{n} \lambda_j x_{ij} \leq \theta^{FDH} x_{io} \qquad i = 1,2,...,m;$$
$$\sum_{j=1}^{n} \lambda_j y_{rj} \geq y_{ro} \qquad r = 1,2,...,s;$$
$$\sum_{j=1}^{n} \lambda_j = 1 \qquad \lambda_j \text{ binary}$$

The output oriented FDH model can be written as

$$\max \phi^{FDH}$$
$$\text{subject to}$$
$$\sum_{j=1}^{n} \lambda_j x_{ij} \leq x_{io} \qquad i = 1,2,...,m;$$
$$\sum_{j=1}^{n} \lambda_j y_{rj} \geq \phi^{FDH} y_{ro} \qquad r = 1,2,...,s;$$
$$\sum_{j=1}^{n} \lambda_j = 1 \qquad \lambda_j \text{ binary}$$

To run the above two FDH models, select the FDH menu item. You will be asked to select the model orientation (see Figure 12.22). The results are reported in the "FDH" sheet.

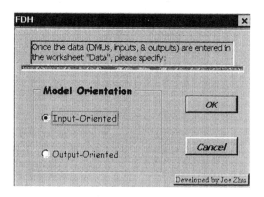

Figure 12.22. FDH Models

12.21   Malmquist Index

Malmquist (1953) first suggests comparing the input of a firm at two different points in time in terms of the maximum factor by which the input in one period could be decreased such that the firm could still produce the same output level of the other time period. This idea lead to the Malmquist input index. Caves, Christensen and Diewert (1982) extend the Malmquist input index to define a Malmquist productivity index. Färe, Grosskopf and Lovell 1994) develop DEA-based Malmquist productivity measures.

Suppose each DMU_j ($j = 1, 2, ..., n$) produces a vector of outputs $y_j^t = (y_{1j}^t, ..., y_{sj}^t)$ by using a vector of inputs $x_j^t = (x_{1j}^t, ..., x_{mj}^t)$ at each time period t, $t = 1, ..., T$. From t to $t+1$, DMU_o's efficiency may change or (and) the frontier may shift. Malmquist productivity index is calculated via

(i) Comparing x_o^t to the frontier at time t, i.e., calculating $\theta_o^t(x_o^t, y_o^t)$ in the following input-oriented CRS envelopment model

$$\theta_o^t(x_o^t, y_o^t) = \min \theta_o$$
subject to
$$\sum_{j=1}^{n} \lambda_j x_j^t \leq \theta_o x_o^t \qquad\qquad (12.1)$$
$$\sum_{j=1}^{n} \lambda_j y_j^t \geq y_o^t$$
$$\lambda_j \geq 0, j = 1, ..., n$$

where $x_o^t = (x_{1o}^t, ..., x_{mo}^t)$ and $y_o^t = (y_{1o}^t, ..., y_{so}^t)$ are the input and output vectors of DMU_o among others.

(ii) Comparing x_o^{t+1} to the frontier at time t+1, i.e., calculating $\theta_o^{t+1}(x_o^{t+1}, y_o^{t+1})$

$$\theta_o^{t+1}(x_o^{t+1}, y_o^{t+1}) = \min \theta_o$$
subject to
$$\sum_{j=1}^{n} \lambda_j x_j^{t+1} \leq \theta_o x_o^{t+1} \qquad (12.2)$$
$$\sum_{j=1}^{n} \lambda_j y_j^{t+1} \geq y_o^{t+1}$$
$$\lambda_j \geq 0, j = 1,...,n$$

(iii) Comparing x_o^t to the frontier at time t+1, i.e., calculating $\theta_o^{t+1}(x_o^t, y_o^t)$ via the following linear program

$$\theta_o^{t+1}(x_o^t, y_o^t) = \min \theta_o$$
subject to
$$\sum_{j=1}^{n} \lambda_j x_j^{t+1} \leq \theta_o x_o^t \qquad (12.3)$$
$$\sum_{j=1}^{n} \lambda_j y_j^{t+1} \geq y_o^t$$
$$\lambda_j \geq 0, j = 1,...,n$$

(iv) Comparing x_o^{t+1} to the frontier at time t, i.e., calculating $\theta_o^t(x_o^{t+1}, y_o^{t+1})$ via the following linear program

$$\theta_o^t(x_o^{t+1}, y_o^{t+1}) = \min \theta_o$$
subject to
$$\sum_{j=1}^{n} \lambda_j x_j^t \leq \theta_o x_o^{t+1} \qquad (12.4)$$
$$\sum_{j=1}^{n} \lambda_j y_j^t \geq y_o^{t+1}$$
$$\lambda_j \geq 0, j = 1,...,n$$

The Malmquist productivity index is defined as:

$$M_o = \left[\frac{\theta_o^t(x_o^t, y_o^t)}{\theta_o^t(x_o^{t+1}, y_o^{t+1})} \frac{\theta_o^{t+1}(x_o^t, y_o^t)}{\theta_o^{t+1}(x_o^{t+1}, y_o^{t+1})} \right]^{\frac{1}{2}}$$

M_o measures the productivity change between periods t and $t+1$. Productivity declines if $M_o > 1$, remains unchanged if $M_o = 1$ and improves if $M_o < 1$.

The following modification of M_o makes it possible to measure the change of technical efficiency and the movement of the frontier in terms of a specific DMU_o.

$$M_o = \frac{\theta_o^t(x_o^t, y_o^t)}{\theta_o^{t+1}(x_o^{t+1}, y_o^{t+1})} \cdot \left[\frac{\theta_o^{t+1}(x_o^{t+1}, y_o^{t+1})}{\theta_o^t(x_o^{t+1}, y_o^{t+1})} \frac{\theta_o^{t+1}(x_o^t, y_o^t)}{\theta_o^t(x_o^t, y_o^t)} \right]^{\frac{1}{2}}$$

The first term on the right hand side measures the magnitude of technical efficiency change between periods t and $t+1$. Obviously, $\dfrac{\theta_o^t(x_o^t, y_o^t)}{\theta_o^{t+1}(x_o^{t+1}, y_o^{t+1})} \underset{>}{\overset{<}{=}} 1$ indicating that technical efficiency improves, remains or declines. The second term measures the shift in the EPF between periods t and t+1.

Similarly, we can develop the Malmquist index based upon the output-oriented DEA models.

To calculate the Malmquist, we can use the envelopment models and the variable benchmarking models. (This allows us to calculate the Malmquist index under non-CRS conditions with an additional constraint on $\sum_{j=1}^{n} \lambda_j$ ($=1, \leq 1, $,or ≥ 1) even if models (12.3) and (12.4) may be infeasible.

The DEA Excel Solver provides a menu item that calculate the Malmquist index based upon models (12.1)-(12.4).

The data for DMUs in each period should be placed in a sheet with a name starting with "Period". For example, "Period1", Period-1", or "Period A". The software will first look for the Period sheets once you select the Malmquist menu item. Select two periods to perform the Malmquist calculation (see Figure 12.23)

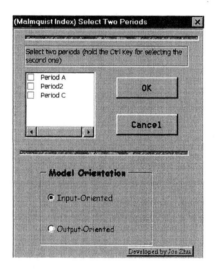

Figure 12.23. Malmquist

The results are reported in the "Malmquist Index" sheet reporting M_o, along with four worksheets related to the results from models (12.1)-(12.4). The names of these four worksheets depend on the periods selected. Suppose "Period A" and "Period2" are selected. Then the name for the four worksheets are (i) "M Period A" (model (12.1)); (ii) "M Period2" (model

(12.2)); (iii) "M Period2-Period A" (model (12.3)); and (iv) "M Period A-Period2" (model (12.3)). For the latter two, the left side of the name after "M" represents the reference set and the right side the period under evaluation.

12.22 Cost Efficiency, Revenue Efficiency and Profit Efficiency

These models need the information on the input and output prices. Consider the Hospital example in Cooper, Tone and Seiford (2000). The input and output data are reported in the "Data" sheet (Figure 12.24), input price are reported in the "Input Price" sheet (Figure 12.25) and the output price are reported in the "Output Price" sheet (Figure 12.26).

	A	B	C	D	E	F
1	Hospital	Doctor	Nurse		Outpat.	Inpat.
2	A	20	151		100	90
3	B	19	131		150	50
4	C	25	160		160	55
5	D	27	168		180	72
6	E	22	158		94	66
7	F	55	255		230	90
8	G	33	235		220	88
9	H	31	206		152	80
10	I	30	244		190	100
11	J	50	268		250	100
12	K	53	306		260	147
13	L	38	284		250	120

Figure 12.24. Hospital Data

	A	B	C	D	E
1	Hospital	Doctor	Nurse		
2	A	500	100		
3	B	350	80		
4	C	450	90		
5	D	600	120		
6	E	300	70		
7	F	450	80		
8	G	500	100		
9	H	450	85		
10	I	380	76		
11	J	410	75		
12	K	440	80		
13	L	400	70		

Figure 12.25. Input Prices

	A	B	C	D	E
1	Hospital	outpat.	Inpat.		
2	A	550	2010		
3	B	400	1800		
4	C	480	2200		
5	D	600	3500		
6	E	400	3050		
7	F	430	3900		
8	G	540	3300		
9	H	420	3500		
10	I	350	2900		
11	J	410	2600		
12	K	540	2450		
13	L	295	3000		

Figure 12.26. Output Price

The cost efficiency and revenue efficiency are discussed in Chapter 4. Table 12.2 summarizes the related models.

Table 12.2. Cost Efficiency and Revenue Efficiency Models

Frontier Type	Cost		Revenue	
	$\min \sum_{i=1}^{m} p_i^o \tilde{x}_{io}$ subject to		$\max \sum_{r=1}^{s} q_r^o \tilde{y}_{ro}$ subject to	
CRS	$\sum_{j=1}^{n} \lambda_j x_{ij} \leq \tilde{x}_{io}$	$i = 1,2,...,m;$	$\sum_{j=1}^{n} \lambda_j x_{ij} \leq x_{io}$	$i = 1,2,...,m$
	$\sum_{j=1}^{n} \lambda_j y_{rj} \geq y_{ro}$	$r = 1,2,...,s;$	$\sum_{j=1}^{n} \lambda_j y_{rj} \geq \tilde{y}_{ro}$	$r = 1,2,...,s$
	$\lambda_j, \tilde{x}_{io} \geq 0$		$\lambda_j, \tilde{y}_{ro} \geq 0$	
VRS	Add $\sum_{j=1}^{n} \lambda_j = 1$			
NIRS	Add $\sum_{j=1}^{n} \lambda_j \leq 1$			
NDRS	Add $\sum_{j=1}^{n} \lambda_j \geq 1$			

In Table 12.2, p_i^o and q_r^o are the unit price of the input i and unit price of the output r of DMU_o, respectively. These price data may vary from one DMU to another. The cost efficiency and revenue efficiency of DMU_o is defined as

$$\frac{\sum_{i=1}^{m} p_i^o \tilde{x}_{io}^*}{\sum_{i=1}^{m} p_i^o x_{io}} \quad \text{and} \quad \frac{\sum_{r=1}^{s} q_r^o y_{ro}}{\sum_{r=1}^{s} q_r^o \tilde{y}_{ro}^*}$$

Note that the revenue efficiency is defined as the reciprocal of the one defined in Chapter 4. As a result, the cost and revenue efficiency scores are within the range of 0 and 1.

The efficiency scores are reported in the "Cost Efficiency" ("Revenue Efficiency") sheet. The optimal inputs (outputs) are reported in the "OptimalData Cost Efficiency" ("OptimalData Revenue Efficiency") sheet.

Table 12.3 presents the models used to calculate the profit efficiency defined as

$$\frac{\sum_{r=1}^{s} q_r^o y_{ro} - \sum_{i=1}^{m} p_i^o x_{io}}{\sum_{r=1}^{s} q_r^o \tilde{y}_{ro}^* - \sum_{i=1}^{m} p_i^o \tilde{x}_{io}^*}$$

Table 12.3. Profit Efficiency Models

Frontier Type	
CRS	$\max \sum_{r=1}^{s} q_r^o \tilde{y}_{ro} - \sum_{i=1}^{m} p_i^o \tilde{x}_{io}$ subject to $\sum_{j=1}^{n} \lambda_j x_{ij} \le \tilde{x}_{io} \quad i = 1,2,...,m$ $\sum_{j=1}^{n} \lambda_j y_{rj} \ge \tilde{y}_{ro} \quad r = 1,2,...,s$ $\tilde{x}_{io} \le x_{io}, \tilde{y}_{ro} \ge y_{ro}$ $\lambda_j \ge 0$
VRS	Add $\sum_{j=1}^{n} \lambda_j = 1$
NIRS	Add $\sum_{j=1}^{n} \lambda_j \le 1$
NDRS	Add $\sum_{j=1}^{n} \lambda_j \ge 1$

The results are reported in the "Profit Efficiency" and "OptimalData Profit Efficiency" sheets.

References

1. Ahn, T.S. and L.M. Seiford (1993), Sensitivity of DEA to models and variable sets in a hypothesis test setting: the efficiency of University operations, In: Y. Ijiri, ed. *Creative and Innovative Approaches to the Science of Management*, 191-208. Quorum Books, New York.

2. Ali, A.I. and L.M. Seiford (1990), Translation invariance in data envelopment analysis, *Operations Research Letters*, 9, 403-405.

3. Ali, A. I., C.S. Lerme and L.M. Seiford (1995), Components of efficiency evaluation in data envelopment analysis, *European Journal of Operational Research*, 80, 462-473.

4. Andersen, P. and N.C. Petersen (1993), A procedure for ranking efficient units in data envelopment analysis, *Management Science* 39, 1261-1264.

5. Anderson, T.R. and G.P. Sharp (1997), A new measure of baseball batters using DEA, *Annals of Operations Research*,73, 141-155.

6. Bakos, J.Y. and C.F. Kemerer (1992), Recent applications of economic theory in information technology research, *Decision Support Systems*, 8, 365-386.

7. Banker, R.D. (1984), Estimating most productive scale size using data envelopment analysis, *European Journal of Operational Research*, 17, 35-44.

8. Banker, R.D., A. Charnes and W.W. Cooper (1984), Some models for estimating technical and scale inefficiencies in data envelopment analysis, *Management Science*, 30, 1078-1092.

9. Banker, R.D. and C.F. Kemerer (1989), Scale economies in new software development, *IEEE Transactions on Software Engineering*, 15, 1199-1205.

10. Banker, ,R.D. and R.C. Morey (1986), Efficiency analysis for exogenously fixed inputs and outputs, *Operations Research*, 34, 513-521.

11. Barr, R.S. and T.F. Siems (1997), Bank failure prediction using DEA to measure management quality, In: R.S. Barr, R.V. Helgason, and J.L. Kennington., eds. *Advances in Metaheuristics, Optimization, and Stochastic Modeling Techniques,* 341-365. Kluwer Academic Publishers, Boston.

12. Belton, V. and S.P. Vickers (1993), Demystifying DEA – a visual interactive approach based on multiple criteria analysis, *Journal of Operational Research Society,* 44, 883-896.

13. Brockett, P.L., W.W. Cooper, H.C. Shin and Y. Wang (1998), Inefficiency and congestion in Chinese production before and after the 1978 economic reforms, *Socio-Economic Planning Sciences,* 32, 1-20.

14. Brynjolsson, E. (1993), The productivity paradox of information technology, *Communications of the ACM,* 36, 67-77.

15. Byrnes, P., R. Färe and S. Grosskopf (1984), Measuring productive efficiency: an application to Illinois strip mines, *Management Science,* 30, 671-681.

16. Camp, R.C., (1995), *Business Process Benchmarking, Finding and Implementing Best Practices.* ASQC Quality Press, Milwaukee, Wisconsin.

17. Caves, D. W., L.R. Christensen and W.E. Diewert (1982), The economic theory of index numbers and the measurement of input, output, and productivity, *Econometric,* 50, No.6, 1939-1414.

18. Charnes, A., W.W. Cooper and E. Rhodes (1978), Measuring efficiency of decision making units, *European Journal of Operational Research,* 2, 429-444.

19. Charnes, A., W.W. Cooper and E. Rhodes (1981), Evaluating program and managerial efficiency: an application of data envelopment analysis to program follow through, *Management Science,* 27, No. 6, 668-697.

20. Charnes, A., W.W. Cooper and R.M. Thrall (1991), A structure for classifying and characterizing efficiencies and inefficiencies in DEA, *Journal of Productivity Analysis,* 2, 197-237.

21. Charnes, A., W.W. Cooper, B. Golany, L.M. Seiford and J. Stutz (1985), Foundations of data envelopment analysis for Pareto-Koopman's efficient empirical production functions, *J. of Econometrics,* 30, 1-17.

22. Charnes, A., W.W. Cooper, A.Y. Lewin, R.C. Morey and J. Rousseau (1985), Sensitivity and stability analysis in DEA, *Annals of Operations Research,* 2, 139-156.

23. Charnes, A., W.W. Cooper, A.Y. Lewin and L.M. Seiford (1994), *Data envelopment analysis: theory, methodology and applications.* Kluwer Academic Publishers, Boston.

24. Charnes, A., S. Haag, P. Jaska and J. Semple (1992), Sensitivity of efficiency classifications in the additive model of data envelopment analysis, *Int. J. Systems Sci.* 23, 789-798.

25. Charnes, A. and L. Neralic (1990), Sensitivity analysis of the additive model in data envelopment analysis, *European Journal of Operational Research,* 48, 332-341.

26. Charnes, A., J. Rousseau and J. Semple (1996), Sensitivity and stability of efficiency classifications in data envelopment analysis, *Journal of Productivity Analysis,* 7, 5-18.

27. Chen, Y. (2002), On infeasibility and super-efficiency DEA," Working paper.

28. Chen, Y. and H.D. Sherman (2002), The benefits of using non-radial versus radial super-efficiency DEA, *Socio-Economic Planning Sciences,* (forthcoming).

29. Chen, Y. and J. Zhu (2001), "Measuring information technology's indirect impact on firm performance," *Proceedings of the 6th INFORMS Conference on Information System & Technology.*

30. Chen, Y. and J. Zhu (2002), Data envelopment analysis interpretation and uses by multiple objective linear programming, working paper.

31. Cheung, K.L. and W.H. Hansman (2000), An exact performance evaluation for the supplier in a two-echelon inventory system, *Operations Research*, 48, 646-653.

32. Chilingerian, J.A. (1995), Evaluating physician efficiency in hospitals: A multivariate analysis of best practice, *European Journal of Operational Research*, 80, 548-574.

33. Cook, W.D., Y. Roll and A. Kazakov (1990), A DEA model for measuring the relative efficiency of highway maintenance patrols, *INFOR*, 28, No. 2, 113-124.

34. Cooper, W.W., R.G. Thompson and R.M. Thrall (1996), Introduction: extensions and new developments in DEA, *Annals of Operations Research*, 66, 3-45.

35. Cooper, W.W., L.M. Seiford and K. Tone (2000), *Data Envelopment Analysis: A Comprehensive Text with Models, Applications, References and DEA-Solver Software*, Kluwer Academic Publishers, Boston.

36. Cooper, W.W., L.M. Seiford and J. Zhu (2000), A unified additive model approach for evaluating inefficiency and congestion with associated measures in DEA. *Socio-Economic Planning Sciences*, 34, No. 1, 1-25.

37. Cooper, W.W., S. Li, L.M. Seiford, R.M. Thrall and J. Zhu (2001), Sensitivity and stability analysis in DEA: some recent developments, *Journal of Productivity Analysis*, 15, 217-246.

38. Deprins, D., L. Simar and H. Tulkens (1984), Measuring labor-efficiency in post offices, In: M. Marchand, P. Pestieau, and H. Tulkens., eds. *The Performance of Public Enterprises: Concepts and Measurement*, 243-267. Elsevier Science Publishers B.V. North-Holland.

39. Desai, A. and J.E. Storbeck (1990), A data envelopment analysis for spatial efficiency, *Computers, Environment and Urban Systems*, 14, 145-156.

40. Doyle, J. and R. Green (1993), Data envelopment analysis and multiple criteria decision making, *OMEGA*, 21, 713-715.

41. Färe, R. and S. Grosskopf (1983), Measuring congestion in production, *J. of Economics*, 43, 257-271.

42. Färe, R., S. Grosskopf and C.A.K. Lovell (1994), *Production Frontiers*. Cambridge University Press.

43. Färe, R., Grosskopf, J. Logan and C.A.K. Lovell (1985), Measuring efficiency in production: with an application to electric utilities, In: R. Färe, S. Grosskopf and C.A.K. Lovell., eds. *The Measurement of Efficiency of Production*, 185-214. Kluwer-Nijhoff Publishing, Kluwer Academic Publishers, Boston.

44. Färe, R. and C.A.K. Lovell (1978), Measuring the technical efficiency, *Journal of Economic Theory*, 19, 150-162.

45. Johnson, S.A. and J. Zhu (2002), Identifying top applicants in recruiting using data envelopment analysis, *Socio-Economic Planning Sciences*, (forthcoming).

46. Joro, T., P. Korhonen and J. Wallenius (1998), Structural comparison of data envelopment analysis and multiple objective linear programming, *Management Science*, 44, 962-970.

47. Kauffman, R.J. and P. Weill (1989), An evaluative framework for research on the performance effects of information technology investment, in *Proceedings of the 10th International Conference on Information Systems*, 377-388. Boston.

48. Keen, P.G.W. (1991), *Shaping the Future: Business Design Through Information Technology*. Harvard Business School Press. Cambridge, MA.

49. Kleinsorge, I.K., P.B. Schary and R.D. Tanner (1989), Evaluating logistics decisions, *International Journal of Physical Distribution and Materials Management*, 19, 200-219.

50. Lee, H.L. and C. Billington (1992), Managing supply chain inventory: pitfalls and opportunities, *Sloan Management Review*, 33, 65-73.

51. Lovell, C.A.K. and J.T. Pastor (1995), Units invariant and translation invariant DEA models, *Operations Research Letters*, 18, 147-151.

52. Malmquist, S. (1953), Index numbers and indifference surfaces, *Trabajos de Estatistica*, 4, 209-242.

53. Mistry, J. J. (1999), Differential Impacts of Information Technology on Cost and Revenue Driver Relationships in Selected Banking Functions. Ph. D. Dissertation, Boston University, Boston, MA

54. Mistry, J.J. and J. Zhu (2001), Data envelopment analysis in measuring the impact of information technology in banking, the 6th Asia Pacific DSI Conference, July 18-21, Singapore.

55. Neralic, L., (1994), Sensitivity analysis in data envelopment analysis: a review, in *Proceedings of the Symposium on Operations Research*, 29-42, SOR '94, V. Rupnik, and M. Bogataj (Eds.), Portoroz.

56. Pastor, J.T. (1996), Translation invariance in data envelopment analysis: a generalization, *Annals of Operations Research*, 66, 93-102.

57. Parlar, M. and Z.K. Weng (1997), Designing a firm's coordinated manufacturing and supply decisions with short product life cycles, *Management Science*, 43, 1329-1344.

58. Ray, S., L.M. Seiford and J. Zhu (1998), Market entity behavior of Chinese state-owned enterprises, *OMEGA*, 26, No. 2, 263-278.

59. Rousseau, J. and J. Semple (1995), Radii of classification preservation in data envelopment analysis, *Journal of the Operational Research Society*, 46, 943-957.

60. Seiford, L.M. and R.M. Thrall (1990), Recent developments in DEA: the mathematical programming approach to frontier analysis, *Journal of Econometrics*, 46, 7-38.

61. Seiford, L.M. and J. Zhu (1998a), An acceptance system decision rule with data envelopment analysis, *Computers and Operations Research*, 25, No. 4, 329-332.

62. Seiford, L.M. and J. Zhu (1998b), On piecewise loglinear and log efficiency measures, *Computers and Operations Research*, 25, No. 5, 389-395.

63. Seiford, L.M. and J. Zhu (1998c), Identifying excesses and deficits in Chinese industrial productivity (1953-1990): a weighted data envelopment analysis approach, *OMEGA*, 26, No. 2, 279-269.

64. Seiford, L.M. and J. Zhu (1998d), Stability regions for maintaining efficiency in data envelopment analysis, *European Journal of Operational Research*, 108, No. 1, 127-139.

65. Seiford, L.M. and J. Zhu (1998e), On alternative optimal solutions in the estimation of returns to scale in DEA, *European Journal of Operational Research*, 108, No. 1, 149-152.

66. Seiford, L.M. and J. Zhu (1998f), Sensitivity analysis of DEA models for simultaneous changes in all the data, *Journal of the Operational Research Society*, 49, 1060-1071.

67. Seiford, L.M. and J. Zhu (1999a), An investigation of returns to scale under data envelopment analysis, *OMEGA*, 27, No. 1, 1-11.

68. Seiford, L.M. and J. Zhu (1999b), Sensitivity and stability of the classification of returns to scale in data envelopment analysis, *Journal of Productivity Analysis*, 12, No. 1, 55-75.

69. Seiford, L.M. and J. Zhu (1999c), Infeasibility of super efficiency data envelopment analysis models, *INFOR*, 37, No. 2, 174-187.

70. Seiford, L.M. and J. Zhu (1999d), Profitability and marketability of the top 55 US commercial banks, *Management Science*, 45, No. 9, 1270-1288.

71. Seiford, L.M. and J. Zhu (2002a), Value judgment versus allocative efficiency: a case of Tennessee county jails, *Studies in Regional & Urban Planning*, (forthcoming)

72. Seiford, L.M. and J. Zhu (2002b), Modeling undesirable factors in efficiency evaluation, *European Journal of Operational Research*, (forthcoming).

73. Sherman, H.D. (1984), Improving the productivity of service businesses, *Sloan Management Review*, 35, No. 3, 11-23.

74. Simonson, I. and A. Tversky (1992), Choice in context: tradeoff contrast and extremeness aversion, *Journal of Marketing Research*, 29 281-295.

75. Stewart, T.J. (1994), Relations between data envelopment analysis and multicriteria decision analysis, *Journal of Operational Research Society*, 44, 883-896.

76. Thanassoulis, E. (2001), Introduction to the Theory and Application of Data Envelopment Analysis: A Foundation Text with Integrated Software, Kluwer Academic Publishers. Boston.

77. Thompson, R.G., P.S. Dharmapala and R.M. Thrall (1994), Sensitivity analysis of efficiency measures with applications to Kansas farming and Illinois coal mining, In: A. Charnes, W.W. Cooper, A.Y. Lewin and L.M. Seiford., eds. *Data Envelopment Analysis: Theory, Methodology, and Applications,* Kluwer Academic Publishers, Boston.

78. Thomas, D.J. and P.M. Griffin (1996), Coordinated supply chain management, *European Journal of Operational Research*, 94, 1-15.

79. Thrall, R.M. (1996), Duality, classification and slacks in DEA, *Annals of Operations Research,* 66, 109-138.

80. Tversky, A. and I. Simonson (1993), Context-dependent preferences. *Management Sciences,* 39 1179-1189.

81. Weber, C.A. and A. Desai (1996), Determination of paths to vendor market efficiency using parallel coordinates representation: a negotiation tool for buyers, *European Journal of Operational Research*, 90, 142-155.

82. Wilkens, K. and J. Zhu (2001), Portfolio evaluation and benchmark selection: a mathematical programming approach, *Journal of Alternative Investments*, 4, No. 1, 9-19.

83. Wilson, P.W. (1993), Detecting outliers in deterministic nonparametric frontier models with multiple outputs, *Journal of Business and Economic Statistics*, 11, 319-323.

84. Wise, R., and D. Morrison (2000), Beyond the exchange: the future of B2B. *Harvard Business Review*, 78, 86-96.

85. Zhu, J. and Z. Shen (1995), A discussion of testing DMUs' returns to scale, *European Journal of Operational Research*, 81, 590-596.

86. Zhu, J. (1996a), Data envelopment analysis with preference structure, *Journal of Operational Research Society*, 47, 136-150.

87. Zhu, J. (1996b), Robustness of the efficient DMUs in data envelopment analysis, *European Journal of Operational Research*, 90, No. 3, 451-460.

88. Zhu, J. (1996c), DEA/AR analysis of the 1988-1989 performance of the Nanjing Textile Cooperation, *Annals of Operations Research*, 66, 311-335.

89. Zhu, J. (1998), Data envelopment analysis vs. principal component analysis: An illustrative study of economic performance of Chinese cities, *European Journal of Operational Research*, 111, No. 1, 50-61.

90. Zhu, J. (2000a), Multi-factor performance measure model with an application to Fortune 500 companies, *European Journal of Operational Research*, 123, No. 1, 105-124.

91. Zhu, J. (2000b), Setting scale efficient targets in DEA via returns to scale estimation method, *Journal of Operational Research Society*, 51, No. 3, 376-378.

92. Zhu, J. (2000c), Further discussion on DEA and linear production function, *European Journal of Operational Research*, 127, No. 3, 611-618.

93. Zhu, J. (2001a), Super-efficiency and DEA sensitivity analysis, *European Journal of Operational Research*, 129, No. 2, 443-455.

94. Zhu, J. (2001b), A multidimensional quality-of-life measure with an application to Fortune's best cities, *Socio-Economic Planning Sciences*, 35, No. 4, 263-284.

Author Index

Topic Index

ABOUT THE CD-ROM

This easy-to-use DEA software, DEA Excel Solver, provides a custom menu of DEA approaches, which include more than 150 different DEA models. This extremely powerful tool can assist decision-makers in benchmarking and analyzing complex operational efficiency issues in manufacturing organizations as well as evaluating processes in banking, retail, franchising, health care, e-business, public services, and many other industries.

The DEA Excel Solver does not set a limit on the number of units, inputs or outputs. With the capacity of Excel Solver, the DEA Excel Solver can deal with large-sized performance evaluation tasks.

DEA Excel Solver Installation Instructions

The CD-ROM contains the DEA Excel Solver* which is a DEA Add-In for Microsoft® Excel. This software **"DEA Excel Solver.xla"** requires Excel 97 or later versions. To use the file "DEA Excel Solver.xla" in the CD-ROM using Windows, you may follow these steps:

Step 1.   Insert the CD-ROM into your computer's CD-ROM drive.
Step 2.   Launch Windows Explore.
Step 3.   Click Browse to browse the CD and find the file "DEA Excel Solver.xla". Copy this file to your hard drive.

For more information about using the DEA Excel Solver, please see Chapter 12.

*May not work on a Macintosh®.